The School Psychologist
An Introduction

Edited by

George W. Hynd

Syracuse University Press   1983

First Edition

Library of Congress Cataloging in Publication Data
Main entry under title:

The School psychologist.

   Bibliography: p.
   Includes index.
   1. School psychologists — Addresses, essays,
lectures. I. Hynd, George W.
LB3013.6.S27 1983   371.2'022   82-19337
ISBN 0-8156-2289-9
ISBN 0-8156-2290-2 (pbk.)

Manufactured in the United States of America

Contents

Contributors

Stephen B. Cannon, M.S. (George Peabody College for Teachers), is a Graduate Assistant, Department of Educational Psychology, University of Georgia.

Ann W. Engin, Ph.D. (University of Michigan), is Professor, School Psychology Program, Department of Psychology, University of South Carolina.

Lawrence C. Hartlage, Ph.D. (University of Louisville), is Professor of Neurology and Pediatrics and Head, Neuropsychology Section, Department of Neurology, Medical College of Georgia.

Stephen E. Haussmann, Ph.D. (University of Georgia), is Instructor, Department of Exceptional Children, University of Georgia.

George W. Hynd, Ed.D. (University of Northern Colorado), is Associate Professor of Educational Psychology and Chair, School Psychology Program, Department of Educational Psychology, University of Georgia, and Assistant Clinical Professor of Neurology, Department of Neurology, Medical School of Georgia.

Alan S. Kaufman, Ph.D. (Columbia University), is Professor of Psychology, California School of Professional Psychology (CSPP), San Diego.

Nadeen L. Kaufman, Ed.D. (Columbia University), is Head, Psychoeducational Clinic, California School of Professional Psychology (CSPP), San Diego.

Roy P. Martin, Ph.D. (University of Texas), is Professor of Educational Psychology, Department of Educational Psychology, University of Georgia.

Barbara A. Mowder, Ph.D. (Indiana University), is Associate Professor, School of Education, University of Colorado at Denver.

Richard J. Nagle, Ph.D. (Columbia University), is Associate Professor and Director, School Psychology Program, Department of Psychology, University of South Carolina.

John E. Obrzut, Ph.D. (University of Minnesota), is Associate Professor of Psychology, Department of Psychology, University of Northern Colorado.

Daniel J. Reschly, Ph.D. (University of Oregon), is Professor of Psychology, Department of Psychology, Iowa State University.

Cecil R. Reynolds, Ph.D. (University of Georgia), is Associate Professor, Department of Educational Psychology, Texas A & M University.

Jacqueline A. Schakel, M.A. (University of Oregon), is a School Psychologist, Anchorage, Alaska.

James E. Ysseldyke, Ph.D. (University of Illinois), is Professor of School Psychology and Director of the Institute for Research on Learning Disabilities, University of Minnesota.

Steve Zucker, M.A. (Fairleigh Dickinson University), is a doctoral student, Department of Psychology, University of Northern Colorado.

Preface

PERHAPS MORE than any other area within applied psychology, school psychology has been receptive to change because of the many social and legal developments of the past decade that have affected it. There can be no doubt that it has been school psychology's ability to meet new professional challenges that has ensured its continued value to children and teachers. This receptivity to change has heralded in a new era in school psychology. Long gone are the days when school psychologists acted alone in identifying, assessing, diagnosing, and prescribing remedial intervention. Considering the problems which arose from this mode of practice, perhaps it is best this era is now history.

As a reflection of our prismatic society, the school psychologist today participates as a valued member of a professional team. Our knowledge about exceptional children continues to develop through active research in a number of fields, so that the school psychologist needs to acquire a solid foundation not only in psychology and education, but also in the fundamentals of law, sociology, and the health sciences. Truly, the school psychologist must be a multifaceted professional in order to meet the demands placed on the practitioner.

This book was developed out of a recognition that no introductory-level book was available that could provide the school psychology student with up-to-date perspectives on the field. Some volumes offer comprehensive coverage of most topics germane to the profession. However, these books were not intended for the beginning-level school psychology student with little or no solid foundation of knowledge upon which to build. This book is intended to provide the foundation upon which more comprehensive understanding can be developed.

In important ways this volume differs from other texts in school psychology. A number of chapters have been devoted to emerging or controversial topics within the field of school psychology. The chapters on national organizations in school psychology, new perspectives on intelligence, brain-behavior relationships and neuropsychological assessment, projective personality assessment, and educational remediation represent important and unique aspects of this volume. In addition to attaining an overall understanding of school psychology as traditionally conceived, the reader of this volume will gain a broader perspective of developments which may influence the future practice of school psychologists.

The format of this book derives from the recognition that no one person could adequately treat all of the topics which should be included. Consequently, widely recognized and highly respected leaders in each area of school psychology were invited to contribute a chapter introducing their particular area of expertise. First and foremost, their goal was to set forth their topics. Then, using this foundation, they were to build a framework for further study. Without exception, the contributors have accomplished this task, and the reader will find the chapters thorough, interesting, and well written.

The organization of this volume required that three sections be included. Recent developments that represent only the present manifestation of a historical process require an introduction to school psychology. The first chapter by Ysseldyke and Schakel traces the influence various national conferences have had on school psychology. Their overview incorporates a summary of the most recently completed conference on the future of school psychology, the Olympia Conference. Chapter 2 by Engin discusses the two most influential organizations that have sought to represent school psychologists. Her discussion of the American Psychological Association (APA) Division 16 and the National Association of School Psychologists (NASP) outlines organizational structure, professional standards, important organizational issues, and areas of commonality and divergence between these two important organizations.

The second section of this book provides the reader with an excellent discussion of pertinent issues related to the practice of school psychology. Chapter 3 by Reynolds discusses at some length the aspects of measurement so critical to school psychology. His overview of reliability and validity in psychological and educational measurement will provide the reader with a foundation upon which to evaluate ideas and concepts discussed in following chapters. Chapter 4 by Reschly examines the legal issues that have affected greatly the practice of school psychology. Kaufman, in Chapter 5, provides an enlightening overview of cognitive ability and the ways in which psychologists have sought to conceptualize and assess its various parameters. In this chapter, the author discusses new perspectives on intelligence and advances made in its measurement.

The third and most comprehensive section is concerned with procedures of psychoeducational intervention. Since the practice of psychoeducational assessment has as its only purpose the gathering of data necessary to formulate intervention strategies, chapters covering assessment and intervention were placed together. Chapter 6 by Hynd, Cannon, and Haussmann on the exceptional child addresses issues related to estimates of prevalence, the intervention process, and differential diagnosis. Chapter 7 by Mowder provides some contrast to the preceding chapter in that the multidimensional nature of assessment is examined in some detail. Nagle, in Chapter 8, critically examines psychoeducational assessment of cognitive abilities and reviews the research on several widely used test instruments. The following chapter (9) by Obrzut and Zucker presents the theory, research, and clinical aspects of projective personality assessment. Although projectives have been criticized for theoretical and empirical reasons, they remain a potentially useful and popular clinical tool. Their defense of projective assessment is strengthened by the inclusion of illustrative case examples.

Chapter 10 by Hynd and Hartlage also presents a review of a controversial area of expertise in school psychology. Discussions of functional neuroanatomy and clinical neuropsychological differentiation are provided with illustrative case reports. Martin, in Chapter 11, discusses consultation in the schools. The various types and stages of consultation as well as research in this area are presented. The concluding chapter (12) by N. Kaufman and A. Kaufman critically evaluates various approaches to remedial intervention and offers insightful recommendations regarding the selection of appropriate remedial practices.

As editor of this volume, I hope that school psychology students will be sufficiently stimulated by the ideas presented here that they will continue to examine—both in their coursework and outside the academic environment—many of the issues and thoughts shared by the authors. Further, it is my hope that the contents of this book may provide the student with a clear understanding of the roots of school psychology, the manifestation of its practice with children, and some of the more critical issues confronting school psychologists. If this is indeed the case, then our efforts have not only been enjoyable but productive as well, especially if exceptional children are eventually better served.

Athens, Georgia
Summer 1982

George W. Hynd

Acknowledgments

SCHOOL PSYCHOLOGY has become a profession so diversified that no one individual could address all of the potential topics and issues relevant to an introductory text. I am indebted to the contributors to this volume who agreed with this basic assumption and gave enthusiastically of their time and expertise. The staff at Syracuse University Press has been very supportive and provided guidance in the development and publication of this book. The reviewers who helped shape the present text are also acknowledged. Finally, a special note of appreciation goes to Betty Randolph and JoAnn Perrin for their patience, competence, and willingness to type various sections of the final manuscript. To all of the children we serve our efforts are dedicated.

The School Psychologist

Section I
Introduction to the Profession

1

Directions in School Psychology

JAMES E. YSSELDYKE AND JACQUELINE A. SCHAKEL

ALTHOUGH there are differences of opinion on how much the actual practice of school psychology has changed since its beginnings in the early 1900s, it is clear that a number of forces have helped determine how school psychologists define their profession. Much, perhaps most, of the impetus for change has come from outside forces. Peterson (1981) points out that, historically, professions have rarely changed until they have had to. Still, psychologists in general, and school psychologists in particular, have made periodic attempts to chart new directions from within their ranks. This chapter includes a discussion of the internal and external forces that have affected the direction of school psychology, and those forces that currently challenge school psychologists in their efforts to plan for future directions.

Because school psychology is tied so closely to both education and psychology, important changes in either discipline potentially affect the profession. Fluctuations in the sociopolitical environment also influence developments in school psychology. At times when outside forces have been most pressing, school psychologists have met to address critical issues. Several conferences on the professional practice of psychology and school psychology have been held, beginning with the Boulder Conference in 1949, the Thayer Conference in 1954, the 1980 Spring Hill Symposium on the Future of Psychology in the Schools, and the Olympia Conference in 1981. At these meetings, leaders in the fields of psychology, school psychology, and such related professions as special education have attempted to clarify issues and address the direction of the profession. Close examination of the issues and questions addressed there is a convenient way to look at the development of school psychology.

This chapter reviews three major professional conferences (Boulder, Thayer, and Spring Hill), looking specifically at the tenor of the time in which each one took place, the major themes of discussion, the participants, and the recommendations made. A section of the chapter is devoted to a description of developments occurring in the twenty-five years between the Thayer Conference and the Spring Hill Symposium. A brief discussion of the Olympia Conference is also included.

THE BOULDER CONFERENCE

The first conference dealing specifically with the applied specialties of psychology was the two-week-long meeting in Boulder, Colorado, in 1949. Although this conference did not focus on school psychology per se, ideas formulated there persist today among institutions that train school psychologists. The major purpose of the Boulder Conference was to discuss procedures for evaluating and approving doctoral training programs in the applied specialties: clinical, counseling, and school psychology (Raimy 1950). Probably the most important and lasting result for the field of school psychology was an increased emphasis on the idea of the applied psychologist as a professional scientist. That is, graduate programs were encouraged to train scientists who practice, not practicing psychologists with backgrounds in scientific psychology. The conference also outlined specific training experiences which participants believed were the necessary components in training a clinician.

At that time, the term *clinician* could be accurately applied to most psychologists working in the schools, for it was from the field of clinical psychology that school psychologists were being placed. In a description of the Boulder Conference Mensch (1966) noted, however, that "clinical psychologists have shown some reluctance to accept the challenge of working with educators and schools to develop effective programs of school psychology, in spite of the admitted great social need for persons especially oriented to work in public schools. Perhaps this social need will only be met when a federal agency begins supporting equally attractive training programs tailored to orient psychologists to work in school settings" (p. 14). Perhaps with impetus from the Boulder Conference, a number of studies and surveys were carried out by the Division of School Psychologists of the American Psychological Association (APA), to investigate school psychology as it existed at that time. The information obtained from these studies and the discussions that followed led to a decision to hold a conference to discuss the evolving profession of school psychology.

THE THAYER CONFERENCE

Context

In the summer of 1954, the first major conference to deal specifically with school psychology was convened at the Hotel Thayer, West Point, New York. The "Thayer Conference," as it is now known, had as its major theme the development of a definite stance on the role and function of the school psychologist, and the specification of the necessary components in training school psychologists. Using the model of the Boulder Conference, participants attempted to delineate the unique aspects of the practice of school psychology and decide on the most appropriate training for this role.

To put the conclusions of the Thayer Conference into perspective, it is important to recognize the professional context in which this meeting was held. School psychology was then a young profession. There were few practitioners identified as school psychologists and few training programs to develop them. School psychology was a profession searching for an initial identity.

Issues Addressed at the Thayer Conference

At the time of the Thayer Conference, "school psychologist" was such a nebulous term that no accurate estimate of the number of people practicing in that capacity could be made. Cutts (1955) used survey data to determine the then-current ratio of school psychologists to pupils. Using as a "proper ratio" a range of one school psychologist for every 1000 to 3000 pupils, she reported a drastic shortage of personnel. According to her summary, "The important fact is that there are now and will be for the immediate future, far too few school psychologists to meet current demands" (p. 4).

A second issue addressed at the Thayer Conference was the fact that opportunities for specific training in school psychology were few. Only five institutions of higher education had formal programs leading to the doctorate in school psychology, and just thirteen institutions offered training at the subdoctoral level.

A third issue discussed extensively at the Thayer Conference concerned inadequate "classification" and certification. School psychologists were called by many different titles; only twenty states and the District of Columbia had certification regulations governing school psychology. Participants at the Thayer Conference also addressed the virtual absence of standards and procedures for accrediting training programs.

The issues addressed were exclusively "guild" issues; focus was on conditions of employment and on the appropriate role and function of school psychologists. Leaders in the profession were concerned with setting standards to assure that enough well-trained persons were available to fill positions. They were worried that "poor service by unqualified people calling themselves school psychologists" would harm children and the profession (Cutts 1955, p. 6).

Organization of the Thayer Conference

Participants in the Thayer Conference were chosen to ensure that trainers of school psychologists and practitioners at various levels of service would be represented, as well as to include different geographic regions and psychological fields of interest. Forty-eight participants were in attendance — twenty-one who were then or had been school psychologists, nine who were supervisors of school psychologists, and nineteen who were trainers of school psychologists. Clinical psychology was the best-represented specialty, with thirty people who were then or had been clinical psychologists.

The first day of the nine-day conference was devoted to preliminary addresses. The five days that followed were taken up with small-group discussions of five issues: (1) definition of functions; (2) specification of competencies; (3) selection, training, and experience; (4) administrative and professional relationships; and (5) professional development, recognition, and accreditation. During the last three days, discussions were reported and critical issues delineated.

Recommendations

Several statements of policy and recommendations for action were formulated as a result of the Thayer Conference. It is worthwhile to summarize them here as a way to demonstrate how the field of school psychology has changed since 1955.

Definition

Agreement on a definition of school psychologists and their functions was one result of the Thayer Conference. They were defined as "psychologist(s) with training and experience in education (who use their) specialized knowledge of assessment, learning, and interpersonal relationships to assist school personnel to enrich the experience and growth of all children and to recognize and deal with exceptional children" (Cutts, 1955, p. 74).

Functions

Although recognizing that school psychologists might apply their special knowledge in a number of ways, several general functions were described as necessary for promoting mental health in school children. Performing assessment and planning remediation based on the assessment data were mentioned as primary activities. Research was described as "both a practical tool and a moral obligation of the school psychologist" (Cutts 1955, p. 175); yet some members of the conference believed that a psychologist practicing in the schools would have little or no time to undertake research.

It was emphasized that, in carrying out these functions, school psychologists were to work with exceptional children of all kinds. However, there was disagreement on the extent to which school psychologists should work with emotionally disturbed children and the kinds of services such children should receive, a debate which continues today.

Finally, it was agreed that the goal of school psychologists should be to facilitate "the best adjustment of the largest possible number of children" (Cutts 1955, p. 174). To do this, in addition to the aforementioned functions, school psychologists would serve as advisors on school curricula and methods, as well as help teachers, principals, and other school personnel to help children.

Qualifications

Qualifications for employment as a school psychologist were not delineated in detail; yet, it was generally agreed that there was need for both doctoral-level school psychologists and individuals with more limited training in school psychology. Therefore, two levels of training were recommended for universities training school psychologists: a four-year doctoral program and a two-year subdoctoral program. It was also strongly recommended that states be encouraged to adopt appropriate certification standards, and that a system of accreditation be set up by the profession to help guarantee the adequacy of training programs.

Training

In addition to the recommendations regarding two levels of training, it was suggested that all training programs include practicum experience in order to provide experiential knowledge of the schools and an appreciation for the work of teachers. Some members of the conference believed that actual teaching experience was a necessity, but most thought a comprehensive understanding of education would be sufficient.

Diversity in training programs was encouraged. Conference participants believed that an infant field like school psychology should test several models of training within general guidelines. A supervised internship was recommended as a necessary component of the doctoral program. For the two-year degree, at least a half year of supervised practicum experience was suggested.

Summary

In her statements summarizing the Thayer Conference, Cutts asserted that "the future of school psychology now depends upon the qualifications and training of those who enter the field and the ability of these persons to become integral parts of the schools" (p. 180). The Thayer Conference set the stage for dealing with the "qualifications and training" part of this statement—the "guild" issues. It was left to the school psychologists to be trained in these new programs to find ways of becoming integral parts of the schools.

The Twenty-Five Years Between Thayer and Spring Hill

In the years since the Thayer Conference, members of the young school psychology profession have spent considerable time, effort, and energy contemplating their role and functions. A number of developments occurring simultaneously in the parent fields of psychology and education, and in the legal, economic, social, and political arenas, influenced the issues under consideration. In this section, conferences which have been held in the past twenty-five years are discussed briefly. This discussion is followed by a look at advances and changes in the field of school psychology and its parent fields, developments which have brought school psychology to a critical juncture and necessitated fresh examinations of the profession at the 1980 Spring Hill Symposium, and the Olympia Conference the following year.

OTHER CONFERENCES

Other professional conferences in psychology and school psychology have served as vehicles for promoting new directions in school psychology. A conference on internships in school psychology was held at the George Peabody College for Teachers in 1963 (Gray 1963). Sponsored by the National Institute of Mental Health, this conference settled some training issues, but raised others—new issues that are still being discussed today. In 1964, the Bethesda Conference was organized by Division 16 of the American Psychological Association. This conference continued many of the discussions begun at Thayer on the role and functions of school psychologists (Bardon 1964-65).

The 1973 National Conference on Levels and Patterns of Professional Training in Psychology (the Vail conference), although not specific to school psychology, provided new direction for training programs by endorsing the Psy.D. degree as an alternative to the Ph.D. model endorsed at Boulder in 1949. This newly proposed doctoral degree was (and continues to be) appealing to many school psychologists, because of its de-emphasis on research and its stress on the development of good practitioner skills. Other implications of the Vail conference for school psychology were the endorsement of multiple training levels and the admission of master's-level psychologists to full APA membership (Korman 1974).

NEW DIRECTIONS IN PSYCHOLOGY

To review all the pertinent developments in the field of psychology is beyond the scope of this chapter. What is important here is to highlight some recent research findings and point out how they have steered school psychology on its current course and may continue to do so. In an unpublished section of a paper ("Recent Developments") delivered at the Spring Hill Symposium, Trachtman discussed the developments of the last few years which he judged likely to affect the practice and theory of school psychology. This section draws from his paper and discusses other influences from the changing field of psychology.

Learning and Cognition

A great deal of current research in cognition is based on information-processing theory, using a computer analogy as a means of understanding human mental processes. The impact of this research on the psychologists' work in the schools has been minimal to date, but the research offers promise as a new means of looking at individual differences in student performance of academic tasks (Yen 1978).

Developmental Psychology

Research in child development, which often cannot be generalized for purposes of school psychologists' work in the schools, is turning more and more to field-based investigations. Field studies, particularly those carried out in the schools, have promise for showing both the extent to which and ways in which schools can enhance development. Recent research and reviews (Hunt 1979; Kagan 1979; Lazar and Darling 1979; Zigler and Valentine 1979) suggest, directly or indirectly, ways the schools can provide experiences that counter a child's early lack of some of the necessary prerequisites for success in school.

Ethological, Ecological and Environmental Psychology

These branches of psychology stress the role of the environment or behavior settings in studying the human organism. Research using these approaches has helped and will continue to help school psychologists to understand and control the effects of the school environment and other interacting systems. School psychologists will probably continue to move toward focusing assessment and intervention on the child in a particular context, and not as an isolated entity (Altman and Wohlwill 1979, Weinstein 1979).

Social and Personality Development

There is movement in this research toward understanding social and personality variables in their interaction with particular situations or classes of situations. As psychology moves away from more traditional theory, perhaps the applied psychologist will begin to prefer new methods of classification and understanding individual differences.

Another area of research with possible impact on school psychology is that of attribution and social comparison. This research shows that whether children (and adults) attribute behavior to their own personalities and efforts or to environmental forces influences how they behave. Such phenomena as "learned helplessness" (when failure is consistently attributed to one's own lack of ability) and the presence or absence of "intrinsic motivation" (Greene and Lepper 1974) have important implications for the schools.

Behavioral Approaches in Psychology

Over the past several years, the influence of behavioral approaches on the practice of school psychology has been tremendous. Recent developments suggest that such tools as behavioral observation are becoming widely used as alternatives to, or to supplement, traditional standard assessments. Behavioral interventions are quite common and "cognitive behavioral approaches," in which children are taught to control their cognitions for social and academic problem-solving, also have promise as new techniques for the school psychologist.

Obviously, many new findings in the field of psychology offer possibilities for affecting what individual school psychologists do and ultimately how school psychology evolves as a profession. Many factors have a bearing on whether and how well these developments can be translated from research into practice, including the climate in the schools and ongoing changes in the field of education. The next section discusses developments in education which may be helping to chart the current and future course of school psychology.

NEW DIRECTIONS IN EDUCATION

Special Education

One development in education which has had, and will continue to have, a tremendous impact on the practice of school psychology is the attempt to serve handicapped students fairly and adequately. Requirements for individualized educational programs and "least restrictive environments," and the extension of education to handicapped persons between the ages of three and five, and eighteen to twenty-one, involve school psychologists in a number of ways. The responsibility to reduce bias in testing and to prevent inaccurate classifications of minority students are also generally assumed by psychologists in the schools.

The term *learning disability* has become very familiar to school personnel, but there is little agreement on its definition, or on appropriate intervention techniques. The "discovery" of learning disabilities, whatever they may be, has probably had as much of an impact on how practicing school psychologists spend their time as has any other educational development. In light of the confusion over learning disabilities, more school psychologists may need to take a leading role in sharing relevant research on learning disabilities with other people in the school system and correcting misperceptions about these and other handicapping conditions.

"Regular" Education

The emphasis in special education on writing individualized programs for students has helped increase professional awareness and appreciation of individual differences. As a consequence, many school psychologists have recommended more diverse services for greater numbers of regular students, in addition to the special services for exceptional children. A challenge which may shape the future role and function of school psychologists may be to find the best means of more efficiently and effectively serving large numbers of students. Providing parent education, designing prevention programs, and planning curricular interventions all have received much attention as possible ways to do this. These demands have also provoked renewed interest among school psychologists in expanding their role as consultants in schools rather than, or in addition to, direct service provision.

Educational Technology

Although, as Trachtman (1981) points out, educational technology, as seen in the schools, has not changed much since 1950, several technological advances have potential applications in the schools. Computer systems that process data on exceptional children and specify instructional needs are being used or considered in some school districts. One wonders if some day they will take over the task of designing interventions so that, as a result, school psychologists will become strictly data gatherers. On the other hand, such a development might free up some of the school psychologists' time for other functions. Good or bad, such changes are possibilities. With the rapid technological growth going on in this country and other parts of the world, techniques may be applied in the schools within the next several years that can only be imagined at this time; or educational techniques may change as little as they have for the last thirty years.

NEW DIRECTIONS WITHIN SCHOOL PSYCHOLOGY

While these changes have been occurring over the last few years in psychology and education, school psychology's parent fields, important changes coming from within the school psychology profession have also guided its current course. A few of these will be discussed here, but only briefly, since they are discussed in greater depth elsewhere in this volume.

Participants at the Thayer Conference in 1954 did not predict the schism that was to occur in school psychology in the late 1960s. A group of school psychologists, who were disillusioned with several American

Psychological Association policies affecting school psychologists, broke away and formed the National Association of School Psychologists (NASP). School psychologists are now represented by two professional associations (See Engin, Chapter 2).

Within both NASP and Division 16 (APA), there has been a relatively recent push to provide continuing education designed to update and upgrade practice. As Drucker (1981) observes, "The fastest growing industry in America today may be the continuing professional education of highly schooled mid-career adults" (p. 20). In addition to continuing education provided by professional associations, the U.S. Office of Special Education has funded a National School Psychology Inservice Training Network, an organization housed at the University of Minnesota, which provides inservice training to practicing school psychologists.

If an interactionist view of the development of school psychology is taken, the relative influences of advances in psychology, new directions in education, and the impetus for change from within the profession itself cannot be isolated. Clearly, though, all these forces are influenced by changes in the broader sociopolitical system in which they occur. The need to discuss ways to face the challenge of providing good school psychological services in a changing society was the impetus for the Spring Hill Symposium on the Future of Psychology in the Schools.

THE SPRING HILL SYMPOSIUM

Changes in American society and the resulting changes in the profession over the years since 1954 provided a very different sociopolitical context for the Spring Hill Symposium than that in which the Thayer Conference took place. Many issues have not changed in that time, but they must be viewed differently in light of the legal, political, economic, and societal changes that have occurred. Whereas school psychology was grappling with the need to establish a professional identity in 1954 (and still is to some extent), the focus of the symposium in 1980 was to discuss providing appropriate services and training school psychologists to meet, and perhaps influence, the demands of society in the decade ahead.

Context

To understand the significance of the Spring Hill discussions, it is important to summarize the broader context in which school psychologists found themselves as the '80s began. Developments in psychology, education, and school psychology during the past few years have already been discussed. Changing societal values and institutions, racial discrimination in a pluralistic society, economic considerations, and litigation and legislation in the "age of accountability" remain to be considered.

Changing Societal Values

Changes in society's values are inevitably reflected in changes in the goals and objectives of schools. Social values, choices, or preferences are never static and as a result, the goals and objectives of education are in a constant state of flux. It is interesting to consider issues that occupied the attention of participants at Spring Hill. They reflected on the fact that schools are increasingly expected to function as the major agent of social change: they are expected to bring about social equality, and eliminate poverty, unemployment, racism, and war.

Repeatedly throughout the discussion at Spring Hill, there was reference to the frustrations that arise when school systems become scapegoats for public frustrations (Hyman 1979). School psychologists expressed frustration at not being able to influence the "system" and not having a clear sense of how best to bring about change, and they expressed strong feelings of helplessness and "burnout."

As Bevan (1981) states, social class will probably always be with us. The problem is how best to free the individual from the limitations of class membership. School psychologists and other school personnel are grappling with this issue.

Changing Social and Political Institutions

There are differences of opinion about whether the family is a dying social institution; but divorce statistics, changing family patterns, and other indications make it clear that the "average American family" is not what it once was. Obviously, these changes have the potential to influence the daily practice of school psychologists in their work with children and their families (see Guidubaldi, 1980). If schools are taking on some of the responsibilities traditionally relegated to the family, as many persons have suggested, and if school psychology as a profession accepts this state of affairs, then there is a need to decide exactly how school psychologists should be involved.

The continued growth of government in the last twenty-five years also has implications for school psychology. Bevan (1981) describes "the wholesale intrusion of government into educational affairs and policy" as the "most worrisome" problem for school psychologists (p. 128). Although recognizing benign intent, he characterizes the increase in governmental regulations, the time spent in bookkeeping and paperwork, and a burgeoning bureaucracy as severely limiting to efficient work in the schools. School psychologists everywhere would no doubt agree that this is a significant problem to be dealt with in the next decade.

Cultural Pluralism and Racial Discrimination

American society has become increasingly "pluralistic," and there have been movements in society and education to recognize and accept a multiracial, multiethnic model. At the same time, there have always been forces resisting this idea and favoring the acceptance of an "Anglo-dominance" model. Bardon (1981) describes the problem this creates for the school psychologist: "At once we are requested to help prepare all pupils to live in the dominant American society, and at the same time, to acknowledge and respect their right not to be judged by a normative standard but, instead, by cultural, ethnic, and racial differences" (p. 299). A related societal condition which has continued down through the years and is reflected in the schools is racism. Sewell (1981) points to racism in the ranks of educational psychology. He also believes that many current diagnostic practices are discriminatory, whether they are intended to be or not. He argues that the fact that many school psychologists tend to look for the causes of problems within an individual creates a discriminatory potential, because the students themselves, their families, or their living situations are likely to be blamed, when the school itself actually needs to be changed. His belief is that the current sociopolitical situation demands a "systems approach" to assessment to avoid such practices.

There were few members of minority racial and ethnic groups in the ranks of school psychology (Abramowitz 1981; Rosenfield 1981) as the '80s began. Why this is true and what to do about it were also issues discussed at Spring Hill.

Economic Considerations

Bevan (1981) described the current economic situation as being of particular importance in the discussions at Spring Hill. In a period of high inflation and high unemployment, education is vulnerable. When governments feel the need to make budget cuts, "education early on is classified among the expendables" (p. 127). When decisions have to be made about where to cut in the educational system, school psychology, often considered a frill, is more likely to be cut than other basic services.

At the same time, Bevan notes, there is increasing dissatisfaction among parents and other taxpayers with the public school system. This will, no doubt, affect the financial future of the schools, as parents turn to private education and taxpayers demand their money's worth. Peterson (1981) asserts that school psychologists must demonstrate that they are not a "costly luxury."

As funds are cut back, school psychologists are being called upon not only to justify their existence in the schools, but also to take on extra duties and additional cases. Those who complain now of being burdened with testing duties and paperwork may find themselves even more so in the future. It may be much more difficult to justify "extras" such as prevention programs and research to administrators facing a budget crisis.

The economic situation may also influence the school psychologists' service delivery system. Many school psychologists have a central office in one location and are assigned to several schools in other locations. Thus, they must travel at least once or twice during a school day to and from schools or office. In some rural areas the situation may be more severe, with school psychologists traveling miles between schools. With ever-rising gasoline prices and unpredictable supplies, this pattern may have to change. The services provided today might have to be cut back to accommodate fiscal constraints.

Another factor of the current economic situation which school psychologists must face is the impact on families of rising unemployment and more difficult financial circumstances. The stress resulting from these factors is bound to affect children directly and indirectly.

Legislation and Litigation

The past few years have seen a sharp increase in the number of court cases and laws pertaining to education. In the past, courts have maintained a hands-off policy toward the schools (Ysseldyke and Algozzine 1982), but according to Bersoff (1979), litigation in the last ten years has dealt with several school issues. Details of these court cases and statutes are discussed elsewhere and will not be reviewed here; however, a brief discussion of the way such forces can influence the direction of school psychology is important.

Many court cases have examined alleged abuses in the process of assessment. *Hanson* v. *Hobson* (1967) ruled unconstitutional ability grouping based on standardized test scores. In *Diana* v. *State Board of Education* (California, 1970), it was determined that children should be tested in their primary language and should not be given test items judged to be culturally biased. The best-known case among school psychologists, that of *Larry P. et al.* v. *Wilson Riles et al. (1 979),* determined that the California schools could not use intelligence tests as a basis for placing black students in classes for the educably mentally retarded. The impact of these cases on the practice of school psychology has been great, since tests have been the school psychologist's most frequently used tool. The reaction of some has been to abandon tests altogether; most school psychologists, however, believe that tests are extremely valuable if used carefully and selectively. In any case, tests have come under considerable scrutiny, and the constraints this places on school psychologists are obvious.

In a recent court case (*Parents in Action on Special Education* [PASE] v. *Joseph P. Hannon* [1980]), it was ruled that intelligence tests are not biased against black students. The determination that the test in question was not biased was based solely on the judge's critical review of the test. It is too early to say whether this signals a new direction in litigation rulings, but the results of this case, viewed in contrast to the *Larry P.* case, make obvious the ease with which school psychology can be affected by outside forces.

Litigation Often Leads to Legislation

Bersoff (1979) pointed out that "when among other reasons, problems need a broader solution than courts can provide or they affect many people, lawmakers enact statutes and administrators promulgate regulations that have comprehensive effect" (p. 77). Any discussion of change in school psychology would have to include the impact of Public Law 94–142, the Education for All Handicapped Children Act of 1975. The purpose of the legislation was to guarantee special education services to any child in need of them, and to ensure that the process of identification and provision of service to such students is fair and appropriate. Since the passage of P.L. 94-142, most school psychologists report spending much more time in evaluating children for possible special education services. Provisions such as the requirement that tests be administered in a child's native language and that tests be judged to be valid for diagnostic purposes have been virtually impossible to meet, and Bevan (1981) suggested that they will continue to be impossible. How are school psychologists to deal with this dilemma?

When discussing changes brought about by legislation and litigation, school psychologists may be inclined to emphasize the negative impact on the profession. It is true, however, that in many cases positive outcomes have occurred both for children and for the profession: P.L. 94-142 resulted in new programs, new jobs for school psychologists, and increased visibility.

Organization

With these pressing issues providing a backdrop, the Spring Hill Symposium was held June 4–8, 1980, at the Spring Hill Conference Center in Wayzata, Minnesota. Sixty-nine school psychologists from twenty-two states, the District of Columbia, and Alberta, Canada, attended. The major consideration in inviting participants was to draw from among the leaders in school psychology a representative group of men and women, educators and practitioners, and minorities. Almost everyone present was currently or had been at one time a practicing school psychologist.

The five-day symposium began with a historical survey by Elizabeth Abramowitz and a keynote address by William Bevan. Following this introductory session, participants met as a large group for three sessions to hear the major invited papers (Trachtman 1981, Grimes 1981, Baer and Bushell 1981), the invited reactions to them (Vensel 1981, Lambert 1981, Sewell 1981, Grubb 1981, Tucker 1981, Keogh 1981), and round-table discussions. The large group of participants was divided into three small groups for two sessions of creative discussion on the future of school psychology; and finally, these group discussions were synthesized (Rosenfield 1981, Bardon 1981, Hodges 1981). Peterson (1981) provided an overall synthesis of the symposium.

Review of Issues Discussed

In the broad framework provided by the introductory session and the invited papers, the discussions in the three groups were remarkably similar. The main concerns of the participants were summarized by Ysseldyke and Weinberg (1981) as : (1) goals and roles for school psychology practice; (2) ethical and legal issues; (3) the professionalism of school psychologists; (4) the content of training programs; and (5) accountability.

Goals and Roles for the Practice of School Psychology

As was true at Thayer, issues of role and function occupied much of the discussion at Spring Hill. Peterson (1981) identified five themes that arose in both the paper presentations and in the small group discussions:

1. What can school psychologists do to serve children and the schooling process as effectively as possible?
2. What are the conditions under which effective services might be provided?

3. How can environmental conditions for the provision of effective services be brought about?
4. What is the appropriate entry level for the practice of professional psychology?
5. We must all work together to help children learn better.

Throughout the discussions at Spring Hill, participants repeatedly addressed ways in which school psychological services could best be provided in the context of then-current social and economic considerations. Reminiscent of the Thayer Conference, participants struggled with the dilemma of serving the largest number of students possible while providing the best possible services for individuals. Perhaps more an issue of debate at Spring Hill than at Thayer was a question of focus: Bardon (1981, p. 301) phrased the question, "Are our goals and purposes best expressed as those of improved mental health in the schools or as improved education?" Strong proponents for both views spoke out during the symposium.

Participants at Spring Hill spoke clearly of a need to document models of exemplary school psychological practice and to communicate those "best practices" to the related professions with which we work. Some (e.g., Lambert 1981) pointed to the specialty guidelines recently published by APA as a model for service delivery; others (e.g., Hodges 1981) spoke of the need to conduct research contrasting alternative models for delivery of services.

Much discussion centered on essential competencies required for the practice of psychology in schools. Discussants recognized that the diversity of current school psychology training programs reflects the variety of beliefs in the profession concerning the skills that are needed to function effectively as a school psychologist. Some participants (Bevan 1981, Trachtman 1981) argued that too much specificity in training would be inappropriate; others (Grubb 1981) argued that a major issue confronting the profession was that too many school psychologists were "overgeneralized generalists."

The need for improved relations with other professionals working in the schools and with advocacy organizations was acknowledged by everyone. Specific suggestions for improving interprofessional relations, especially with administrators, were made (Grimes 1981).

Finally, several different opinions were expressed on the ability of school psychologists to control their professional destiny. Bevan (1981) expressed the belief that school psychologists will have much to say about their future roles if they are able to work effectively within the political system. Grimes (1981) called for controlling the professional future by improving everyday practice and demonstrating the contributions of school psychologists to the welfare of students and schools. Sewell (1981) and Tucker (1981) expressed doubt that school psychologists will be able to direct their own destiny, indicating that first it must be demonstrated that psychologists can answer important educational questions. Rosenfield (1981) spoke of barriers (e.g., our perception of a knowledge-practice gap) to taking control of the future, and called on the profession to develop psychologists who think like professionals rather than technicians.

Ethical and Legal Issues

Considerable attention at Spring Hill focused on the extent to which professional standards and/or competencies are compromised in efforts to respond to current litigation and legislation. Participants expressed the concern that Public Law 94-142 was forcing an increased emphasis on psychometric testing at the expense of activities that would have greater payoff for individual students. At issue was whether school psychologists could best maintain professional standards by working within the law (Grimes 1981), whether they might find it necessary to resort to confrontation to keep from compromising professional standards (Grubb 1981) or whether they could best response by working to change laws found to be impracticable (Bevan 1981).

A major ethical issue addressed at Spring Hill concerned responsibility for making decisions about students. A kind of "my turf–your turf" discussion focused on responsibility for classifying students, for deciding who should be assessed, and for specifying diagnostic procedures to be used.

It was clear that practicing school psychologists face a major ethical dilemma as they endeavor to work in schools and at the same time try to change "system" practices they view as inappropriate. There was general agreement on the need to specify who the client is (student, parent, school) and to work to eliminate mediocrity in education (Baer and Bushell 1981).

Professionalization of School Psychology

Participants at Spring Hill focused on several issues related to the professionalization of school psychology: the extent to which school psychology is a unique professional discipline; the role that professional school psychology organizations should play; school psychologists' role in influencing policy and legislation; problems of credentialing in school psychology; and both inter- and intra-professional communication. While

there was general agreement that school psychology is a unique professional discipline that should not overidentify with either parent group,
there was also appreciation and acceptance of professional pluralism
(Rosenfield 1981).

Participants at Spring Hill were very concerned with issues related to a breakdown in communication within the profession and with
other professions. While the discussion was probably triggered by the introductory remarks of Abramowitz (1981) and Bevan (1981), Peterson
ended the symposium by urging school psychologists to work together to
influence public policy, with primary attention to how policy can benefit
children and schools and only secondary emphasis on benefits to the
profession.

Training Issues

Abramowitz (1981) began the symposium with a challenge, stat-
ing that "the field has contributed little to the application of psychology
to resolving rather than describing critical recurring problems" (p. 126).
Bevan (1981), in his keynote address stated that

> we are doing an increasingly poor job of educating graduate students in
> psychology as a whole. In my opinion, our graduates are excessively nar-
> row specialists, long on technique and short on grasp of the fundamen-
> tals of our field, short on an understanding of its intellectual base, and
> short on a knowledge of its historical traditions. Such persons are likely
> to be effective when textbook solutions are readily evident, but found
> wanting when the problem solving calls for versatility — that is, for those
> overarching intuitive insights that professional settings more often than
> not require. If I were to pick two verbs to summarize my layman's advice
> about the curriculum, I would say *broaden* and *diversify* (p. 135).

Participants throughout the symposium were critical of current
training efforts, though two different viewpoints were expressed. There
were those who called for increasing specialization in technique and
action-oriented training programs; others called for increasing scope and
diversification. In the context of this discussion, the notion of nationally-
standardized training was raised and dismissed.

Accountability

School psychologists were concerned about the extent to which
they are accountable for the validity of their own practice. All agreed on

the need to start validating practices and document the effectiveness of their work.

Recommendations

The organizers of the Spring Hill Symposium hoped that the conference would help "begin an intensive process of serious thought and attention to the future of psychology in the schools." For this reason, the conference was organized mainly to promote discussion and clarification of contemporary issues, and not to make formal recommendations. The editors of the proceedings stated:

> If neither the "right" answers nor the paths to their discovery were found at Spring Hill, we can take comfort in the knowledge that the sample of trainers, practitioners, and administrators who gathered there for five days raised the appropriate questions. Piaget has taught us that the kinds of questions children ask tell us a great deal about their cognitive development and the ways they view the world. In the same way, we believe that the questions raised about their profession by its members are indicative of the professional posture and issues that are important at a particular time.
>
> (Ysseldyke and Weinberg 1981, p. 119)

THE OLYMPIA CONFERENCE

Planned as a follow-up to the Spring Hill Symposium, the Olympia Conference was held a year later, in the fall of 1981, at the Olympia Resort in Oconomowoc, Wisconsin. Participants continued the process begun at Spring Hill of examining the future of school psychology, focused by the conference theme, "School Psychology Can Make a Difference in the Future." The social, economic, and political issues underlying this conference had changed little since the preceding year, but a downturn in the nation's economy and a new federal Administration's threat of changes in the nation's priorities for education loomed as pressing issues for conference participants.

Invited to the conference were 350 participants representing the leadership of NASP, Division 16 (APA), and each state, and including all who participated in the Spring Hill Symposium. Unlike other school psychology conferences, the Olympia Conference began with speakers and activities designed to provide perspective on personal, economic, and political futures. It was not until the second day of the conference that participants began to consider possible futures for school psychology. This was accomplished in small groups of ten, where alternative scenarios of the future were designed and action statements on selected critical issues facing school psychologists were generated. The day's activities concluded with addresses by the presidents of NASP and Division 16 of APA and a mock U.S. Senate hearing, in which a proposal to eliminate funding for school psychology was debated. On the third morning of the conference, participants formed "networks" to consider possible actions in their areas of special interest. Concluding speeches were given by the presidents-elect of NASP and Division 16 and by Gilbert Trachtman. As was true at Spring Hill, no specific recommendations were generated at the Olympia Conference; but organizers and participants stressed the hope that the energy generated at Olympia for planning the future of school psychology would carry forward into action. The importance of the Olympia Conference was that it provided the participants with a better understanding of possible futures and the forces that will shape them, and offered the opportunity for attenders to work together and form networks for future action.

SUMMARY

It is clear that the issues in contemporary school psychology are complex, and no simple solutions to the problems are likely to be found. It is possible that twenty-five years from now, when another professional conference is held at another critical point in the history of the profession, the same issues will be discussed and participants will bemoan the fact that school psychology has made so few strides. But it is more likely that school psychologists will have to chart new directions in the next few years to keep their profession alive and to continue making worthwhile contributions to schools and school children. Whether the impetus will come from within the profession or from outside forces remains to be seen.

REFERENCES

Abramowitz, E. A. School psychology: A historical perspective. In J. Ysseldyke & R. Weinberg (Eds.), The future of psychology in the schools: Proceedings of the Spring Hill Symposium. *School Psychology Review,* 1981, *10,* 121–126.

Altman, I., & Wohlwill, J. F. (Eds.) *Children and the environment. Vol. 3 of Human Behavior and Environment: Advances in Theory and Research.* New York: Plenum, 1979.

Baer, D. M., & Bushell, D. Jr. The future of behavior analysis in the schools? Consider its recent past and then ask a different question. In J. Ysseldyke & R. Weinberg (Eds.), The future of psychology in the schools: Proceedings of the Spring Hill Symposium. *School Psychology Review,* 1981, *10,* 259–270.

Bardon, J. I. (Ed.). Problems and issues in school psychology—1964: Proceedings of a conference on "New Directions in School Psychology" sponsored by the National Institute of Mental Health. *Journal of School Psychology,* 1964–65, *3,* 1–44.

Bardon, J. I. Small group synthesis, Group C. In J. Ysseldyke & R. Weinberg (Eds.), The future of psychology in the schools: Proceedings of the Spring Hill Symposium. *School Psychology Review,* 1981, *10,* 297–306.

Bersoff, D. Regarding psychologists testily: The legal regulation of psychological testing in the public schools. *Maryland Law Review,* 1979, *39.*

Bevan, W. On coming of age among the professions. In J. Ysseldyke & R. Weinberg (Eds.), The future of psychology in the schools: Proceedings of the Spring Hill Symposium. *School Psychology Review,* 1981, *10,* 127–137.

Cutts, N. E. (Ed.). *School psychologists at mid-century.* Washington: American Psychological Association, 1955.

Diana v. State Board of Education, C-70, 37 RFP, District Court for Northern California (February 1970).

Drucker, P. The coming changes in our school systems. *Wall Street Journal,* 1981, *61,* 20.

Gray, S. W. (Ed.). *The internship in school psychology: Proceedings of the Peabody Conference.* Nashville, Tenn.: Department of Psychology, George Peabody College for Teachers, 1963.

Greene, D., & Lepper, M. R. Effects of extrinsic rewards on children's subsequent intrinsic interest. *Child Development,* 1974, *45,* 1141–45.

Grimes, J. Shaping the future of school psychology. In J. Ysseldyke & R. Weinberg (Eds.), The future of psychology in the schools: Proceedings of the Spring Hill Symposium. *School Psychology Review,* 1981, *10,* 206–231.

Grubb, R. D. Shaping the future of school psychology: A reaction. In J. Ysseldyke & R. Weinberg (Eds.), The future of psychology in the schools: Proceedings of the Spring Hill Symposium. *School Psychology Review,* 1981, *10,* 243–258.

Guidubaldi, J. (Ed.). Families: Current status and emerging trends. *School Psychology Review,* 1980, *9* (whole issue).

Hobson v. Hanson, 269F. Supp. 401 (1967).

Hodges, W. Small group synthesis, Group B. In J. Ysseldyke & R. Weinberg (Eds.), The future of psychology in the schools: Proceedings of the Spring Hill Symposium. *School Psychology Review,* 1981, *10,* 290–296.

Hunt, J. McV. Psychological development: Early experience. *Annual Review of Psychology,* 1979, *30,* 103–44.

Hyman, I. A. Psychology, education and schooling: Social policy implications in the lives of children and youth. *American Psychologist,* 1979, *34,* 1024–29.

Kagan, J. Family experience and the child's development. *American Psychologist,* 1979, *34,* 886–91.

Keogh, B. K. Ask a different question: Expect a different answer. In J. Ysseldyke & R. Weinberg (Eds.), The future of psychology in the schools: Proceedings of the Spring Hill Symposium. *School Psychology Review,* 1981, *10,* 278–284.

Korman, M. National conference on levels and patterns of professional training in psychology: The major themes. *American Psychologist,* 1974, *29,* 441–49.

Lambert, N. School psychology training for the decades ahead or rivers, streams, and creeks—Currents and tributaries to the sea. In J. Ysseldyke & R. Weinberg (Eds.), The future of psychology in the schools: Proceedings of the Spring Hill Symposium. *School Psychology Review,* 1981, *10,* 194–205.

Larry P., et al. v. *Wilson Riles, et al.* United States District Court, Northern District of California, Case No. C-71-2270 RFP, 1972, 1974, 1979.

Lazar, I., & Darling, R. B. *Lasting effects after preschool.* Washington, D.C.: U.S. Government Printing Office, 1979.

Mensch, I. N. *Clinical psychology: Science and profession.* New York: Macmillan, 1966.

Parents in Action on Special Education v. *Joseph P. Hannon.* U.S. District Court, Northern District of Illinois, Eastern Division, No. 74, (3586), July, 1980.

Peterson, D. R. Overall synthesis of the Spring Hill Symposium on the Future of Psychology in the Schools. In J. Ysseldyke & R. Weinberg (Eds.), The future of psychology in the schools: Proceedings of the Spring Hill Symposium. *School Psychology Review,* 1981, *10,* 307–314.

Raimy, V. C. (Ed.). *Training in clinical psychology.* Englewood Cliffs, N.J.: Prentice-Hall, 1950.

Rosenfield, S. Small group synthesis, Group A. In J. Ysseldyke & R. Weinberg (Eds.), The future of psychology in the schools: Proceedings of the Spring Hill Symposium. *School Psychology Review,* 1981, *10,* 285–289.

Sewell, T. Shaping the future of school psychology: Another perspective. In J. Ysseldyke & R. Weinberg (Eds.), The future of psychology in the schools: Proceedings of the Spring Hill Symposium. *School Psychology Review,* 1981, *10,* 232–242.

Trachtman, G. On such a full sea. In J. Ysseldyke & R. Weinberg (Eds.), The future of psychology in the schools: Proceedings of the Spring Hill Symposium. *School Psychology Review,* 1981, *10* 138–181.

Tucker, J. The emperor's new clothes are hand-me-downs. In J. Ysseldyke & R. Weinberg (Eds.), The future of psychology in the schools: Proceedings of the Spring Hill Symposium. *School Psychology Review,* 1981, *10,* 271–277.

Vensel, D. Assuming responsibility for the future of school psychology. In J. Yssel-dyke & R. Weinberg (Eds.), The future of psychology in the schools: Proceedings of the Spring Hill Symposium. *School Psychology Review,* 1981, *10,* 182–193.

Weinstein, C. S. The physical environment of the school: A review of the research. *Review of Educational Research,* 1979, *49,* 577–610.

Yen, W. M. Measuring individual differences with an information-processing model. *Journal of Educational Psychology,* 1978, *70,* 72–86.

Ysseldyke, J., & Algozzine, R. *Critical issues in special and remedial education.* Boston: Houghton-Mifflin, 1982.

Ysseldyke, J., & Weinberg, R. (Eds.). The future of psychology in the schools: Proceedings of the Spring Hill Symposium. *School Psychology Review,* 1981, *10.*

Zigler, E., & Valentine, J. *Project Head Start: A legacy of the War on Poverty.* New York: Free Press, 1979.

2

National Organizations
Professional Identity
ANN W. ENGIN

ORGANIZATIONS of any kind serve multiple purposes—from meeting social affiliative needs and facilitating communication to serving as high-powered problem-identification and problem-solving forums on the local, state, or national level. At the base of the attraction of organizations is an ancient, simple, and yet cogent truth: in numbers there is strength and power. The power may derive from a greater number of minds and cognitive styles to interact synergistically on a conceptual, philosophical or practical agenda, or it may simply consist of the force of numbers in the ballot box or in a letter-writing campaign. The awesome power of small but effectively engineered special interest groups in the halls of the United States Congress aptly illustrates the point that organized, planned, well-orchestrated efforts yield results that sheer numbers alone cannot produce.

Professional organizations always serve the self-interest of the profession as well as working to improve services to the public. The self-interest or guild functions protect or enhance the profession. In principle, all professional organizations place service to the public as the paramount concern, but many activities are related to furthering the prestige or influence of the profession. Often the two interests go hand in hand. For instance, since professions offer a service which requires special expertise, the untrained public is ofttimes ill equipped to judge the effectiveness of an individual professional in comparison with his or her peers or with the standards of the profession. Thus, an elaborate system of ensuring minimal standards has evolved over time, largely as a function of professional organizations. Training programs and/or institutions are accredited to indicate to those who are seeking to be trained or to those who are planning to hire graduate trainees that the training program has been objectively evaluated against a uniform set of standards or criteria. The credentials of individual professionals indicate that they have met the minimal standards to practice the profession.

The two kinds of credentials of interest to the school psychologist are: (1) certification, which is generally administered by state teacher certification agencies and allows the holder to practice in the public schools of the state; and (2) licensure, which is generally controlled by state boards of psychology and permits the holder to practice in the private domain, to work independently of an agency or school district, and to charge fees for the delivery of psychological services. Accreditation and credentialing bodies receive their authority from legal statutes. In essence, then, the professions through their organizations interface with the legal and regulatory systems of local, state, and national government, and they influence and are influenced by governmental laws, regulations, and standards. Brown (1979a, 1980) and Brown, Horn, and Lindstrom (1977, 1980) thoroughly discuss the accreditation and credentialing processes and current status in the field of school psychology.

Professional organizations have played a superordinate role in the development and evolution of school psychology as a specialty or profession. (As we shall soon see, whether school psychology is defined as a specialty of psychology or as an independent profession is one of the basic disputes at issue in school psychology.)

There are two major national professional associations for school psychologists, the American Psychological Association (APA) and the National Association of School Psychologists (NASP). Both organizations are of importance to school psychologists, but each has a different overall emphasis and mission. In order to understand fully the present status of school psychology as an emerging entity, it is imperative to have a perspective on the history of the two professional organizations, their beginnings, the present and potential future conflicting interests, their differing styles of organizational behavior, and membership patterns.

THE AMERICAN PSYCHOLOGICAL ASSOCIATION

The American Psychological Association was founded in 1892 and represents all of psychology. With a humble beginning of 26 members, the APA was formed at Clark University, held its first meeting at the University of Pennsylvania, and had G. Stanley Hall as its first president. Indeed, the association was organized in a conference in Hall's study at Clark. Several benchmarks illustrate the growth of American organized psychology. By 1910 APA had grown to 228 members. In 1930 there were approximately one thousand members and in 1950 approximately six thousand (Boring 1950). The current membership is 53,000 (Perloff, 1981).

Psychology is generally conceded to have emerged from three disciplines: philosophy, physics, and physiology. The history of American psychology is replete with conflicting theories, views and emphases, but two interrelated trends are particularly noteworthy for school psychologists: (1) the ongoing struggle within organized generic psychology between academic-scientific and applied-professional interests, and (2) the steadily increasing diversity of interests within the APA.

Academic-Scientific versus Applied-Professional Interests

Organized psychology has almost incessantly grappled with the question of whether the primary essence of psychology should be rooted in a scientific or a professional orientation. The academic-scientific interests are largely concerned with the production and dissemination of scholarly psychological knowledge, whereas the applied-professional interests are primarily concerned with service delivery to specified target populations. There are four recognized psychology specialties: clinical, counseling, school, and industrial-organizational psychology. The specialty guidelines for service delivery were adopted by the APA Council of Representatives in January 1980 and represent official policy relative to delivery of psychological services (Committee on Professional Standards, 1981). The specialty guidelines were based on the generic "Standards for Providers of Psychological Services" which were adopted in January of 1977 (APA, 1977).

At times the diverse interests were actually represented by separate organizations, concrete evidence of the schism. For example, in 1936 the American Association of Applied Psychology (AAAP) was founded as a separate organization from the APA, which was then left primarily as a scientific body. Following World War II, the two organizations merged, and once again APA represented both scientific and professional interests. In approximately another decade, a group of experimentalists left APA and created the Psychonomic Society in reaction to their perception that professional concerns were paramount in APA, and that experimental interests required an organizational structure without any divergent claims for attention. The tension is still present in APA today. A recent, poignant example of the continued conflict was the resignation from membership in the organization of Lloyd Humphreys in a letter to the editor of the *APA Monitor* in October 1981. The long-standing organizational divergences prompted several factions to recommend a new organizational structure for the APA, in order that the organization may on the one hand continue to represent all of psychology and speak "with one voice" in the legislative and public policy arenas, yet acknowledge and program maximally for the existing diversity of interests and purposes on the other ("Five-year Report of the Policy and Planning Board," 1980, 1981).

The difficulty is further compounded by the fact that many psychologists across the scientific and professional ranks possess strong social consciences and have urged the APA to take action in social policy arenas both within and outside the organization. Reflecting this trend are several recent developments, including the creation of a Board of Ethnic Minority Affairs, increased involvement in external legal issues as *amicus curia,* the establishment of a Psychology Defense Fund to support membership needs, the creation of the National Institutes of Psychological Policy Studies (NIPPS), the divestiture of APA holdings in five corporations with direct involvement in South Africa, a proposed Board of Women's Issues in Psychology (BWIP), and the refusal to hold conventions in non-ERA-ratified states. While many concur with these developments, a large number of psychologists are dissatisfied with some or all of them and feel strongly that APA has confused the mission of a professional organization and has overstepped reasonable bounds of organizational behavior.

Diversity of Interests in APA

Concurrent with the reorganization of APA in 1944 and 1945 was the development of a divisional structure to represent the specialized interests within psychology (Wolfe 1946). There are currently forty-two divisions within APA. They are as follows:

1. General Psychology
2. Teaching of Psychology
3. Experimental Psychology
*4. Psychometric Society (which decided not to become a Charter division)
5. Evaluation and Measurement
6. Physiological and Comparative Psychology
7. Developmental Psychology
8. Personality and Social Psychology
9. The Society for the Psychological Study of Social Issues (SPSSI)
10. Psychology and the Arts
*11. Abnormal Psychology and Psychotherapy (absorbed into Division 12)
12. Clinical Psychology
13. Consulting Psychology
14. Industrial and Organizational Psychology

*Of the 42 divisions two, Division 4 and 11, are no longer functioning.

15. Educational Psychology
16. School Psychology
17. Counseling Psychology
18. Psychologists in Public Service
19. Military Psychology
20. Adult Development and Aging
21. Society of Engineering Psychologists
22. Rehabilitation Psychology
23. Consumer Psychology
24. Theoretical and Philosophical Psychology
25. Experimental Analysis of Behavior
26. History of Psychology
27. Community Psychology
28. Psychopharmacology
29. Psychotherapy
30. Psychological Hypnosis
31. State Psychological Association Affairs
32. Humanistic Psychology
33. Mental Retardation
34. Population and Environmental Psychology
35. Psychology of Women
36. Psychologists Interested in Religious Issues
37. Child and Youth Services
38. Health Psychology
39. Psychoanalysis
40. Clinical Neuropsychology
41. Psychology and the Law
42. Psychologists in Independent Practice

Much concern has been expressed within APA about the proliferation of divisions. Six new divisions have been added just in the last five years. It is interesting to note that the most recently added divisions relate to professional as opposed to academic-scientific interests.

APA Organizational Structure

The Council of Representatives is the policy-making body of APA and consists of approximately 100-120 members. An annual apportionment ballot determines how many representatives the divisions and state associations will have for the year (Committee on Structure and Function of Council, 1981). There are five officers: president, president-elect, past president, recording secretary and treasurer. The officers and six other elected members constitute the Board of Directors, which serves as the executive committee of the Council. There are eight standing Boards with their own committees that report to the Council through the Board of Directors. The central office, headed by the executive officer, facilitates and coordinates the work of the overall governance structure. A good overview of the governance structure is found in Pallak's (1980) first executive report to the membership. Each June issue of the *American Psychologist* contains a list of the current officers, boards, committees, and representatives, as well as important reports of annual activities.

APA Membership Requirements

Full members must possess a doctoral degree. Associate membership is available to psychologists without the doctoral degree, but many prerogatives of full membership are not available to these members, such as voting and eligibility to serve as elected officials of the association.

Division 16

Division 16 (the Division of School Psychology) was included as a charter division in the 1944 reorganization (Tindall 1979) and it currently has approximately 2500 members (Van den Bos, Stapp, and Pallak 1981). In contrast to APA proper, Division 16 permits full membership to school psychologists possessing a master's degree or a specialist degree in school psychology or a related area. The majority of its membership is at the doctoral level, however. Trainers and school psychologists from the Northeast and Far West, areas of the country where school psychology evolved directly from clinical psychology (Brown 1979a), constitute the majority of Division 16 membership.

In the early years of school psychology, Division 16 played an important role in defining the practice of school psychology by developing guidelines for the certification and training of school psychologists (Bardon 1963); sponsoring the Thayer Conference, which provided the conceptual base for the training and practice of school psychology, even into the present (Cutts 1955); and representing the school psychology specialty to generic psychology (see Ysseldyke and Schakel, Chapter 1).

Within the APA structure, Division 16 has represented a small and not politically potent force in comparison with the large memberships and accompanying political power in the clinical and counseling divisions, particularly the former area of professional psychology. Several Division 16 members, however, have played leading roles in APA governance and have enhanced the image of school psychology through their efforts. Of particular note are Jack Bardon, Virginia Bennett, and Nadine Lambert, although many other names could be mentioned.

THE NATIONAL ASSOCIATION OF SCHOOL PSYCHOLOGISTS

The National Association of School Psychologists (NASP) was formed largely to meet the professional needs of practicing school psycholgists, most of whom were nondoctoral and who deemed the American Psychological Association unable to meet their needs. The catalyst for the inception of NASP was an active group of school psychologists in the Ohio School Psychologists Association who perceived a need, assessed the leadership in other states, and organized a planning meeting in March of 1968 in Columbus, Ohio. This meeting set the stage for the convention in St. Louis in March of 1969 at which NASP was officially launched.

The 1969 conference, which was attended by over 400 people from twenty-four states, identified several important issues:

1. Even though school psychology was an established professional entity in many states, communication networks across states were poor or nonexistent;

2. The overall picture of the profession was one of disorganization, confusion, and haphazard growth due to its uneven development among the states and the lack of human and financial resources to remedy the situation;

3. In spite of great potential for enhancing the mental health and educational development of children and youth, national school psychology in practice was without a general purpose and unified set of goals;

4. Nondoctoral school psychology practitioners were in need of a national identity and a means of dealing with the problems and issues facing the profession.

NASP Organizational Structure

The Delegate Assembly is the policy-making body of NASP and consists of one elected representative from each state and representatives from regions in Canada. The five officers are the president, president-elect, past president, secretary and treasurer. Eleven regional directors and the officers form the Executive Board, which conducts the continuing affairs of the organization. NASP has a unique managerial system,

consisting of four part-time executive managers with clearly differenti-
ated responsibilities. The functions are Convention, Executive Board-
Delegate-Committee Services, Fiscal-Membership, and Public Relations.
Standing committees do a large part of the organizational business. The
Executive Board meets separately two times a year and twice with the Del-
egate Assembly.

NASP Membership Requirements

Membership in NASP is open to anyone certified as a school psychologist, as well as to students. It is one of the few organizations where
students possess both full voting rights and the right to participate in the
governance structure in any role but president. The majority of NASP
members are nondoctoral school psychologists employed in the school,
but many trainers also belong, some in addition to membership in APA
and others in lieu of APA membership (Ramage 1979).

The preceding was a brief overview of the history of the two organizations and serves as an important prelude to a discussion of their
differing positions concerning standards for training and practice. The
relative brevity of the section on NASP, in comparison to that on APA,
should not be construed as reflecting lesser importance. Rather, NASP
has a significantly shorter history and its singularity of professional identity also renders its inner workings far less complex than those of APA.

A concise comparison of the differences and similarities of the
two organizations is now in order. APA is much larger, older, and more
complex than NASP and is widely known nationally as the organization
of psychologists. APA is also more diverse and thus must weigh "the
greatest good for the greatest number of people" in a totally different way
than does NASP. APA policymaking proceeds slowly, whereas NASP has
the capability of responding quickly in matters concerning policy as well
as action. Trachtman (1981) offered some interesting and controversial
views on the strengths and weaknesses of each organization related to
organizational structure and modus operandi. APA speaks for all of psychology, while NASP represents but one professional area. The differences are great, but both organizations are alike in one important, fundamental sense: each has a large cadre of talented, dedicated leaders and a
lasting commitment to promote excellence in all areas of organizational
endeavor.

APA AND NASP POSITIONS ON PROFESSIONAL STANDARDS

Both APA and NASP have developed and published clearly articulated positions on the training of school psychologists, accreditation of training programs, standards for service delivery, credentialing of school psychologists, and ethical standards for professional practice. All school psychologists should be familiar with the contents of each of the documents. Table 2.1 presents a list of the important documents of the APA and NASP relative to standards and school psychology. The APA and NASP standards documents are discussed at length in Pryzwansky (1982) and Engin and Johnson (1983).

Basically, the two organizations have taken dissimilar stands on

TABLE 2.1

APA and NASP Standards Documents for School Psychologists

	American Psychological Association	National Association of School Psychologists
Training or accreditation standards	American Psychological Association. *Criteria for accreditation of doctoral training programs and internships in professional psychology.* Washington, D.C.: Author, 1979 (amended 1980). American Psychological Association. *Accreditation handbook.* Washington, D.C.: Author, 1980.	National Association of School Psychologists. *Standards for field placement programs in school psychology.* Washington, D.C.: Author, 1978. National Association of School Psychologists. *Standards for training programs in school psychology.* Washington, D.C.: Author, 1978.
Service delivery and credentialing standards	American Psychological Association. *Standards for providers of psychological services* (Rev. ed.). Washington, D.C.: Author, 1977. American Psychological Association. *Specialty guidelines for the delivery of services by school psychologists.* Washington, D.C.: Author, 1980.	National Association of School Psychologists. *Standards for credentialing in school psychology.* Washington, D.C.: Author, 1978. National Association of School Psychologists. *Standards for the provision of school psychological services.* Washington, D.C.: Author, 1978.
Ethical standards	American Psychological Association. *Ethical principles of psychologists* (Rev. ed.). Washington, D.C.: Author, 1981.	National Association of School Psychologists. *Principles for professional ethics* (Rev. ed.). Washington, D.C.: Author, 1980.

key professional issues, a phenomenon which is a logical offshoot of their divergent histories, traditions, and orientations. The answers they give to four basic professional questions simultaneously delineate their conflicting viewpoints and define the challenge of effecting a unified professional agenda for the future. Those four key questions are:

1. Is the school psychologist primarily a psychologist or an educator?
2. Is school psychology a specialty of professional psychology or an independent profession?
3. What is the appropriate entry level of training required for the unsupervised practice of school psychology?
4. Who is entitled to the title of "school psychologist"?

Genealogy of School Psychology

The APA position strongly asserts that school psychologists are psychologists first and foremost, albeit psychologists who happen to function in the school setting. Thus, school psychology is viewed as evolving directly from generic psychology with deep and inextricable roots in its lineage. NASP, on the other hand, views school psychology as a hybrid or blend of psychology and education, rather than a direct offshoot of either one. School psychologists are therefore both psychologists and educators. It is instructive to compare the chronicles of school psychology's evolution presented by Tindall (1979) and Brown (1979a), who present the APA and the NASP viewpoints respectively. Tindall stressed the roots in psychology, whereas Brown credited the multiple sources in a different manner and stated that school psychology is equally rooted in the mainstreams of education and generic psychology. In the vernacular, NASP maintains that school psychology is of mixed parentage, while APA characterizes school psychology with clear bloodlines and a pedigree.

Specialty or Profession

Closely related to the parentage issue is the question of whether school psychology is a specialty of professional psychology or an independent profession. The APA view is presented informally by Bardon (1979a) in a parable in which he equates the school psychologist to the school physician and maintains that a physician is a physician first and foremost and a school physician only by virtue of the work setting; so, indeed, is a school psychologist a specialist of psychology practice rather than a practitioner of a unique professional role. Brown (1979a, 1979b), on the contrary, expresses the NASP view of school psychology as an independent profession linked to both psychology and education but dependent on neither for its identity. Thus, Brown (1979b) optimistically hails the future of school psychology as an autonomous profession, while Bardon (1979b) prophesies doom and gloom if an autonomous movement prevails.

Other views on this issue are also present in the professional literature. Trachtman (1981), using pragmatic, psychological reasoning (as opposed to a purely philosophical reflection), accepts that ideally school psychology is and should remain a part of generic psychology, but believes that this situation could and should change if the APA rigid doctoral stance is unaltered. Likening school psychology to an adolescent in identity crisis, Trachtman suggests that the school psychology "adolescent" is receiving contradictory, double-bind statements from the "parent" (APA), to the effect that not all of the adolescent is worthwhile or belongs in all respects to the family. The message either has to be denied or the "bad parts" of the adolescent removed to prevent the inevitable schizophrenia. Through confrontative arbitration or family therapy or both, the adolescent may struggle to retain familial identity while simultaneously preserving personal integrity. If one's basic integrity is threatened, however, a healthy but still developing adolescent has little choice but to leave home and embark on a separate, emancipated course. The freed adolescent cannot discard genes or early childhood learnings but is able to create new intimate relationships and to build an independent future.

Trachtman is in essence agreeing philosophically with APA regarding the genealogy of school psychology, affirming the pragmatism of NASP's independent course, and exhorting APA to revise its standards for providers of psychological services to prevent an exodus. Tucker (1981), on the other hand, suggests that we as professionals allow the consumer to decide these issues in the marketplace. Let us next consider the respective standards.

Entry Level for Unsupervised Practice

Prior to a discussion of the differences in NASP and APA policy, it will be helpful to point out where they do agree. Both NASP and APA consider the entry level for the delivery of school psychological services to be at the sixth year or specialist level of training. Therefore, a master's level of training or less is regarded by both as insufficient to meet the multiple demands and expectations of the field. The two associations part company, however, when the issue becomes one of entry level for *unsupervised* practice.

For the APA, only doctoral-level practitioners may work without supervision. Since the guidelines for all four professional psychology specialties are based on the generic "Standards for Providers of Psychological Services" (APA 1977), which stipulates the doctoral level for independent, unsupervised practice, all four specialties are uniform in this requirement. The APA perspective, succinctly stated, is that the question of who is a psychologist must be answered in a generic sense based on a consensual definition across subareas. The specialties, therefore, cannot define individual criteria but are bound by the generic definition in the "Standards," which preceded and takes precedence over the subsequent "Specialty Guidelines for the Delivery of Services" (APA 1981). APA representatives point to the need for depth and breadth in training and for the inculcation of a scientific way of thinking in all types of practice. Such training, they maintain, can only be assured by doctoral-level programs.

For NASP, the entry level for unsupervised practice in the public schools and the private domain is the sixth year or specialist level. The NASP maintains that quality training and practice can be and are assured at the sixth-year level, and that there is no empirical evidence to suggest that a doctoral-level practitioner is in any way a better, more competent practitioner. While recognizing that more is generally better than less, NASP asserts that additional training above the already substantial, required curriculum would not be functionally related to job responsibilities. The demand in the schools is for the sixth-year level of training rather than the doctoral level, and the majority of school psychologists themselves, regardless of associational affiliation, choose the sixth-year level as the preferred entry level (Ramage 1979).

NASP and APA also differ in their views regarding the supervision of school psychologists. APA "Specialty Guidelines" call for all nondoctoral service providers to be supervised by doctoral-level professional psychologists. Whereas APA asserts that the depth and breadth of doctoral-level training provides a strong base for supervisory practice, NASP notes that there is a body of literature on the theory and practice of supervision which is not included in all doctoral training program curricula, so that supervisory skills cannot be assumed of recipients of the doctoral degree. NASP further maintains that professional supervisors should be chosen on the basis of demonstrated competencies rather than degree level.

School Psychology Title

The issue of title may seem a minor one; after all, what's in a name? Yet, hard as it may be to believe, this may be the most emotionally laden aspect of the APA's position on nondoctoral school psychologists. The APA "Standards" (1977) and the subsequent "Specialty Guidelines" (1981) define a professional psychologist as one with a doctoral degree. While recognizing service providers with lesser training, APA policy states that they are not to be called psychologists; rather, the word *psychological* is to be used as an adjective with another noun, as the proposed titles of "school psychological examiner," "school psychological technician," or "school psychological assistant." By APA definition, "specialist in school psychology" is the designated title for the sixth year or specialist-level school psychologist. Bardon (1979a) proposed the NASP change its name from the National Association of School Psychologists to something like the "National Association of School Psychological Personnel," with the acronym NASPP. There are a few limited exemptions for school psychologists which serve to grandparent a large number of currently functioning school psychologists in a transition period. All beginning students now and in the future, however, must obtain the doctorate in school psychology in order to possess the title of "professional school psychologist," according to APA policy. NASP questions the legitimacy and efficacy of this policy, as professional titles are bestowed by state legislatures rather than by professional organizations.

Accreditation: Challenge and Opportunity

APA and NASP are both involved in school psychology accreditation. APA accredits at the doctoral level only. In 1981, the APA had given full accreditation to sixteen doctoral-level school psychology programs and four had been provisionally approved. NASP does not directly accredit training programs but is a constituent member of the National Council for Accreditation of Teacher Education (NCATE), which accredits schools of education and programs that lead to practice in the public schools. NCATE has been accrediting school psychology programs since 1953 (Brown 1979a) and has accredited at the master's, sixth year, and doctoral levels. Currently approximately 125 school psychology programs are accredited by NCATE.

In 1978, the APA and NASP came into direct conflict when the APA Board of Professional Affairs, as a logical consequence of the policy in the generic "Standards" (APA 1977), attempted to assume exclusive authority to accredit school psychology programs at the doctoral level. In order to facilitate a resolution to this issue (as well as those pertaining to titling and credentialing, entry level for the independent practice of school psychology, and related concerns), both organizations agreed to create an APA/NASP Task Force composed of six individuals, three from each organization, to study the points of disagreement and propose resolutions to the respective governing bodies.

The task force proved to be extremely productive and proposed a trial joint accreditation project by NASP, NCATE and APA, with an implementation plan for a collaborative accreditation process. Since accreditation policies eventually determine the level and quality of training, this cooperative effort is viewed as an important first step towards resolving other professional issues which find the two associations in philosophical and/or political conflict. One recent development was the request by the Board of Directors of APA for the task force to confine its activities to joint *doctoral*-level accreditation, while exploration of the possible APA role in accreditation at the nondoctoral level continues (Abeles 1981). In this connection, it is interesting that the APA Policy and Planning Board recommended the establishment of a commission to consider issues associated with the master's degree in psychology (Five-year report of the Policy and Planning Board 1980). The nondoctoral issue is far from resolved, even within APA.

APA and NASP: Friendly Enemies or Cooperative Builders?

The long history of APA and short story of NASP bring us to the present, where all of us must face some difficult questions. Even a brief reflection on the events of the last three to four years brings into dramatic focus the advances APA and Division 16 and NASP have made in building communication networks and promoting cooperative, mutually beneficial activities. The APA/NASP Task Force, the Spring Hill Symposium, the National School Psychology Inservice Training Network, the Olympia Conference, and a number of smaller but no less significant interorganizational committee activities have opened doors that were only cracked before. Forbidding personal and organizational barriers have been found unnecessary and removed. The stage is now set for a future of cooperative building, but the potential for friendly enmity is still among us.

The outlook of school psychologists generally tends to be one of optimism, sometimes beyond reasonable bounds. Bardon (1981) cautions us not to expect or to demand miracles of our professional organizations singly or in concert, but instead to determine sensible and workable agendas, so we do not doom ourselves to failure even before our activities are begun. Conversely, however, we cannot afford to defer our professional hopes and dreams until we have thoroughly examined all possibilities for achievement. We all recognize the need and should be willing to work for a unified professional identity and a better fusion of professional commitment, resources, and activities for the common good. The ideal is laudable; now, how can it be realized?

IMPLICATIONS FOR TRAINERS, PRACTITIONERS, AND STUDENTS

I hesitate to state the obvious, because it is in many respects an overworked cliché, but it is necessary for a common starting point: school psychology like many other professions, and perhaps like American domestic and foreign affairs, is at a crucial crossroads, a crisis point. As we all know, crises represent a call to action, a challenge to develop new strategies and to bring new coping mechanisms into play. At this time we need all of the people and financial resources we can muster to confront our challenges most effectively. This requires that each of us belong to and become involved in our national, state, and local school psychology organizations. Furthermore, we must use our influence to attract new, unaffiliated school psychologists to the organizational folds. Too many of our colleagues fail to realize the importance of organizations and of their own participation in them for personal and professional gain. Personal influence is a far more potent motivator than paper invitations to join. Two groups are of utmost consequence: established practitioners who have never joined organizations or who dropped out because they felt they were not getting their money's worth, and students in training. The former group is in need of renewed enthusiasm for the field and may indeed have much to offer the organization once special interests are kindled. The latter group represents the leaders of tomorrow and should be indoctrinated early in the social and professional advantages of professional organizations. Membership patterns reveal that students tend to maintain membership past student days, while most nonmember students continue their unaffiliated status once in the field.

Beyond the decision to join and a concern for what professional organizations are doing for us, we need to consider what we as individuals may have to contribute to our organizations and to our profession. If nothing else, all members should take seriously their responsibility to give feedback to the elected representatives, conveying both positive and negative feedback in the most constructive fashion possible. The most helpful feedback, of course, contains concrete suggestions for change. Very few people realize the frustration of elected or appointed officials who eagerly seek input only to discover that few (in some cases, none) of those served can find the time to give the requested feedback. Most leaders would far prefer to be given honest, negative feedback than to receive silence, which is the most distressing feedback of all, indicating lack of interest in the matter at hand.

Perhaps the most helpful, although time consuming, contribution to professional organizations is to volunteer your services in a capacity which interests you. Do not assume that you will be asked if you are wanted; rather take the initiative. Familiarize yourself with the organization, find the activities which are best suited to your talents, and then actively volunteer. Professional organizations are able to accomplish a variety of work activities only by dint of their unpaid volunteers. Expect to start as a committee member and be prepared, if you work hard and well, to be rewarded by more work, perhaps the honor and recognition of serving as committee chair. Nearly all who participate actively and fully as volunteers in professional organizations find personal rewards, satisfactions, friendships, and a shared sense of community which is unparalleled in other activities. Volunteer workers can also take pride in the fact that they are an important albeit small part of the history of the profession. Each effort counts in the overall scheme of advancement of professional maturity.

In many senses school psychologists are still grappling with the same issues we faced when the profession first began, but the issues have become more complex and intertwined with sociological, economic and political forces we are only recently acknowledging, even as we struggle to predict and control them. On a positive note we are more active than was ever true in our previous history, and we have affirmed the urgent necessity of affecting the all-important policy issues in our lives as perhaps the single most provocative conclusion of the Spring Hill Symposium and the most cogent challenge for our professional organizations working in concert.

REFERENCES

Abeles, N. Proceedings of the American Psychological Association, Incorporated, for the year 1980. Minutes of the Annual Meetings of the Council of Representatives. *American Psychologist,* 1981, *36,* 552–586.

American Psychological Association. *Standards for providers of psychological services* (Rev. ed.). Washington, D.C.: Author, 1977.

American Psychological Association. Approved doctoral programs in clinical, counseling and school psychology: 1981. *American Psychologist,* 1981, *36,* 1516–1518.

Bardon, J. I. Proposals for state department of education certification of school psychologists. *American Psychologist*, 1963, *18*, 711–714.

Bardon, J. I. Debate: Will the real school psychologist please stand up? I. How best to establish the identity of professional psychology. *School Psychology Digest*, 1979, *8*, 162–167. (a)

Bardon, J. I. Reactions to the Debate: Will the real school psychologist please stand up? Commentary on Brown and Hyman. *School Psychology Digest*, 1979, *8*, 181–183. (b)

Bardon, J. I. Small group synthesis, Group C. In J. Ysseldyke & R. Weinberg (Eds.), The future of psychology in the schools: Proceedings of the Spring Hill Symposium. *School Psychology Review*, 1981, *10*, 297–306.

Boring, E. G. *A history of experimental psychology* (2nd ed.). New York: Appleton-Century-Crofts, 1950.

Brown, D. T. Issues in accreditation, certification, and licensure. In G. D. Phye & D. J. Reschly (Eds.), *School psychology: Perspectives and issues*. New York: Academic Press, 1979, 49–82. (a)

Brown, D. T. Debate: Will the real school psychologist please stand up? II. The drive for independence. *School Psychology Digest*, 1979, *8*, 168–173. (b)

Brown, D. T. Current trends in certification and licensure. *NASP Communique*, 1980, *8*(6), 1.

Brown, D. T., Horn, A. J., & Lindstrom, J. P. *The handbook of certification/ licensure requirements for school psychologists* (3rd ed.). Washington, D.C.: National Association of School Psychologists, 1980.

Brown, D. T., Sewall, T. J., & Lindstrom, J. P. *The handbook of certification/ licensure requirements for school psychologists* (2nd ed.). Washington, D.C.: National Association of School Psychologists, 1977.

Committee on Professional Standards. Specialty guidelines for the delivery of services. *American Psychologist*, 1981, *36*, 639–681.

Committee on Structure and Function of Council. Composition of the Council of Representatives: Report on the apportionment ballot for representation year 1982. *American Psychologist*, 1981, *36*, 610–615.

Cutts, N. E. (Ed.). *School psychologists at mid-century*. Washington, D. C.: American Psychological Association, 1955.

Engin, A. W., & Johnson, R. School psychology training and practice: The NASP perspective. In T. R. Kratochwill (Ed.), *Advances in school psychology* (Vol. III). Hillsdale, New Jersey: Lawrence Erlbaum Associates, 1983, in press.

Five-year report of the Policy and Planning Board: 1980. *American Psychologist*, 1981, *36*, 547–551.

Pallak, M. S. Report of the Executive Officer: 1979. *American Psychologist*, 1980, *35*, 485–496.

Perloff, R. Report of the treasurer: 1980. *American Psychologist*, 1981, *36*, 543–546.

Pryzwansky, W. B. School psychology training and practice: The APA perspective. In T. R. Kratochwill (Ed.), *Advances in school psychology* (Vol. II). Hillsdale, N. J.: Lawrence Erlbaum Associates, 1982.

Ramage, J. C. National survey of school psychologists: Update. *School Psychology Digest,* 1979, *8,* 153-161.

Tindall, R. H. School psychology: The development of a profession. In G. D. Phye, & D. J. Reschly (Eds.), *School psychology: Perspectives and issues.* New York: Academic Press, 1979, 3-24.

Trachtman, G. M. On such a full sea. *School Psychology Review,* 1981, *10,* 138-181.

Tucker, J. The emperor's new clothes are hand-me-downs. *School Psychology Review,* 1981, *10,* 271-277.

Van den Bos, G. R., Stapp, J., & Pallak, M. S. (Eds.). Editorial: About the Human Resources in Psychology special issue. *American Psychologist,* 1981, *36,* 1207-1210.

Wolf, D. The reorganized American Psychological Association. *American Psychologist,* 1946, *1,* 3-6.

Section II
Practice of School Psychology
Issues

3

Foundations of Measurement in Psychology and Education

CECIL R. REYNOLDS

AT ALL LEVELS of practice, school psychologists are in some way involved in measurement, assessment, and evaluation. Central to the adequate performance of the school psychologist's role in public school, mental health, or university settings is a good command of the basic foundations of measurement theory. This entails understanding at least three measurement concepts: reliability, validity, and scaling. The single most prevalent function of the school psychologist remains the administration and interpretation of psychological tests (Goldwasser, Meyers, Christenson, and Graden 1981). Without an adequate understanding of basic measurement theory, accurate test interpretation is not possible. In many smaller districts, the school psychologist is often looked upon as the resident expert in a variety of the psychological sciences, including measurement. School psychologists are called upon to help choose tests for use in the district and to consult with teachers on test selection (and sometimes even test development) for individual classrooms. Reliability and validity are two basic characteristics of mental measures that must always be evaluated in the test selection process.

Research in the human social sciences almost always includes the measurement of some psychological construct with a specially designed test or a more widely available commercial scale. The reading and appraisal of research in school psychology will require an understanding of measurement theory as well. As should now be evident, measurement permeates nearly all aspects of the school psychologist's training and job functions. The present chapter is intended to provide an introduction to the most basic elements of measurement theory as they relate specifically to test interpretation and evaluation. A grasp of basic measurement theory early in the graduate career should facilitate one's training as a school psychologist and enable one to achieve a better understanding of the psychological literature in general. However, this chapter should not be thought of as a substitute for a comprehensive course in measurement.

RELIABILITY

Psychological tests are the principal tools of measurement and assessment. The administration of a standardized test typically yields some quantifiable result expressed as a score. Psychological tests only sample the domain of possible behaviors or problems that a person could experience. Whenever less than the total number of possible behaviors in a domain is observed, sampling error can occur. Psychological tests are thus less than perfect measures of any psychological construct, trait, or ability. Psychological test scores can contain error for a variety of other reasons as well, including numerous situational factors. When attempting to interpret a test score, it is imperative to have some idea of the relative accuracy or reliability of the test involved.

Error due to domain sampling is the greatest contributor to the total amount of error involved in a test score (Nunnally 1978) and is the type of error about which measurement theory has the greatest concern. Fortunately, this type of error is the easiest to estimate and can also be more accurately estimated than other contributions to a total error term. Error due to domain sampling is determined from the degree of homogeneity of the items in the test, i.e., how well the various items correlate with one another and with an individual's true score on the trait being assessed. The relative accuracy of a test is typically represented by a reliability coefficient symbolized as r_{xx}. Since r_{xx} is based on the homogeneity or consistency of the individual items of a test and no outside criteria or information are necessary for its calculation, r_{xx} is frequently referred to as internal consistency reliability or as an estimate of item homogeneity. Error due to domain sampling is also sometimes estimated by determining the correlation between two parallel forms of a test (forms that are designed to measure the same construct with items sampled from the same item domain and believed to be equivalent). The correlation between the two equivalent or alternate forms is then taken as the reliability estimate and is usually symbolized as r_{xx}, r_{ab}, or r_{xy} (although r_{xy} is more generally used to represent a validity coefficient). The size of the correlation between alternate forms (r_{ab}) of a test is restricted as a function of the square root of the product of the internal consistency reliability coefficients of each test taken singly ($\sqrt{r_{xx_1} \cdot r_{xx_2}}$) and in actual practice will typically be smaller than r_{xx}.

A variety of methods are available for the estimation of r_{xx}. By far the most prevalent method of estimation is by what has come to be known as Cronbach's coefficient alpha (Cronbach 1951) or simply coefficient alpha. Coefficient alpha can be used with test items where the item scores can take multiple values (e.g., items that are scored 0, 1, or 2 depending on the quality of the response). When dichotomous items are used, a special case of alpha known as KR_{20} is used because it is computationally simpler. Coefficient alpha is computed as follows:

$$\sigma = (\frac{K}{K-1}) \frac{\sigma_x^2 - \Sigma \sigma_i^2}{\sigma_x^2} \qquad (1)$$

where: K = number of test items
σ_x^2 = variance of the total test score
$\Sigma \sigma_i^2$ = sum of the variances of each item.

Coefficient alpha can also be used as an estimate of the correlation between the test and a hypothetical yet true alternate form of a scale. Coefficient alpha has many practical uses and is most helpful in evaluating the psychometric properties of a scale. Alpha should be routinely calculated and reported for all tests except in special cases, such as tests which place a priority on speeded performance.

Split-half reliability estimates can also be determined for any specific test as a measure of internal consistency. Split-half reliability is typically determined by correlating each person's score on the first half of the items with his or her score on the latter half of the test, with a correction (by the Spearman-Brown formula) for the original length of the test. Predetermined or planned split-half comparisons such as correlating scores on odd-numbered items with scores on the even-numbered items may take advantage of chance or other factors resulting in spuriously high estimates of reliability. Alpha is a better method for estimating reliability since it can be shown to be the mean of all possible split-half correlations, thus expunging any sampling error due to the method of dividing the test for purposes of calculating a correlation between each half.

As noted earlier, a number of techniques exist for estimating reliability. Throughout this chapter, reliability has been referred to as estimated. This is because the absolute or "true" reliability of a psychological test can never be determined. Alpha and all other methods of determining reliability are, however, considered to be lower-bound estimates of the true reliability of the test. One can be certain that the reliability of a test is at least as high as the calculated estimate and possibly even higher. Figure 3.1 provides a schematic representation of the relationship between each of a variety of methods of estimating reliability and their relationship to the test's true reliability. The pictorial relationship is a general one and may change under special conditions.

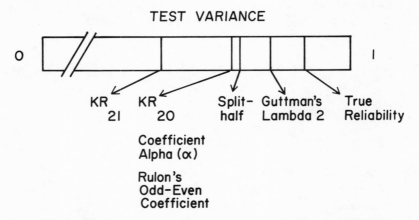

Figure 3.1 Relative standing of a variety of methods for calculating internal consistency reliability estimates with regard to each other and to the "true" reliability of the test.

Once the reliability of a test has been estimated, it is possible to calculate a sometimes more useful statistic known as the standard error of measurement (S_{em}). Since there is always some error involved in the score a person obtains on a psychological test, the obtained score (X_i) does not truly represent the individual's standing with regard to the trait in question. Obtained scores are only estimates of an individual's true score on the test, the score that would be obtained if there was no error involved in the measurement. Since this is not possible, the true score (X_∞) is defined as the mean score of an individual if he or she were administered an infinite number of equivalent forms of a test and there were no practice effects or other intervening variables. The standard error of measurement is the standard deviation of the individual's distribution of scores about his or her true score. To determine the (S_{em}) it is necessary to know only the standard deviation (SD) and the reliability (preferably an internal consistency estimate) of the test in question. The (S_{em}) can then be quickly calculated by application of equation 2.

$$S_{em} = SD\sqrt{1 - r_{xx}} \qquad (2)$$

The calculation of X_∞ and S_{em} are only estimates however, since the conditions for determining a true score never actually exist.

Since the distribution of obtained scores about the true score is considered to be normal, one can establish a degree of confidence in test results by banding the estimated true score by a specified number of S_{em}s. A table of values associated with the normal curve quickly tells us how many S_{em}s are necessary for a given level of confidence. In a normal distribution, about 68% of all scores fall within 1 SD of the mean, and about 95% of all scores fall within 2 SDs of the mean. Therefore, if one wanted to be 68% certain that a range of scores contained a person's true score, X_∞ would be banded by $\pm 1\ S_{em}$. To be 95% certain that a range of scores contained the true score, a range of $X_\infty \pm 2\ S_{em}$s would be necessary.

Frequently in psychological reports and a variety of other sources, one sees the obtained score of the individual banded by 1 or 2 S_{em}s and a probability statement made. The confidence interval about the

TABLE 3.1

Standard Errors of Measurement for Given Values
of Reliability Coefficient and Standard Deviation

SD	Reliability Coefficient					
	.95	.90	.85	.80	.75	.70
30	6.7	9.5	11.6	13.4	15.0	16.4
28	6.3	8.9	10.8	12.5	14.0	15.3
26	5.8	8.2	10.1	11.6	13.0	14.2
24	5.4	7.6	9.3	10.7	12.0	13.1
22	4.9	7.0	8.5	9.8	11.0	12.0
20	4.5	6.3	7.7	8.9	10.0	11.0
18	4.0	5.7	7.0	8.0	9.0	9.9
16	3.6	5.1	6.2	7.2	8.0	8.8
14	3.1	4.4	5.4	6.3	7.0	7.7
12	2.7	3.8	4.6	5.4	6.0	6.6
10	2.2	3.2	3.9	4.5	5.0	5.5
8	1.8	2.5	3.1	3.6	4.0	4.4
6	1.3	1.9	2.3	2.7	3.0	3.3
4	.9	1.3	1.5	1.8	2.0	2.2
2	.4	.6	.8	.9	1.0	1.1

This table is based on the formula $SE_M = SD \sqrt{1 - r_{xx}}$. For most purposes the result will be sufficiently accurate if the table is entered with the reliability and standard deviation values nearest those given in the test manual. Be sure the standard deviation and the reliability coefficient are for the same group of people.

Source: Test Service Bulletin No. 50, published by The Psychological Corporation, New York.

X_i is not symmetrical and such reporting is technically in error. The S_{em} is added and subtracted *around X_∞ only* in a symmetrical fashion. However, it may be better in actual practice to continue to band X_i whenever reporting scores to a psychometrically unsophisticated audience such as classroom teachers to avoid confusion, so long as r_{xx} is large (i.e., approaching .90 or higher). One can of course report X_i and a range of scores that would be symmetrical about X_∞. This requires knowing X_∞ and S_{em}. Although S_{em} can be estimated by equation 2, it is directly related to r_{xx} and the test's SD. Table 3.1 shows this relationship in tabular form and may be useful in estimating S_{em} or in comparing S_{em}s for tests with varying SDs. To obtain X_∞, the obtained score must be regressed toward the test mean. An obtained score is considered to be a biased estimate of X_∞. This means that X_i contains constant or systematic error with regard to X_∞; this error causes X_i to err away from the test mean. To estimate X_∞, equation 3 may be applied.

$$X_\infty = [r_{xx} (X_i - \overline{X})] + \overline{X} \qquad (3)$$

Applying equation 3 to a test with a mean of 100 and r_{xx} of .90 may be helpful as an example. If an individual earned an X_i of 110 on this test, his or her X_∞ becomes 109.

$$X_\infty = [.90 (110 - 100)] + 100$$
$$X_\infty = [.90 (10)] + 100$$
$$X_\infty = 9 + 100 = 109$$

When evaluating a test, the reliability estimate should be carefully examined. If comparing several tests, the reliability estimate should also be a principal concern and generally, the higher the r_{xx} the better. Curiously, some test manuals only report the S_{em} for a test and not r_{xx}. However, if S_{em} is known, r_{xx} can be calculated with equation 2 if one also knows the SD. Direct comparisons of S_{em}s across tests cannot be made unless the SDs of the tests are equivalent.

It is also important to ascertain just what type of reliability estimate is being reported. S_{em}s should be calculated from an internal consistency estimate. Comparisons of reliability estimates across tests should be based on the same type of estimate. For example, one should not compare the reliability of two tests using a KR_{21} estimate for one test and estimation by coefficient alpha for the other. Test-retest correlations, also frequently referred to as reliability coefficients, should not be confused with measures of the accuracy or precision of a test at a given point in time.

Test-retest "reliability" is one of the most-often-confused concepts of psychometric theory. Even Anastasi (1976), in introducing reliability, refers to reliability as a measure of the degree to which a person would obtain the same score if tested again at a later time. In the earlier stages of development of psychology, when traits were considered to be quite static, test-retest reliability was considered to be a proper characteristic of the test, and indeed was believed to be an indication of the degree to which a person would obtain the same score if tested again. Test-retest reliability speaks only to the stability of the trait being measured and has little to do with the accuracy or precision of measurement, unless the psychological construct in question is considered to be totally unchangeable. Given that traits such as anxiety and even intelligence do in fact change over time and that testing from one time to the next is positively correlated, it is still possible to use the test-retest correlation to estimate the score a person would obtain upon retesting. Internal consistency estimates however, should not be interpreted in such a manner.

VALIDITY

Reliability refers to the degree of precision or accuracy of a test score, that is, the degree to which the true score is reflected in the obtained score. Validity refers to what the test measures and not specifically to how well the test measures a particular trait. Reliability of a measure enters into the evaluation and determination of validity but only indirectly; reliability is a necessary but insufficient condition for validity. As with reliability, validity is not typically a dichotomous characteristic of tests but exists on a continuum. The question of validity for a test is whether the test measures what it is purported to measure. For a test such as the Wechsler Intelligence Scale for Children-Revised (WISC-R) (Wechsler 1974) to be considered valid, it must be demonstrated to measure intelligence. A test without reliability cannot be valid but a reliable test may or may not be a valid measure of the claimed trait. This becomes a problem for empirical investigation at both the pre- and postpublication stages of a test. The validation of a test requires considerable research, for ". . . to validate is to investigate" (Cronbach 1971, p. 433). The validation process also is not a static one, as it may be perceived by many: validation is more than the corroboration of a particular meaning of a test score; it is a process for developing better and sounder interpretations of observations that are expressed as scores on a psychological test (Cronbach 1971).

Just as reliability may take on a number of variations, so may va-

lidity. Quite a bit of divergent nomenclature has been applied to test validity, with Messick (1980) recently listing some seventeen "different" types
of validity that are referred to in the technical literature. In research on
test bias, it has become popular to break validity into two broad categories: internal validity and external validity (Jensen 1980, Reynolds
1982). External validity refers to the relationship between performance on
the test and outside criterion measures such as job performance or grade
point average in college. Internal validity refers to an evaluation of the
internal psychometric properties of a test in the absence of any external
criteria. More traditionally, validity has been broken into three major categories, termed content, construct, and predictive or criterion-related validity. These are the three types of validity distinguished and discussed in
the joint *Standards for Educational and Psychological Tests* (American
Psychological Association 1974). Content validity is most clearly related
to the internal properties of a test, while construct validity cuts across
both of the broader categories and criterion-related validity is definitely a
question of external validity.

     The content validity of a test is determined by how well the test
items and their specific content sample the set of behaviors or subject
matter area about which inferences are to be drawn from the test scores.
The content validity of a test should be ensured from the beginning of the
test development process by carefully designing a table of specifications
for the instrument that clearly details the domain of content to be sampled and the type of questions to be ascertained. Content validity is related to the internal consistency reliability estimates of a test since, if the
test items do in fact measure a particular domain of behavior, the items
should prove to be homogeneous. Content validity eventually resolves to
a question of how well one can generalize from the particular sample of
test questions asked by the examiner to the larger population of all possible items. This is a difficult question to answer from a purely statistical
basis, and much of the evaluation of content validity occurs through expert opinion and circumstantial evidence (such as evaluation of inter-item
correlations and other statistical measures that can only provide indirect,
inferred support for the test's content validity).

     Criterion-related or predictive validity refers to comparisons of
test scores on the measure in question with performance levels on an accepted criterion of the construct in question, or the level of prediction of
performance at some specified future time on an accepted criterion believed to provide a direct measure of the trait purported to be measured
by the test. Predictive validity is usually at issue with tests of aptitude
such as are used in admissions to colleges or universities or for certain
types of employment. The military services undertake considerable test-

ing to predict how well recruits will perform in various job training programs. Criterion-related and predictive validity are determined by the degree of correspondence between the test score and the individual's performance on the criterion. If the correlation between these two variables is high, no further evidence may be considered necessary (Nunnally 1978).

Construct validity of psychological tests is one of the most complex issues facing the psychometrician and permeates all aspects of test development and use. Psychology for the most part deals with intangible constructs. Intelligence is one of the most intensely studied constructs in the field of psychology, yet it cannot be directly observed or evaluated. Intelligence can only be inferred from the observation and quantification of what has been agreed upon as "intelligent" behavior. Personality variables such as dependence, succorance, need for achievement, depression, and on through the seemingly endless list of personality traits that psychologists have "identified" cannot be directly observed. Their existence is only inferred from the observation of behavior. Construct validity thus involves considerable inference on the part of the test developer and the researcher; construct validity is evaluated by investigating just what psychological properties a test measures.

As befits the complexity of the concept of construct validity, many methods must be applied to the determination of a test's construct validity. Construct validity permeates all other aspects of validity as well. Every investigation of test validity, no matter which of the seventeen types identified by Messick is being evaluated, bears at least indirectly on the construct validity of the measure. If there can be a single, unifying theme in the study of test validity, surely it is construct validity. Some of the most popular methods for examining construct validity include factor analysis and the examination of a multi-trait, multi-method validation matrix.

Factor analysis of test items on subscales of a larger test battery can be used to reduce performance on the test to the "lowest common denominator" of traits being tapped by the scale. Performance on the twelve subtests of the WISC-R, for example, seems to be adequately explained by three basic, underlying factors. Factor analysis is a purely internal procedure that examines patterns of item or subtest intercorrelations among the components of the test itself. Multi-trait, multi-method validation is an external validation procedure that makes predictions about what a test will correlate well with and, of equal importance, what the test will not correlate with well if at all. Care is also taken to ensure that any observed correlations are not an artifact of the method of measurement by including multiple types of assessment of each trait being considered.

When establishing correlations between test scores and criterion measures, whether they are other tests or other types of performance ratings or status variables, the relationship between reliability of a test and the validity of the test becomes clearer. The influence of the reliability of the criterion measure, which is infrequently reported and often unknown, on the validity coefficient, as such a correlation is known, also becomes clear. The validity coefficient between a test and a criterion is restricted as a function of the square root of the product of the reliabilities of the test and the criterion ($\sqrt{r_{xx} \cdot r_{yy}}$). Thus, if the reliability of the criterion is low, as is frequently the case with such variables as grade point average, the validity of the test may appear considerably lower than if the criterion measure were a perfectly reliable indicator of the individual's true standing on the criterion variable.

Frequently in discussions of test validity, different types of validity are emphasized for different types of psychological tests. Traditionally, content validity has been considered the central issue for an achievement test; predictive validity is usually emphasized for aptitude measures; and, for personality, interest, and related scales, construct validity has been seen as most important. In actuality, construct validity should be the single most central issue in test development and validation. If a test has adequate construct validity, all other aspects of validity will fall into place. If an "intelligence" test has construct validity (i.e., actually does measure intelligence), it must have accurately sampled the domain of intelligent behaviors, and, if intelligence is related to school achievement, it will predict academic attainment. It is possible to construct tests that make predictions for no apparent reasons. As a test whose validity is being investigated, this may be acceptable; but, such a test should not be used in decision making about individuals or about programs that affect individuals. Blind empiricism can only be justified over the short term and then only in an exploratory sense if at all. Test score interpretation should be guided by the nomothetic nature of theory, which necessarily is wrapped up in the issues of construct validity.

As has been noted by Cronbach (1971) and others, the term "test validation" can cause some confusion. In thinking about and evaluating validity, it must always be kept in mind that one does not ever actually validate a test but only the interpretation that is given to the score on the test. Any single test may have many applications, or a test originally having a singular purpose may prove promising for other applications. Each application of a test or interpretation of a test score must undergo validation. Whenever one hears or reads that a test has been validated, it is necessary to know for what purpose it has been validated, and what interpretations of scores from the instrument in question have been empirically shown to be justifiable and accurate.

UNITS, SCORES, AND NORMS

The term *measurement* has been used throughout this chapter without proper definition. Much discussion could be given to the various philosophical views of what actually constitutes measurement, especially as it is related to psychological constructs. I myself am in agreement with Nunnally (1978) that in the end, "measurement consists of rules for assigning numbers to objects in such a way to represent quantities of attributes" (p. 3). A psychological measurement device provides us with a set of rules (the test questions, directions for administration, scoring, etc.) for assigning numbers to an individual that are believed to represent some underlying or latent trait possessed by the individual.

The understanding and interpretation of these numbers depends on a variety of factors, many of which have been discussed previously in this chapter. Another important variable in attaching meaning to an individual's score on a psychological measurement device is the scale of measurement that is being employed. Different scales and units of measurement have quite different properties. The four basic scales of measurement are nominal, ordinal, interval, and ratio scales. As one moves from a nominal scale upward to a ratio scale, increasingly sophisticated measurement becomes possible.

A *nominal scale* is a qualitative system of categorization that groups individual observations into classes or sets. Diagnostic categories of mental illness such as schizophrenia, manic-depressive disorder, or anxiety neurosis represent nominal scaling categories. Differentiation by gender is another example of a nominal scale. However, nominal scales provide so little quantitative information about the members of the categories that some writers prefer to exclude nominal scales from the general rubric of measurement (e.g., Hays 1973). As Hays points out, the term *measurement* is usually reserved for a situation in which each individual is assigned a number. Since we are unsure of the quantitative relationship between each nominal category, many statistical tests that are commonly applied in psychology cannot be employed with nominal scale data. However, since nominal scales do allow for classification into discrete categories, many writers (e.g., Nunnally 1978) include nominal scaling as one type of measurement, albeit one that provides little quantitatively distinguishable information about the members of the class.

Ordinal scales provide considerably more quantitative information about people or events than do nominal scales. Ordinal scales allow the researcher at least to rank objects or people according to the quantity of a particular attribute they may possess. Ordering usually takes the form of a range from the "most" to the "least" amount of the attribute in question. If children in a classroom were each weighed and then ranked from the heaviest to the lightest, with the heaviest child assigned an ordinal rank of one and the next heaviest a two, and so on until each child had been assigned a number, the resulting measurement would be on an ordinal scale. While an ordinal scale provides certain quantitative information about each individual, it does not tell how far apart each person is from the next one. It is quite likely in this example that between each adjacent pair of ranks, there is a different weight difference being represented. Ordinal scales thus provide us with a method only for designating relative positions among individuals, an advancement over nominal scaling, but still a crude procedure with regard to the possible statistical treatments that can be meaningfully applied to the data. Means and standard deviations, the most basic of all statistics, cannot be applied to ordinal scales.

Interval scales afford far more information about individuals and can be mathematically manipulated with far greater confidence and precision than nominal or ordinal scales. To have an interval scale of measurement it is necessary to know not only the information provided by an ordinal scale, but also how far apart each person is on the attribute being measured. What distinguishes an interval scale from an ordinal scale is knowledge of the distance between subjects in terms of the quantity of the attribute in question. Most of the measurement scales and tests used in psychology and education are interval scales. Intelligence tests are a good example of measurement using interval scales and they also provide a good illustration of the distinction between interval and ratio scales. Although nearly all statistical methods can be applied to measurements taken on an interval scale, the interval scale has no true zero point, where zero designates a total absence of the attribute under consideration. (If one were to earn a zero on an intelligence test, by failing to answer a single question correctly, this would not indicate an *absence* of intelligence, for without intelligence no human could remain alive.)

Ratio scales possess the attributes of the ordinal and interval scales but also have a true zero point. In the case of a ratio scale, a score of zero indicates the complete absence of the attribute under consideration. There is relatively little use of ratio scales in psychology outside of measurement of simple sensory and motor functions. Nevertheless, ratio scales do have many quantitative features that make them useful. While with an interval scale such as intelligence tests possess it would be incorrect to state that a person with an IQ of 100 is twice as intelligent as a person with an IQ of 50, a ratio scale makes such comparisons appropriate. Fortunately, it is not necessary to have ratio scales to attack the vast majority of research problems in the social sciences.

The foregoing discussion of scales of measurement has necessarily been limited to the most basic elements and distinctions among scales. The reader who desires to explore this topic will find an extensive mathematical presentation of scales of measurement in Hays (1973).

After determining that one is dealing with an interval scale, as will be the case with nearly all tests used by the school psychologist, one must, to understand more fully an individual's score on the test, evaluate the score relative to some reference group. Raw scores, determined by adding up the correct responses to test items, are quite tedious to work with and to interpret accurately. Raw scores are typically transformed into what are referred to as scaled scores or standard scores, based on the responses of a large sample of the test population (the standardization sample). Making raw scores into scaled scores involves creating a scale with a known mean and standard deviation that remain constant across such variables as age or perhaps even across tests.

The mean score on a test is simply the sum of all the scores obtained by the individuals in the standardization sample divided by the number of people in the sample ($\Sigma X_i / N$). The mean has a number of interesting properties that make it useful. The most useful property is related to the principle of least squares that you will learn about in some detail in your study of statistics. If each person's score in the standardization sample was to be subtracted from some constant value and the differences squared and then summed, no constant value would yield a smaller number than would the mean. In a normal distribution of scores (to be described below) the mean also breaks performance on the test into two equal halves, with half of those taking the test scoring above the mean and half scoring below the mean. The median score is formally defined as the point which breaks a distribution into two equal halves; in a normal distribution, the mean and median are the same score.

The standard deviation (SD) is another extremely useful statistic in describing and interpreting a test score. The SD is a measure of the dispersion of scores about the mean. If a test has a mean of 100 and an individual earns a score of 110 on the test, we still have very little information except that the individual did not perform at a below average level. Once the standard deviation is known (if the distribution of scores approaches normality), it can be determined how far from the mean the score of 110 falls. A score of 110 takes on far different meaning depending upon whether the SD of the scores is 5, 15, or 30. The SD is relatively easy to calculate once the mean is known. The standard deviation is determined by first subtracting each score from the mean, squaring the result, and adding up this quantity for each person. This sum of squared deviations from the mean is then divided by the number of subjects (some divide by

N-1, and the argument over whether N or N-1 is more appropriate is unlikely to be settled soon, but with large numbers of subjects it makes little
difference in practice). The resulting number is known as the variance of
the test scores, and the square root of the variance is the standard deviation. This calculation is illustrated in equation 4.

$$SD = \sqrt{\frac{\Sigma (X_i - \bar{X})^2}{N}}$$

(4)

Once the mean and standard deviation of test scores are known,
the individual's standing relative to others on the attribute in question can
be determined. The normal distribution or normal curve (or sometimes
called the bell curve because of its shape) is most helpful in making these
interpretations. Figure 3.2 displays the normal curve and shows its relationship to various standard score systems. A person whose score falls
one SD above the mean performs at a level exceeding about 84% of
the population of test takers. Two SDs will be above 98% of the group.
The relationship is the inverse below the mean. A score of one SD below
the mean indicates that the individual exceeds only about 16% of the population on the attribute in question. Approximately two-thirds (68%) of
the population will score within one SD of the mean on any psychological
test.

Standard scores such as those shown in Figure 3.2 (z-scores,
T-scores, etc.) are developed for ease of interpretation. Raw score means
and SDs are inconvenient to use and also may not be perfectly normally
distributed. Though standard scores are typically linear transformations
of raw scores to a desired scale with a predetermined mean and SD, nor-
malized scaled scores can also be developed. In a linear transformation of
test scores to a predetermined mean and SD, equation 5 must be applied
to each score.

$$\text{Scaled Score} = SD_{ss} \left(\frac{X_i - \bar{X}}{SD_x} \right) + \bar{X}_{ss}$$

(5)

where: X_i = raw score
$\bar{X}$ = mean of the raw scores
SD_x = standard deviation of the raw scores
SD_{ss} = standard deviation scaled scores are to have
$\bar{X}_{ss}$ = mean scaled scores are to have.

Most tests designed for use with children and some adult tests standardize
scores within age groups, so that a scaled score at one age has the same

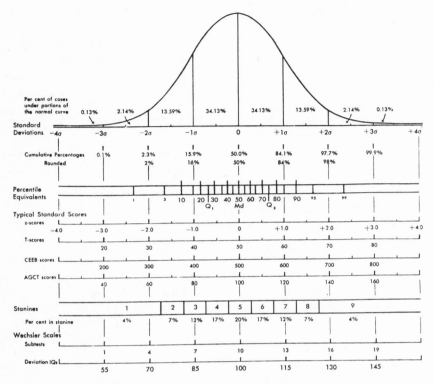

Figure 3.2 Relationships between the normal curve, percentiles, and several common systems of standard scores.

meaning at all other ages. Thus a person aged ten who earns a scaled score of 105 on the test has the same percentile rank within his or her age group as a twelve-year-old with the same score has in his or her age group. That is, the score of 105 will fall at the same point on the normal curve in each case.

Not all scores have this property. Grade equivalents are one type of score that is much abused because they are assumed to have scaled score properties, when they in fact only represent an ordinal scale of measurement. Grade equivalents ignore the dispersion of scores about the mean when the dispersion is constantly changing from grade to grade. Under no circumstances do grade equivalents qualify as standard scores. The calculation of a grade equivalent is quite simple. When a test is administered to a large group of children, the mean raw score is calculated at each grade level and this mean raw score then is called the "grade equivalent" score for a raw score of that magnitude. If the mean raw score for beginning fourth graders (grade 4.0) on a reading test is 37, then any person earning a score of 37 on the test is assigned a grade equivalent score of 4.0. If the mean raw score of fifth graders (grade 5.0) is 38, then a score of 38 would receive a grade equivalent of 5.0. A raw score of 36 could represent a grade equivalent of 3.8, 38 could be 4.0, and 39, 5.0. Thus, differences of one raw score point can cause dramatic differences in the grade equivalent received, and the differences will be inconsistent across grades with regard to magnitude of the difference in grade equivalents produced by constant changes in raw scores.

Table 3.2 illustrates the problems of attempting to use grade equivalents in evaluating a child's academic standing relative to his or her peers. As seen in Table 3.2, a child with a grade equivalent score in reading two years below the appropriate grade placement for his or her age may or may not have a reading problem. At some ages, this is well within the average range. Grade equivalents have a tendency to become standards of performance as well, which they clearly are not. Contrary to popular belief, grade equivalent scores on a test also do not indicate what level of reading text a child should be using. Grade equivalent scores on tests simply do not have a one-to-one correspondence with reading series.

Grade equivalents are also inappropriate for use in any sort of discrepancy analysis of an individual's test performance and for use in many statistical procedures for the following reasons (Reynolds, in press):

1. The growth curve between age and achievement in basic academic subjects flattens out at upper grade levels. This can also be observed in Table 2, where it is seen that there is very little change in standard score values corresponding to two years below grade level for age after about grades seven or eight. In fact, grade equivalents have almost no meaning at this level, since reading instruction typically stops by high school and grade equivalents really only represent extrapolations from earlier grades. An excellent example of the difficulty in interpreting grade equivalents beyond about grades ten and eleven has been provided by Thorndike and Hagen (1977) using an analogy with age equivalents. Height can be expressed in age equivalents, just as reading can be expressed as grade equivalents. But while it might be helpful to describe a tall first grader as having the height of an 8½ year-old, what happens to the 5'10", 14 year-old female? At no age does the mean height of females equal 5'10". Since the average reading level in the population changes very little after junior high school, grade equivalents at these ages become virtually nonsensical, with large fluctuations resulting from a raw score difference of 2 or 3 points on a 100-item test.

TABLE 3.2

Standard Scores and Percentile Ranks Corresponding to Performance "Two Years Below Grade Level for Age" on Four Major Reading Tests

Grade Placement	Two Years Below Placement	Wide Range Achievement Test		Peabody Individual Achievement Test[a]		Woodcock Reading Mastery Test[b]		Stanford Diagnostic Reading Test[b]	
		SS[c]	%R[d]	SS	%R	SS	%R	SS	%R
1.5	Pk.5	65	1	—		—		—	
2.5	K.5	72	3	—		—		—	
3.5	1.5	69	2	—		64	1	64	1
4.5	2.5	73	4	75	5	77	6	64	1
5.5	3.5	84	14	85	16	85	16	77	6
6.5	4.5	88	21	88	21	91	27	91	27
7.5	5.5	86	18	89	23	94	34	92	30
8.5	6.5	87	19	91	27	94	34	93	32
9.5	7.5	90	25	93	32	96	39	95	37
10.5	8.5	85	16	93	32	95	37	95	37
11.5	9.5	85	16	93	32	95	37	92	30
12.5	10.5	85	16	95	37	95	37	92	30

[a]Reading Comprehension subtest only.
[b]Total test.
[c]All standard scores in this table have been converted for ease of comparison to a common scale having a mean of 100 and a standard deviation of 15.
[d]Percentile rank.

Source: Reynolds, C.R. The fallacy of "two years below grade level for age" as a diagnostic criterion for reading disorders. *Journal of School Psychology*, in press.

2. Grade equivalents assume that the rate of learning is constant throughout the school year and that there is no gain or loss during summer vacation.

3. As partially noted above, grade equivalents involve an excess of extrapolation, especially at the upper and lower ends of the scale. However, since tests are not administered during every month of the school year, scores between the testing intervals (often a full year) must be interpolated on the assumption of constant growth rates. Interpolations between sometimes extrapolated values on an assumption of constant growth rates is at best a highly perilous activity.

4. Different academic subjects are acquired at different rates and the variation in performance varies across content areas so that "two

years below grade level for age" may be a much more serious deficiency in math, for example, than in reading comprehension.

5. Grade equivalents exaggerate small differences in performance between individuals and for a single individual across tests. Some test authors even provide a caution on test record forms that standard scores only, and not grade equivalents, should be used for comparison purposes.

The primary advantage of standardized or scaled scores lies in the comparability of score interpretation across age. By standard scores, of course, we refer to scores scaled to a constant mean and SD such as the Wechsler Deviation IQ, and not to ratio IQ types of scales employed by the early Binet and current Slosson Intelligence Test, which give the false appearance of being scaled scores. Ratio IQs or other types of quotients have many of the same problems as grade equivalents and should be avoided for many of the same reasons. Standard scores of the deviation IQ type have the same percentile rank across age, since they are based not only on the mean but the variability in scores about the mean at each age level. For example, a score that falls ⅔ of a standard deviation below the mean (90 on a Wechsler scale) has a percentile rank of 25 at every age. A score falling ⅔ of a grade level below the average grade level has a different percentile rank at every age.

Standard scores are more accurate and precise. When constructing tables for the conversion of raw scores into standard scores, interpolation of scores to arrive at an exact score point is typically not necessary, whereas the opposite is true of grade equivalents. Extrapolation is also typically not necessary for scores within three standard deviations of the mean, which accounts for more than 99% of all scores encountered.

A normative sample or reference group is also necessary for test interpretation. With certain special exceptions (and even many of these are questionable exceptions, e.g., criterion-referenced testing), psychological test scores only take on true meaning when the amount of an attribute in question can be considered relative to that possessed by other individuals. This comparison or reference group (known also as the standardization sample) is necessary for a variety of reasons, the major ones being the lack of ratio scales for most tests and psychology and society's interest in knowing how individuals compare to one another on a variety of traits and how differences in psychological traits affect behavior. Other types of test interpretation are feasible and appropriate under certain circumstances. In planning educational programs, ipsative score interpretation has been advocated (Kaufman 1979; Reynolds and Clark, in press), i.e., interpretation which makes an individual his or her own "normative" group, with performance on a variety of tests compared to the individual's own mean level of performance.

CONCLUSION

Many factors affect an individual's response to a psychological test. The process of accurate test interpretation requires a broad understanding of measurement theory as well as psychological theories of individual differences. The purpose of the present chapter has been to provide only the most basic understanding of those measurement concepts necessary for learning about tests and for reading the professional literature on testing. Far more must be learned before a full understanding can be obtained. Test development and standardization procedures must be studied. The present work has focussed on "true score" theory, also called classical or traditional measurement theory. Newer methods are developing daily, latent-trait or item characteristic curve theory being one prominent example, and these methods too will need to be mastered as they begin to impact more and more on the school psychologist's daily functions. Continuing education in measurement theory will be an asset to the school psychologist, not only during the graduate career but throughout his or her professional life.

REFERENCES

American Psychological Association. *Standards for educational and psychological tests.* Washington, D.C.: Author, 1974.

Anastasi, A. *Psychological testing* (4th ed.). New York: Macmillan, 1976.

Cronbach, L. J. Coefficient alpha and the internal structure of tests. *Psychometrika,* 1951, *16,* 297–334.

Cronbach, L. J. Test validation. In R. L. Thorndike (Ed.), *Educational Measurement* (2nd ed.). Washington, D.C.: American Council on Education, 1971.

Goldwasser, E., Meyers, J., Christenson, S., & Graden, J. *National survey on the impact of PL 94-142 on the role of school psychologists.* Unpublished manuscript (1981).

Hays, W. L. *Statistics for the social sciences.* New York: Holt, Rinehart, and Winston, 1973.

Jensen, A. R. *Bias in mental testing.* New York: The Free Press, 1980.

Kaufman, A. S. *Intelligent testing with the WISC-R.* New York: Wiley-Interscience, 1979.

Messick, S. Test validity and the ethics of assessment. *American Psychologist,* 1980, *35,* 1012–1027.

Nunnally, J. *Psychometric theory.* New York: McGraw-Hill, 1978.

Reynolds, C. R. The problem of bias in psychological assessment. In C. R. Reynolds & T. B. Gutkin (Eds.), *The handbook of school psychology*. New York: Wiley, 1982.

Reynolds, C. R. The fallacy of "two years below grade level for age" as a diagnostic criterion for reading disorders. *Journal of School Psychology,* in press.

Reynolds, C. R., & Clark, J. Cognitive assessment of the preschool child. In K. D. Paget & B. Bracken (Eds.), *Psychoeducational assessment of the preschool and primary aged child*. New York: Grune & Stratton, in press.

Thorndike, R. L., & Hagen, E. P. *Measurement and evaluation in psychology and education* (4th ed.). New York: Wiley, 1977.

Wechsler, D. *Wechsler Intelligence Scale for Children-Revised*. New York: Psychological Corporation, 1974.

4

Legal Issues in
Psychoeducational Assessment

DANIEL J. RESCHLY

LEGISLATION AND LITIGATION have increasingly exerted an influence on school psychology over the past decade. Psychoeducational assessment instruments and practices, in contrast to other services provided by school psychologists, have been the principal issues in court cases and legislative action. Today a variety of legal guidelines, sometimes overlapping and occasionally inconsistent, affect the delivery of psychoeducational assessment services by school psychologists. In this chapter, legal principles, recent litigation and legislation, and legal requirements concerning assessment practices will be discussed. It should be noted at the outset that legal guidelines are often ambiguous and subject to differing interpretations. Court opinions on the same issues are not always consistent. Legislation is enacted, revised, sometimes interpreted differently by the courts, sometimes ignored by agencies and professionals, and occasionally repealed! In short, legal guidelines are dynamic and continuing changes in the future should be anticipated.

A short digression to the pre-1970 world of school psychology may assist in giving the reader an appreciation for the changes which have been brought about by legal developments over the past decade. In one sense, school psychology has always been acutely affected by legal factors, and particularly by state legislation. (School psychologists have generally been employed by school districts, legal entities which are created by state governments.) Throughout the twentieth century, the growth of school psychology in the U.S. has closely paralleled the enactment of funding for special education programs for exceptional children (Tindall 1979, Wallin and Ferguson 1967). Prior to various precedent-setting legal cases in the early 1970s regarding the educational rights of exceptional children, provision of special education (and the associated development of school psychology) was very much dependent upon state legislatures. A few states had very strong legislation and funding to develop programs for exceptional children, many provided for some but not all exceptional children, and a few states provided little or no support. With very few exceptions, the number of school psychologists in a state was closely related to the nature and funding of special education legislation, and the number and ratio of school psychologists to students varied widely from state to state (Kicklighter 1976).

Although the existence of school psychology has been and, to a considerable degree, continues to be affected by state legislation, legal developments in the 1970s increasingly influenced the kinds of services provided. For example prior to the 1970s, decisions about whether to refer a child for possible special education placement, the nature and extent of the preplacement evaluation, the involvement of specialists such as school psychologists, the nature and extent of psychoeducational assessment, and the child's ultimate placement in alternative educational programs were, in most states, the legal prerogative of the school district and designated school officials. In many instances, school psychologists acted as one-person placement committees by developing the vast majority, if not all, of the information leading to exceptional classification and special education placement. In many instances there were few, if any, legal guidelines concerning what areas were to be assessed, how they were to be assessed, and so on. Finally, parent involvement in the entire process often was at the discretion of school officials and, depending on state legal guidelines, varied from no involvement at all to rudimentary forms of notification and consent. Through the application of several concepts of constitutional law to educational classification and placement decisions, the entire process of referral, psychoeducational assessment, and placement was radically changed in the 1970s.

LEGAL PRINCIPLES

In high school or college political science classes, or perhaps in the popular media, the reader has probably seen the United States Constitution depicted as a "living document." The interpretation and application of various constitutional principles are refined and often extended through the evolution of case law. This clearly has been the case with the related concepts of due process and equal protection, which were used in several cases involving the education of exceptional students in the 1970s (Bersoff 1981).

Due Process

The basic constitutional right of due process is established in the Fourteenth Amendment, which prohibits the state from depriving ". . . any persons of life, liberty, or property, without due process of law." A good synonym for due process is "procedural fairness." The due-process right protects citizens from arbitrary and capricious government actions. Several good sources now exist concerning the meaning and application of due-process rights in educational settings (Abeson, Bolick, and Hass 1975; Bersoff 1978; Buss 1975).

The concept of due process may seem less academic if the reader considers this question: What protections and procedural safeguards would you suggest if someone representing a governmental agency (such as a school) proposed to classify you or your child as mentally retarded and intended to change your (his or her) educational program from a regular class to a special class with other retarded children — or, even more serious, proposed to exclude you or your child completely from public education because of a handicap? First, would these actions constitute deprivation of life, liberty, or property? While life itself may not be threatened, clearly liberty is involved since your association with other people, especially normal peers, would be limited through exclusion or alternative placement. "Property" would certainly be affected as well, since with educational opportunities limited, career choice would probably be limited too and potential adult earnings accordingly reduced. Note that these ill effects of classification and placement would become likely only if the decision to classify and place was wrong or, in the case of exclusion, if the person in question would have been able to learn and thereby profit from an education.

If you concede that educational exclusion, or special education classification and placement, especially if incorrect, could constitute deprivation of liberty and "property," then the issue of procedural fairness becomes paramount. Specific due-process procedures and their influence on psychoeducational assessment are described in a later section.

Equal Protection

The Fourteenth Amendment also includes the equal protection clause, which prohibits states from denying "to any person . . . equal protection of the laws." Bersoff (1981) noted that equal protection has been interpreted in several court cases as protecting equal educational opportunity and prohibiting discrimination on the basis of race, gender, and handicapping conditions. Court use of the equal protection clause has been very complex, and legal guidelines for equal protection analyses are far from clear (Bersoff 1981). For our purposes it is sufficient to note that since 1972, courts have consistently viewed the exclusion of children from public education due to handicapping conditions as a denial of equal protection and, with some inconsistency, have also viewed overrepresentation of minority children in special classes for the mildly retarded as a denial of equal protection. Although these concepts may seem far removed from psychoeducational assessment in school psychology, litigation and legislation in the 1970s established both as central concerns in the daily work of school psychologists.

LITIGATION

Two distinctly different types of court cases in the 1970s markedly influenced both legislation at the state and federal levels and the work of school psychologists. Both types of cases were decided on the basis of the due process and equal protection concepts. However, while the right-to-education cases led to a dramatic expansion of special education and increased emphasis on individual psychoeducational assessment, the placement-bias cases at least implied reduced use of special education placement, as well as intense doubt about the fairness of traditional psychoeducational assessment.

Right to Education

Two cases in the early 1970s—*Pennsylvania Association for Retarded Children* (PARC) v. *Commonwealth of Pennsylvania* in 1971, and *Mills* v. *Board of Education of the District of Columbia* in 1972—led to the rapid development of special education services for the handicapped. The *PARC* case was a class-action suit in which thirteen mentally retarded students (on behalf of all other mentally retarded students) sued the state of Pennsylvania because they had been excluded from public education. They claimed that the exclusion violated their constitutional rights both to equal protection and to due process. They claimed that it was fundamentally unfair for the state to provide financial support for the education of some of its citizens (normal children) while excluding others (handicapped children). Moreover, this unfair treatment was carried out without elementary due-process protection (Gilhool 1976). In a far-reaching decree, a federal district court agreed with both claims and mandated that the state provide an *appropriate* education for all mentally retarded students at public expense.

The *PARC* decision, a monumental breakthrough regarding the rights of handicapped students, was further reinforced by the *Mills* case just one year later. Both cases clearly established the right to education of the handicapped as well as due-process rights concerning classification and placement decisions. Perhaps even more important for school psychologists were the requirements that educational services be designed to meet individual needs, thereby implying careful assessment of the individual, and that educational programming be provided in as normal an environment as possible (Weintraub and Abeson 1974). The decisions in the *PARC* and *Mills* cases quickly prompted the development of similar cases in almost every state. Most of these cases did not reach the courts because nearly every state legislature enacted and funded mandatory special education legislation between 1972 and 1974.

It is somewhat ironic that the major legal breakthrough occurred in Pennsylvania, a state which for that time had fairly progressive special education and school psychological services. The problem was that the legislation was not mandatory. School districts were encouraged but not required to develop special education programs through enabling legislation and partial reimbursement from the state for the additional costs. Some districts developed very comprehensive programs, while others did very little in educating the handicapped. Thus, whether a specific handicapped child received educational services depended on the arbitrary and capricious circumstances of his or her place of residence within the state, precisely the sort of unequal treatment prohibited by the equal protection clause according to the court. Nearly all the states had similar or even worse inequities.

Some of the effects of the *PARC* decision on psychoeducational assessment were not immediately apparent. Clearly, there was a need for expanded assessment services and more school psychologists. The unforeseen consequence was that specific populations of handicapped children, rarely if ever served in the public schools previously, were now to be included and would require comprehensive psychoeducational evaluations. Among these new populations in most school districts around the country were children with severe disabilities, including profound levels of mental retardation, blindness, deafness, and multiple handicaps. However, traditional assessment instruments often were ill suited for these children, and conventionally educated school psychologists typically had little or no preparation in providing services to them (Gerken 1979, *School Psychology Digest* 1979). Considerable activity in recent years has been devoted to providing continuing education for school psychologists in assessment and intervention with the more severely handicapped.

Placement Bias

Considerable litigation has focused on the overrepresentation of minority students in special classes for educable mentally retarded (EMR) children. Minority students, including blacks, Hispanics, and American Indians, have been and, in most instances, continue to be classified and placed in EMR programs in disporportionate numbers, sometimes at three to four times the rate for white students. The fact of overrepresentation is indisputable. Debate concerning the reasons for overrepresentation has consumed considerable time and attention over the past decade and has been the focus of much litigation (Mercer 1973, Reschly 1979, 1980a, 1981).

The litigation concerning overrepresentation can be divided into two phases, 1970–1975 and 1975–1980, depending on whether the major cases were resolved through consent decrees or through court opinions based on trials. In both phases, the critical issues were the fairness of IQ tests to minority students and the appropriateness of the EMR classification for minority students with low IQ scores.

1970–1975 Consent Decrees

Diana v. *State Board of Education* (California, 1970) and *Guadalupe* v. *Tempe Elementary School District* (Arizona, 1972) were very similar cases. Both were filed by civil rights organizations on behalf of bilingual students overrepresented in special classes for the mildly retarded. Data cited in *Diana* indicated that Spanish-surnamed students constituted about 18 percent of the total student population in Monterey County, California, but one-third (33 percent) of the enrollment in EMR classes. Both cases involved allegations that IQ tests administered in English were unfair and biased, and that verbal IQ tests were the primary basis for classification and placement decisions. In addition, the *Diana* and *Guadalupe* plaintiffs made a number of other allegations about the quality of EMR programs, the absence of elementary due-process protections, the competence and training of the special class teachers and assessment personnel, and the thoroughness and breadth of psychoeducational assessment. In both cases there were many conditions and procedures that are best described simply as bad practices (MacMillan 1977, Reschly 1979).

Diana and *Guadalupe* were resolved by consent decrees — agreements negotiated among the plaintiffs and defendants, who were state departments of education and local school districts. The agreements were then accepted and put into the form of a legal mandate by the courts. For obvious reasons, the defendants chose to avoid a trial on the merits of each case. However, in view of the many problems represented in the two cases, it was somewhat surprising that the court order focused primarily on the process and content of psychoeducational assessment. Issues concerning the quality and effectiveness of the special class EMR program were largely ignored, despite the fact that these issues were the plaintiffs' primary concern.

The consent decree in *Diana* required: (1) assessment of a child's primary language competence and, if found to be other than English, that the tests used were to be nonverbal, translated, or administered with an interpreter; (2) that unfair portions of English-language tests were to be deleted and more emphasis placed on the results of nonverbal tests. The *Guadalupe* consent decree also mandated similar revisions in testing practices, with the additional requirements that: (1) IQ tests were not to be the exclusive nor the primary basis for EMR classification and placement; (2) adaptive behavior outside of school was to be assessed; (3) due-process procedures were to be instituted *prior* to individual psychoeducational assessment and prior to classification and placement; and (4) special education programming was to be provided in as normal an environment as possible.

Since *Diana* and *Guadalupe* were settled by consent decree, there were no legal analyses of the constitutional and statutory rights they had established. However, the consent decrees had clear implications for the process (procedural safeguards, involvement of parents) and content (primary language, adaptive behavior) of psychoeducational assessment. Both cases appeared to exert a strong influence on legislation enacted in the mid-1970s.

1975–1980: IQ on Trial

In the late 1970s, court action on the placement-bias issue took a different turn. The issues were defined more narrowly, plaintiffs requested an outright ban on IQ tests, and two potentially landmark cases were decided by judicial opinions following trials.

The cases of *Larry P. et al.* v. *Wilson Riles et al.* (California, 1972, 1974, 1979) and *Parents in Action on Special Education* (PASE) v. *Joseph P. Hannon* (Illinois, 1980) dealt with issues regarding overrepresentation of black students in EMR classes which the plaintiffs alleged were caused by biases in IQ tests. Unlike the earlier cases, the defendants sought to justify conventional psychoeducational assessment practices in court. Expert testimony from a number of prominent psychologists, some defending IQ tests and others very critical of them, was prominent in both cases. In *Larry P.,* California Federal District Court Judge Robert

F. Peckham agreed with plaintiffs that IQ tests were the primary cause of overrepresentation and that IQ tests were biased. On the basis of constitutional and statutory law, the judge banned the use of IQ tests with black students. In sharp contrast, Judge John F. Grady, for an Illinois federal district court, concluded that IQ tests were largely unbiased, that they were a small part of EMR diagnosis, and that no constitutional or statutory rights were violated either by overrepresentation of black students in EMR classes or by the use of IQ tests with black students. Thus, students, educators, and school psychologists are caught between the contradictory opinions on IQ tests reached by two different federal district court judges who examined essentially identical evidence and testimony. Both *Larry P.* and *PASE* are in the appeal process, which could result in a U.S. Supreme Court decision on IQ tests in the mid-to-late 1980s. The contradictory opinions in these cases set the stage for us to consider the broader issues involved in placement-bias litigation.

PLACEMENT BIAS: ISSUES AND ASSUMPTIONS

The lengthy judicial opinions in *Larry P.* and *PASE,* major portions of which were devoted to analyses of the issue of bias, have been discussed and criticized by psychologists (Bersoff, 1982; Reschly 1980a; Sattler 1980; *School Psychology Review* 1980). In neither opinion was the use of psychological evidence on bias particularly systematic or insightful, as Bersoff argues in a scathing commentary on the opinions:

> "Judge Grady's eventual holding that the black plaintiffs in *PASE* had failed to prove that the tests were discriminatory was based on *his* estimation of bias. The method by which he reached that judgment was embarrassingly devoid of intellectual integrity [emphasis added]. . . .
>
> What has been found with regard to standardized tests generally, or individual tests specifically, does not support Judge Peckham's conclusions. . . .
>
> If Judge Peckham's analysis of the issues of cultural bias was scanty and faulty, Judge Grady's can best be described as naive."

The report card prepared by Bersoff suggests rather low marks to date for the federal judiciary concerning legal analyses of the bias issue. Two general reasons explain the rather poor performance of the judiciary regarding this issue. One has to do with the judicial mechanism and the other with the way that the IQ-bias issue was framed in the court proceedings.

Court proceedings are typically resolved in an unequivocal, all or none fashion. The placement-bias cases brought the courts into the rather murky world of social science theory and research which, in most cases, yield somewhat ambiguous results. This is particularly true with respect to IQ test bias. In science, truth is always approximate and does not easily yield clear right or wrong value judgments. (We are prone to say "especially the social sciences," but that is not necessarily true.) In any event, the judicial process, by nature, is ill equipped to deal with issues in the social sciences which are by nature ambiguous and impossible to resolve unequivocally. The efforts of the courts to deal with the placement-bias cases were further complicated by a number of other issues and assumptions that are inherent in the cases, but which were largely ignored in testimony and the formal opinions. Several of these implicit issues and assumptions are more important to the development of effective psycho-educational assessment services than the simple issue of bias.

Concepts of Bias

The concepts of bias used in the placement-bias litigation have been rather narrow and nontechnical. Mean differences, which do exist among groups, often are cited as indicating bias, under the assumption that a fair test of "potential" would yield identical distributions and means for all cultural groups. However, IQ tests are not direct measures of innate potential, a point of agreement among both proponents and critics of IQ tests. The causes of the mean differences among groups, and particularly between blacks and whites, have been discussed at great length in psychology for many years, with no final resolution (Loehlin, Lindzey, and Spuhler 1975).

A wide variety of technical criteria for assessing bias in tests has appeared in the measurement literature (Flaugher 1978). Research applying these criteria to various IQ and achievement tests has flourished in recent years. Conventional tests are nearly always found to be largely unbiased on the basis of such criteria as internal psychometric properties, factor structure, item content, atmosphere effects, and predictive validity (Cleary, Humphreys, Kendrick, and Wesman 1975; Jensen 1980; Reschly 1981). In the measurement literature, conventional tests are usually defended on the basis of predictive validity and other technical criteria, and improper or unwise test use is implicated as causing any bias that may exist (Cleary et al. 1975).

The issue of bias in tests is not simple. The conclusion one reaches in examining any test depends in large part on the definition of bias being used and is further complicated by the fact that any test can be used unwisely and unfairly. This misuse can occur when tests are used for purposes for which they were not intended, with inappropriate populations, and by ill-prepared examiners. The complexity of this issue and the research evidence, some of which is very clear, have not been reflected well in the court opinions.

Nature-Nurture

The possibility that more than IQ tests and overrepresentation was involved in the *Larry P.* case is suggested in the following statements, all of which were part of the plaintiff's testimony and were accepted by the court: IQ tests are biased and should be banned; IQ tests and standardized achievement tests are the same; customary uses of standardized achievement tests are acceptable (Reschly 1980a). The seemingly illogical reasoning behind these assertions can only be understood in light of other issues, one of which is the nature-nurture debate.

Most psychologists and educators who use IQ tests reject genetic explanations of group differences in unequivocal terms. Nevertheless, concern with this hypothesis, called "notorious" by Judge Peckham, has been just below the surface in court considerations and prominent in the placement-bias literature. Overrepresentation of black students in programs for the mildly retarded has been tied to racist views of their intellectual potential by Jones and Wilderson (1976), as well as others. The implicit assumption is that those who are involved with conventional uses of IQ tests, and educational systems having disproportionate classifications of minorities, are proponents of a genetic explanation of race differences. Extreme positions occasionally have been prompted by critics who suggest that the only alternatives for professional psychologists are to accept pluralistic norms or to subscribe to discriminatory practices (Mercer 1979), or that the only alternative to racist practices is to ban IQ tests (Hilliard 1980).

In view of the social policy implications of the nature-nurture debate (Cronbach 1975), professional psychologists should not be surprised by the attempts of many minority psychologists and public advocacy professionals such as civil rights attorneys, to resolve the issue through the courts. A court opinion that IQ tests are culturally biased and should be banned is a powerful resolution to the genetic hypothesis debate, at least in the broader social and political arena. The problem is that the wrong defendants are in court and the wrong issues are addressed: the actual defendants are not proponents of the genetic hypothesis, and the focus on whether the tests are biased ignores the educational needs of minority students who fail in regular classrooms. The principal, but unnamed, defendants in *Larry P.* and like cases are the proponents of genetic explanations of race differences such as Arthur Jensen (1969) and William Shockley (1971). The crucial but ignored issue is the educational and psychological development of economically disadvantaged minority students.

Role of Tests

In several court cases and in much of the placement-bias literature, it has been implicitly assumed that IQ tests were the primary if not the sole basis for the classification of students as mildly retarded (Mercer 1973). The role of standardized tests in the classification process has been exaggerated. From reading this literature one might reach the conclusion that classified and placed children were performing well until a psychologist came along and ensnared them in a pernicious psychometric net. However, the single most important determinant of classification is academic failure or behavioral difficulties in the regular classroom which lead to referral. It is only in this context that individual IQ tests are given and classification is even considered. Research conducted with randomly selected samples of students reveals that some children who would meet eligibility requirements are never referred, so that classification and placement (and IQ testing) are never considered. Disproportionate numbers of minority (as well as economically disadvantaged and male) students are referred because of academic or behavioral problems. Although research on the entire process is somewhat meager, the available data suggest that IQ tests either have a neutral effect on overall disproportionality, or perhaps actually reduce the degree of overrepresentation that would result from teacher referral alone (Reschly 1979). Overall, IQ test use protects students in all racial and social categories, boys as well as girls, from erroneous and inappropriate classification. An IQ test ban by itself would have little effect on overrepresentation.

Overrepresentation Data

Actual data on the degree of overrepresentation are confusing, easily distorted, and have perhaps been misunderstood by the courts. The percentage of enrollment in various programs broken down by minority and white students typically is presented, rather than the percentage of each group enrolled in various programs. The numbers, although obviously related, create quite a different impression. For example, in California over the past decade or so, the enrollment in special classes for the mildly retarded has been about 25 percent black while the total student population has been about 10 percent black (*Larry P.* 1979). A recent analysis in New Jersey revealed that black and Hispanic students were 18 percent and 7 percent respectively of the total student enrollment, but constituted 43 percent and 14 percent respectively of the enrollment in programs for the mildly retarded (Manni, Winikur, and Keller 1980). These data are typical of many states. Simply adding up the minority-student percentages of enrollment in programs for the mildly retarded has led some to the erroneous conclusion that a large percentage, perhaps even the majority, of minority students are labeled as mildly retarded. Examination of the data based on the percentage of each group classified and placed in programs for the mildly retarded leads to a much different perspective. In California, the actual percentage of the total black student population placed in special classes for the mildly retarded was just over one percent (Reschly 1980a). In New Jersey, the percentages of the total black and Hispanic student population classified and placed in programs for the mildly retarded were 1.9 percent and 1.4 percent, respectively. The comparable percentages for white students were about 0.5 percent in both states. The difference between program enrollment percentages and percentage of total student population enrolled in programs is substantial because only a very small percentage of the total student population or the minority student population is classified as mildly retarded. Minority students are indeed overrepresented in these classifications which are based in part on standardized test results. However, a very small percentage of minority students are classified and placed disproportionately in programs for the mildly retarded or in other mildly handicapping classifications and programs.

Effects of Classification

Economically disadvantaged students who come from a minority background are disproportionately placed in many educational programs, not just ones for mild mental retardation. For example, overrepresentation is much greater in the Head Start, Follow Through, and Title I programs. However, the mild mental retardation classification is much less acceptable because of prevailing assumptions about the meaning of this classification and the effectiveness of programs for the mildly retarded.

For the last decade increased concern has been expressed regarding the possibly negative consequences of formal classification. Many of the alleged negative effects of "labeling" have probably been exaggerated and have been difficult to document, including concerns about self-fulfilling prophecy and diminished motivation. However, ample evidence confirms that the mildly handicapping classifications are often misunderstood by students and parents and are regarded as inaccurate and humiliating by those who are classified (MacMillan 1977). The mental retardation classification appears to be the least acceptable and the most widely misunderstood. The classifications of learning disability or emotional disturbance (even with its connotation of "crazy") are regarded as less damaging. Although classification is inevitable, and informal, often very negative labeling occurs in all social settings, mild or educable mental retardation has a uniquely detrimental connotation.

Mild mental retardation (the educational equivalent being educable mental retardation) is the least severe of the four levels recognized in the current American Association on Mental Deficiency (AAMD) classification system (Grossman 1977). Mildly retarded persons are believed to constitute the vast majority of the mentally retarded. Unfortunately, the characteristics of the more severely retarded are frequently attributed to the mildly retarded, who differ from them on at least three crucial dimensions. Mild mental retardation, in contrast to the moderate, severe, or profound levels, typically is not associated with biological anomaly, is not permanent or life long, and is not comprehensive in the sense of causing incompetence across most social roles and settings. Mild mental retardation is typically identified only in the public school context, which establishes demands for abstract cognitive skills. (It is sometimes referred to as "six hour" retardation.)

Discovery of the overrepresentation of economically disadvantaged minority students in the mild mental retardation classification, coupled with confusion over what mild mental retardation means, has led to efforts to separate "true" from pseudo- or quasi-retardation, and to demands that bias in assessment be eliminated (*Larry P.* 1979, Mercer 1973, 1979). Mild or educable mental retardation is regarded as an illegitimate classification, since mental retardation is incorrectly understood to involve biological anomaly, permanent disability, and comprehensive incompetence. The problem is partly due to widespread ignorance of the AAMD classification system, in which mental retardation is conceptualized as referring to the current status of the individual, with no direct implications for prognosis (permanence) or etiology, which may be biological or psychosocial. However, the confusion over the meaning of mental retardation is in large part inherent in the current classification system, which attempts to organize all levels of mental retardation on the same continuum. However, mild mental retardation, where overrepresentation occurs, is vastly different from the other levels of mental retardation in terms of the comprehensiveness or breadth of the handicap and its etiology and prognosis. One obvious solution to this confusion is to change the classification system terminology so that mild mental retardation is clearly separated from the more severe levels of mental retardation (Reschly 1981).

Effectiveness of Special Classes

The special education program that has usually been provided for students classified as mildly retarded is the self-contained special class. This pattern of special education programming continues to prevail despite mandates to deliver services in as normal an environment as possible. In addition to its different connotation, mild mental retardation differs from learning diability in that the latter more often leads to part-time special education involving individual tutorial services, with the child's full participation in the regular classroom and school program during most of the school day. Self-contained special classes often involve a larger degree of separation from the regular school program and curriculum and less contact with "normal" students. The recent emphasis on "mainstreaming" suggests reduced use of special classes for the mildly retarded, a trend fostered in part by court opinions viewing overrepresentation of minorities in special classes as constituting unlawful segregation of students by race.

The weakest link in any argument to justify current patterns of overrepresentation is the effectiveness of the self-contained special classes for the mildly retarded. Although the research problem is extremely complex, precious little empirical support exists for these classes at the elementary and junior high school grade levels. Any benefits which do exist appear to be in the areas of social and personal adjustment, not academic achievement. The doubts about special classes in the research literature (e.g., Dunn 1968) were repeated in many other articles in the 1970s and accepted as fact by the *Larry P.* court decision. In the *Larry P.* opinion, special classes were characterized at least twenty-seven times as "dead-end," "inferior," etc. If these programs were as poor as alleged, then no student, regardless of race or social class, should have been placed in them. However, the negative characterization of special classes may be overdrawn. The benefits of special classes at the high school level involving work-study experiences are supported by evidence, and the common-sense experiences of educators suggest that self-contained special classes are a desirable and beneficial alternative for some students.

Summary

A cursory reading of the placement-bias litigation might lead to the naive conclusion that the only implication for psychoeducational assessment is whether IQ tests should be used. Far more than IQ tests is involved, and, as we have seen, the legal conclusions on that question are inconsistent. The overall influence of litigation, further reinforced by recent legislation, affects the entire process, content, and outcome of psychoeducational assessment.

LEGISLATION

Legislation at the state and federal levels is a second form of legal influence on psychoeducational assessment. In this chapter, less space is devoted to a discussion of legislation for several reasons. First, the status of federal legislation concerning education for the handicapped may change drastically in the near future. Second, nearly everything in federal legislation regarding assessment practices appeared in or was implied in court opinions or consent decrees (Turnbull 1978). Thus, even if the federal legislation is changed or repealed, the legal mandates concerning assessment practices would continue, though in a weakened form. State legislation varies considerably, making a discussion of all state legislation impossible in a chapter of this length. Some states provide rather precise requirements concerning assessment; other provide few if any guidelines.

A distinction between actual legislation and rules and regulations is important to this discussion. Laws or legal statutes passed by Congress or a state legislature typically are relatively brief statements of general principles and legislative intent. The laws typically are implemented through rules and regulations developed by the appropriate agency in the executive branch of government, e.g., the Federal Bureau of Education for the Handicapped or a state Department of Education. Rules and regulations usually have the effect of law after approval by the appropriate legislative committee. It should be noted that rules and regulations, in contrast to statutes, usually are changed more frequently and with less difficulty.

Federal Legislation: Public Law 94-142

Although several federal laws influence assessment practices, the most important by far is the Education for All Handicapped Children Act of 1975 (PL 94-142). PL 94-142 is in essence a grant-giving statute providing financial benefits to states if certain requirements are met. The requirements involve first a set of general principles regarding education of the handicapped: right to an appropriate education at public expense in the least restrictive environment, individualized educational programming, due process, protection in evaluation procedures, and confidentiality of information. All of these principles appeared earlier in court cases (Turnbull 1978). Secondly, PL 94-142 establishes a set of complex rules and regulations for implementing these principles (Federal Register 1977). Legislation and funding patterns proposed by the Reagan Administration would repeal PL 94-142 and combine current PL 94-142 monies with other programs in block grants to states. Regardless of the fate of PL 94-142, the law has been and likely will continue to be influential in assessment practices. Many of the features of PL 94-142 have been incorporated in state legislation and state rules and regulations. Because of the legal precedents described earlier, along with other reasons, it is unlikely that state legislation will be changed drastically.

Although all of the major principles and accompanying rules and regulations of PL 94-142 have implications for assessment, the most important are the sections on "Procedural Safeguards" (due process) and "Protection in Evaluation Procedures" (Federal Register 1977). In Table 4.1 the major principles and implications for assessment are presented.

Due Process

Earlier in this chapter, the basic concept of due process was discussed and readers encouraged to consider the procedures that should be followed if a significant decision was to be made about them or a child of theirs. The due-process regulations resulting from PL 94-142, court decisions, and state legislation represent efforts to ensure that significant decisions are made in a fair manner. The critical elements constituting due process are:

1. *Informed Consent.* Written notice to the parents is required prior to the initiation of preplacement evaluation procedures and prior to classification and placement in a special education program. If the parents refuse consent at either stage, appeal and hearing procedures can be initiated by the educational agency or the parent.

2. *Access to Records.* Parental rights to examine all records pertaining to the evaluation, classification, and placement, and to educational programming are guaranteed by due-process legal guidelines. Further, schools are required to maintain the confidentiality of these records and to release the information only with parental notice and consent. Parents also have the right to challenge the content of any record.

3. *Independent Evaluation.* Parents have the right to obtain an independent evaluation conducted by a "qualified examiner." The results of an independent evaluation must be considered in classification and

TABLE 4.1

Legal Principles Affecting Education of the Handicapped:
Implications for Assessment

Principle	Effects	Implications for Assessment
Right to education	— More students classified as handicapped. — New populations of handicapped students entered the public schools.	— Greatly increased need for individual psychoeducational assessment. — Need for specialized skills in assessment of low incident and more severely handicapped.
Least restrictive environment	— Handicapped students served in as normal an environment as possible, including regular class-rooms with support ser-vices or part-time special education.	— More emphasis on assessment in the natural environment through observation, etc., and the development and evaluation of interventions in the natural environment.
Individualized educational program	— Development of detailed plans to guide interven-tions with learning or behavior problems. — Annual reviews of effects of interventions.	— More emphasis on description of specific educational needs and problem behaviors. — More emphasis on use of as-sessment information to design interventions and to monitor progress.
Due process	— Formal procedures to ensure fairness through informed consent, access to records, appeal, and hearing.	— Greater scrutiny of the entire decisionmaking process, in-cluding psychoeducational assessment. — More emphasis on open com-munication with parents con-cerning instruments, results, and recommendations based on assessment data.
Protection in evaluation procedures	— Numerous guidelines concerning the preplace-ment and reevaluation of handicapped students: multifactored assess-ment, multidisciplinary team, valid procedures, appropriate in terms of handicap, primary lan-guage, nondiscrimina-tion, etc.	— More emphasis on adaptive be-havior, sociocultural status, and primary language, and less em-phasis on global measures such as IQ. — More emphasis on determina-tion of specific educational need, and less emphasis on un-derlying dynamics. — Assessment tailored to nature of child. — Assessment conducted by a team of professionals.

placement decisions by school personnel and can be used as evidence by the parent at a hearing.

    4. *Appeal and Hearing.* Complex procedures are established concerning appeal and hearing rights. These procedures, although oriented toward protecting the due-process rights of parents and students, also are available to the school if the parent refuses consent for evaluation or placement. The hearings must be impartial.

    Attempts to ensure fairness, although cumbersome, are critical to guaranteeing basic rights. These procedures can be viewed as legal entanglements which get in the way of effective psychological services, which they are in certain instances, or as a process which facilitates communication and fosters cooperation between home and school. The importance of these procedures becomes more apparent if we apply them to our personal situation and imagine that a classification and placement decision is being made about us or our children.

Protection in Evaluation Procedures

    The "Protection in Evaluation Procedures" (PEP) section of PL 94-142 established a number of standards concerning both the content and process of assessment. Unlike the due process procedures, which are firmly based on several court cases, the PEP provisions, for the most part, are related to litigation in a general way. The specific PEP provisions and brief comments follow. (Quoted statements and phrases are from the PL 94-142 "Rules and Regulations," Federal Register 1977, pp. 42496 and 42497.)

    1. A "full and complete *individual evaluation*" must be conducted by trained personnel prior to classification and placement.

    2. *Nonbiased assessment* was required in a sweeping statement that "testing and evaluation materials and procedures used for the purposes of evaluation and placement of handicapped children must be selected and administered so as not to be racially or culturally discriminatory." This deceptively simple requirement reflects in part the placement-bias litigation discussed earlier.

    3. The assessment must be conducted using "the child's *native language* or other mode of communication unless it is clearly not feasible to do so."

    4. Assessment procedures are to be "*validated* for the specific purpose for which they are used."

    5. Specific *educational need* must be assessed in the preplacement evaluation. Evaluation procedures and placement decisions must be

based on a wide variety of information, i.e., *multifactored assessment,* and no single measure such as IQ can be used as the sole criterion.

6. A *multidisciplinary team* is required in the preplacement evaluation and in the placement decision. Although the members of the team are specified only in a general sense, the clear implication is that no single individual or professional discipline is to have the sole authority over classification and placement.

7. Special attention is drawn to the needs of low-incidence handicapped students by the requirement that tests not merely reflect the sensory, manual, or speaking skills of the child, but rather, accurately reflect the child's aptitude or achievement level.

8. *Placement decisions* must be made by a multidisciplinary team, must be based on a multifactored assessment, must be made "in conformance with the least restrictive environment rules," and must be accompanied by an individualized educational program which specifies the special education *and* related services needs of the child.

9. A complete *reevaluation* of children classified as handicapped and placed in special programs must be conducted at least every three years. The reevaluation must meet the standards discussed in this section.

The federal legislation discussed in this section has many implications for graduate education programs as well as for the practice of school psychology. The specific legislation, even if revised or repealed, reflects both litigation and professional standards for best practices. Moreover, state legislation, discussed briefly in the next section, is generally consistent with PL 94-142 requirements.

State Legislation

The uncertainties concerning the future of PL 94-142 make state legislation concerning the handicapped and psychoeducational assessment even more important. The evolution of state legislation concerning the handicapped and a large expansion of school psychological services closely paralleled the right-to-education litigation. Mandates to serve the handicapped, along with funding mechanisms and program requirements, were passed by nearly every state between 1970 and 1975 (Abeson and Ballard 1976). The date the mandates were to be effective (i.e., fully implemented) varied somewhat, with most in the mid-to-late 1970s.

State legislation exerts a powerful influence on school psychology and psychoeducational assessment in a number of ways. First, and most basic, there is the question of whether school psychologists are required as members of multidisciplinary teams. Most states have such requirements for at least some handicapping conditions. Second, levels of funding for school psychological services vary considerably among states, with ratios as low as one psychologist per 1500 students and as high as one psychologist per 5000 or more students (Kicklighter 1976). The ratio has an obvious effect on the number of students seen by school psychologists and the types of services provided.

States generally define handicapping conditions in legislation, with specific diagnostic criteria spelled out in special education rules and regulations. The state rules and regulations also may specify the areas to be assessed for each handicap, who is responsible for conducting the assessment, and the specific instruments that can be used (Mercer, Forgnore, and Wolking 1976, Patrick and Reschly 1982). These latter requirements have an obvious effect on psychoeducational assessment. For example, some states have defined diagnostic criteria for learning disabilities in terms of an underlying disorder in psychological processes related to learning, requiring the use of assessment techniques to measure these processes, e.g., auditory discrimination and visual-motor integration. In contrast, other states have defined learning disability as a severe discrepancy between actual achievement and apparent potential, which places less emphasis on processing factors and more emphasis on measures of achievement and intelligence (Mercer et al. 1976). States may suggest or require the use of specific instruments in certain areas such as intelligence or adaptive behavior, and may specify the professional personnel responsible for certain areas of assessment (Patrick and Reschly 1982).

There is considerable variation among states in the way services are organized, the personnel required or recommended, and the nature and specificity of guidelines for assessment practices. These state-by-state variations influence how certain basic principles are implemented, not whether the principles are established. All states must work toward non-discriminatory assessment and placement, must observe due process, and so on.

CURRENT TRENDS IN PSYCHOEDUCATIONAL ASSESSMENT

There is every reason to believe that legal influences on psychoeducational assessment, already enormous, will continue to evolve in the future. The dynamic relationships among litigation based on constitutional principles, legislation based on the results of litigation, and then litigation prompted by that legislation have been described by Bersoff (1981). Legislation and accompanying rules and regulations are passed, amended, revised, and sometimes even repealed. Court decisions typically are somewhat ambiguous, sometimes inconsistent from court to court, and also subject to the evolution of legal principles and legislation. Nevertheless, the legal influences to date have clear implications for psychoeducational assessment which, in a general sense, are unlikely to change significantly over the next decade. In addition, many of the changes discussed in this section were already underway due to the influence of psychological theory and research (Reschly 1980b).

Accountability

A major trend in psychoeducational assessment which has been fostered by legal influences is accountability. The due-process procedures and other legal guidelines establish the potential for close scrutiny of nearly all aspects of the work of school psychologists. Psychological reports, regarded a decade ago, as confidential documents which were not shown to parents are now among the educational records which parents can examine. Information in the reports can be challenged by parents through their submission of additional information or by requesting a hearing. Classification decisions, interpretations of behavior, and recommendations are now open to question. The validity and fairness of tests and other assessment devices can be challenged on the basis of due-process protections and on other legal grounds.

Some very desirable effects of this increased scrutiny of psychoeducational assessment practices are a greater use of behavioral assessment procedures, more objective presentation of information in reports, and reduced use of broad inferences based on minimal information. These trends, also prominent in research, theories, and graduate education relating to school psychology (Reschly 1980b), have been furthered by the legal influences. School psychology shares, in part, the unfortunate tradition in clinical psychology of combining "clinical insight" with very minimal data to arrive at global descriptions of persons. These global descriptions, particularly of presumed underlying dynamics, typically reflect analogical reasoning—assuming that a logical relationship exists between observed behavior and the supposed underlying dynamics (See Obrzut and Zucker, Chapter 9). For example, a common interpretation of dark, heavy lines in reproductions of Bender-Gestalt designs is repressed hostility (Koppitz 1975, p. 85). This analogy between observed behavior (the dark, heavy lines) and underlying dynamics (repressed hostility) has very weak empirical support. Similar interpretations of behaviors observed during formal assessment have been common in psychological reports, even though the interpretation is rarely supported by other observations. Increased scrutiny of these interpretations and the reliability and validity of commonly used assessment devices will lead to a very desirable outcome, namely, conservative interpretation and a greater use of measures which are known to be valid.

The major problem is level of inference, or the relationship between the behavior observed and the interpretation of that behavior. Interpretations which involve a high level of inference — i.e., in which the seriousness of the inferred condition exceeds the sophistication of the available diagnostic tools — are more vulnerable to challenge, particularly if they do not lead to interventions and are not firmly supported by empirical evidence. A psychologist, depending on graduate education and theoretical orientation, may interpret poor performance in copying the Bender designs as indicating weak visual-motor skills (a low-level inference), as suggestive of maturational lag (a middle-level inference), or as suggestive of neurological dysfunction (a high-level inference). The high-level inference in this example is not directly related to an intervention or treatment and has weak empirical support (See Hynd and Hartlage, Chapter 10). The interests of both the psychologist and the child are served best by avoidance of high-level inferences which, in reality, are far more speculative than scientific.

Sensitivity to Sociocultural Differences

Among human services professionals, school psychologists always have been in the forefront of efforts to understand and deal effectively with sociocultural differences. The issues raised in the placement-bias litigation broadened these issues to include concerns about the effectiveness of special education programs, the fairness of tests, the social consequences of testing, and so on. These are important concerns that are understood best in the context of attempts to enhance the competencies and opportunities of minority students through educational programs (Reschly 1981). Psychoeducational assessment practices are part of the answer, but even more important are efforts to ensure that the outcomes of testing and assessment are positive for the individual. Even if we had the perfect culture-free or culture-fair test, recognized now as an impossibility, the consequences of testing could be negative if special programs or other interventions were ineffective.

Increased sensitivity to sociocultural differences is reflected in the kinds and variety of assessment instruments used, the interpretations of performance on these instruments, and the recognition of environmental influences on performance. Several examples will illustrate these points. It is now very unlikely that a bilingual child, who may be less fluent in the English language, will have "intelligence" measured with a test that assesses only the verbal factor, such as the Stanford-Binet. Moreover, measures of intelligence are nearly universally supplemented by other measures, such as individually administered formal tests, interviews with significant others, observation in key settings, etc. The classification and placement decisions that may result from psychoeducational assessment are based on a broad variety of information. Interpretation, especially of IQ tests, now is more conservative and more closely related to validity data. Nearly all school psychologists are knowledgeable about environmental and cultural influences on IQ measures. This knowledge is increasingly reflected in interpretation: IQ test information is important, but limited in scope; IQ scores are reliable, but can change for individuals; IQ scores do not reflect innate potential nor measure some global index of worth, but rather predict fairly well the somewhat limited criterion of academic success. These changes, brought about through increased sensitivity to minority students, are beneficial for all students.

Assessment for Intervention

A subtle shift in emphasis in psychoeducational assessment has been stimulated by the combined influences of psychological theory, research on the effects of special education programs, and legal guidelines. The major purpose of psychoeducational assessment increasingly is viewed in terms of intervention or treatment, rather than merely describing or understanding behavior. Intervention and understanding, of course, are not mutually exclusive; but the relative emphasis on one or the other has important implications for the focus of assessment activities. The "understanding" purpose, when applied to assessment of children with learning or adjustment problems, typically involves attempts to determine what underlies or accounts for problem behaviors. This research for causes serves to focus assessment activities on the developmental history, family dynamics, and intrapersonal personality factors. Although understanding of developmental influences and family dynamics may be worthy goals in developing a comprehensive picture of the individual, this information often is irrelevant to treatment or intervention in an educational setting. In most instances, there is little that educational personnel, including school psychologists, can do about family dynamics, developmental factors, etc.

Assessment for intervention typically focuses more attention on a precise description of specific problem behaviors. Learning problems are analyzed in terms of specific educational skills that have been mastered and those that need to be taught. Adjustment problems are analyzed in terms of the frequency, intensity, and duration of specific behaviors that may be inappropriate due to situational factors, may be inappropriate due to the nature of the behavior, or may reflect deficits in skills. In addition to precise descriptions of behavior, assessment activities are focused on the specific situation in which problems occur, with attempts to determine antecedent and consequent conditions that maintain the problem behavior. Based on this assessment information, interventions are designed, implemented, and evaluated. This basic approach has been applied both to rather specific problems which occur in one setting and to broad ranges of problems that require long-term interventions such as special classes (Bergan 1977).

The behavioral-assessment techniques used in assessment for intervention typically involve greater use of structured interview, observation in the natural setting, and criterion-referenced tests. All of these measures are used to assess the *current* situation and to design interventions. The interpretation of traditional norm-referenced measures such as IQ tests also is oriented to describing the current situation and designing interventions (Nelson 1980). In contrast, the "understanding" purpose typically involves greater use of unstructured interviews, projective tests, and personality inventories. These assessment techniques are rich sources of hypotheses concerning the underlying causes of problem behaviors. Unfortunately, the hypotheses are usually difficult to confirm or disconfirm, the assessment techniques have questionable reliability and validity, and the information gathered is difficult to translate into specific interventions. For all of these reasons, this kind of assessment is unlikely to meet legal challenges or be in the best interests of children.

The assessment-for-intervention trend, which usually involves behavioral assessment techniques, is consistent with legal guidelines emphasizing individualized planning and evaluation of the effects of special programs. This trend also is consistent with efforts to ensure that classification is beneficial to the individual (Cromwell, Blashfield, and Strauss 1975) and that special education programs are effective (Gallagher 1972). A major implicit assumption in the placement-bias litigation discussed earlier was that special-class programs were ineffective. Assessment for intervention should enhance the planning, implementation, and evaluation of all types of special education programs.

CONCLUSION

Legal influences have been important in hastening the pace of change in the content and process of psychoeducational assessment. The major trends, greater accountability, increased sensitivity to sociocultural differences, and greater emphasis on assessment for interventions are positive changes that are in the best interests of all children (and school psychology). Considerably greater emphasis on the outcomes of assessment now is apparent. The legal influences, although ambiguous and often cumbersome in practice, have fostered the further development of effective services to children.

REFERENCES

Abeson, A., & Ballard, J. State and federal policy for exceptional children. In F. Weintraub, A. Abeson, J. Ballard, & M. LaVor, *Public Policy and the Education of Exceptional Children*. Reston, Va.: Council for Exceptional Children, 1976.

Abeson, A., Bolick, N., & Hass, J. *A primer on due process*. Reston, Va.: Council for Exceptional Children, 1975.

Bergan, J. *Behavioral consultation*. Columbus, Ohio: Charles E. Merrill, 1977.

Bersoff, D. Procedural safeguards. In L. Morra (Ed.), *Due Process*. Washington, D.C.: U.S. Office of Education, Bureau of Education for the Handicapped, 1978.

Bersoff, D. The legal regulation of school psychology. In C. Reynolds & T. Gutkin (Eds.), *The handbook of school psychology*. New York: Wiley, 1982.

Bersoff, D. *Larry P.* and *PASE:* Judicial report cards on the validity of individual intelligence tests. In T. Kratochwill (Ed.), *Advances in school psychology* (Vol. II). Hillsdale, N.J.: Erlbaum, 1982.

Buss, W. What procedural due process means to the school psychologist: A dialogue. *Journal of School Psychology, 1975, 13,* 298–310.

Cleary, T. A., Humphreys, L., Kendrick, A., & Wesman, A. Educational uses of tests with disadvantaged students. *American Psychologist, 1975, 30,* 15–41.

Cromwell, R., Blashfield, R., & Strauss, J. Criteria for classification systems. In N. Hobbs (Ed.), *Issues in the classification of children*. San Francisco: Jossey-Bass, 1975.

Cronbach, L. Five decades of public controversy over mental testing. *American Psychologist, 1975, 30,* 1–14.

Diana v. *State Board of Education,* C-70 37 RFP, District Court for Northern California (February 1970).

Dunn, L. Special education for the mildly retarded: Is much of it justifiable? *Exceptional Children, 1968, 35,* 5–22.

Federal Register, August 23, 1977, p. 42474–42518. Education of handicapped children. Regulations Implementing Education for all Handicapped Children Act of 1975 (Public Law 94–142).

Flaugher, R. The many definitions of test bias. *American Psychologist,* 1978, *33,* 671–679.

Gallagher, J. The special education contract for mildly handicapped children. *Exceptional Children,* 1972, *38,* 527–535.

Gerken, K. Assessment of high-risk preschoolers and children and adolescents with low-incident handicapping conditions. In G. Phye & D. Reschly (Eds.), *School psychology: Perspectives and issues.* New York: Academic Press, 1979.

Gilhool, T. Education: An inalienable right. In F. Weintraub, A. Abeson, J. Ballard, & M. LaVor (Eds.), *Public policy and the education of exceptional children.* Reston, Va.: Council for Exceptional Children, 1976.

Grossman, H. (Ed.). *Manual on terminology and classification in mental retardation.* Washington, D.C.: American Association on Mental Deficiency, 1977.

Guadalupe v. *Tempe Elementary School District,* 71-435, District Court for Arizona, January 1972.

Hilliard, A. Cultural diversity and special education. *Exceptional Children,* 1980, *46,* 584–588.

Jensen, A. How much can we boost IQ and scholastic achievement? *Harvard Education Review,* 1969, *39,* 1–123.

Jensen, A. *Bias in mental testing.* New York: Free Press, 1980.

Jones, R., & Wilderson, F. Mainstreaming and the minority child: An overview of issues and a perspective. In R. Jones (Ed.), *Mainstreaming and the minority child.* Reston, Va.: Council for Exceptional Children, 1976.

Kicklighter, R. School psychology in the U.S.: A quantitative survey. *Journal of School Psychology,* 1976, *14,* 151–156.

Koppitz, E. *The Bender Gestalt Test for young children. Vol. 2. Research and application, 1963–1973.* New York: Grune & Stratton, 1975.

Larry P. et al. v. *Wilson Riles et al.* United States District Court, Northern District of California, Case No. C-71-2270 RFP, 1972, 1974, 1979.

Loehlin, J., Lindzey, G., & Spuhler, J. *Race differences in intelligence.* San Francisco: Freeman, 1975.

MacMillan, D. *Mental retardation in school and society.* Boston: Little, Brown, 1977.

Manni, J., Winikur, D., & Keller, M. *A report on minority group representation in special education programs in the state of New Jersey.* Trenton, N.J.: State Department of Education, 1980.

Mercer, C., Forgnone, C., & Wolking, W. Definitions of learning disabilities used in the United States. *Journal of Learning Disabilities,* 1976, *9,* 376–386.

Mercer, J. *Labeling the mentally retarded.* Berkeley, Calif.: University of California Press, 1973.

Mercer, J. *Technical manual: SOMPA — System of multicultural pluralistic assessment.* New York: Psychological Corporation, 1979.

5

Intelligence
Old Concepts — New Perspectives
ALAN S. KAUFMAN

INTELLIGENCE TESTING and the IQ concept are controversial topics, and these controversies not only occupy much professional journal space, but also appear frequently in lay magazines and newspapers (Kaufman 1979b). Litigation involving IQ tests was common in the 1970s, most notably the *Larry P.* decision (Prasse 1980), and there is every indication that similar legal cases will continue and probably multiply in the 1980s. In this chapter, the history of individual intelligence testing is summarized and explored as a means of better understanding the contemporary assessment scene. With the past and present firmly in perspective, new directions for intelligence testing are then considered, with particular emphasis on the development and rationale of the Kaufman Assessment Battery for Children (K-ABC; Kaufman and Kaufman 1983).

THE HISTORY OF INTELLIGENCE TESTING

Not surprisingly, the study of intelligence and its measurement traces its roots to physicians, educators, and psychologists who were deeply involved with populations at the two extremes of the intellectual continuum. Jean Esquirol (1838) and Edouard Seguin (1866) were committed to the study of mentally retarded individuals, and Sir Francis Galton (1869) was fascinated by the mental abilities of men of genius. The separate contributions of these pioneers have been profoundly felt in the field of intelligence testing; however, it was the innovative research investigations of Alfred Binet (1903), who focused on the mental abilities of typical or average children at each age, which have had the longest lasting and most direct effect on individual intelligence testing as we know it today.

Esquirol made several important contributions, most notably by distinguishing "between the idiot, whose intelligence does not develop beyond a very low level, and the demented person" (Peterson 1925, p. 163). This distinction between mental retardation and emotional disturbance reflected a vital breakthrough for assessment and indicates the primitive state of the art in the early nineteenth century. Esquirol also described a hierarchy of retardation (or feeble-mindedness, as it was known in earlier times) with "idiots" occupying the bottom rung, followed by "imbeciles," and peaking with "morons" (Peterson 1925). He was indeed well ahead of his time in concluding that the use of language was the most dependable criterion for inferring a retarded individual's intelligence level (Anastasi 1976), and Esquirol (1828) is also credited with developing a precursor of the mental-age concept by pointing out that "an idiot is incapable of acquiring the knowledge common to other persons of his own age" (Peterson 1925, p. 183).

Seguin was heavily influenced in his work with mentally retarded individuals by Jean Itard, of *Wild Boy of Aveyron* fame; in turn, Seguin's methodology had a profound influence on the educational techniques of Maria Montessori. Like Esquirol, Seguin tried to establish criteria for distinguishing between different levels of retardation, although Seguin (1866) focused on sensory discrimination and motor control. Optimism regarding treatment of retarded individuals characterized Seguin's approach, and he instituted a comprehensive program of sense-training and muscle-training techniques, much of which lives on in present-day institutions for the mentally retarded (Anastasi 1976). In addition, tests developed by Seguin, such as the Seguin Form Board, which requires the rapid placement of various wooden geometric shapes into their proper holes, are still included in contemporary nonverbal performance tests, e.g. the Arthur Point Scale (Arthur 1947).

Not only were Esquirol and Seguin pioneers in individual intellectual assessment, but their efforts helped bring the world out of a dark age, engendering more humane treatment of retarded and insane people. Prior to the nineteenth century, "neglect, ridicule, and even torture had been the common lot of these unfortunates" (Anastasi 1976, p. 5). However, one arguably negative legacy of their focus on differentiating levels of retardation is the prevalent practice of labelling individuals in various special-education categories. The Esquirol tradition has substituted euphemisms for terms like "imbecile," as evidenced by the American Association on Mental Deficiency's (AAMD) classification scheme, which distinguishes among mild, moderate, severe, and profound levels of retardation. To this day, I find occasional case reports in the folders of retarded individuals which use archaic and offensive labels, such as "low-grade moron." Yet, regardless of whether a person is considered to suffer from "idiocy" or "profound retardation," the use of unpleasant, pigeon-holing labels remains an unfortunate by-product of the otherwise great contributions of the pioneers in the field of retardation.

Francis Galton, studying people at the opposite end of the ability spectrum, transformed his enthusiasm for gifted men of genius and the study of the genetics of intelligence into the development of what is apparently the first comprehensive individual intelligence test. Galton's tests, administered for a small fee (threepence or fourpence) in his Anthropometric Laboratory, required sensory discrimination and sensory-motor coordination. Based on Galton's (1883) belief that intelligence must be intimately related to sensory abilities because environmental knowledge comes to us via the senses, he developed a series of tests such as weight discrimination, reaction time, visual discrimination, steadiness of hand, keenness of sight, and strength of squeeze. His empirical justification for this test battery came from comparisons between gifted and retarded individuals which — not surprisingly, in view of Seguin's work — showed obvious superiority in favor of the gifted (Peterson 1925).

Galton's laboratory was established in the 1880s, first at the International Health Exhibition in South Kensington, England, and later in the South Kensington Museum. His laboratory was popular, but Galton's influence spread far beyond the museum, as Galton-type tests were developed throughout Europe and in the United States as well. James McKeen Cattell, an assistant at Galton's Anthropometric Laboratory, set up a laboratory in 1890 at the University of Pennsylvania and moved it to Columbia University the following year. It was he who coined the term "mental tests." Galton's influence was clearly evidenced in Cattell's 40–60 minute, individual examination: the tests included keenness of hearing, reaction time, after-images, color vision, sensitivity to pain, and the like (Peterson 1925). However, Cattell's (1890) work was not merely an imitation of Galton's tests. Cattell elaborated upon and improved his mentor's methodology by emphasizing the vital notion that administration procedures must be standardized to obtain results that are strictly comparable from person to person and time to time.

In the meantime, a challenge was being issued to the Galton view of sensory and motor intelligence by Alfred Binet in France. In collaboration with Theóphile Simon and Victor Henri, Binet conducted numerous investigations of complex mental tasks, rejecting the Galton notion that performance on elementary sensory discrimination and motor coordination tasks equates with intelligent behavior. Although Binet and his co-workers developed numerous tests of higher mental processes not long after the time that Galton's laboratory was founded, these tasks of memory, imagination, comprehension, moral sentiments, and so forth did not have an immediate impact on the field of intellectual measurement. In fact, Cattell considered carefully the arguments for "tests of a strictly psychological nature" put forth by Binet and others, but rejected these arguments in favor of "more definite and simple tests" since "measurements of the body and of the senses come as completely within our scope as the higher mental processes" (Cattell and Farrand 1896; Peterson 1925, p. 79).

The downfall of the Galton-Cattell approach and the concomitant upswing of the Binet methodology came, oddly enough, as the result of two very flawed investigations. Stella Sharp (1898–99), who conducted her research in Tichener's Cornell laboratory, directly compared sensory discrimination tests with tests of complex mental functions and concluded that the simplest mental processes yield comparatively unimportant information, whereas the tests of Binet and Henri showed much value in assessing "individual psychical differences." However, these well-respected conclusions were based on a sample of only seven advanced college students in psychology, along with a "control group" of less advanced undergraduate members of an experimental psychology course. Apart from the small and homogeneous nature of the sample, the methodology was weak and only partially quantified.

The second study that spelled doom for the Galton approach was Clark Wissler's (1901) correlational analysis at Barnard College, based on data for 250 first-year students and 35 seniors. The tests and anthropometric measures obtained at Cattell's laboratory "showed little more than a mere chance relation" when correlated with each other or when correlated with academic marks (Wissler 1901). However, the highly selected groups evaluated were extremely restricted in range, which would have depressed coefficients for any tests, including highly complex ones. It is ironical that studies with serious methodological shortcomings would help mark the downfall of the Galton movement. A further irony is that Galton developed a statistical method that was the forerunner of the coefficient of correlation, which was perfected by his friend Karl Pearson. As indicated, low Pearsonian correlations obtained by Wissler were instrumental in a swing toward the Binet tests.

Even though initial reaction to the two studies was predominantly anti-*testing,* causing a lack of enthusiasm for the Galton-Cattell as well as the Binet-Henri approach in the United States, the methodology of Binet eventually triumphed, first throughout Europe and finally in America (Peterson 1925). Thus, support was finally given to what we now know axiomatically to be true, namely, the claims repeatedly made by Binet and his collaborators in his own journal (*L'Année Psychologique,* founded in 1895): that efficiency in simple sensory-motor tests bears only a small relationship to other criteria of intellect (Binet used teachers' estimates of ability), and that the tests of higher mental processes, though they give more variable and unstable results than simple tests, are more significant and therefore distinguish between the everyday activities of different individuals (e.g., Binet and Henri 1896; Binet and Simon 1905). Indeed, the willingness of Binet to accept *error* in measurement as a necessity for proper intellectual assessment constitutes one of his most dynamic contributions to the field.

In addition to recognizing the inevitability of some variability in test performance, Binet "discarded the specific test for the specific ability and took a group of tests which seemed to cover in general the chief psychological characteristics that go to make up intelligence. And, furthermore, as the norm or standard of intelligence he took what the average child at each age could do" (Pintner and Paterson 1925, p. 7). Although Binet's first group of tests (the 1905 scale, which was constructed to separate mentally retarded from normal children in the Paris public schools) was not arranged by year level, the landmark 1908 Binet-Simon scale did follow this systematic and novel format. The 1908 intelligence test included three to eight brief tasks at eleven age levels between three and thirteen years. The tasks at the three-year-level, (e.g., asking the child to repeat sentences of six syllables, to give the family name) were passed by the normal child of three; those at the seven-year-level (e.g., telling what is missing in unfinished pictures, naming four common coins) were passed by typical seven-year-olds; those at the eleven-year-level (e.g., pointing out absurdities in contradictory statements, naming sixty words in three minutes) were passed by the average eleven-year-old; and so forth (Peterson 1925).

This age-level approach characterizes the Stanford-Binet Intelligence Scale (Terman and Merrill 1973) to this day, and the nature of the tasks developed by Binet and his colleagues is extremely similar to the specific tasks constituting every major intelligence test in current use. The extent of Binet's influence is discussed in the next section.

THE LEGACY OF ALFRED BINET IN THE UNITED STATES

The Binet-Simon scale, including the 1911 revision which extended through adulthood, was welcomed in Europe and the United States, and its translation and adaptation were begun almost immediately. Town directly translated the Binet-Simon scale into English in 1913; early revisions and adaptations were developed by Bobertag in Germany, Johnston and Winch in England, and by several investigators in the United States: Goddard, Kuhlmann, Wallin, Terman, and Yerkes (Pintner and Paterson 1925).

Terman's (1916) Stanford Revision and Extension of the Binet-

Simon Intelligence Scale, later shortened to Stanford-Binet, emerged victorious, despite the earlier appearance of competing scales like the Goddard-Binet (Goddard 1911) and Kuhlmann-Binet (Kuhlmann 1912), and the later publication of revised Binet batteries (e.g., Herring Revision of the Binet-Simon Tests, Herring 1922).

Terman's success was not due to luck or coincidence. After publishing a revision of the Binet Scale that he termed "tentative" (Terman and Childs 1912), he spent four years painstakingly and thoroughly standardizing the scale. He was specifically trying to meet the needs of the growing number of practitioners in the field whose demand "for more and more accurate diagnoses . . . raised the whole question of the accurate placing of tests in the scale and the accurate evaluation of the responses made by the child" (Pintner and Paterson 1925, p. 11). Terman also introduced the term *IQ* (intelligence quotient) in his 1916 scale, borrowing Stern's (1914) concept and making his revised Binet even more attractive to individual mental examiners.

Despite the many advantages of Terman's scale over its competitors, there was still much room for improvement: adult intelligence was not adequately measured, standardization was not representative enough, directions for administering and scoring some tasks were unclear, and too many of the tasks were verbal (Sattler 1974). The 1937 revision of the Binet (Terman and Merrill 1937) produced two Forms (L and M) and corrected many of the problems with the earlier version. For example, more nonverbal tests were added at the preschool age levels, the standardization was much improved, and additional levels were added at the lower and upper ends of the scale.

The two most recent Binet revisions have been very disappointing. In 1960, Forms L and M were combined into the present Form L-M, and the deviation IQ (a standard score with a mean of 100 and standard deviation of 16) replaced the ratio IQ (Terman and Merrill 1937). Astonishingly, there was no restandardization of the 1960 Stanford-Binet. Instead, data from a nonrepresentative sample of 4,498 children, tested in the early 1950s, were used to determine changes in item difficulties obtained in the 1930s. This technique was less than satisfactory as a substitution for a new standardization (Berger 1970).

The 1972 Stanford-Binet represented a restandardization of the instrument, but it made no modifications of existing items (except for a couple of trivial substitutions) nor switching of tasks from one level to another. Consequently, tests that are placed at year-level five, for example, are now solved by the average four-and-a-half-year-old, a demonstration of — among other things — the impact of mass media on the mental functioning of preschool children. The result is the misplacement of numerous tasks and the total loss of meaning of the mental-age (MA) concept. For example, a child of four who earns an MA of four obtains an IQ of 88 instead of the expected 100! It is ironical that Terman's rigor in determining accurate placements for tasks in his 1916 scale was instrumental in the triumph of his Binet revision over the versions developed by his competitors; yet the lack of rigor in this same important endeavor, conducted more than a half-century after Terman's initial work and about fifteen years after his death, has been instrumental in the diminished usage of the once-venerated Stanford-Binet. To be sure, the Binet is still used by practitioners throughout the country (Goh, Teslow, and Fuller 1980), but this one-score, unrevised battery has clearly been superseded in everyday practice by Wechsler's scales, notably the Wechsler Intelligence Scale for Children — Revised (WISC-R, Wechsler 1974) for school-aged youngsters.

Although on the wane in terms of its frequency of use in present-day schools and clinics, the Stanford-Binet's impact is evident in every contemporary instrument, including the WISC-R. As new tests were developed in the 1920s and 1930s, Terman's adaptations and revisions of the tests developed by Binet and his collaborators became the prototypes of tasks in new instruments. Frequently, an identical format and even the same items characterized many tasks in "new" test batteries.

An illustration of this impact is presented in Table 5.1, which shows that one of the most popular current tests for preschool children, the McCarthy Scales of Children's Abilities (McCarthy 1972), traces its roots directly to the 1916 Binet revision. This table also demonstrates that Goodenough, Maurer, and Van Wagenen's (1940) Minnesota Preschool Scale is primarily a collection of Binet tasks, modified only slightly. The Minnesota tasks are listed in sequence in the center of Table 5.1. To the left are listed the Binet tasks which were adopted or modified by Goodenough and her colleagues. To the right are the McCarthy analogs of Binet and Minnesota tasks. In her test manual, Dorothea McCarthy (1972, p. iii) acknowledges "the astute tutelage of Dr. Florence L. Goodenough" during her early training. The influence of Goodenough on the McCarthy subtests is clearly evident if one compares the McCarthy General Cognitive Scale to the Minnesota Preschool Scale. The similarity extends to the item level for some subtests (e.g., McCarthy's Puzzle Solving and the Minnesota's Picture Puzzles). In addition, two Minnesota analogs were included in the tryout version of the McCarthy (Paper Folding, Verbal Absurdities), and the Goodenough Draw-A-Man test (Goodenough and Harris 1950) was clearly the precursor of McCarthy's Draw-A-Child subtest.

Thus, the influence of the Binet on the McCarthy Scales, indirectly through Goodenough and directly from the Terman and Merrill

TABLE 5.1

The Influence of the Binet Tradition
on Contemporary Preschool and Primary-Grade Assessment

Stanford-Binet (1916 and 1937 Revisions)	Minnesota Preschool Scale (1940)	McCarthy Scales of Children's Abilities: General Cognitive Scale (1972)
Pointing to parts of the body (1916, III)	I. Pointing out parts of body	
Enumeration of objects in pictures (1916, III)	II. Pointing out objects in pictures	4. Word knowledge, Part I, item 1
Naming familiar objects (1916, III)	III. Naming familiar objects	4. Word knowledge, Part II, items 2–5
Copying a square, diamond (1916, IV, VII)	IV. Copying drawings	12. Draw-A-Design, items 4–9
Drawing a vertical line, cross (1937, Form M, III, & Form L, III-6)	V. Imitative drawings	12. Draw-A-Design, items 1–3
Block building: tower, bridge (1937, Form L, II & III)	VI. Block building	1. Block building
Description of pictures (1916, VII)	VII. Response to pictures	
– – – –	VIII. Knox cube imitation	6. Tapping sequence
Obeying simple commands (1937, Form L, II & Form M, II-6)	IX. Obeying simple commands	
Comprehension (1916, IV, VI, VIII, X)	X. Comprehension	
Discrimination of forms (1916, IV)	XI. Discrimination of forms	

Note: The Stanford-Binet subtests are divided according to age levels, indicated by Roman numerals (e.g., III-6 would indicate a test a normal child 3 years, 6 months of age should pass). The McCarthy Scales and Minnesota Preschool Scale are not so organized but consist of a series of subtests administered to most children.

Note: Tasks from Form L and Form M of the 1937 Revision of the Stanford-Binet are included in this table only when analogous tasks were *not* included in the 1916 version of the Stanford-Binet. Only Binet tasks at years II-X were considered for this table.

TABLE 5.1 *(continued)*

Stanford-Binet (1916 and 1937 Revisions)	Minnesota Preschool Scale (1940)	McCarthy Scales of Children's Abilities: General Cognitive Scale (1972)
Naming objects from memory (1937, Form L, IV)	XII. Naming objects from memory	3. Pictorial memory
Picture memories (1937, Form L, III)	XIII. Recognition of forms	
Naming colors (1916, V)	XIV. Colors	
Maze tracing (1937, Form L, VI)	XV. Tracing a form	
Patience: Pictures (1937, Form M, III-6)	XVI. Picture puzzles: rectangular series	2. Puzzle solving, cow, bear
Finding omissions in pictures (1916, VI)	XVII. Incomplete pictures	
Repeating 3, 4, 5, and 6 digits (1916, III, IV, VII, X)	XVIII. Digit span	14. Numerical memory, Part I
The Game of patience (1916, V)	XIX. Picture puzzles: diagonal series	2. Puzzle solving, cat, pear, bird
Paper Folding: triangle (1937, Form L, V)	XX. Paper folding	
Detecting absurdities (1916, X)	XXI. Absurdities	
Finding omissions in pictures (1916, VI)	XXII. Mutilated pictures	
Vocabulary (1916, VIII, X)	XXIII. Vocabulary	4. Word knowledge, Part II
Opposite analogies (1937, Form L, IV-6 & Form M, IV)	XXIV. Giving word opposites	17. Opposite analogies
– – – –	XXV. Imitating position of clock hands	

TABLE 5.1 *(continued)*

Stanford-Binet (1916 and 1937 Revisions)	Minnesota Preschool Scale (1940)	McCarthy Scales of Children's Abilities: General Cognitive Scale (1972)
Word combinations (1937, Form L, II & Form M, II)	XXVI. Speech	
Giving the number of fingers, making change (1916, VII, IX)		5. Number questions
Repeating 6–7, 12–13, 16–18, and 20–22 syllables (1916, III, IV, VI, X)		7. Verbal memory, Part I
Memory for stories: The Wet Fall, The School Concert (1937, Form L, VIII & Form M, X)		7. Verbal memory, Part II
Distinguishing right and left (1916, VI)		8. Right-left orientation
Picture completion: Man (1937, Form L, IV)		13. Draw-A-Child
Repeating 3, 4 digits reversed (1916, VII, IX)		14. Numerical memory, Part II
Word naming: animals (1937, Form M, X)		15. Verbal fluency
Counting 4, 13 pennies (1916, IV, VI); Number concepts (1937, Form L, VI & Form M, IV, V, VI); Matching objects (1937, Form M, III-6)		16. Counting and sorting
Comparison of lines, naming colors (1916, IV, V); Comparison of sticks, balls (1937, Form L, III-6 & Form M, III-6); Sorting buttons (1937, Form M, III-6)		18. Conceptual grouping

tasks, is quite profound, despite the fact that McCarthy offers a six-scale profile instead of a single, global score. Yet, McCarthy is to be commended for offering a profile that seems to have much value for psychoeducational assessment, for producing an attractive set of materials that is child-oriented and holds the interest of young children (e.g., McCarthy innovatively adapted the Minnesota's Knox Cube Imitation task to one involving tapping a toy-like xylophone), and for developing a scale that yields no significant race differences for preschool children (Kaufman and Kaufman 1977).

WECHSLER, WORLD WAR I, AND PERFORMANCE SCALES

The biggest challenge to the Stanford-Binet monopoly came from David Wechsler in 1939, when he published the Wechsler-Bellevue Scale (Wechsler 1939). Present-day instruments which trace their heritage to Form I and Form II of the Wechsler-Bellevue are the WISC-R, Wechsler Preschool and Primary Scale of Intelligence (WPPSI, Wechsler 1967), and Wechsler Adult Intelligence Scale-Revised (WAIS-R, Wechsler 1981). All Wechsler scales include ten to twelve separate subtests, each considerably longer than virtually all the Binet tasks, with about half included on a Verbal Scale and half on a Performance Scale. Three IQs are yielded — a Verbal IQ, a Performance IQ, and a Full Scale IQ, the latter being a composite of the various verbal and nonverbal subtests. The yielding of a global IQ, despite the separate subtests and scales, is consistent with Wechsler's (1958) notion about the existence of the construct of global intelligence. He stated:

> The grouping of subtests into Verbal . . . and Performance, . . . while intending to emphasize a dichotomy, as regards possible types of ability called for by the individual tests, does not imply that these are the only abilities involved in the tests. Nor does it presume that there are different kinds of intelligence, e.g., verbal, manipulative, etc. It merely implies that these are different ways in which intelligence may manifest itself. The subtests are different measures of intelligence, not measures of different kinds of intelligence, and the dichotomy into Verbal and Performance areas is only one of several ways in which the tests could be grouped. (Wechsler 1958, p. 64)

Wechsler was thus basically accepting of the Terman-Binet definition of intelligence as a global entity, but he used a different type of methodology to measure it. Rather than employ a plethora of brief tasks organized by age level, such that any individual would get an arbitrary sampling of these tasks based on his or her age and ability level, Wechsler limited his scale to a smaller number of reliable tasks, predetermining that all people would be administered all tasks. He selected nonverbal tests, conspicuously absent at most age levels of the Stanford-Binet, to constitute fully half of his intelligence scale.

Wechsler followed four procedures before selecting eleven subtests for his original 1939 Wechsler-Bellevue scale: (1) careful analysis of all existing standardized tests regarding functions measured and reliability, (2) empirical assessment of each test's validity claims, (3) subjective judgment of each test's clinical value, and (4) tryout data collected over a two-year period on individuals with known levels of intelligence (Wechsler 1958, p. 63). By limiting his tests to those already in existence, Wechsler selected the best measurement tools available in the mid-1930s; in actuality, all of his tasks were developed not later than the early 1920s.

Many Wechsler tasks were taken directly from the work of Binet and the Americans who adapted the Binet scales during the first ten or fifteen years of the twentieth century. These include several direct analogs, namely, Comprehension, Similarities, Vocabulary, Digit Span, and Picture Completion, and some that are closely similar to Binet tasks, including Arithmetic (Making Change) and Object Assembly (Patience Pictures). In addition to Binet's work, the other main sources of Wechsler subtests were the Army examinations developed during World War I. Extremely similar versions of Wechsler's Information, Arithmetic, and Comprehension subtests appeared in Army Group Examination Alpha; close analogs of Mazes, Digit Symbol (Coding), and Picture Completion appeared on Army Group Examination Beta; and the direct ancestors of Object Assembly, Digit Symbol (Coding), Mazes, Picture Arrangement, and Picture Completion constituted half of the Army Individual Performance Scale Examination (Yoakum and Yerkes 1920). Whereas a cousin of Wechsler's Block Design subtest appeared on the Army individual test (Cube Construction), Wechsler's task follows directly from the test originated by Kohs (1923).

Thus, all of the subtests in the WISC-R and WAIS-R were developed and used at least sixty years ago. They were constructed without benefit of a theoretical model at a time when diverse and comprehensive theories of learning, cognition, and intelligence had not yet germinated. Since the 1920s, impressive theories and research investigations have emerged from separate disciplines such as cognition, learning, child development, and neuropsychology, much of which relates directly to the measurement of intelligence. The work of Piaget, Cattell-Horn, Guil-

ford, Gagne, Luria, Bruner, Sperry, Hebb, and many others has been bla-
tantly ignored by the publishers of individual tests of intelligence. The
tradition as well as the tasks developed by Alfred Binet and the World
War I-era psychologists are alive and well in all popular, present-day individual assessment tools for measuring the intelligence of adults, as well as
that of preschool, elementary school and high school students.

These assertions are not intended to diminish the genius of Alfred Binet and David Wechsler. Binet was a man of vision and a true inno-
vator and pioneer. Wechsler, whose death in May 1981 was a deep loss to
psychology, had the clinical insight to provide verbal and nonverbal scales
and the empirical sophistication to select and standardize tasks with exceptional psychometric properties. Many others had developed primarily
verbal scales (the Binet adaptions) or performance scales (Cornell and
Coxe 1934; Pintner and Paterson 1925), but Wechsler was the one who realized just how clinically valuable a verbal-nonverbal comparison would
be for all individuals if derived from well-standardized scales.

Binet and Wechsler were both courageous. Binet had the courage
to speak out strongly against the sensory-motor view of intelligence that
had attained almost worldwide acceptance. Wechsler was bold enough to
challenge the Stanford-Binet monopoly in the United States: to many
psychologists, a Binet age scale was synonymous with *intelligence test*.
Both men ultimately triumphed.

Binet's victory, with an assist from Terman, led to the supremacy
of the Stanford-Binet in the U.S. for about a half-century. Wechsler settled for second place for many years. However, while the Stanford-Binet
failed to respond to a changing environment (the 1960 version was not
even renormed, and the 1972 version was not revised), Wechsler did, indeed, try harder. The two forms of the Wechsler-Bellevue were replaced
by improved models known as the WISC and WAIS. As these scales became outmoded, they were replaced by the WPPSI, WISC-R, and WAIS-
R, test batteries with better and more representative norms, updated content, and greatly improved psychometric properties.

With the increasing stress on the psychoeducational assessment
of learning disabilities in the 1960s, and on neuropsychological evaluation
in the 1970s, the Verbal-Performance (V-P) IQ discrepancies and subtest
profiles yielded by Wechsler's scales were waiting and ready to overtake
the one-score Binet. The WISC and WISC-R have been used widely with
exceptional populations, and their value has been documented in hundreds of research investigations. However, the accruing data from clinical
practice and empirical study suggest that the value of the Wechsler scales
for psychoeducational assessment resides primarily in describing the
strong and weak areas of handicapped children. Unfortunately, the effi-

cacy of Wechsler profiles and indexes of scatter for differential diagnosis of learning disabilities is dubious (Kaufman 1981b), and their value for educational intervention is also under severe challenge (Salvia and Ysseldyke 1978).

Now, in the 1980s, the continued attack on current intelligence tests demands that alternate approaches be developed to meet the needs of both the examiners and children.

THE CONTEMPORARY STATE OF INTELLECTUAL ASSESSMENT

The quality of individual mental assessment is no longer simply a question of an instrument's empirical or psychometric characteristics. High reliability and validity coefficients, a meaningful factor structure, and normative data obtained by stratified random sampling techniques do not ensure that an intelligence test is valuable for all or even most assessment purposes.

Children are labeled learning disabled, mentally retarded, slow learners, and so forth, in large part based on IQs derived from an individual intelligence test. IQs are also instrumental in the placement of children in exceptional classes or special programs, placements which invariably select out disproportionate numbers of minority children and boys (Richmond 1980). These educational decisions have social consequences, and social inequities bring to the fore issues of test fairness or bias; unfortunately, these issues are complex and cannot be solved by simple application of formulas and other empirical criteria. (Flaugher 1978).

The social implications of test use and abuse demand that we challenge the nature of the intelligence tests that are used for decision making. Several questions come quickly to mind: Shouldn't intelligence tests be based on current theories rather than on arbitrary selections of tasks developed sixty to one hundred years ago? Is it reasonable to say that someone has retarded potential or below average ability, when so much of IQ measurement is based on tasks that are really measures of verbal achievement (e.g., verbal fluency, knowledge of facts)? Should evaluation of intelligence be so dependent on verbal expression, in view of the large proportions of bilingual children placed in special classes and of the vital roles that personality and culture (see Labov 1970) play in a child's expression?

Research results based on the volumes of investigations with Wechsler's various scales also raise concerns regarding the ways intelligence is measured. Factor analysis gives support to Wechsler's Verbal and

Performance Scales, but the emergence of a third factor — variously referred to as Freedom from Distractibility, Number Ability, Attention-Concentration, Memory, or Sequencing Ability in most analyses (Kaufman 1979b, 1981a) — does not conform to Wechsler's simple dichotomy. Similarly, the characteristic profiles obtained for many groups of mentally retarded children, and the profiles found for groups of reading and learning disabled children, are both readily explainable in terms of Bannatyne's (1971, 1974) four-category regrouping of WISC-R subtests but not Wechsler's two-category approach (Kaufman 1979b). All of these unexplained consistencies in the research question the meaning of the Verbal IQ, Performance IQ, Full Scale IQ, and the V-P IQ discrepancy for numerous children, especially those with school-related problems.

Some who are concerned about the fair assessment of minority children, especially blacks, have also raised pertinent questions about conventional intelligence tests. The more extreme professionals in this area accuse the IQ tests of crimes against black children and see the elimination of all such scales as the first step towards sanity (Hilliard 1979, Williams 1974). The failure of Wechsler to include blacks in the standardization of the 1949 WISC was a rallying cry for the anti-testing forces in the 1960s and early 1970s, but this problem was supposedly remedied by including a proportional representation of nonwhites in the normative sample of the 1974 WISC-R. However, this solution was treated by some professionals as akin to tokenism, and even illogical in a statistical sense because of the blending of disproportionate bimodal distributions (e.g., Mercer 1977). In fact, Mercer has been a strong advocate of the need for separate pluralistic norms, based on a child's sociocultural and ethnic background, to interpret properly a child's intelligence test scores (Mercer and Lewis 1978).

Some other questions concerning the use of intelligence tests for minority children include (1) whether many youngsters really understand what is expected of them on numerous items or subtests (Hardy, Welcher, Mellits and Kagan 1976; Kaufman 1978); (2) if there is sufficient measurement of black children's "right-hemisphere" skills (Kaufman 1979a, 1979b); and (3) whether subtle biases and communication problems between white examiner and black examinee serve systematically to depress scores earned by blacks on the verbal expression items (Hewitt and Massey 1969). Supporting the latter point, empirical evidence shows that experienced teachers assigned higher grades to the verbal responses of whites than blacks, even when their answers to the typical school questions used identical wording (Crowl and MacGinitie, 1974). In addition, Sattler and his colleagues found that ambiguous responses on WISC and WAIS Similarities, Vocabulary, and Comprehension subtests were assigned higher scores when given by individuals believed to have high IQs than when given by individuals thought to be dull (Sattler, Hillix and Neher 1970, Sattler and Winget 1970).

The concerns of professionals and the lay public, whether based on empirical data or personal experience, and whether rational or emotional, have to be respected by test publishers and psychologists. New instruments are needed to provide examiners with more choices before making decisions that often have profound consequences.

THE DEVELOPMENT OF THE K-ABC

The K-ABC (Kaufman and Kaufman 1983) is a theory-based test of the intelligence and achievement of children aged 2½ to 12½ years. My wife and I developed this battery for the American Guidance Service in an attempt to provide a relevant alternative to the Wechsler scales and Stanford-Binet for many contemporary assessment purposes.

The theoretical rationale stems from a convergence of findings, derived independently by researchers in cognitive psychology and neuropsychology, which stress two modes of solving problems and processing information. From cognitive psychology, Neisser (1967) refers to these modes as sequential vs. parallel or serial vs. multiple; from neuropsychology, cerebral specialization theorists (e.g., Bogen 1969; Gazzaniga 1975) distinguish between analytic-sequential and gestalt-holistic processing, and Luria (1966) identified a successive-simultaneous dichotomy. Operating from a Luria framework, Das, Kirby, and Jarman (1975, 1979) have provided much factor-analytic support for the existence of two modes of processing information, which they label successive and simultaneous.

Intelligence, as defined by the K-ABC, thus concerns an individual's efficiency in solving problems and is divided into two scales: Sequential Processing and Simultaneous Processing. The Sequential Processing Scale requires the child to solve problems by arranging the stimuli in sequential or serial order; illustrative tasks are repeating a sequence of hand movements tapped by the examiner, and pointing to pictures that were named by the examiner after first performing an "interference" activity (i.e., naming colors). The Simultaneous Processing Scale, usually spatial or analogic in nature, requires the simultaneous, gestalt-like integration of stimuli to solve the problems. Examples are recalling the spatial locations of stimuli, solving abstract analogies, and identifying an object from a partially complete "inkblot" drawing.

Whereas Wechsler's scales are organized by the *content* of the

tasks (verbal or nonverbal), the two K-ABC intelligence scales are dichotomized by the *process* required for correct solution, regardless of content. Several investigations have supported the effectiveness of using a
person's preferred style of information processing as the basis for selecting the most appropriate educational intervention (Biggs 1978; Krashen,
Seliga and Hartnett 1973; Snow, Federico, and Montague 1980).

The K-ABC intelligence scales, which are supported by factor
analysis at ages 3-4½, 5½-6½, 7½-8½, and 10½-12½ (Kaufman,
Kaufman, Kamphaus, and Naglieri 1981), are primarily nonverbal and
utilize child-oriented, concrete materials. These scales, taken together,
call upon the kinds of abilities that Horn and Cattell (1966) have referred
to as *fluid intelligence,* namely, the capacity to be flexible and adaptable
when faced with unfamiliar problems. Rather than use only abstract stimuli for the processing tasks, as are typically included in "pure" tests of
fluid intelligence, several K-ABC tasks involve meaningful, relevant stimuli. In choosing these stimuli, however, care was taken to include objects,
scenes, and faces which are easily accessible to all people living in the U.S.
Effort was also made to construct new subtests and to adapt tasks which
appear frequently in the psychological literature but are not included in
conventional intelligence tests. Although some variants of tests with great
clinical and neuropsychological value (e.g., Wechsler's Block Design) are
included in the K-ABC, this new battery does not trace very many of its
roots to the Binet–World War I tradition.

Probably the biggest departure from the existing approach for
measuring intelligence is the exclusion of traditional tests of verbal ability
from the K-ABC intelligence scales. Many of these tasks are really measures of past acquisitions, notably Information, Vocabulary, Comprehension, and Arithmetic on Wechsler's scales, and a host of tasks on the
Stanford-Binet. These tasks yield important data, but should not be used
to help label a child mentally retarded or learning disabled and then lead
to alternate class placement, especially for minority children. Consequently, tests related to Verbal IQ or Binet IQ subtests are included in the
K-ABC, but on the third scale: Achievement. This scale is never used to
infer a child's mental functioning, and the Wechsler-like tasks are joined
on the Achievement Scale by conventional tests such as reading.

Whereas the two K-ABC intelligence scales were designed to
measure abilities akin to fluid intelligence, the Achievement Scale assesses
skills more closely aligned to the Cattell-Horn notion of "crystallized ability," i.e., skills acquired primarily through education and formal training.
Conventional achievement measures, whether included in test batteries
labeled *intelligence* or *achievement,* are typically highly verbal in nature.
In the K-ABC, emphasis was placed on developing Achievement tasks

with a strong visual-spatial component, and requiring other so-called right-hemisphere functions as well, such as gestural communication. Thus, the general information portion of the K-ABC Achievement Scale requires identification of famous faces and places (e.g., Popeye, pyramids, John F. Kennedy), and one of the reading subtests demands acting out written commands to demonstrate comprehension.

The inclusion of several tasks with presumed right-hemisphere involvement enables children with a "right-brain cognitive style" to demonstrate this strength on achievement tasks as well as on the Simultaneous Processing Scale. Importantly, there is some evidence to support the hypothesis that blacks, as a group, may have a relative tendency toward a right-hemispheric style of thinking and learning (Kaltsounis 1974; Kaufman 1979a, 1979b; Torrance 1977). Although some completely verbal tasks are included in the K-ABC Achievement Scale, the responses are one or two words in length and are objective to score. There is considerable evidence that subjective judgment in scoring tests such as Vocabulary or Comprehension can lead to wide variations in the scores assigned by different examiners (Sattler 1974).

The three scales on the K-ABC were normed in 1981 on a nationwide sample, with proportional representation of blacks, Hispanics, and exceptional children. The latter group included speech-and language-impaired, learning disabled, mentally retarded, emotionally disturbed, and gifted children, and other handicapped samples. The exclusion of exceptional children from the standardization samples of most major norm-referenced instruments has been a point of contention for many professionals, in view of the fact that exceptional children are the most frequently assessed in psychological and psychoeducational evaluations.

A large additional sample of black children was tested to permit the development of supplementary norms by race and socioeconomic background. Scores based on these sociocultural norms are intended to augment (not replace) information provided by national norms, thereby enabling examiners to take into account the potential effects of a child's ethnic and cultural heritage on the obtained test scores. Further to ensure fairness, all tasks on the two intelligence scales include three items (an unscored sample and the first two items per task) which are designated as "teaching items." During the administration of these items, examiners follow up wrong responses by teaching the task, using almost any means imaginable (foreign languages, writing, gestures, illustrations, and so forth) to communicate to the child precisely what is expected of him or her.

CONCLUDING COMMENTS

Intelligence testing and the IQ concept have had a long and colorful history. Whereas the IQ will not be missed by very many people if this concept is allowed to pass out of existence, the future of intelligence testing promises to be bright. We do not see the K-ABC as the solution to the present dilemmas involving intelligence and its assessment, but rather as a reasonable alternative to contemporary instruments. There will be no single or simple solution to so complex a set of problems. However, the many questions raised by involved professionals and a concerned lay public can be answered if other psychologists and test publishers continue to challenge the existing monopoly by providing diverse alternatives to the measurement of intelligence.

Neuropsychological or cognitive processing theory is but one of many candidates for providing a sound theoretical model or rationale for an intelligence test. Cattell and Horn's fluid vs. crystallized intelligence, Piaget's developmental approach, Guilford's three-dimensional model, Jensen's memory-reasoning hierarchy, Vernon's factor-analytic method, Sternberg's metacomponents, and countless other systems offer suitable and potentially exciting foundations for future intelligence tests. If well normed and psychometrically sound, theory-based tests are sensitive to sociocultural issues and keep achievement out of the measure of so-called potential to the degree possible, and if the derived scores are translatable to educational intervention, then the future of mental assessment is indeed bright.

Ideally, examiners should be able to choose the best test or combination of tests for their purposes during any given evaluation, much the way a therapist can apply Freud, Horney, Adler, Sullivan, Rogers, or an eclectic approach to meet the needs of each client. However, this choice of instruments only becomes meaningful when there are good tests to choose from. The WISC-R has enjoyed a long and successful run, and the wealth of research and clinical experience with Wechsler's batteries guarantees that it will remain at or near the top for years to come. There is plenty of room, however, for many other well-designed individual intelligence tests to join the WISC-R (and the Stanford-Binet as well) on the examiner's shelf.

REFERENCES

Anastasi, A. *Psychological testing* (4th ed.). New York: Macmillan, 1976.
Arthur, G. *A Point Scale of Performance, Revised Form II: Manual for administering and scoring the tests.* New York: Psychological Corporation, 1947.

Bannatyne, A. *Language, reading, and learning disabilities.* Springfield, Ill.: Charles C. Thomas, 1971.

Bannatyne, A. Diagnosis: A note on recategorization of the WISC scaled scores. *Journal of Learning Disabilities,* 1974, *7,* 272–274.

Berger, M. The third revision of the Stanford-Binet (Form L-M): Some methodological limitations and their practical implications. *Bulletin of the British Psychological Society,* 1970, *23,* 17–26.

Biggs, J. B. Genetics and education: An alternative to Jensenism. *Educational Researcher,* 1978, *7,* 11–17.

Binet, A. *L'étude expérimentale de l'intelligence.* Paris: Schleicher, 1903.

Binet, A., & Henri, V. La psychologie individuelle. *L'Année Psychologique,* 1896, *2,* 411–465.

Binet, A., & Simon, T. Methodes nouvelles pour le diagnostic du niveau intellectuel des anormaux. *L'Année Psychologique,* 1905, *11,* 191–244.

Bogen, J. E. The other side of the brain: Parts I, II and III. *Bulletin of the Los Angeles Neurological Society,* 1969, *34,* 73–105; 135–162; 191–203.

Cattell, J. M. Mental tests and measurements. *Mind,* 1890, *15,* 373ff.

Cattell, J. M., & Farrand, L. Physical and mental measurements of the students of Columbia University. *Psychological Review,* 1896, *3,* 618–648.

Cornell, E. L., & Coxe, W. W. *A Performance Ability Scale: Examination manual.* New York: World Book Co., 1934.

Crowl, T. K., & MacGinitie, W. H. The influence of students' speech characteristics on teachers' evaluations of oral answers. *Journal of Educational Psychology,* 1974, *66,* 304–308.

Das, J. P., Kirby, J., & Jarman, R. F. Simultaneous and successive syntheses: An alternative model for cognitive abilities. *Psychological Bulletin,* 1975, *82,* 87–103.

Das, J. P., Kirby, J. R., & Jarman, R. F. *Simultaneous and successive cognitive processes.* New York: Academic Press, 1979.

Esquirol, J. E. D. Observations pour servir a l'histoire de l'idiotie. *Les maladies mentales,* 1828.

Esquirol, J. E. D. *Des maladies mentales considerées sous les rapports médical, hygiénique, et médico-légal* (2 vols.). Paris: Baillière, 1838.

Flaugher, R. L. The many definitions of test bias. *American Psychologist,* 1978, *33,* 671–679.

Galton, F. *Hereditary genius: An inquiry into its laws and consequences.* London: Macmillan, 1869.

Galton, F. *Inquiries into human faculty and its development.* London: Macmillan, 1883.

Gazzaniga, M. S. Recent research on hemispheric lateralization of the human brain: Review of the split-brain. *UCLA Educator,* 1975, *17,* 9–12.

Goddard, H. H. A revision of the Binet scale. *Training School,* 1911, *8,* 56–62.

Goh, D. S., Teslow, C. J., & Fuller, G. B. Psychological test usage among school psychologists. Paper presented at the meeting of National Association of School Psychologists, Washington, D.C., 1980 (*NASP Convention Proceedings,* pp. 47–48).

Goodenough, F. L., & Harris, D. B. Studies in the psychology of children's drawings: II. 1928–1949. *Psychological Bulletin,* 1950, *47,* 369–433.

Goodenough, F. L., Maurer, K. M., & Van Wagenen, M. J. *Minnesota Preschool Scale: Manual.* Minneapolis: Educational Test Bureau, 1940.

Hardy, J. B., Welcher, D. W., Mellits, E. D., & Kagan, J. Pitfalls in the measurement of intelligence: Are standard intelligence tests valid instruments for measuring the intellectual potential of urban children? *Journal of Psychology,* 1976, *94,* 43–51.

Herring, J. P. *Herring Revision of the Binet-Simon Tests: Examination manual— Form A.* London: World Book Co., 1922.

Hewitt, P., & Massey, J. O. *Clinical clues from the WISC.* Palo Alto, Calif.: Consulting Psychologists Press, 1969.

Hilliard, A. G. Standardization and cultural bias as impediments to the scientific study and validation of "intelligence." *Journal of Research and Development in Education,* 1979, *12,* 47–58.

Horn, J. L., & Cattell, R. B. Refinement and test of the theory of fluid and crystallized intelligence. *Journal of Educational Psychology,* 1966, *57,* 253–270.

Kaltsounis, B. Race, socioeconomic status and creativity. *Psychological Reports,* 1974, *35,* 164–166.

Kaufman, A. S. The importance of basic concepts in the individual assessment of preschool children. *Journal of School Psychology,* 1978, *16,* 207–211.

Kaufman, A. S. Cerebral specialization and intelligence testing. *Journal of Research and Development in Education,* 1979, *12,* 96–107. (a)

Kaufman, A. S. *Intelligent testing with the WISC-R.* New York: Wiley-Interscience, 1979. (b)

Kaufman, A. S. The impact of WISC-R research for school psychologists. In C.R. Reynolds and T.B. Gutkin (Eds.), *A handbook for school psychology.* New York: Wiley, 1981. (a)

Kaufman, A. S. The WISC-R and LD assessment: State of the art. *Journal of Learning Disabilities,* 1981, *14,* 520–526. (b)

Kaufman, A. S., & Kaufman, N. L. *Clinical evaluation of young children with the McCarthy Scales.* New York: Grune & Stratton, 1977.

Kaufman, A. S., & Kaufman, N. L. *Kaufman Assessment Battery for Children (K-ABC) Interpretive Manual.* Circle Pines, Minn.: American Guidance Service, 1983.

Kaufman, A. S., Kaufman, N. L., Kamphaus, R. W., & Naglieri, J. A. *Developmental changes in sequential-simultaneous processing at ages 3–12½.* Paper presented at the meeting of the American Psychological Association, Los Angeles, August 1981.

Kohs, S. C. *Intelligence measurement.* New York: Macmillan, 1923.

Krashen, S., Seliga, R., & Hartnett, D. Two studies in adult second language learning. *Kritikon Litterarum,* 1973, *3,* 220–228.

Kuhlmann, F. A revision of the Binet-Simon system for measuring the intelligence of children. *Journal of Psycho-Asthenics Monograph Supplement,* 1912, *1,* 1–41.

Labov, W. The logic of nonstandard English. In F. Williams (Ed.), *Language and poverty*. Chicago: Markham, 1970.

Luria, A. R. *Higher cortical functions in man*. New York: Basic Books, 1966.

McCarthy, D. *Manual for the McCarthy Scales of Children's Abilities*. New York: Psychological Corporation, 1972.

Mercer, J. R. The struggle for children's rights: Critical juncture for school psychology. *School Psychology Digest*, 1977, *6*, 4–19.

Mercer, J. R., & Lewis, J. F. *System of Multicultural Pluralistic Assessment (SOMPA)*. New York: Psychological Corporation, 1978.

Neisser, U. *Cognitive psychology*. New York: Appleton-Century-Crofts, 1967.

Peterson, J. *Early conceptions and tests of intelligence*. Chicago: World Book Co., 1925.

Pintner, R., & Paterson, D. G. *A Scale of Performance Tests*. New York: Appleton & Co., 1925.

Prasse, D. P. (Ed.). The *Larry P.* decision. Special issue of *School Psychology Review*, 1980, Volume 9, 111–167.

Richmond, B. O. Comparative incidence of educable mental retardation: Racial and sexual composition. In *The future of educable mental retardation: Analysis of Larry P.* Symposium presented at the meeting of the American Psychological Association, Montreal, 1980.

Salvia, J., & Ysseldyke, J. E. *Assessment in special and remedial education*. Boston: Houghton-Mifflin, 1978.

Sattler, J. M. *Assessment of children's intelligence* (Rev. ed.). Philadelphia: Saunders, 1974.

Sattler, J. M., Hillix, W. A., & Neher, L. A. Halo effect in examiner scoring of intelligence test responses. *Journal of Consulting and Clinical Psychology*, 1970, *34*, 172–176.

Sattler, J. M., & Winget, B. M. Intelligence testing procedures as affected by expectancy and IQ. *Journal of Clinical Psychology*, 1970, *26*, 446–448.

Seguin, E. *Idiocy: Its treatment by the physiological method* (Reprinted from original edition of 1866). New York: Bureau of Publications, Teachers College, Columbia University, 1907.

Sharp, S. E. Individual psychology: A study in psychological method. *American Journal of Psychology*, 1898–99, *10*, 329–391.

Snow, R. E., Federico, P., & Montague, W. E. *Aptitude, learning, and instruction* (2 vols.). Hillsdale, N.J.: Lawrence Erlbaum, 1980.

Stern, W. *The psychological methods of testing intelligence*. Baltimore: Warwick and York, 1914.

Terman, L. M. *The measurement of intelligence*. Boston: Houghton-Mifflin, 1916.

Terman, L. M., & Childs, H. G. A tentative revision and extension of the Binet-Simon Measuring Scale of Intelligence. *Journal of Educational Psychology*, 1912, *3*, 61–74; 133–143; 198–208; 277–289.

Terman, L. M., & Merrill, M. A. *Measuring intelligence*. Boston: Houghton-Mifflin, 1937.

Terman, L. M. & Merrill, M. A. *Stanford-Binet Intelligence Scale*. Boston: Houghton-Mifflin, 1960.

6

The Exceptional Child

GEORGE W. HYND, STEPHEN B. CANNON,
AND STEPHEN E. HAUSSMANN

PERHAPS NO OTHER professional psychologist is so closely tied to the forces of change as the school psychologist. Although clinical and school psychology share a common history, the practice of psychology in the schools has undergone more radical change than its clinical counterpart. It has been suggested that it is this receptivity to change that has ensured the continued growth and professional development of school psychology (Bardon 1976). Certainly the ability of any profession to adapt and modify its practice in response to social, political, and legal changes is the key to its survival. The Thayer Conference, Spring Hill Symposium, and the Olympic Conference testify readily to the continuing development of our profession (see Ysseldyke & Schakel, Chapter One).

While the debates regarding what constitutes appropriate professional practice and about guild and survival issues are important (Trachtman 1981), in reality, it is how well the school psychologist can provide services to exceptional children, their parents, and teachers that will determine the future of the profession. If school psychologists are no longer needed in identifying the exceptional child, providing consultant services to teachers, and in performing research and evaluation services, then, as a profession, school psychology will not need to exist.

Since school psychology is so closely tied to how we perceive, identify, and treat the exceptional child, this chapter was included in the present volume. In an introductory book, it is critically important to discuss the basics, including who the exceptional children are, what the general process is in their identification, how one differentially diagnoses these children, and what contributes to the manifestation of the conditions of exceptionality? This chapter is intended to serve as an introduction to the general principles of intervention, and since the role of the school psychologist is so closely tied to clinical assessment (Goh 1977, Ramage 1979), the focus will be on understanding how these children are typically identified. For a more complete discussion of the practices and issues only mentioned here (e.g., assessment of cognitive and emotional functioning, legal issues, consultation), the reader is referred to the chapters which specifically discuss these topics.

The authors acknowledge that the focus of this chapter is on categorical identification and placement. For instance, under this approach it is assumed that a child must be diagnosed and labeled "learning disabled" before he or she can be placed in a resource room setting that provides needed educational services. Within the past decade other conceptualizations have been advanced (e.g., Bergen 1981, Cancelli and Kratochwill 1981, Senf 1981) that tie assessment more closely to direct intervention. The diagnostic-prescriptive approach is a good example of this paradigm. The value in such an approach is obvious, but the authors would argue that as long as categorical funding determines the parameters of school psychological services, traditional differential diagnosis will be the standard in practice. We would argue that fewer labels are not the solution to the problems associated with categorical labeling; rather, more refined and differential subcategorizations are needed to maximize the potential benefits of treatment more in tune with a child's unique inter- and intraindividual qualities. To some this is a controversial point, but we acknowledge our bias and propose to those who differ in orientation that one must first understand the framework presented herein to disagree intelligently. For an excellent critical discussion representing a different perspective than that presented here, the reader is referred to Senf (1981) or Mercer and Ysseldyke (1977). The following chapter by Mowder also discusses the multidimensional nature of assessment and intervention as it relates to school psychological services.

HISTORICAL PERSPECTIVES

From what little we know of the treatment of the exceptional child in ancient times, it seems as though there was a general interest in them and their well-being in early Egypt, Greece, and China. During the reign of Thebes in Egypt (1500 B.C.), a document was published which discussed treatment and care for the intellectually exceptional. In Greece, it was Plato who first formally recognized the potential contribution the gifted could make in the betterment of society. Confucius was interested in "weak-minded" individuals and believed them to have a justified claim on society. He believed it was the responsibility of society to care for their health and education and find useful employment for them (L'Abate and Curtis 1975). Interestingly, and perhaps reflecting this early attitude, the mentally retarded in China today seem to be well integrated into society and serve meaningful and productive lives (Hittman 1978).

While these are certainly attitudes to be admired, the attitude of the general public seemed marked by neglect, contempt, and intentional abandonment of anyone born with an obvious deficit. It can be argued, however, that history has vacillated between neglect and abuse to expressions of compassion, especially in the case of the intellectually superior child. Suleiman the Magnificent, during the sixteenth century, directed his advisors to travel throughout the Turkish empire in an effort to find the most capable, handsome, and intelligent youth, who were to receive an exceptionally enriched education (Gearhart 1974). During the late eighteenth century, Charlemagne proposed the idea of training the gifted at state expense. Under the direction of Alcuin, his court became a center for learning.

In England during the Middle Ages, "idiots" (probably equivalent to someone today with an IQ of less than 55 or 60) were made wards of the king and often found themselves employed as court jesters or fools. Without a doubt, though, there were those who were interested in helping and caring for the retarded, handicapped and the generally less fortunate. The work of Saint Vincent de Paul, the Sisters of Charity, Pedro Ponce de Leon and Valentine Hauy are indeed significant. These individuals and others like them began a reformation in the way in which the exceptional individual was perceived.

The attitudes towards the exceptional that prevailed until the early eighteenth century can at best be described as paternalistic. The limited achievements of these individuals, coupled with the efforts of Itard with Victor, the "wolf boy" who was found in the woods of southern France, encouraged Seguin to develop his "physiological method" for the treatment of the retarded. These were the first documented attempts at education of the retarded. Esquirol's work in differentiating between mental illness and retardation was equally important. The value of the work of Binet and Simon (see A. Kaufman, Chapter Five) in constructing their scales is widely recognized. Perhaps equally important but often ignored today was Binet's plea that the situation of the intellectually handicapped was not without hope. Disturbed by those who argued that intellectual ability was fixed, Binet eloquently responded:

> Some recent philosophers appear to have given their moral support to the deplorable verdict that the intelligence of the individual is a fixed quantity, a quantity which cannot be augmented. We must protest and act against this brutal pessimism. . . . A child's mind is like a field for which an expert farmer has advised a change in the method of cultivating, with the result that in place of desert land we now have a harvest. It is in this particular sense, the only one that is significant, that we say that the intelligence of children may be increased . . . namely the capacity to learn, to improve with instruction (quoted by Skeels and Dye 1939).

It was indeed upon this philosophical foundation that educators everywhere developed, modified, and applied programs aimed at training the exceptional child to participate and contribute to society. Mandatory education of the retarded was initiated in the United States in 1911 by the state of New Jersey. By 1952, all states (except Nevada and Montana) had enacted provisions for the identification and education of the intellectually disabled child. Complementing this increased interest in the retarded was an increasing commitment to the education of other exceptional children, including the blind, deaf, emotionally disturbed, gifted, brain damaged, and more recently, the learning disabled. More than any time in the past, the exceptional child has a secure place in the educational system and is guaranteed a chance in participating and contributing to society.

PREVALENCE OF EXCEPTIONALITY

Accompanying the continued refinement and acceptance of our perceptions of exactly who comprises the population of exceptional children is a set of closely related assumptions. First and foremost, we assume that the condition or conditions that contribute to and characterize the various categories of childhood exceptionality are (a) identifiable and (b) constant over time. Second, and closely related, we assume that we can differentially diagnose exceptionality in a reliable and valid manner. Finally, an assumption is made that differential diagnosis is essential to differential treatment (Wolfensberger 1965). Thus we presume that, as school psychologists, we have the ability to diagnose a specific handicapping condition, hypothesize in a reasonable fashion as to its etiology, and provide optimal therapeutic intervention.

For these assumptions to prove of value, it should be obvious that a workable and generally agreed upon definition of childhood exceptionality must exist. There are practical as well as conceptual reasons for our developing definitions, which in turn can lead to estimations of prevalence. For one, accurate estimates of enrollment need to be made so that the schools can adequately prepare to meet the needs of these unique children. In addition to planning purposes at the district level, colleges and universities need to determine how many teachers to train to meet the needs of the educational community. Also, local school districts receive reimbursement from the state and federal government based on the number of children enrolled in each aspect of the special education program (*if* they are in compliance with P.L. 94-142). Furthermore, there must be some continuity between districts, so that if a child is diagnosed as learning disabled in one district, he or she will be similarly placed in another school district should his or her family relocate. A final reason why a serviceable estimation of prevalence must be attempted is so that when research is conducted, the results can have meaning to others studying the same problem. Again, continuity in our conceptualization of childhood exceptionality is critical.

These are indeed important reasons for the consideration of definitions of childhood exceptionality and their prevalence. Every school psychologist should be aware that, in all likelihood, his or her position as a valued member of the psychoeducational team is to a large degree dependent on our profession's definitions and estimates of prevalence. Should the definitions be too restrictive, there will be a proportionately smaller population to serve and children truly in need will be neglected. On the other hand, should our diagnostic criteria be too flexible, then an inappropriate number of children not really needing special education services will be placed.

Even if the psychological, educational, and medical community could agree on the "perfect" definition, we would still be plagued by other difficulties. Definitions, to those who use them, suggest invariance in our criterion measures. In other words, our criteria for differential diagnosis appear absolute, much the way a high fever is indicative of biological disorder. For example, consider the school district that has established a criterion of an IQ of 130 as being necessary for entry into the gifted program. This criterion does not take into account the literature on the variability of IQ scores (see Reynolds, Chapter 3). McCall (1970) and McCall, Appelbaum, and Hogarty (1973) found in a population of 114 children tested repeatedly from age 2½ to 17 that the average *range* of individual IQ scores was 28.5 points (nearly two standard deviations)! One out of three children's IQ scores shifted more than 30 points. This incredible fact is complicated by an apparent interaction according to sex. Boys' IQs were more likely to show an increase over time than girls. It is likely that a given child could qualify at one testing and be disqualified on a later assessment simply because of variability in our appraisal.

One might think that behavioral criteria are less variable than psychometric criteria. But with behavioral criteria, one runs into the problem of interpretation or subjective judgment. Rubin and Balow (1971) found that first grade teachers when asked to identify children evidencing learning-disabled characteristics referred 41 percent of their first grade classes—clearly an overestimation of the numbers of children in need of special education services.

In addition to definitional issues and related problems, other factors can affect the accuracy of prevalence estimates. These include geographical considerations, environmental/sociocultural concerns, and genetic or nutritional factors, among others. For instance, in the south-west United States, the Native American population seems highly sus-pectible to otitis media. These middle ear infections during early life seem to be correlated with later auditory processing deficits (Howie 1980) char-acteristically found in certain subtypes of learning-disabled children. Consequently, it might be reasonable to expect a significantly higher inci-dence of learning disabilities among southwest Native American children. German measles (rubella) during pregnancy is known to cause birth de-fects including retardation. A community experiencing an outbreak of ru-bella affecting a significant proportion of expectant mothers could rea-sonably expect an increased need for their special education program for the retarded. Conversely, a community with a large university and a strong commitment to an enriched life-style might expect that the genetic pool and sociocultural environment could produce an unusually high per-centage of children achieving in the gifted range.

Because of the problems associated with definitions of exception-ality and resulting prevalence estimates, the figures presented in Table 6.1 should serve only as a rough guide in gauging the frequency with which one might encounter various childhood exceptionalities. It is generally agreed that between twelve and fifteen percent of the school-age popula-tion is in need of some special education services (Gaddes 1976, Gaddes 1980, Kirk 1972, Mackie 1969). It should be pointed out that the percent-ages for each category of childhood exceptionality may (and in fact should) change based on the factors previously discussed.

The Pro's and Con's of Labeling and Categorizing Children

Labeling is probably one of the most controversial issues within special education. As noted previously, excellent discussions of this topic abound. Hobbs (1975) and others have noted the following reasons for *not* labeling a child:

1. Placing a label on an individual may prejudice the response to him or her by teachers, peers, family, and society. This discourages a sensitiv-ity to change in the child's behavior.
2. Labeling creates a new level of fear of the implied condition (MR, BD, LD, etc.) and can expose children unnecessarily to changes associ-ated with the treatment (e.g., inappropriate peer models).
3. Labels focus on the negative aspects of the child and imply that the problem is within the child. Labels tend to refer to a segmented sample of behavior.

TABLE 6.1

Prevalence Estimates of Exceptional Children*

Exceptionality	% of Population
Deaf and hard of hearing	.5– .7
Emotionally disturbed	2.0–3.0
Gifted and creative	2.0–4.0
Learning disabled	2.0–3.0
Mentally retarded (EMR and TMR)	2.0–3.0
Speech handicapped	3.0–4.0
Visually handicapped and blind	.1
Multihandicapped	.5– .7
Crippled and other health handicapped	.5

*Based on estimated 1980 census figures.

4. Labels tend to neglect individual differences and obscure the services needed to meet the child's particular strengths and weaknesses; they can lead to placement, which often results in exclusion rather than remediation.

5. Labels facilitate the self-fulfilling prophecy; they lower the individual's self-esteem and personal expectancy.

Although the arguments against labeling children appear convincing, Kolstoe (1972) and Gaddes (1980, 1981) have presented equally viable arguments in favor of diagnostic labels. Their reasons, and others, include the following:

1. Labeling has made it possible for society to identify special problems and to marshal vast resources of money, facilities, and talent to attack problems.

2. The cleavage between the child with special needs and his or her peers exists whether or not the label is applied. The label is not the prob-

lem; rather, it is the intolerance of others for "different" behavior in children that creates problems.

3. Labeling has been useful in promoting employability and self-management in post-school years.

4. The negative effects associated with labeling have not been proven; the notion of the self-fulfilling prophecy has not been substantiated by research.

5. If special education programs geared to fit the abilities and needs of children and youth are ineffective, how can general educational programs, with their enormous problems, provide the appropriate services?

From experience, we can testify that labels help not only to identify a child in need of special services, but help to bring a sense of order and consistency in a world marked by ambiguity. This sense of order is a false one, and this uncomfortable fact must be remembered when applying labels and attempting to treat educational and behavioral disorders. Since a number of factors (including error variability due to measurement, achievement gains made by children in special programs, and developmental growth) can affect the validity of the diagnosis, continued reevaluation of children labeled is necessary to insure the accuracy of the diagnosis.

THE INTERVENTION PROCESS

Although they are alluded to in other chapters in this volume, it would be prudent briefly to review the steps that are typically undertaken by the school psychologist and other school personnel in referring, evaluating, staffing, and treating the child in need of special services. It should be stated at the outset that these sequential procedures, which ensure the child's right to due process, are rather recent developments (see Reschly, Chapter 4). Less than a decade ago, it was quite the norm for a teacher to make a referral directly to the school psychologist, who would evaluate the child; only then would someone contact the parents regarding what had been determined as the appropriate placement. In many cases children were assessed without parental consent or knowledge. Spanish-speaking children were assessed in English and, on the basis of their performance, diagnosed as mentally retarded (Reschly 1977). Furthermore, the assessment batteries which were typically used a decade ago might only qualify as minimal (if that) screening batteries today. While this may seem to be a summary of "worst case" instances and a gross over-simplification of actual practice, many of the landmark court decrees so well reviewed by Reschly (Chapter 4) are a direct result of such inadequate practices.

In fact, many of the changes in assessment practices which have occurred in the past fifteen years can be directly tied either to litigation or to legislation. Some of these changes include:

> 1. It is no longer considered appropriate to use group ability tests to track students (*Hobson* v. *Hansen,* 1967). 2. An assessment of primary language should be conducted prior to the assessment of ability. If the primary language is other than English, appropriate steps should be taken. 3. Culturally biased test items or portions of tests should be eliminated with a concurrent emphasis in assessment on nonverbal performance measures (*Diana* v. *State Board of Education,* 1970). 4. IQ tests should *not* be the primary instrument for identifying retarded children. 5. No child should be placed in a class for the retarded unless his or her IQ score is at least two standard deviations below the mean. 6. Assessment of adaptive behavior must be done in all cases of placement for the mentally retarded (*Guadalupe* v. *Tempe Elementary School District,* 1972).

Other changes regarding the right to due process can be traced to court decrees and later federal legislation (e.g., PL 94-142).

These few examples should serve to alert the school psychology student that serious attention should be paid to professional psychological, educational, and associated legal issues regarding differential clinical diagnosis and treatment. Clearly, the court decrees and judicial mandates regarding what constitutes appropriate intervention have made a significant impact on the lives of school psychologists (see Reschly 1979). The following outline for conducting a nonbiased clinical evaluation should exemplify those practices and procedures deemed necessary and appropriate in the assessment of most cases of exceptionality in school-age children.

Initial Referral Phase

The classroom teacher is the most important individual in providing the impetus for the identification of children in need of services. While the parents, the child, or any interested individual may initiate a referral, the classroom teacher is the one who typically uses his or her knowledge about normal child development, intuition, and experience with children in spotting a child in need. Once a teacher decides that traditional educational approaches applied in the regular classroom setting may not be appropriate or effective, permission from the child's parent for evaluation is obtained prior to a referral to the school psychologist. The intervention process, in accordance with due-process procedures, begins when a child is suspected of needing exceptional educational services, beyond those found in the regular classroom.

In many school districts, it is at this point that the school psychologist becomes directly involved and he or she may (1) interview the teacher and parents; (2) obtain a complete medical/developmental history; (3) collect work samples of the child; (4) review educational and medical records that may be available; and (5) observe the child in a variety of settings, both at school and at home. The data generated from these activities are then presented to a preplacement, multidisciplinary team meeting. Individuals who may, and perhaps should be involved, include: the referring teacher, a special education teacher, the parent(s), the school psychologist, and other persons who may provide additional insight into a discussion of the child. It is the responsibility of this preplacement staffing committee to recommend avenues of further evaluation and to assign responsibility for follow-up. Optimally, this phase should be completed in about thirty days from the date of the initial referral (Abeson, Bolick and Hass 1975).

The Evaluation Phase

After the preplacement staffing committee makes its determination that a more complete evaluation is required, the school psychologist initiates the evaluation phase. Similar to the first phase, this phase of intervention should not exceed more than a month's time. Prior to the formal psychological assessment, the school psychologist will need to determine language dominance and check to see that sensory screening including audition and vision has been completed. If there are manifested difficulties in vision or hearing, or if the dominant language is other than English, then the assessment practices will need to be modified accordingly.

It is at this point that the school psychologist's clinical-psychometric expertise becomes important, as he or she will probably be required to assess abilities and competencies in the areas outlined in Table 6.2. Frequently used assessment instruments and procedures are noted under each area of clinical concentration.

The assessment should be multifaceted such that all skills and abilities related to the area of possible handicap are addressed. Furthermore, no single criterion (e.g., IQ) may be utilized as the determining agent in placement. Once the evaluation results are available, the evalua-

TABLE 6.2

Areas of Assessment and Procedures and Tests Typically Utilized
in the Psychoeducational Evaluation

I. Cognitive and intellectual ability	IV. Sensory-Perceptual-Motor
Kaufman Assessment Battery for Children	Bender-Gestalt
McCarthy Scales of Children's Abilities	Berry VMI
Peabody Picture Vocabulary Test—Revised	Finger-tip Number Writing
Slosson Intelligence Test	Lateral Dominance Exam
Stanford-Binet	Tactile Finger Recognition Test
Wechsler Intelligence Scale for Children—	Raven's Matrices
Revised (WISC-R)	(vision and hearing screening)
Wechsler Preschool and Primary Scale of	
Intelligence (WPPSI)	V. Social-Emotional
	Drawing Techniques
II. Adaptive behavior	Draw-A-Person (D-A-P)
AAMD—School Version	House-Tree-Person (H-T-P)
Children's Adaptive Behavior Scale	Kinetic Family Drawing (KFD)
Vineland Social Maturity Scale—Revised	Sentence Completion
	Picture Story Techniques
III. Achievement	Thematic Apperception Test (TAT)
Boder Diagnostic Spelling Test	School Apperception Method (SAM)
Formal Reading Inventories	Children's Apperception Test (CAT)
Illinois Test of Psycholinguistic Ability	Rorschach
Keymath	Word Association Test
Peabody Individual Achievement Test	(observation)
Woodcock Reading Mastery Scales	(behavior checklists)
Wide Range Achievement Test (WRAT)	
(task analysis)	

tion is deemed complete as prescribed by the preplacement committee, and the third phase of intervention is undertaken.

The Multidisciplinary Staffing (Individual Education Plan) Meeting

It is here that all interested parties gather to consider every source of available information in an attempt to reach some agreement as to how best to serve the referred child's needs. The committee should include those previously involved as well as the special education administrator, principal or vice-principal, school nurse, counselor, and any others who may be able to contribute to the committee's decision process (e.g., physician, speech therapist). The first task of this committee is to examine the accumulated data and consider its completeness and relevance to the decision process. If the information is deemed complete, a discussion follows to consider the child's particular needs, abilities, and current status. Everyone including the parent(s) should have imput into this process. In many cases, it will fall to the school psychologist to chair the staffing or case conference, but the chair may also rotate among the members of the multidisciplinary team or remain the responsibility of the psychology or special education coordinator.

A final responsibility at this committee meeting is to identify the area of need, prescribe an individual educational plan (IEP) designed to meet the child's unique psychoeducational needs, and determine an appropriate placement based upon these needs. The notion is that a group decision based on nonbiased or multifaceted assessment procedures (Mercer 1972, Mercer and Lewis 1978, Ysseldyke 1978) will be less open to individual or psychometric bias than one arrived at individually or with a limited scope of data.

Implementation and Follow-up

A final formal phase in which the school psychologist is likely to be involved is in the implementation of the IEP and ongoing follow-up. Ideally the child is placed in the least restrictive environment (LRE) appropriate for his or her individual needs; the regulations of P.L. 94-142 require the integration of special children into the mainstream "to the fullest extent possible." Ideally, the child is placed in special programs designed to meet his or her individual needs, and the remaining time is spent in regular class placement. The effects of mainstreaming exceptional children are assumed to be beneficial. It is assumed that integrating them with normal children will lessen any stigmatizing effect, and they will learn to cope in the real world.

The school psychologist, as well as the regular classroom teacher, must be aware of how he or she feels about exceptional children and the effects of attitudes of those who interact with special children. The mere fact that the child is identified as needing special services may pose problems, as these children are often viewed and treated as different (Gillung and Rucker 1977, Harasymiw 1976, Otoole and Weeks 1978, Shears and Jensema 1969, Smith and Greenberg 1975). In fact, there is evidence that the perceptions others have of exceptional children may be related to (1) how visible their disability is; (2) whether or not it affects communication; (3) the social stigma attached to it; (4) the reversibility of the condition; and (5) the difficulty the child experiences in daily living (Shears and Jensema 1969). Hence, a child with severe cerebral palsy who is confined to a motorized wheelchair may be perceived more unfavorably than a child with a mild hearing loss in one ear.

In the follow-up phase it is the school psychologist's as well as the teacher's responsibility to monitor carefully not only academic progress, but social-emotional adjustment as well. Social-skills training may serve as a means to facilitate more positive interactions between the regular students and mainstreamed students (Gresham 1982). A reevaluation of the IEP must be done at least once a year, and a comprehensive psychoeducational evaluation should be completed at no more than three-year intervals.

Professional Considerations

While this brief outline of what should occur during the intervention process is reasonably complete, it should be stressed that, despite the mandates of public law, court decisions, and decrees, each school district is going to develop its own unique procedures under which the school psychologist will be required to conduct professional services. Furthermore, not all the steps outlined above are necessary or even desired for all children initially thought to be in need of special services.

Whatever the district procedures and policies or variation in the provision of psychoeducational services in the schools, the school psychologist should keep in mind that (1) the procedures of due process must be adhered to; (2) the parents or legal guardians must be involved in the process and must be privy to *all* records and reports used in considering their child's placement; (3) there are procedural safeguards for appeal of placement decisions and avenues for obtaining an independent psychoeducational evaluation; (4) an individualized, nonbiased assessment must be conducted, taking into account dominant language and adaptive behavior; and (5) a multidisciplinary team must be involved in reaching some consensus as to the best avenues for intervention considering the child's unique needs.

DIFFERENTIAL DIAGNOSIS

As previously noted, the very idea of differential diagnosis is predicated on the assumption that an identifiable condition exists and can be adequately defined. Also, it seems obvious that if we can differentially diagnose a condition, we should be able to treat it differentially and thus optimize the probabilities for success. Tests have been developed for this very purpose and educators have made abundant use of them in the United States.

For instance, in 1969 it was estimated that over 250,000,000 tests were administered annually (Brim, Glass, Neulinger, Firestone, and Lerner 1969)! One can only wonder what this figure might be today. While there are many criticisms regarding the use and misuse of tests (Laosa 1973, Laosa 1977) and many alternative approaches to intervention (see Peter 1965, Resnick, Wang, and Kaplan 1973, Ysseldyke and Salvia 1974, Wallace and Larsen 1978), the use of standardized assessment practices is likely to continue. However, due to the legal developments within the profession during the past decade or so, behavioral and multifactorial assessment procedures are more likely to be used as *added* safeguards. The chapters by Nagle and Reschly (this volume) expand on these ideas.

The purpose of this section is to provide an overview of characteristics typically associated with various categories of exceptional children. Because of the introductory nature of this volume and also to avoid overlap with other chapters (e.g., Nagle, and Obrzut and Zucker in Chapters 8 and 9), the following sections will be necessarily brief.

Deaf, Hard of Hearing, and Speech Handicapped

Hearing deficits are perhaps the most difficult to detect and the most serious disorders to overlook, since speech and language development are so closely tied to normal hearing. Most children who have hearing impairments are able to adjust to their disability, often without being aware that anything is wrong. With hearing, however, it is possible to specify some reasonable criteria which relate to varying levels of deficit. It is generally agreed that hearing loss of more than 90 decibels in the least impaired ear is a profound hearing loss. Less significant but nonetheless very severe loss falls in the range of 60–90 decibels in the better ear. Electronic aids can be of great benefit to such an individual, whereas with a 90-decibel-loss amplification is useless. Mild hearing loss involves a deficit of 30–45 decibels, and difficulty hearing normal speech will be apparent. Near-normal hearing is between 15–30 decibels, and some difficulty with speech may be apparent (L'Abate and Curtis 1975).

A clinical audiologist is usually responsible for screening children at the beginning of the school-year, so most instances of hearing loss should already be identified once the school psychologist is called in to see a particular child. Sometimes, however, these children are overlooked. Any child who (1) seems listless or fails to attend, (2) has poor oral production, (3) speaks loudly, (4) has other odd voice qualities, and/or (5) has any obvious ear discharge or deformity should receive an audiological examination prior to any formal psychometric assessment. Audiological screening takes no more than five or ten minutes, and the school psychologist can easily perform this task using an audiometer. Psychometrically, the mildly impaired child may evidence slightly lower IQ scores overall and, again, the factor of adaptive behavior becomes important in estimating functioning levels.

Speech deficits may or may not be associated with hearing loss. Deficits in speech or language development can be due to environmental, genetic, emotional, cognitive, or neurological factors. Differential diagnosis is important here because if a child's speech defect is related to behavioral or emotional problems, then counseling or some form of therapy may relieve the symptoms. However, counseling or behavioral intervention will serve no direct benefit should the defect be due to neurological problems. Developmental aphasia is the most serious of speech disorders and refers to an inability to develop normal speech and language abilities in accordance with expected developmental milestones. It is usually related to neurological deficit, much the same as many cases of stuttering may be. Stuttering, may also be a developmental disorder: some studies suggest that up to 40 percent of all children stutter at some point in their development (Kessler 1966). While the school psychologist may work with these children, their diagnosis and intervention usually is the responsibility of the speech therapist or audiologist. A good knowledge of physiology as well as psycholinguistic development is essential in providing services to these children or specialists. The school psychologist may be called upon to assess intelligence or social-emotional adjustment, or assist in the development of the I.E.P. Consultation with the parents or teacher may also be required.

The Emotionally Disturbed

The emotionally disturbed child probably represents one of the greater challenges in terms of the application of clinical skills. In working with these children, one becomes impressed with the variety of symptoms that may be manifest. These behaviors can include withdrawal, rage reactions, fantasy, enuresis, anorexia nervosa, language problems, tics, schizophrenic behavior, and so on. Clearly the school psychologist's therapeutic skills, whether behavioral or dynamic in orientation, will be tested. Because of the insecurity of these children and the manifest anxiety present, they may do poorly on many measures of cognitive, behavioral, and academic tasks, especially timed or reflective tasks. Consequently, they are difficult in many cases to differentiate from learning disabled children. Behavioral checklists, projective assessment (see Obrzut and Zucker, Chapter 9) and direct observation may provide some clue as to whether the origin of the difficulty in school is emotional or neurological. One point should be stressed: emotional disturbance, giftedness, and learning disabilities do not always occur as separate clinical entities. Thus, it is very possible to find a gifted child who is experiencing a learning difficulty because of emotional problems.

The Gifted and Creative

Historically, the needs of the gifted child probably have been the poorest met by the educational system (Hildreth 1966). The studies done by Terman at Stanford would suggest that the truly gifted somehow survive, despite the best efforts of schools to avoid working with them. This has been a popular notion which is only now being challenged.

Terman's studies at Stanford do deserve special note. Terman (1925) was interested in superior students and specifically in their characteristics, why they succeeded, and what they eventually did with their lives. In 1921, he asked teachers to rate the three brightest young children in their classes. Then, based on IQ testing, he selected 1528 students who were just shy of puberty on the average. Data was collected on their development, health, school history, family, and personality, and they were followed over decades, receiving periodic evaluations. At the initial testing all had IQs in excess of 140. Generally, his results showed that the gifted were physically superior, had an enriched family background, and tended to be several grades ahead of their actual placement in school. His studies and others (Oden 1968, Sears 1977, Sears and Barbee 1977) demonstrated that these children tended to become successful professional people, were as mentally healthy as the normal population, and lived more healthy lives.

The work of Guilford (1967) and his Structure of Intellect Model and Torrance's (1977) work with the creative helped to demonstrate the narrowness of our previous conceptualizations of giftedness and creativity. While many school districts still use the criterion of two standard deviations above the mean (IQ > 130), most would agree that multiple criteria best suit these unique children. Consequently, exceptional performance in intellectual matters, academic skills, creative thinking, leadership, visual or performing arts, or psychomotor ability might qualify a child for entry into a gifted or talented program (Marland 1971). As Treffinger, Pyryt, Hawk, and Houseman (1979) suggest, the school psychologist can assist the teacher in screening and identifying these children, consulting in locating appropriate resources for their enrichment, and in helping in program evaluation.

The Learning Disabled

Newell Kephart's (1960) book on the slow learner marked the beginning of our focus on what Samuel Kirk later defined as the "learning disabled" (Nazzaro 1977). Together with the child identified as gifted, the learning disabled child is in good company: there is evidence that Thomas Edison, Woodrow Wilson (who did not read until he was eleven), Nelson Rockefeller, and Albert Einstein may have been learning disabled (Lerner 1976). According to the first widely accepted definition, the learning-disabled child suffers

> . . . a disorder in one or more of the basic psychological processes involved in understanding or in using language, spoken or written, which may manifest itself in an imperfect ability to listen, think, speak, read, write, spell, or do mathematical calculations. The term includes such conditions as perceptual handicaps, brain injury, minimal brain dysfunction, dyslexia and developmental aphasia (*Federal Register,* 1976, p. 56977).

As McCarthy (1975) pointed out, a definition such as this implies: (1) that, despite adequate intelligence, these children do not learn; (2) the concept of discrepancy—i.e., that there is a difference between where these children should perform and their actual performance; and (3) the concept of deviation—that their discrepancy is severe enough to warrant intervention. Many states required the learning disabled child to evidence a "significant" discrepancy between ability and performance before they could be so diagnosed (e.g., a sixth grader with an IQ of 100 performing at the fourth grade level in reading). Other states have left it up to the staffing committee to decide what specific conditions qualify, considering the general criteria noted above. Still other states required not only the significant discrepancy in some specified area, but also that the "basic psychological processes involved" be described (e.g., visual discrimination). While the definitions vary from state to state, the concept of basic ability (IQ = > 80 or 85) and a "significant" discrepancy in actual achievement remain paramount in diagnosis. Consequently, an assessment of intelligence, sensory-perceptual-motor ability, achievement, and other related areas must be conducted.

The definition which appeared in the *Federal Register* in 1976 was acknowledged to be imperfect. Controversy has continued almost unabated as to how a more precise definition could be developed. In 1981 the six organizations which constituted the National Joint Committee for Learning Disabilities (NJCLD) agreed on a model definition of learning disabilities. The organizations which participated in this unique and most challenging professional endeavor included the American Speech-Language-Hearing Association (ASHA), the Association for Children and Adults with Learning Disabilities (ACLD), the Council for Learning Disabilities (CLD), the Division for Children with Communication Disorders (DCCD), the International Reading Association (IRA), and the Orton Dyslexia Society. Their efforts resulted in the following definition:

> *Learning disabilities* is a generic term that refers to a heterogeneous group of disorders manifested by significant difficulties in the acquisition and use of listening, speaking, reading, writing, reasoning, or mathematical abilities. These disorders are intrinsic to the individual and presumed to be due to central nervous system dysfunction. Even though a learning disability may occur concomitantly with other handicapping conditions (e.g., sensory impairment, mental retardation, social and emotional disturbance) or environmental influences (e.g., cultural differences, insufficient/inappropriate instruction, psychogenic factors), it is not the direct result of those conditions or influences (Hammill, Leigh, McNutt, and Larson 1981, p. 336).

It will indeed be interesting to see exactly what impact this well-endorsed definition will have on the diagnosis and treatment of learning disabilities. While the concept of learning disability is meaningful, it is now recognized that there are probably various subtypes of specific learning disabilities. This has yet to be recognized in any formal definition of learning disabilities. The work of Rourke and his colleagues (Fisk and Rourke 1979, Rourke and Finlayson 1978) as well as Pirozzolo (1979 and 1981) is especially important in this regard. In fact, Pirozzolo (1979) has provided convincing experimental as well as clinical evidence for the existence of two categories of dyslexia roughly equivalent to Boders' (1973) dysphonetic (auditory-linguistic deficit) and dyseidetic (visual-spatial deficit) dyslexics. Chapter 10 by Hynd and Hartlage elaborates on these ideas.

The Mentally Retarded

In 1977, Grossman put forth a new, narrower definition of mental retardation: "Mental retardation refers to the significant subaverage intellectual functioning existing concurrently with deficits in adaptive behavior and manifested during the developmental period."

This definition carried with it two very important points for school psychologists to consider prior to diagnosing a child as mentally retarded. The first is that there must be *significant* subaverage intellectual functioning present. Typically associated with IQ, this level of intellectual functioning must be at least two standard deviations below the mean score for the assessment instrument. The second point is that the student must demonstrate a concurrent deficit in adaptive behavior. The level of adaptive behavior should be equal to that level of functioning indicated on the intelligence test for a diagnosis of mentally retardation to be made.

There is a multitude of genetic factors (e.g., Down's syndrome, cri du chat syndrome, neurofibromatosis), as well as environmental (rubella, head injury, lead encephalopathy) and gestational (prematurity) ones which can lead to mental retardation (Berg 1974). These individuals have always been at a disadvantage, and it is common for them to be confused with the mentally ill by the unknowledgeable public (Gardner and Veno 1979). Advocates for the mentally retarded have in many cases successfully addressed civil issues important to guaranteeing the rights of these people. These include: (1) financial security and economic self-determination; (2) housing; (3) due process within the criminal system; (4) equal educational opportunity; (5) guardianship; (6) voting rights; and (7) involuntary sterilization (Massachusetts State Commission on the Legal and Civil Rights of the Developmentally Disabled 1977).

While the identification of the profoundly or severely retarded does not present special problems from a diagnostic standpoint, the diagnosis of the educable mentally retarded brings with it a considerable challenge in terms of recent court decisions. This and other important related issues are addressed in detail by Nagle in Chapter 8. (See also Reschly, Chapter 4.)

The Visually Handicapped and Blind

The incidence rate for visual impairments is relatively low, yet research and public support in this area have always been considerable (L'Abate and Curtis 1975). The causes of blindness (correctable vision no better than 20/200 in the better eye) are many, but typically include glaucoma, cataracts, retrolental fibroplasia, trauma, tumor, and genetic diseases. The major causes of visual impairment (no better than 20/70 in the best eye) include infections, injuries, tumors, and brain damage. Clinically, these children are not as likely to evidence the severe deficits that the deaf child often does, although they do seem to be somewhat slower than the normal child in developing their verbal abilities (Brieland 1966). Intellectually, they seem to evidence normal development (Bateman 1963). The child who is developing vision difficulties may manifest chronic eye irritations, visual blurring, headaches, rapid blinking, and peculiar reading postures. These behaviors should suggest that consideration be given to a thorough vision examination.

CONCLUSION

The intent of this chapter has been to provide an overview of the exceptional child. Historical perspectives, incidence rates, the process of intervention, and differential clinical diagnosis have been discussed, with an acknowledged emphasis on categorical placement. Since this chapter needed to encompass a wide range of topics, it has been impossible to dwell on temendously important professional issues related to the provision of school psychological services to children in need. An attempt has been made, however, to note basic assumptions which underlie much of our practice. Important issues have been raised and references chosen carefully so that the interested reader can pursue a more in-depth examination of topics of controversy within special education and school psychology. With the basic conceptual framework presented in this chapter, it is now appropriate to focus on more specific aspects of school psychology practice in the remaining chapters in this volume.

REFERENCES

Abeson, A., Bolick, N., & Hass, J. *A primer on due process: Education decisions for handicapped children.* Reston, Va.: The Council for Exceptional Children, 1975.

Bardon, J. I. The state of the art (and science) of school psychology. *American Psychologist,* 1976, *31,* 785–791.

Bateman, B. *Reading and psycholinguistic processes of partially sighted children.* Unpublished doctoral dissertation, University of Illinois, 1963.

Berg, F. M. Aetiological aspects of mental subnormality: Pathological factors. In A. M. Clarke & A. D. B. Clarke (Eds.), *Mental deficiency: The changing outlook.* New York: The Free Press, 1974.

Bergen, J. R. Path-referenced assessment in school psychology. In T. R. Kratochwill (Ed.), *Advances in school psychology (Vol. 1).* Hillsdale, N.J.: Lawrence Erlbaum, 1981.

Boder, E. Developmental dyslexia: A diagnostic approach based on three atypical reading-spelling patterns. *Developmental Medicine and Child Neurology,* 1973; *15,* 663–687.

Brieland, D. M. A comparative study of the speech of blind and sighted children. *Speech Monographs,* 1966, *17,* 99–103.

Brim, O. G., Jr., Glass, P. C., Neulinger, S., Firestone, I. J., & Lerner, S. C. *American beliefs and attitudes about intelligence.* New York: Russell Sage Foundation, 1969.

Cancelli, A. A., & Kratochwill, T. R. Advances in criterion-referenced assessment. In T. R. Kratochwill (Ed.), *Advances in School Psychology (Vol. 1).* Hillsdale, N.J.: Lawrence Erlbaum, 1981.

Diana v. *State Board of Education,* United States District Court, Northern District of California. Case # C-70-37 RFP. (1970).

Fisk, J. L., & Rourke, B. P. Identification of subtypes of learning disabled children at three age levels: A neuropsychological, multivariate approach. *Journal of Clinical Neuropsychology,* 1979, *1,* 289–310.

Gaddes, W. H. Prevalence estimates and the need for definition of learning disabilities. In R. M. Knights & D. J. Bakker (Eds.), *The neuropsychology of learning disorders.* Baltimore: University Park Press, 1976.

Gaddes, W. H. *Learning disabilities and brain function: A neuropsychological approach.* New York: Springer-Verlag, 1980.

Gaddes, W. H. An examination of the validity of neuropsychological knowledge in educational diagnosis and remediation. In G. W. Hynd & J. E. Obrzut (Eds.), *Neuropsychological assessment and the school-age child: Issues and procedures.* New York: Grune & Stratton, 1981.

Gardner, J. M., & Beno, A. Public views of the surplus population. *Mental Retardation,* 1979, *17,* 231–236.

Gearheart, B. R. *Organization and administration of educational programs for exceptional children.* Springfield, Ill.: Charles C Thomas, 1974.

Gillung, T. B., & Rucker, C. H. Labels and teacher expectation. *Exceptional Children,* 1977, *43,* 464–465.

Goh, D. S. Graduate training in school psychology. *Journal of School Psychology,* 1977, *15,* 207–217.

Gresham, F. M. Misguided mainstreaming: The case for social skills training with handicapped children. *Exceptional Children,* 1982, *48,* 422–435.

Grossman, H. (Ed.). *Manual on terminology and classification in mental retardation* (Rev. ed.). Washington, D.C.: American Association on Mental Deficiency, 1977.

Guadalupe v. *Tempe Elementary School District,* District Court of Arizona, 71–435, 1972.

Guilford, J. D. *The nature of human intelligence.* New York: McGraw-Hill, 1967.

Hammill, D. D., Leight, J. E., McNutt, G., & Larsen, S. C. A new definition of learning disabilities. *Learning Disability Quarterly,* 1981, *4,* 336–342.

Harasymiw, S. J. Disability social distance hierarchy for populations subgroups. *Scandinavian Journal of Rehabilitation Medicine,* 1976, *8,* 33–36.

Hildreth, G. H. *Introduction to the gifted.* New York: McGraw-Hill, 1966.

Hittman, S. *China's approach to mental retardation.* Paper presented at the World Congress on Future Special Education, Stirling, Scotland, 1978.

Hobbs, N. *The futures of children.* San Francisco: Jossey-Bass, 1975.

Hobson v. *Hansen.* 269 F. Supp. 401, 1967.

Howie, V. M. Developmental sequence of chronic otitis media: A review. *Journal of Developmental and Behavioral Pediatrics,* 1980, *1,* 34–38.

Kephart, N. *The slow learner in the classroom.* Columbus, Ohio: Charles E. Merrill, 1960.

Kessler, J. W. *Psychopathology of childhood.* Englewood Cliffs: Prentice-Hall, 1966.

Kirk, S. *Educating exceptional children.* Boston: Houghton-Mifflin Company, 1972.

Kolstoe, O. P. Programs for the mildly retarded: A reply to the critics. *Exceptional Children,* 1972, *39,* 51–56.

L'Abate, L., & Curtis, L. T. *Teaching the exceptional child.* Philadelphia: W. B. Saunders, 1975.

Laosa, L. M. Reform in educational and psychological assessment: Cultural and linguistic issues. *Journal of the Association of Mexican-American Educators,* 1973, *1,* 19–24.

Laosa, L. M. Non-biased assessment of children's abilities: Historical antecedents and current issues. In T. Oakland (Ed.), *Psychological and Educational Assessment of Minority Children.* New York: Brunner/Mazel Publishers, 1977.

Lerner, J. W. *Children with learning disabilities* (2nd ed.). Boston: Houghton-Mifflin Company, 1976.

Mackie, R. D. *Special education in the United States: Statistics 1946–1966.* New York: Teachers College Press, 1969.

Marland, S. D. *Education of the gifted and talented.* Washington, D.C.: U. S. Government Printing Office, 1971.

Massachusetts State Commission on the Legal and Civil Rights on the Developmentally Disabled. Boston, 1977.

McCall, R. B. IQ pattern over age: Comparison among siblings and parent–child pairs. *Science,* 1970, *170,* 644–648.

McCall, R. B., Appelbaum, M. I., & Hogarty, P. S. Developmental changes in mental performance. *Monographs of the Society for Research in Child Development,* 1973, *38,* 1–84.

McCarthy, J. M. Children with learning disabilities. In J. J. Gallagher (Ed.), *The application of child development research to exceptional children.* Reston, Va.: Council for Exceptional Children, 1975.

Mercer, J. R. *Sociocultural factors in the educational evaluation of Black and Chicano children.* Paper presented at the 10th Annual Conference on Civil and Human Rights of Educators and Students, Washington, D.C., 1972.

Mercer, J. R., & Lewis, J. F. *System of Multicultural Pluralistic Assessment (SOMPA).* New York: The Psychological Corporation, 1978.

Mercer, J. R., & Ysseldyke, J. Designing diagnostic-intervention programs. In T. Oakland (Ed.), *Psychological and educational assessment of minority children.* New York: Brunner/Mazel, 1977.

Nazzaro, J. N. *Exceptional time-tables: Historical events affecting the handicapped and gifted.* Reston, Va., Council for Exceptional Children, 1977.

Oden, M. H. The fulfillment of promise: 40-year follow-up of the Terman gifted group. *Genetic Psychology Monographs,* 1968, *77,* 3-93.

Otoole, E. J., & Weeks, C. *What happens after school? A study of disabled women and education.* Washington, D.C.: Department of Health, Education, and Welfare, 1978.

Peter, L. J. *Perscriptive Teaching.* New York: McGraw-Hill, 1965.

Pirozzolo, F. J. *The neuropsychology of developmental reading disorders.* New York: Praeger Publishers, 1979.

Pirozzolo, F. J. Language and brain: Neuropsychological aspects of developmental reading disability. *School Psychology Review,* 1981, *10,* 350-355.

Ramage, J. C. National survey of school psychologists: Update. *School Psychology Review,* 1979, *8,* 153-161.

Reschly, D. J. *School psychologists and assessment in the future.* P. O. Wagner Memorial Address delivered at the Ohio School Psychologists Association meeting, November 1977.

Reschly, D. J. Nonbiased assessment. In G. D. Phye & D. J. Reschly (Eds.), *School psychology: Perspective and issues.* New York: Academic Press, 1979.

Resnick, L. B., Wang, M. C., & Kaplan, J. Task analysis in curriculum design: A hierarchly sequenced introductory mathematics curriculum. *Journal of Applied Behavior Analysis,* 1973, *6,* 679-710.

Rourke, B. D., & Finlayson, M. A. J. Neuropsychological significance of variations in patterns of academic performance: Verbal and visual-spatial abilities. *Journal of Abnormal Child Psychology,* 1978, *6,* 121-133.

Ruben, R., & Balow, B. Learning and behavior disorders: A longitudinal study. *Exceptional Children,* 1971, *38,* 293-299.

Sears, P. S., & Barbee, A. H. Career and life satisfactions among Terman's gifted women. In J. C. Stanley, W. C. George, & C. H. Salano (Eds.), *The gifted and creative: A fifty-year perspective.* Baltimore: Johns Hopkins University Press, 1977.

Sears, R. R. Sources of life satisfaction of the Terman gifted men. *American Psychologist,* 1977, *32,* 119-128.

Senf, G. M. Issues surrounding diagnosis of learning disabilities: Child handicap versus failure of child-school interaction. In T. R. Kratochwill (Ed.), *Advances in school psychology* (Vol. 1). Hillsdale, N.J.: Lawrence Erlbaum, 1981.

Shears, L. M., & Jensema, C. J. Social acceptability of anomalous persons. *Exceptional Children,* 1969, *36,* 91–96.

Skeels, H. M., & Dye, H. B. A study of the effects of differential stimulation on mentally retarded children. *Proceedings of the American Association of Mental Deficiency,* 1939, *44,* 114–136.

Smith, I., & Greenberg, S. Teacher attitudes and the labeling process. *Exceptional Children,* 1975, *41,* 319–324.

Terman, L. M. Mental and physical traits of a thousand gifted children. *Genetic studies of genius* (Vol. 1). Stanford: Stanford University Press, 1925.

Torrance, E. P. Creatively gifted and disadvantaged students. In J. C. Stanley, W. C. George, & C. H. Salano (Eds.), *The gifted and creative: A fifty year perspective.* Baltimore: Johns Hopkins University Press, 1977.

Trachtman, G. On such a full sea. *School Psychology Review,* 1981, *10,* 138–181.

Treffinger, D. J., Pyryt, M. C., Hawk, M. M., & Houseman, E. D. Education of the gifted and talented: Implications for school psychology. In G. D. Phye & D. J. Reschly (Eds.), *School psychology: Perspectives and issues.* New York: Academic Press, 1979.

U.S. Department of Health, Education, and Welfare. *Education of handicapped children and incentive grants program.* Federal Register, 1976, *41,* 46977.

Wallace, G., & Larsen, S. C. *Educational assessment of learning problems: Testing for teaching.* Boston: Allyn & Bacon, 1978.

Wolfensberger, W. Diagnosis is diagnosed. *The Journal of Mental Subnormality,* 1965, *11,* 62–70.

Ysseldyke, J. Non-discriminatory assessment: Is it achievable? *Centerfold,* 1978, *3.*

Ysseldyke, J., & Salvia, J. A. A critical analysis of the assumptions underlying diagnostic-prescriptive teaching. *Exceptional Children,* 1974, *41,* 181–195.

7

Assessment and Intervention in School Psychological Services

BARBARA A. MOWDER

THIS CHAPTER provides an overview of two aspects of school psychologists' functioning—assessment and intervention. Although these are not the only functions of school psychologists, they are undeniably important services. The previous chapter briefly addressed this topic. In this chapter, assessment and intervention are presented through an examination of their definitions, underlying assumptions, component processes, and caveats regarding each activity. Before extensively reviewing assessment and intervention, however, a brief preliminary discussion will help to clarify what the terms mean and the activities they entail, and to establish their importance in the delivery of school psychological services.

To the layperson, assessment is often thought to be synonymous with psychological testing. For school psychologists, though, the term has a much broader meaning. Assessment, or an assessment process, may be defined as the planning, collection, and evaluation of information pertinent to a psychoeducational concern. Thus, assessment has three facets: the first is planning the assessment to obtain comprehensive, accurate data which fully portray the concern; the second is the act of collecting the data; and the third is the evaluation, interpretation, or meaning the school psychologist gives the data.

Psychological testing, then, is but one form of data gathering (others include activities such as observations and interviews), and data collection is but one part of an assessment process. It should be mentioned, however, that some psychologists use the term *assessment* differently, reserving that word exclusively for data gathering (e.g., test administration) while employing the term *evaluation* for the interpretation of the data. As used in this chapter, though, assessment refers to both of these activities, as well as including a planning factor, because they are all interdependent functions. For instance, planning gives direction and meaning to the assessment process by pinpointing the concerns brought forward, guiding the data collection through a predetermined course of action, and helping to place the data evaluation in context.

Intervention frequently is spoken of as the companion piece to assessment; indeed, they are presented together in this chapter. Oftentimes intervention does follow assessment. This occurs when an assessment prompts those concerned to conclude that a problem exists, and an action or change is sought. Assessment does not always lead to intervention, however. When an assessment inclines those involved to believe that no action or change is necessary, then no intervention is planned. For example, if there is a concern about a child's academic progress, yet the assessment reveals that the child's school achievement is at the appropriate grade level, then little might be planned in the way of intervention.

Rhodes (1977) proposes that intervention be defined as "a mediational process which enters into the variant reciprocity between a child and his world, to affect that reciprocity, and to promote a different outcome than would have been expected without such interposing" (p. 22). In other words, Rhodes is proposing that intervention refers to affecting the interaction between a child and the child's world to bring about a different end than would have occurred without interference. That definition may be broadened so that it refers not only to a child and the child's world, but also, for instance, to a classroom, school environment, or whatever concern (in possible need of change) presents itself to the school psychologist. Broadly conceived, school psychological service intervention may be defined as a mediational procedure which enters into some aspect of the psychoeducational process in order to affect that process and promote a different outcome than would be expected without such interposing.

Like assessment, intervention is composed of several elements, commencing with a planning phase. The planning process identifies the intervention target, clearly establishes the intervention goal, determines an intervention method (i.e., who is going to intervene, how, when, and where), and delineates an intervention evaluation plan. The anticipated intervention activity then takes place and, depending on the planned evaluation, is evaluated during and/or following the intervention. (Intervention evaluation activities may be conceptualized as akin to formative and summative evaluation; that is, they may occur during and affect an ongoing intervention, and/or happen following an intervention [see, e.g., Mowder and Prasse 1982]). For instance, if a school psychologist evaluates an ongoing behavior modification program which does not seem to be gaining the desired results, the reinforcement may be changed, with the evaluation of the program continuing. In this example, the school psychologist would be employing a formative evaluation mode. On the other hand, if the psychologist evaluates the program at its conclusion, the school psychologist is relying on a summative evaluation.

The intervention elements or components are every bit as intertwined and interdependent as the assessment facets. The plan gives direction and meaning to the intervention activity and determines an appropriate evaluation strategy. In addition, an intervention implies action—action which depends on the goal (given by the plan) and requires evaluation to see if it accomplishes the intervention objectives.

ASSESSMENT

Much has been written about assessment (see e.g., Kaufman 1979, Maloney and Ward 1976, Phye and Reschly 1980, Salvia and Ysseldyke 1981). The assessment process itself begins after someone identifies a possible psychoeducational problem. Frequently this occurs in the form of a request or referral for school psychological services. Less frequently, school psychologists themselves identify a concern and commence an assessment. Regardless of the specific situation, the process begins after someone has pointed out a possible difficulty and this has been brought to the attention of the school psychologist. Subsequently, a careful planning process begins which leads toward data collection and evaluation. Each of the three assessment components (i.e., planning, data collection, and evaluation) is essential and must occur in sequence, because each component depends and builds upon the previous one. But before discussing the assessment process, it is important to examine the assumptions on which the process is based. The underlying assumptions shed light on the purpose of assessments and why certain assessment decisions arise, giving meaning to much of the assessment process.

Assessment Assumptions

It is appropriate to begin this discussion with the assumption about what purpose the assessment will serve. The assumed purpose of an assessment is to provide comprehensive, accurate psychoeducational information which addresses someone's concern. To this end, the school psychologist plans, obtains, and evaluates information which is as comprehensive and complete as possible, and facilitates educational decision making as well as an understanding of the concern. The emphasis, therefore, is on planning, obtaining, and evaluating valid, reliable information as a basis for educational decision making rather than, for example, providing a label for an individual, behavior, or situation.

A second assumption is that anyone or anything in the educational system may be a concern and, likewise, the object of a psychoeducational evaluation. Thus, a student is not necessarily the focus of an assessment (even though this is frequently the case); the concern as easily may be toward some other person in the educational system. In addition, the assessment focus is not necessarily an individual; it may be a group, an educational policy, or some other aspect of the educational system. For example, parents may express concern over the textbooks used in a fifth grade social studies class. In this case, not only might the textbooks be assessed, but also the curriculum decision-making process.

A third assumption is that, regardless of the specific assessment concern, individuals, groups, behaviors, and situations are multidimensional. Assessment reflects this fact; assessment, too, is multidimensional. It is assumed that no single set of information, reporting source, assessment method, time or place is adequate in effecting a comprehensive, accurate psychoeducational assessment. Behavior, for instance, has numerous manifestations, including verbal and nonverbal aspects. It encompasses everything from facial expressions and motor coordination to interactions with others. Behavior may be situational, vary over time, and be perceived differently depending on the particular observer. Psychoeducational assessments mirror a multidimensional view of individuals, groups, situations, and their interactions, in order to be as comprehensive and precise as possible.

The final, but nonetheless important, assumption regarding assessment is that there is no presupposition that a concern brought forward is a "problem." In other words, the school psychologist's goal is to plan, obtain, and evaluate data relative to a stated concern, without a priori regarding that concern as a problem. The designation "problem" or "difficulty" is applied *after* the assessment process is complete. (A planning team or case conference committee usually makes this determination after the assessment is finished.)

Assessment Planning

The assessment plan is the foundation upon which the entire process rests, and of necessity it represents a thoughtful process. During this time, the school psychologist refers to the stated concerns and available related material (e.g., the information on the referral form). In addition, and depending on the specific circumstance, the school psychologist may seek other available information by examining secondary information sources (e.g., school files, informal interviews). Based on the stated concerns and available related material, the school psychologist makes numerous decisions, including:

1. What information to obtain (e.g., data on a child's cognitive development, data on teacher-classroom interactions);
2. What persons may be able to contribute useful information (e.g., child, parent, teacher, administrator);
3. How to obtain the information (e.g., observation, interview, administration of a standardized assessment instrument);
4. Where to obtain the information (e.g., in the school psychologist's office, in the classroom, on the playground); and
5. When to obtain the information (e.g., during a scheduled appointment or meeting, during reading class, during recess).

To have confidence in each assessment plan decision, the school psychologist must know why each decision is made. The guiding, central consideration in the decision making is to develop a plan which leads to as comprehensive and exact a portrayal of the concern as possible. To this end, there are two primary factors to consider. First, there is a recognition of the multidimensional scope of behavior, perceptions, and situations, including the realization that these factors may change over time. Thus, the school psychologist's assessment plan reflects a multidimensional view of psychoeducational concerns. And second, validity and reliability are weighed heavily in determining what information to obtain, from whom to obtain it, and how, when, and where to obtain the information so that the data adequately reflect the significant features of the matter.

The charge, to develop a plan which gives a comprehensive, accurate view of the stated concern, is neither simple nor easy. This means a recognition at the very beginning that individuals, groups, and situations may be looked at in a number of different ways, may change over time, and do not exist in isolation. There are always variables in an educational setting which are relevant to any stated concern; these must be considered in planning and carrying out an assessment so that the school psychologist not only has data on the concern, but also the time frame and context in which the concern occurs.

What Information to Obtain

There are numerous assessment areas to explore, largely depending on what the assessment focus is (i.e., an individual, group, or some aspect of the educational system). If the educational concern focuses on an individual, what information to obtain may depend on whether the individual is a student (and within that category, whether a preschooler, elementary school student, adolescent, or adult), teacher, parent, administrator, or some other person in the education system. If the concern regards a group, the relevant information to obtain may likewise vary according to the makeup of the group (e.g., elementary school students, a staff group, or a teacher group). And if there is a system concern, the plan may address student concerns (e.g., scheduling of courses), teacher concerns (e.g., availability of support staff), parental concerns (e.g., reading curriculum), or administrator concerns (e.g., the school environment or atmosphere). Some of the primary dimensions within each of these three areas will be presented to provide examples of the array of factors which may be explored in an assessment.

Because the assessment focus is frequently an individual, and most often a student, it is appropriate to begin a discussion of assessment dimensions here. Students are referred for school psychological services primarily (but not necessarily) by teachers, usually because of a concern about the student's school progress. For any concern of this type, there is a host of variables which the school psychologist may explore. The variables may be categorized, somewhat arbitrarily, into five major areas: physiological-biological, developmental, educational, home, and any other relevant areas.

1. *Physiological, Biological Information.* If the concern has medical overtones (e.g., the slow academic progress of a seizure-prone student), physiological, biological information may be sought. Examples of the type of information which may be desired include data on neurological, physical, and physiological development, motor coordination, and sensory acuity (see e.g., Hynd, Quackenbush, and Obrzut 1980, Lezak 1976, Obrzut 1981). Chapter 10 by Hynd and Hartlage elaborates on this theme.

2. *Developmental Data.* If the concern has developmental aspects (a child's disruptive classroom outbursts), developmental information may be sought. For example, it may be important to consider psychomotor development, language development, cognitive development, intellectual development, social-emotional development, behavior development, personality development, and neuropsychological development (see, e.g., Knobloch and Pasamanick 1974, Maloney and Ward 1976).

3. *Educational Information.* If the concern has academic aspects (e.g., a student's poor reading ability), educational data may be sought. Examples of the kind of information which may be important to consider are reading ability and achievement, math ability and achievement, study habits, classroom behavior, student-teacher interaction, student-student interaction, and, in the case of older students, vocational interests (see, e.g., Sabatino and Mauser 1978, Salvia and Ysseldyke 1981).

4. *Home Data.* If the concern is possibly related to a child's home (e.g., a child who consistently comes to school in tears), information on the home may be sought. For example, it may be important to

consider the child's adaptive behavior, home behavior, the family's communication patterns, the family's cultural background, and the stability of the home (see, e.g., Oakland 1977, Oakland and Matuszek 1977).

5. *Other Relevant Areas.* Other factors also may be appropriate to consider. For instance, the child may have lost a close playmate or been involved in a natural disaster, an occurrence which now is affecting the child educationally.

Depending on the particular concern, it may be necessary to obtain information in more than one area. Indeed, this is more frequently than not the case. Two or more areas of information are often sought to provide the comprehensive information necessary to develop a multidimensional psychoeducational assessment.

While concerns related to students represent the most frequent request for school psychological services, they are not the only possible concerns regarding individuals. A concern may be expressed regarding a teacher, for instance. In a situation such as this, the data sought may relate to a number of variables. The individual's interactions with students, parents, and educational professionals may be considered, as well as other factors such as personal adjustment, medical background, and social-emotional maturity. System concerns (e.g., the referral system's effectiveness, curricular decision making) may also be considered along a number of lines. Different individuals' and groups' perceptions of the situation may be examined, as well as various other characteristics, including how the situation has or has not changed over time.

What Persons May Be Able to Contribute Useful Information

Assessment information may be obtained from any number of sources. The choice of source depends to a great extent on what information is being sought (e.g., home data usually is sought through an interview with the student's parents) and on the individual's ability to give useful and relevant, valid and reliable information. Information may be solicited from individuals (e.g., students, parents, teachers, administrators, etc.), groups (e.g., team teachers, a school's math staff, etc.), and from samples of groups (e.g., a survey of parents' attitudes toward the school lunch program). In essence, information is sought from those who can provide valid, reliable data which facilitates a thorough record of the concern.

How to Obtain the Information

Once the school psychologist determines what information is required and from whom, the next decision is how to obtain it. In determining the method, the school psychologist again applies the criterion of appropriateness in adding to a complete picture of the concern. Data are primarily obtained through three basic mechanisms: observation, administration of assessment instruments, and interviews. Any one or all of these methods may be employed to obtain data on individual, group, or system concerns.

1. *Observations.* Much has been written on the use of observation information (e.g., Hunter 1977, Irwin and Bushnell 1980, Lynch 1977, MacDonald and Tanabe 1973, Madsen, Becker, and Thomas 1968, McMillan 1980, Medinnus 1976, Sackett 1976, 1978; Sitko, Fink, and Gillespie 1977, Stallings 1977) in psychoeducational assessments.

Individuals and groups as well as systems may be observed, and the observations may be either direct or indirect. School psychologists obtain indirect observation material by examining secondary sources (e.g., reviewing teachers' anecdotal notes on students' performance as found in school files). Direct observations, on the other hand, are those which school psychologists obtain firsthand; they are made as school psychologists conduct interviews, or are spectators of or participants in an ongoing activity. Direct and indirect observations vary along a number of lines, such as in the degree of influence the psychologist may exert on the observation, and possibly in their validity and reliability.

There are numerous kinds of observations. They vary from the casual, informal observation to the highly structured, tightly controlled experimental observation, and include: (a) informal observations, (b) naturalistic observations, (c) clinical or case study observations, (d) standardized observations, (e) interview observations, and (f) experimental observations. By far the least structured is the informal observation; here, the observer casually notes an activity, situation, setting, etc. For the most part, the observation is unstructured and undirected. A naturalistic observation, on the other hand, maintains more focus than an informal observation. In a naturalistic observation, a school psychologist carefully notes as much as possible to capture the relevant features of an individual, group, ongoing activity, and/or situation.

A clinical or case study observation deviates from the previous two observations in that the focus is distinctly on the past. Clinical observations might include such things as previous clinical records and case study material (e.g., information on past performance gained through interviews). In contrast, standardized observations usually focus on current activities and are characterized by their format. Usually instructions for completing the observation and the observation format are standardized, and frequently, when the standardized observation is published by a professional test-publishing company, validity and reliability data on the instrument are provided. Interview observations are those made by the school psychologist during an interview situation. Observations made during an interview might include such things as individuals' verbalizations, facial expressions, gestures, demeanor, etc. The most highly controlled observation is the experimental observation. In this case, the school psychologist controls as many variables as possible, then manipulates an independent variable (e.g., instructional material) to observe the effects on a dependent variable (e.g., student performance).

2. *Assessment Instruments.* Assessment instruments represent materials developed to assess a characteristic or variable directly (see, e.g., Kaufman 1979, Maloney and Ward 1976). They may focus on cognitive development, consider social-emotional behavior, measure math skills, or assess reading ability, for example (See Table 6.2 in Hynd, et al., Chapter 6). Assessment instruments may be informal (and usually unstandardized), classroom developed, or standardized. The most popular of the three is the standardized assessment instrument category, primarily because standardized instructions and format, validity, reliability, and norm data (when appropriate) are usually provided.

An informal assessment instrument may be one which the school psychologist has developed. For example, if the school psychologist is exploring a concern for which there is no appropriate standardized instrument (e.g., the cognitive abilities of a severely cerebral palsied child), the psychologist may develop an informal assessment instrument. Likewise, when exploring a concern which is directly classroom related (e.g., cursive writing ability), the school psychologist may elect to develop a classroom assessment instrument (e.g., an informal sample of classroom cursive writing ability). The major drawbacks of these instruments are that they have not been fully tried and tested, and may have severely limited validity and reliability.

There is a sizable number of standardized assessment instruments covering everything from intellectual development (e.g., the Wechsler scales, Stanford-Binet), adaptive behavior (e.g., the Adaptive Behavior Inventory for Children), and self-concept (e.g., the Coopersmith, Piers-Harris), to reading and math achievement (e.g., the Peabody Individual Achievement Test). Although all published, standardized assessment materials should meet standards such as those published by the American Psychological Association and the National Council on Measurement in Education, this is not always the case. Therefore, the published data regarding standardization of the particular instrument must always be reviewed prior to utilization to determine such things as appropriateness of the instrument to a given concern, the age range for test takers, the qualifications necessary to administer the test, norm data, and validity and reliability information.

3. *Interviews.* The interview is another method of data collec-

tion. It is probably one of the oldest techniques for clinicians to gather data and collect observations (Maloney and Ward 1976). Interviews range from a relatively unstructured format to a highly structured, sometimes standardized one. This is often referred to as the direct question-and-answer approach, which offers the advantages of wide flexibility in terms of data content and the opportunity to make close-range observations of the interviewee, and allows for information of historical significance.

When to Obtain Information

School psychologists also consider when to schedule an assessment because time may be a relevant factor in the assessment process. If a concern occurs during one part of the day and not the other, for example, it may be worthwhile exploring the importance of the time factor. Likewise, school psychologists are aware of the possibility of differences in assessment information gathered during different times of the day, week, month, semester, and year, with different individuals and groups (e.g., preschoolers, high school students, teachers), and different activities (e.g., classroom behavior, academic performance, professional meetings). Thus, the time dimension is an important one to consider in the assessment plan.

Where to Obtain Information

Where to obtain the assessment information is another factor to be determined in the planning process. Depending on the information desired and from whom, how, and when it is sought, one place may be preferable to another. Typical locations for data collection include the psychologist's office, the classroom, playground, and school conference room. One should keep in mind that different information may be obtained depending on where it is sought. For instance, charting behavior on the playground may yield different information than recording it in the classroom.

Assessment Data Collection

Data collection, as the second step in the assessment process, involves obtaining the information called for in the assessment plan. In essence, an assessment blueprint has already been drawn; subsequently, during data collection, that blueprint or plan is followed. Therefore, the school psychologist knows what information to obtain, from whom to obtain it, the method to be used to collect the data, and when and where the information is to be obtained. School psychologists follow the plan as closely as possible.

This does not mean that the plan may not be modified as the result of information gained during data collection. If the data yield information which makes a reconsideration of the plan appropriate, then the plan is reevaluated and may be modified. The criteria applied in a reconsideration of the plan are the same as those originally employed in the plan development — usefulness in adding to a complete, accurate record of the concern, its validity, and reliability. Thus, the school psychologist follows the assessment plan as long as it is appropriate to do so. When it appears that the plan is no longer appropriate, it is reevaluated, possibly modified, and the revised (or reevaluated) plan is then followed.

Evaluation of Assessment

The evaluation portion of the assessment process is the step in which all of the data which have been collected are related back to the assessment concern, and some interpretation of the concern and the data is made. Thus, there are two parts to the evaluation: (1) a multidimensional view of the concern is developed, as well as (2) an interpretation of that view. While both aspects of the evaluation are data-based, the latter includes a somewhat subjective interpretation of the data by the school psychologist.

The multidimensional view of the concern, developed during the evaluation, depends almost exclusively on what the assessment plan mapped out and the data which were then collected. The evaluation includes an objective presentation of the data which clarifies the stated concern (e.g., what the concern is and why it is a concern, whose concern it is and why, and when and where the concern occurs) and provides substantive data related to the concern (e.g., significant characteristics, relevant features of the concern related to individuals' and groups' expectations, differing perceptions of the concern, etc.).

The interpretation aspect of assessment evaluation is the part in which the school psychologist pinpoints what, in his or her judgment, the difficulty is and why. The psychologist coalesces all the assessment data plus any clinical intuitions based on data, and develops an interpretation of the data and the concern. The school psychologist relies on knowledge, for example, of child development, learning theory, social-emotional and personality development, social psychology of education, and educational curriculum and instruction in developing an interpretation.

Assessment Caveats

The assessment process is not an independent activity; it is tied in with a series of events and individuals and may be influenced by them. Any one of many factors involving the context in which assessment occurs may affect the process. The context includes such variables as the individual who makes the referral, the referral process itself, the school psychologist, the school system, and even the community in which the school system exists. Any one of a number of contextual variables, beginning with individual perceptions of the psychoeducational process and extending through school and community expectations, may significantly affect an assessment and likewise any subsequent intervention.

For instance, an assessment is usually planned after someone informs the school psychologist of the existence of a possible problem. That communication represents one person's perceptions about a person or situation—perceptions which are based on the individual's educational background, past experiences, opinions and value system, and their own personal adjustment, among many things. It is conceivable that a referred concern may be more a reflection of the person making the referral than an actual psychoeducational problem. This might affect an assessment if the school psychologist builds an assessment plan solely around one individual's concerns, concerns which do not accurately present the "problem."

In addition, one should not neglect the well-researched factor of the possible differences in perception of a problem which may exist. There is ample evidence from the attribution-theory literature about divergences in opinions of behavior depending upon who is considering the behavior (i.e., the observer or the actor, the teacher or the student). There is a tendency for an observer (e.g., the teacher) to attribute a happening to the individual characteristics of the person being observed, while that individual tends to place heavy emphasis on existing situational variables. Thus, a situation perceived as problematic and caused by a student, may be viewed quite differently by the student. For example, a teacher who observes an unruly class may perceive that the problem is caused by a particular disruptive student. The student, however, may view the situation as confining (i.e., no time allowed to visit with other students, sharpen one's pencil, or move about the classroom independently) and not view him- or herself as the problem.

Further, differences in perception often occur between teachers and psychologists. Much research exists documenting that problem characteristics identified by teachers are not necessarily the same as those perceived by psychologists (Morris and Arrant 1978, Walsh and O'Connor 1968). Therefore, school psychologists may look for data different from that which the teacher feels is important, and, further, may weight certain data more heavily than other information.

Another example of how the context may affect an assessment can be discerned by examining the referral system. Referrals often go through some process (e.g., a school or district committee, or an administrator who reviews referrals) before they reach the school psychologist. Some districts, school review committees, administrators and/or school psychological services staff prioritize referrals, placing a high priority on some (e.g., those which may have placement implications) and relegating others to a low priority status. The prioritization may influence what data are sought, as well as how that information is interpreted; the affect may be subtle, but nonetheless influential. For example, the school psychologist may seek achievement and classroom data, to the exclusion of possibly relevant developmental and home data, if a concern has been determined to have possible placement implications.

The fact that the school psychologist is in the employ of the school district or educational system is another element which should not be neglected in evaluating the context in which assessment occurs. Financial remuneration and economic security can be powerful forces influencing the assessment process. That is, the school psychologist may be predisposed to weigh school data and information from education personnel more heavily than home data in evaluating the presence and disposition of a problem.

The aforementioned examples, contextual factors influencing or possibly affecting an assessment, are but a sample of what could be presented. Let it suffice to note that there are variables present (outside the confines of the assessment itself) which may influence the assessment process. Factors such as these need to be kept in mind as assessments are planned, and data gathered and evaluated so that the school psychologist remains as objective and comprehensive as possible when engaging in the assessment activity.

INTERVENTION

The intervention process begins after an assessment is complete, a problem is identified and described, and a change in the projected outcome is sought. Intervention, like assessment, has three components and begins with a planning process. A plan is developed which establishes the intervention goals and objectives, specifies the intervention focus, delineates the intervention method (what the intervention entails and how it will be employed in the particular circumstance, who will intervene, and when and where the intervention will occur), and details an evaluation to determine whether the intervention meets its goals and objectives. The next aspect is the intervention activity itself, and the final element is the evaluation of the intervention (in light of the targeted goals and objectives).

Intervention Assumptions

The assumed purpose of an intervention is to effect a change in an anticipated psychoeducational outcome. An alteration is desired when an assessment leads those involved to conclude that there is a problem and, if uninterrupted, the problem will continue. The companion assumption is that intervention will make the outcome better than what would be expected without such an intervention.

A further assumption is that facilitating students' growth and development is at the heart of any intervention strategy. Therefore, the best interests of students are kept in mind as interventions are planned (regardless of the specific intervention target). For example, rather than regarding things such as school procedures or teacher convenience as primary, students' psychoeducational growth and development is the tantamount consideration.

Another assumption is that anything in the psychoeducational milieu that is relevant to the problem may be the target of an intervention. For example, even though there may be a problem with a child's school progress, the focus of an intervention may be on the teacher, rather than the child. The teacher may be taught alternative instructional strategies to better facilitate the child's academic progress.

Furthermore, it is assumed that there may be more than one intervention target and more than one intervention activity, based on the fact that problems (like behaviors, situations, and perceptions) are multidimensional. For example, the intervention target for a child whose poor academic progress is of concern may not only be the teacher and the teacher's instructional repertoire, but also the teacher's and parents' expectations for the child's academic achievement. In addition, the intervention target may be an *interaction* (e.g., teacher-student), rather than a specific individual or group.

Intervention Planning

The intervention plan is heavily dependent on the assessment and the subsequent team meeting or case conference in which the original concern and the assessment are discussed. In this meeting, there is typically a clarification of what the concern is, to whom it is a concern, and why, when, and where the concern arises. Those involved determine if the concern is a problem and why. If there is a problem *and* a change in a projected outcome is sought, then an intervention plan is developed. Either the involved group or the school psychologist may be responsible for developing the intervention plan. Regardless of the specific makeup of the planning group (e.g., resource teacher, school social worker, administrator), the intervention decision making includes:

1. determining the goals and objectives of the intervention (e.g., increased teacher proficiency, improved student academic achievement);
2. determining the intervention target (e.g., student, teacher, parent);
3. determining the intervention method (e.g., behavioral, consultation, physiological-biochemical);
4. determining who is going to intervene (e.g., the school psychologist, teacher, school nurse); and
5. determining when and where the intervention is going to occur (e.g., in the classroom, during reading instruction).

Acknowledged in this process is that any one intervention activity may produce a number of different outcomes and, likewise, any number of interventions may lead to the same desired change. A matching process occurs by which the method most likely to lead to the desired goals and objectives is selected. Weighed in this process are the validity and reliability characteristics of various intervention strategies.

Determining Goals and Objectives

Determining the intervention goals and objectives is a significant first step in intervention planning, and is accomplished by reviewing what the problem is, whose problem it is, and why, when, and where the problem occurs, and what the projected outcome is without intervention. Because the focus is on changing the projected outcome, those involved need to determine what a desirable alternative outcome would be. The desired outcome provides the basis for the intervention goals and objectives.

Determining the Intervention Target

The target selection depends, to a great extent, on what the desired outcome is. If the goal is something like providing improved instructional materials to a child with a severe reading difficulty, the target might be the teacher (and getting the teacher appropriate instructional materials to use with the child). If, on the other hand, the goal is something like improved classroom behavior (i.e., behavior appropriate to the classroom situation), the target might well be the child whose behavior is the object of concern.

Determining the Intervention Method

Selecting an intervention method is also dependent upon the goals and objectives. Selection is the determination of how the desired change is going to take place. Psychologists have discussed and conceptualized interventions in a number of different ways (e.g., Anastasiow and Mowder 1980, Rhodes and Tracey 1977, Millman, Schaefer, and Cohen 1980, Ross 1980, 1981; Sabatino and Mauser 1978). Interventions may be placed into one of several categories, depending on their intervention focus:

1. Physiological, biochemical, and pharmacological interventions
2. Counseling and psychotherapy
3. Behavioral interventions
4. Consultation
5. Milieu interventions

Some of the interventions are distinctly suitable for student or individual interventions, some for groups, and others for the system or milieu. It is beyond the scope of this chapter to review each of the intervention frameworks extensively. But even a brief description of each will clarify their usefulness in effecting change (depending on the intervention focus).

1. *A physiological, biochemical, or pharmacological intervention* is one which is usually directed at an individual and typically involves some medical attention. The intervention may include the administration (reduction or elimination) of medication, a change in diet, nutritional supplements, and/or an array of other physiological-biological manipulations. If, for example, a student is taking medication to control a seizure disorder but is extremely lethargic in class, the medication or amount of medication may need to be altered to obtain a subsequent change in the child's classroom behavior. The school psychologist's role in this type of intervention might be one of observer, monitor, and/or intermediary among teachers, parents, and medical personnel. (For an extensive review of biophysical interventions in child deviation, see Kameya 1977).

2. *Counseling or psychotherapy* is another possible intervention. This intervention, too, may be directed at the student having educational difficulties, and/or it may be recommended for other individuals (e.g., parent, teacher). For example, a counseling situation may provide a

forum to discuss a child's and others' expectations, as well as educational realities. It should be noted that a basic distinction is usually made between counseling and psychotherapy. Counseling generally deals with the kind of day-to-day problems that many people commonly encounter. Frequently there is a situational component to a particular problem. Psychotherapy, on the other hand, is reserved for severe, more pervasive social, emotional, and behavioral difficulties. A variety of counseling and psychotherapy philosophies and techniques exist (see, e.g., Carkhuff and Berenson 1967). The school psychologist skilled in offering therapeutic services may directly provide this intervention or, more usually, will refer the individual to another professional for clinical help.

3. *A behavioral intervention* may have as its primary target an individual's behavior, a group's behavior, or something in the milieu which is reinforcing the inappropriate behavior, (or not reinforcing the appropriate behavior) of one, several or many individuals. In each of these instances some part of a behavioral sequence is modified. The antecedent or stimulus conditions or the consequences of the behavior might be changed. Or, a behavioral intervention might focus on some aspect of the student's milieu in need of modification. Whether directed toward individuals or some aspect of the environment, a resultant behavior is targeted and identified in observable, measurable terms. Some alteration of the behavior is expected once the intervention is in place. The school psychologist's role in this process might be one of designing the behavioral intervention, implementing the program, monitoring the program's progress, and/or evaluating the program. (For further discussions of behavioral interventions, see, e.g., Ackerman 1972, Carter 1972, Madsen et al. 1968, O'Leary and O'Leary 1972, Ross 1980, 1981; Tharp and Wetzel 1969, Thomson and Holmberg 1974.)

4. *Consultation* is often conceptualized as an indirect intervention, one which is focused toward others in a particular individual's life, or toward the broader system or milieu in which the person operates. For example, the school psychologist may consult with a teacher who is having difficulty with one particular child in the classroom about ways to teach the child better or more effectively. Or, in this same instance, the school psychologist may consult with the administrator in the school to discuss options for changing the school environment to better accommodate for children with different learning needs and styles. Consultation is a frequently mentioned and acknowledged role for the school psychologist. (For a further review of consultation see, e.g., Conoley 1981, Heron and Catera 1980, Langhorne, Paternite, and Loney 1979, Meyers, Parsons, and Hyman 1979, Meyers, Parsons, and Martin 1979, Schein 1969.) See also Martin (Chapter 11).

5. *Milieu interventions.* Like counseling and psychotherapy,

there is no one milieu-based intervention. Here the focus is distinctly on the environment which the child acts. Family interventions, therapeutically designed environments, work with street-clubs, and organizational development are diverse examples of milieu interventions. The school psychologist's role in milieu interventions may vary widely, and can include making direct environmental manipulations, referring children or others to therapeutic environments, designing preventative educational or mental health programs, and setting up remedial treatment programs. (See, e.g., Owens 1981, Sabatino and Mauser 1978, Wagner 1977, for a review of environmental interventions.)

Interventions have been treated as if they are one dimensional; that is, the intervention is either directed at an individual, a group, or the psychoeducational milieu. Conceptualizing the problem and the subsequent intervention in this way simplifies the discussion of intervention strategies. But it also obscures the reality that a problem can reside in more than one place. Often it is not the individual, others significant in the individual's life, a group, or the situation per se that is the difficulty, but the *interaction* among these factors. Thus, interventions can be directed at one or more factors contributing to a problem situation, and/or toward the interaction among those factors.

Determining Who is Going to Intervene

Determining who is going to intervene is another important decision. The decision depends upon the goal of the intervention, the target and the method, as well as who has the expertise to perform the intervention.

Determining When and Where to Intervene

Determining when and where to intervene hinges on the goal, the target, the intervention method, and the intervener. One location may be preferable over another (e.g., the school psychologist's office rather than the playground), as well as one time over another (e.g., the morning rather than the afternoon). These are additional factors to weigh in the development of an intervention plan.

Conducting the Intervention

The implementation of the planned intervention is the second step in the intervention process. The intervention activity directly follows the intervention plan: the designated intervener, at the preselected time and place, carries out the intervention activity. The intervention activity is carefully documented to provide data which will facilitate the evaluation of the intervention.

Shaffer (1980) offers some valuable thoughts on implementation. While she specifically addresses program implementation concerns and calls implementation the neglected step between planning and evaluation, her insights can easily be applied to the broader area of intervention. She enumerates significant hazards to accuracy in implementation, makes suggestions for ensuring accurate implementation, and offers methods of evaluating implementation.

Evaluating the Intervention

The intervention evaluation determines how effective the intervention is in bringing about the stated intervention goals and objectives. There are any number of ways to evaluate an intervention. The variety of evaluation methods includes the use of questionnaires (Fullen and Pomfret 1977), single subject research designs (Kratochwill 1978), observation (Fullen and Pomfret 1977), interviews (Hall and Loucks 1977), and broad evaluation systems (Borich and Jemelka 1982, Fairchild 1980, House 1980, Maher 1980, Mowder and Prasse 1982). To some extent the intervention focus will help determine the evaluation strategy (e.g., individual, group, system concerns). Several evaluation modes may be applied simultaneously, particularly if there is more than one target, method, intervener, and/or intervention time and place.

Intervention Caveats

The intervention plan and activity can be significantly affected by how the "problem" is perceived by the school psychologist, planning team, and/or intervener. Rhodes (1977, p. 35) states that an intervention takes somewhat different forms depending on whether the difficulty is seen as (1) emanating from a disability, (2) the result of a deviation from the norm, or (3) an alienation from people and/or the situation.

If one takes the approach that the problem represents a disability, the tendency is to seek a biophysical intervention, though behavioral, psychotherapeutic, and consultation interventions may also be considered. The deviance perspective tends to lead one toward behavioral, interpersonal, intrapersonal, and milieu-systems interventions. And the perception that alienation is the reason for a problem may point toward psychotherapeutic, consultation, and milieu-based interventions.

SUMMARY

Assessment and intervention represent two significant school psychological service functions. The activities are both broad and complex. When a school psychologist undertakes a psychoeducational assessment, an assessment plan is developed, the assessment activity (i.e., collection of data) carried out, and an evaluation made of the assessment information. And in effecting an intervention, the school psychologist (and/or team planning committee) details an intervention plan, the intervention activity then transpires and is evaluated. Although serious criticisms have been raised about certain aspects of the processes (most notably testing [e.g., Bersoff 1973] and largely for possible bias against minority students [e.g., Oakland 1977, Oakland and Matuszek 1977]), no one has seriously questioned the importance of these activities. Many of the chapters in this book detail different assessment issues and areas.

REFERENCES

Ackerman, J. M. *Operant conditioning techniques for teachers.* Glenview, Ill.: Scott, Foresman, 1972.

Anastasiow, M., & Mowder, B. A. Intervention resources from three conceptual frameworks. NASP *Communiqué,* 1980, *10,* 6–7.

Bersoff, D. N. Silk purses into sows' ears: The decline of psychological testing and suggestion for its redemption. *American Psychologist,* 1973, *28,* 892–899.

Borich, G. D., & Jemelka, R. P. *Programs and systems, an evaluation perspective.* New York: Academic Press, 1982.

Carkhuff, R. R., & Berenson, B. G. *Beyond counseling and therapy.* New York: Holt, Rinehart, and Winston, 1967.

Carter, R. *Help! These kids are driving me crazy.* Champaign, Ill.: Research Press, 1972.

Conoley, J. C. *Consultation in schools, theory, research, procedures.* New York: Academic Press, 1981.

Fairchild, T. STEPPS: A model for the evaluation of school psychological services. *School Psychology Review,* 1980, *9,* 252–258.

Fullen, M., & Pomfret, A. Research on curriculum and instruction implementation. *Review of Educational Research,* 1977, *47,* 335–397.

Hall, G., & Loucks, S. A developmental model for determining whether the treatment is actually implemented. *American Educational Research Journal,* 1977, *14,* 263–276.

Heron, T. E., & Catera, R. Teacher consultation: A functional approach. *School Psychology Review,* 1980, *9,* 283–289.

House, E. R. *Evaluating with validity.* Beverly Hills: Sage Publications, 1980.

Hunter, C. P. Classroom observation instruments and teacher inservice training by school psychologists. *School Psychology Monograph,* 1977, *3,* 45–88.

Hynd, G. W., Quackenbush, R., & Obrzut, J. E. Training school psychologists in neuropsychological assessment: Current practices and trends. *Journal of School Psychology,* 1980, *18,* 148–153.

Irwin, D. M., & Bushnell, M. M. *Observational strategies for child study.* New York: Holt, Rinehart, and Winston, 1980.

Kameya, L. I. Biophysical interventions in emotional disturbance. In Rhodes, W. C. and Tracy, M. L. *A study of child variance: Volume 2, Interventions.* Ann Arbor: University of Michigan Press, 1977.

Kaufman, A. S. *Intelligent testing with the WISC-R.* New York: John Wiley and Sons, 1979.

Knobloch, H., & Pasamanick, G. *Gesell and Amatruda's developmental diagnosis* (3rd ed.). Baltimore: Harper and Row, 1974.

Kratochwill, T. R. *Single-subject research: Strategies for evaluating change.* New York: Academic Press, 1978.

Langhorne, J. E., Jr., Paternite, C., & Loney, J. An alternative teacher consultation model: A case study. *School Psychology Digest,* 1979, *8*(2), 235–239.

Lezak, M. D. *Neuropsychological assessment.* New York: Oxford University Press, 1976.

Lynch, W. W. Guidelines to the use of classroom observation instruments by the school psychologist. *School Psychology Monograph,* 1977, *3,* 1–22.

MacDonald, W. S., & Tanabe, G. (Eds.). *Focus on classroom behavior.* Springfield, Ill.: Charles C. Thomas, 1973.

McMillan, J. H. *The social psychology of school learning.* New York: Academic Press, 1980.

Madsen, C. H., Becker, W. C., & Thomas, D. R. Rules, praise and ignoring: Elements of elementary classroom control. *Journal of Applied Behavior Analysis,* 1968, *1,* 139–150.

Maher, C. A. Evaluating organizational effectiveness of special service departments: Comparison of two models. *School Psychology Review,* 1980, *9,* 259–266.

Maloney, M. P., & Ward, M. P. *Psychological assessment: A conceptual approach.* New York: Oxford University Press, 1976.

Medinnus, G. R. *Child study and observation guide.* New York: John Wiley and Sons, 1976.

Meyers, J., Parsons, R. P., & Hyman, I. *School consultation.* Springfield, Ill.: Charles C. Thomas, 1977.

Meyers, J., Parsons, R. P., & Martin, R. *Mental health consultation in the schools.* San Francisco: Jossey-Bass, 1979.

Millman, H. L., Schaefer, C. E., & Cohen, J. J. *Therapies for school behavior problems.* San Francisco: Jossey-Bass, 1980.

Morris, J. D., & Arrant, D. Behavior ratings of emotionally disturbed children by teachers, parents, and school psychologists. *Psychology in the Schools,* 1978, *15,* 450–455.

Mowder, B. A. Competency-based education and school psychology. In T. Kratochwill (Ed.), *Advances in school psychology,* Volume II. Hillsdale, N.J.: Erlbaum Associates, 1982, 41–59.

Mowder, B. A., & Prasse, D. P. An evaluation model for school psychological services. *Evaluation and Program Planning,* 1982, *4.*

Oakland, T. (Ed.). *Psychological and educational assessment of minority children.* New York: Brunner/Mazel, 1977.

Oakland, T., & Matuszek, P. Using tests in nondiscriminatory assessment. In T. Oakland (Ed.), *Psychological and educational assessment of minority children.* New York: Brunner/Mazel, 1977.

Obrzut, J. E. Neuropsychological assessment in the schools. *School Psychology Review,* 1981, *10,* 331–342.

O'Leary, K. D., & O'Leary, S. G. (Eds.). *Classroom management: The successful use of behavior modification.* Elmsford, N.Y.: Pergamon, 1972.

Owens, R. G. *Organizational behavior in education* (2nd ed.). Englewood Cliffs, N.J.: Prentice-Hall, 1981.

Phye, G. D., & Reschly, D. J. (Eds.). *School psychology: Perspectives and issues.* New York: Academic Press, 1980.

Rhodes, W. C. Overview of intervention. In Rhodes, W. C. and Tracy, M. L. (Eds.), *A study of child variance: Volume 2, Interventions.* Ann Arbor: University of Michigan Press, 1977.

Rhodes, W. C., & Tracy, M. L. (Eds.). *A study of child variance: Volume I, Conceptual models.* Ann Arbor: University of Michigan Press, 1977.

Rhodes, W. C., & Tracy, M. L. (Eds.). *A study of child variance: Volume II, Interventions.* Ann Arbor: University of Michigan Press, 1977.

Ross, A. O. *Psychological disorders of children: A behavioral approach to theory, research, and therapy.* New York: McGraw-Hill, 1980.

Ross, A. O. *Child behavior therapy: Principles, procedures, and empirical basis.* New York: John Wiley and Sons, 1981.

Sabatino, D. A., & Mauser, A. J. *Intervention strategies for specialized secondary education.* Boston: Allyn and Bacon, 1978.

Sackett, G. P. (Ed.). *Observing behavior: Volume 1, Theories and applications in mental retardation.* Baltimore: University Park Press, 1976.

Sackett, G. P. (Ed.). *Observing behavior: Volume 2, Data collection and analysis methods.* Baltimore: University Park Press, 1978.

Salvia, J., & Ysseldyke, J. E. *Assessment in special and remedial education* (2nd ed.). Boston: Houghton-Mifflin, 1981.

Schein, R. *Process consultation: Its role in organization development.* Reading, Mass.: Addison-Wesley, 1969.

Shaffer, M. B. Implementation: The neglected step between program planning and program evaluation. *School Psychology Review,* 1980, *9,* 247–251.

Sitko, M. C., Fink, A. H., & Gillespie, P. H. Utilizing systematic observation for decision making in school psychology. *School Psychology Monograph,* 1977, *3,* 23–44.

Stallings, J. A. *Learning to look: A handbook on classroom observation and teaching models.* Belmont, Calif.: Wadsworth Publishing Company, 1977.

Tharp, R. G., & Wetzel, R. J. *Behavior modification in the natural environment.* New York: Academic Press, 1969.

Thomson, C., & Holmberg, M. A brief report on a comparison of time-sampling procedures. *Journal of Applied Behavior Analysis,* 1974, *7,* 623–626.

Wagner, M. Environmental interventions in emotional disturbance. In Rhodes, W. C. and Tracy, M. L. (Eds.), *A study of child variance: Volume 2, Interventions.* Ann Arbor: University of Michigan Press, 1977.

Walsh, J. F., & O'Connor, J. D., Sr. When are children disturbed? *The Elementary School Journal,* 1968, *68,* 353–356.

8

Psychoeducational Assessment
Cognitive Domain
RICHARD J. NAGLE

As THE PROFESSION of school psychology has evolved, there has been a great deal of discussion regarding the expanded role and function of the school psychologist. Psychoeducational assessment has been the earliest and most prominent of the services provided by the psychologist working in the schools (Monroe 1979). Historically, school psychology emerged out of the mental testing movement associated with special education programming (Sarason 1976, Tindall 1979). In recent years, there has been increased controversy over the use of tests in schools, particularly those appraising individual intelligence. Much of this controversy has focused on the use of intelligence tests for special class placement among minority group children. It has been argued that many minority children do poorly on intelligence tests because they lack opportunities to acquire the cognitive skills and knowledge necessary to perform well on such tests (Mercer 1975). Various litigations and legislative actions (e.g., Public Law 94-142), have forced a closer consideration among school psychologists of their discipline's ethical guidelines and standards as they relate to the general issues of reliability and validity of the test instrument, particularly with reference to the child's social and ethnic background.

In response to the various legal and legislative actions, school psychologists have begun to expand the focus of their assessment methods. The multidimensional nature of these methods will be discussed in a later section of this chapter. An additional impetus for change in the assessment activities of school psychologists has come from teachers who have become increasingly dissatisfied by the limitations in the kinds and quality of current assessment activities (Ysseldyke 1979). As Ysseldyke (1979) has pointed out, many teachers view the school psychologist as a tester and "number getter whose sole usefulness is his or her authority to remove a deviant youngster from a classroom" (p. 106). Teachers, for the most part, are relatively unconcerned with test scores, per se, and are more concerned with an appraisal of the child's strengths and weaknesses and what remedial or intervention strategies should be undertaken to maximize the child's educational development. Thus, the scope of assessment activities should include both an evaluation of the child's skill development and suggested individualized instructional or intervention strategies. This makes assessment information and recommendations based on assessment data more relevant both to classroom teachers and to parents. As we will see later in this chapter, this is of utmost importance in educational decision making. With the increase in the number of handicapped children "mainstreamed" in regular classrooms, many teachers will need the assistance of school psychologists and other special personnel to formulate appropriate classroom instruction. Parents, on the other hand, have a right, mandated by Public Law 94-142, to develop an individualized educational program for their child together with school personnel. Thus, test findings and suggested interventions must be couched in terms which are comprehensible to parents, so they may intelligently participate in these educational decision making procedures for their child.

Many of the criticisms lodged against assessment procedures are actually directed toward testing in general. The difference between assessment and testing is more than semantic. Assessment is the process of solving problems and answering questions in which psychological tests are often used as methods of acquiring relevant data (Maloney and Ward 1976). Assessment within the context of schools is a multifaceted process of collecting data for making decisions for and about students (Salvia and Ysseldyke 1981) which will enhance their educational development. According to Salvia and Ysseldyke (1981), assessment procedures are undertaken in educational settings for at least five basic reasons; these include screening, classification and placement decisions, planning of educational programs, program evaluation, and evaluation of individual pupil progress. Certainly, these different reasons for assessment are not mutually exclusive and, in fact, one type of assessment information can supplement or be a prerequisite for another. Although school psychologists may be involved in any of these five areas, the most common assessment activity involves classification and placement decisions, since many of the evaluation procedures used in these activities require specialized training in psychoeducational diagnostics. Broadly speaking, the cognitive domain of psychoeducational assessment entails the use of intellectual and achievement measures.

The present chapter will outline cognitive assessment procedures as they are carried out within the broader context of psychoeducational assessment. The historical perspectives of the development of intelligence tests, legal aspects of assessment, and specific remedial methods will not be discussed in this chapter since these topics have been discussed in other parts of this book. The primary focus of the current chapter will be on the process of assessment with individually administered cognitive tests.

GROUP VERSUS INDIVIDUAL TESTING

Just as there are distinct purposes for assessment, there are also some basic format differences among cognitive assessment devices. Both intellectual and achievement tests have been designed to be administered in group or individual formats. In deciding between group or individually administered tests, the school psychologist must be cognizant of both the advantages and disadvantages of each approach. Several advantages of group testing have been discussed by Anastasi (1976). First, and perhaps most obvious, is that more than one person can be tested at a time; thus testing can be undertaken efficiently both in terms of cost and time. Second, the role of the examiner is quite simplified when compared to individually administered tests such as the Stanford-Binet or Wechsler Scales, which require extensive training or experience. Therefore, following some preliminary training, various school personnel are able to administer such tests. In conjunction with ease of administration, the scoring of group tests is highly objective because of the usual multiple-choice format.

The disadvantages of group testing, however, limit their usefulness in certain education decisions. First, since the role of the examiner is minimal, there is virtually no opportunity for the examiner to establish rapport or maintain a child's motivation. Any atypical behaviors or transient behavioral conditions, such as fatigue, lapses in attention or task persistence, or illness can easily go undetected by the examiner (Anastasi 1976). Children referred for possible special educational placement are much more likely to exhibit these behaviors, which would interfere with optimal test performance. A second limitation involves the inability of the examiner to observe the strategies or methods a child uses in problem solving. Thus, any qualitative interpretation is not possible and can only be observed systematically through individually administered tests. Another significant problem with group tests is their inflexible procedural format (Anastasi 1976). That is to say, each examinee is tested on all items. Such procedures, according to Anastasi, enhance the likelihood of frustration and anxiety when a child is beyond his or her ability level. Also, boredom may result from working on items which may be too easy. These problems can be avoided somewhat on individually administered tests, since items are dependent on the examinee's prior responses.

The selection of a group or an individually-administered test should be based primarily on the decision to be drawn from the test results and the efficiency with which the purpose of assessment can be achieved accurately (Salvia and Ysseldyke 1981). In general, decisions involving program evaluation, screening, and some types of program planning are most appropriately accomplished through group tests (Salvia and Ysseldyke, 1981). When decisions about individual students are made, such as placement decisions or the design of individual program plans, individually administered tests are most appropriate. In fact, individual assessment is required by law in making placement decisions in special education programs (Salvia and Ysseldyke 1981).

THE PROCESS OF INDIVIDUAL ASSESSMENT IN THE SCHOOL

The purpose of individual assessment is to explicate the nature of a child's difficulty in school and then to implement appropriate intervention strategies to maximize the child's educational development. The process of assessment is interrelated with intervention; assessment without intervention is a futile effort.

The process of individual assessment does not have a fixed sequence of steps. The methods of data collection should largely be a function of the nature of the referral problem and the amount of existing information available to the school psychologist. The majority of children are referred for psychoeducational evaluation by their teachers or parents because of poor academic progress. Referrals may also be made based on the results of screening programs which may indicate that a particular child is "at risk" for academic problems.

Early Stages of Assessment: Problem Clarification

The usual initial step in the assessment process is the referral. Once a referral is received by the school psychologist, it should be carefully reviewed and any ambiguity or points which need elaboration should be clarified by the referral source. For example, it is not uncommon for the school psychologist to receive a referral that states that the child shows "poor school progress." Clearly, this provides very little information to the psychologist. Questions which may clarify the child's problem may be, "Does the child experience difficulty in all subject areas?" "What type of effort does the child show?" And so on.

A logical next step would be to schedule interviews with the child's teacher and parents. These interviews have several purposes, and regardless of the psychologist's theoretical orientation, the interview is still a universal device to obtain valuable information about the behavior of children and their environments (Marholin and Bijou 1978). It is important to determine (a) how teachers and parents perceive the referral problem, (b) what alternative strategies have been tried to alleviate the problem, (c) their role in the present maintenance of the problem, and (d) their role and level of cooperation in the future alleviation of the problem (Ciminero and Drabman 1977). Parent interviews also provide an excellent opportunity to acquire background information in terms of developmental, medical, behavioral, and environmental factors as they relate to the child's referral problem. It is also an opportune time to explain to the parents informed-consent procedures, how you will likely proceed with the evaluation of their child, and the possible ways in which the assessment data may be used. The teacher interview should clarify any issues related to the reason for referral. Also, the teacher interview provides an excellent opportunity for the school psychologist to establish rapport with the teacher, since it is very likely that the school psychologist will wish to observe the child in the classroom setting. At this time, it is also desirable to discuss the purpose of the observation and arrange for a mutually agreeable time that the observation may be carried out. Frequently, comments made by both teachers and parents alert us to important behaviors which we may observe in the classroom or the formal test situation, behavior which affects the child's performance as well as the design of our assessment strategies.

There are also circumstances in which information gathered during the interview helps the assessor formulate solutions to the referral problem. In these instances resolution of the problem may only require that the assessor share psychological knowledge with the teacher or parent to formulate intervention strategies to alleviate the child's difficulties.

Classroom Observation

Classroom observations are an important component in psychoeducational assessment. First, it is generally acknowledged by most psychologists that behavior observed during testing is frequently not generalizable to the classroom setting. Second, systematic observation in the classroom can provide the school psychologist with potential avenues for intervention or remedial strategies, since it will be in the classroom that such strategies will ultimately be carried out. As Lidz (1981) suggests, classroom observation is one of the best responses to teacher concerns and criticisms about the oversimplicity or irrelevancy of psychological evaluations.

What behaviors are eventually selected to be observed in the classroom will largely be a function of the areas of concern articulated by the referral source (Lidz 1981). Based upon the nature of the behavior to be observed, the assessor decides upon procedures for the observational session (Boehm and Weinberg 1977). Methodologies for classroom observations vary considerably, ranging from a continuous, diary-like recording of ongoing behavior, to very sophisticated behavior code sampling systems. (See Ciminero and Drabman, 1977, for a discussion of various behavioral observation techniques.) Regardless of the observational method used, such behavioral assessment techniques may help delineate target behaviors to change, what environmental conditions contribute to the target behavior, possible strategies which may alleviate the referral problem, and how to evaluate treatment effects (Ciminero and Drabman 1977). The psychologist should attempt to observe the child in a variety of settings and activities to discern the cross-situational nature of his or her behavior. At this juncture, the psychologist may again suggest some remedial strategies, particularly if the observational data suggest that more extensive assessment is not warranted. For example, a child's poor performance in reading may be due to motivational problems, and thus it may be most appropriate to intervene with methods aimed at enhancing the child's motivation. On the other hand, if the assessor observed that a child was failing in reading because of an inability to master simple letter-sound associations, despite strong effort, it would be appropriate to proceed with other assessments to explain these deficiencies.

Psychoeducational Evaluation: Testing Procedures

Formal testing procedures including tests of intelligence, achievement, and social functioning are undertaken when the referred child is suspected of mental retardation or a learning disability. Most federal and state guidelines place a great deal of importance on intellectual functioning in the classification and placement of handicapped children. The most widely accepted definition of mental retardation is the American Association on Mental Deficiency's (AAMD) (Grossman 1977, p. 5), in which "mental retardation refers to significantly sub-average, general intellectual functioning existing concurrently with deficits in adaptive behavior and manifested during the developmental period." Significantly subaverage intellectual functioning refers to IQ scores 2 or more standard deviation units below the mean on an individually administered IQ test. Deficits in adaptive behavior refer to deficiencies in the effectiveness or degree to which an individual meets the standards of personal independence and social responsibility expected of his or her age and cultural group. It can readily be seen that this definition places a strong emphasis on measurement.

Recent federal regulations (*Federal Register,* December 29, 1977) have stated that a child could be diagnosed with a specific learning disability if the child did not achieve commensurate with age and ability level in one or more specified areas of achievement (e.g., oral expression, listening comprehension, written expression, basic reading skill, reading comprehension, mathematics calculation, and/or mathematical reasoning) when provided with learning experiences appropriate for the child's age and ability level. Furthermore, the difference between a child's achievement and intellectual ability must show a significant discrepancy (usually 1.6 standard deviation units, although local school district guidelines may differ somewhat). The discrepancy between ability and achievement cannot be primarily a function of other handicapping conditions, including sensory and motor handicaps, mental retardation, emotional disturbance, and/or environmental, social, or economic disadvantage. As with definitional guidelines for mental retardation, it can be readily noted that this definition of a specific learning disability also emphasizes cognitive assessment.

Given that intellectual and achievement tests are required in the placement procedures for children suspected of various handicapping conditions, the school psychologist is confronted with the important task of test selection. With the information that the psychologist has gathered about the child from various interviews and school records and knowledge of the child's background, the selection of the most valid and reliable instruments from those available should be made. The examiner should have a thorough understanding of the *Standards for Educational and Psychological Tests* (American Psychological Association 1974) to be able to choose tests, interpret scores, and make decisions based on the test scores. It is also incumbent on the examiner to determine what behavioral domains should be assessed and what type of test data will aid most in the understanding of the referral problem.

An issue which has long been debated among psychologists has been the difference between intelligence or aptitude and achievement. According to Nunnally (1972), aptitude is the capacity to learn, a prediction of how well a student can achieve under favorable conditions. Achievement, on the other hand, measures a student's actual level of attainment within specific subject areas. Aptitude and achievement are somewhat inseparable, in that we judge aptitude by how well people have mastered their cultural environments up to a specific point in time. As a consequence, many items from intelligence tests are similar to items from achievement tests (Nunnally 1972). Regardless of one's conceptualization of aptitude, it is reasonable to assume that it is influenced by the richness of educational as well as cultural experiences.

Once the psychologist has chosen the most appropriate evaluation tools, the more formal or traditional testing begins. Unlike other steps in the overall assessment process, we now begin to sample behavior under a set of highly structured or standardized procedures (Ciminero and Drabman 1977, Salvia and Ysseldyke 1981). In the case of intelligence testing, we are sampling behaviors believed to measure intelligence. We know that success on items included in these tests usually corresponds to success in school.

INTELLIGENCE TESTING

The development and history of intelligence testing has been discussed previously, in the chapter by A. Kaufman. Kaufman astutely points out that there has been little change in the content of commonly used IQ tests in the last century; thus, knowledge gleaned from broad areas of child development research has been virtually neglected in test construction. It is apparent that there tends to be a gap between testing technology and psychological theory.

Despite this present state of affairs, the school psychologist must work within the constraints of available testing instruments. The two most commonly used individual intelligence tests with school-aged children are the Stanford-Binet Intelligence Scale (S-B; Terman and Merrill 1973) and the Wechsler Intelligence Scale for Children-Revised (WISC-R; Wechsler 1974).

Stanford-Binet Intelligence Scale

The Stanford-Binet Intelligence Scale was originally devised as an age scale. The scale is comprised of 142 items or tests which are administered separately to the examinee. The tests are grouped into age levels from age two through superior adult. From ages two to five, the tests are divided by half-year intervals. This was done to accommodate the rapid changes in intellectual development during these early years. For ages six to fourteen, the age levels are partitioned into one-year intervals. Following these levels are the Average Adult level and Superior Adult levels I, II, and III. Each age level is comprised of six tests, except Average Adult, which contains eight tests. The tests at each level are approximately of similar difficulty and increase in difficulty with each successive age level. At each age level, an alternate test is also included. Alternate tests are used when one of the regular tests is spoiled because of administrative problems or errors, or because of the characteristics or handicap of the examinee which would make administration inappropriate (i.e., a motor test for a cerebral palsied child).

In practice with the Stanford-Binet, no person takes all the tests. Testing is usually begun at a given age level after consideration of the child's chronological age, performance on the initial vocabulary test of the Binet, background information, and the reason for referral or testing (Sattler 1982). Once a starting point has been determined, the examiner first must establish a *basal age,* which is the age level at which the child passes all six items. The examiner then continues upward, giving the child credit for each item passed until an age level is reached in which the child fails all six items. This is called the *ceiling age.* At this point, the test is discontinued. The total amount of credit is then calculated and converted into a *Mental Age* (MA). The child's Mental Age score is then compared to others of the same chronological age, which results in a single deviation IQ score. The mean IQ for the Binet is 100 with a standard deviation of 16.

An examinee will generally show some degree of scatter in his or her pattern of successes and failures among adjacent age levels. It should be kept in mind that the MA score is an average composite of the child's successes and failures; thus children will both pass items above their MA and fail items below their MA.

Our major task in intelligence testing is to determine the child's overall level of intellectual functioning and to discern any meaningful strengths or weaknesses which may be derived from the analysis of the child's profile of scores.

There are a number of important issues which need to be considered when interpreting the Stanford-Binet. First, content and factorial analyses of the Binet reveal that the distribution of test content varies considerably within the lower age levels; thus different age levels may measure different aspects of intelligence. Additionally, while the Binet is factorially more complex at lower age levels, with increasing age, it becomes more of a primarily verbal-factor test (Anastasi 1982, Sattler 1982). In an attempt fo classify the types of behaviors assessed on the Binet and therefore aid in interpretation, various classification systems have been proposed. These include: Sattler's (1965) Binetgram, which groups items into the seven categories of language, memory, conceptual thinking, reasoning, numerical reasoning, visual-motor, and social intelligence; Valett's (1964) classification of six item groupings of general comprehension, visual-motor ability, arithmetic reasoning, memory and concentration, vocabulary and verbal fluency, and judgment and reasoning; and

Meeker's (1969) classification based on Guilford's (1967) Structure of the Intellect model. These classification systems allow the psychologist to examine the child's pattern of successes and failures in different functions and may provide helpful clues for further clinical exploration (Anastasi 1982). Information gathered from these types of procedures should be treated cautiously since, in most cases, the categories were generated on an intuitive rather than empirical basis. In addition, several functions are represented by only a small number of tests and content sampling varies greatly from one age level to another. For example, on the Binetgram, only one numerical reasoning task is contained from year two to eight, whereas language contained fifteen.

A second interpretative task involves determining the relative significance of a child's successes or failures. That is to say, relative to himself or herself (intraindividual comparison) or to other children his or her age (intergroup comparison), do the obtained high and low scores reflect significant strengths or weaknesses, or do these scores represent chance fluctuations? Sattler (1974) initially developed the Standard Deviation (SD) technique for the Binet, which is based on the assumption that tests passed or failed within one SD of the child's chronological age or mental age represent normal fluctuation in ability. Tests failed below one SD are potential weaknesses, whereas those passed above are potential strengths. Both Kaufman and Waterstreet (1978) and Chase and Sattler (1980) have refined Sattler's initial technique and have provided convenient tables in which normal bands of variability (± 1 SD) are cited for both MA or intraindividual and chronological age (CA) or intergroup comparison points. The reader is referred to these articles for a more detailed explanation of the SD method.

A third point involves the interpretation of the MA. As previously pointed out in the A. Kaufman chapter, as well as by a variety of other authors (Fischman, Proger, and Duffy 1976, Thompson 1977, Salvia, Ysseldyke, and Lee 1975), the MA concept of the Stanford-Binet lost its meaning with the 1972 restandardization. That is to say, MA no longer corresponds numerically to CA (Sattler 1982). Thus, if a five-year-old child earned an MA of 5-0, his or her IQ would be 91. In order to earn an IQ of 100, the child would have to earn an MA of 5-6. In order to correct for this disparity between CA and MA, Shorr, McClelland, and Robinson (1977) calculated a table of statistically adjusted MA scores, so that there is a better correspondence between MA and CA, as existed in previous forms of the Binet. These adjusted MA scores allow for a more accurate description of the age-level performance of the child.

The Stanford-Binet performance of various groups of excep-

TABLE 8.1

Description of WISC-R Subtests*

Verbal Scale	
Information	This subtest measures the fund of general factual knowledge acquired primarily through cultural and educational experiences.
Similarities	Items require abstract or categorical thinking skills in identifying commonalities between two verbal concepts.
Arithmetic	This subtest assesses numerical reasoning in which the child demonstrates mental computational skills in response to orally presented arithmetic problems.
Vocabulary	The vocabulary subtest assesses language development and word knowledge based on the child's ability to define words.
Comprehension	This subtest assesses the ability to show common sense and judgment within social situations.
Digit Span	Items require immediate auditory memory for orally presented strings of digits.

Performance Scale	
Picture Completion	The test assesses the ability to detect missing parts from a familiar object.
Picture Arrangement	This subtest measures the ability to anticipate, sequence, and comprehend social realities by requiring the child to order pictures in a correct sequence to produce a logically correct story.
Block Design	This task requires visual organization and analysis in reproducing abstract designs from blocks.
Object Assembly	This task measures part-whole understanding in solving a puzzle.
Coding	The Coding subtest involves learning number-symbol associations and copying them on paper.
Mazes	This measures the capacity for foresight and the ability to follow a visual pattern in working with progressively difficult mazes.

*Adapted in part from Kaufman (1979a) and Salvia and Ysseldyke (1981).

of robust Verbal Comprehension and Perceptual Organization factors across a wide variety of normal and exceptional populations of differing age groups. The Verbal Comprehension factor was comprised of the five regularly administered verbal subtests with the Arithmetic showing the lowest factor loading. The Perceptual Organization factor was comprised on all performance subtests except Coding. In addition, in eight of the ten factor analytic studies cited by Kauman, a Freedom from Distractibility factor was found to emerge, consisting of the Arithmetic, Digit Span, and Coding subtests.

These results suggest that for groups of normal and exceptional children, Wechsler's Vebal-Performance dichotomy reflects real and meaningful differences in domains of cognitive abilities, thereby suggesting that profile analysis should begin with comparisons of the Verbal and Performance IQs which generally resemble these factors. The Freedom from Distractibility factor, which was found to be much less robust than the Verbal Comprehension and Perceptual Organization factors, was found to emerge in the majority of factor analytic studies. However, the third factor should be considered in WISC-R interpretation, particularly when these scores deviate from their respective Scale means. Excellent guidelines for the interpretation of the Freedom from Distractibility factor are provided by Kaufman (1979a, 1979b).

Many studies have examined Verbal-Performance IQ differences among various groups of exceptional children. However, as Kaufman (1979b) asserts, we must first be aware that in the WISC-R standardization sample, the average child showed a Verbal-Performance discrepancy of nearly 10 points. Within this frame of reference, Kaufman believes that it is only when the discrepancy is significant or rare, does the Verbal-Performance discrepancy have possible diagnostic meaningfulness. Additionally, a difference in Verbal-Performance scores may be suggestive of real differences concerning the child's functioning in nonverbal and verbal abilities, which may have educational rather than diagnostic significance by possibly suggesting one type of remedial strategy over another (Kaufman 1979b). Summaries of research dealing with Verbal-Performance IQ discrepancies of learning disabled (Kaufman 1979b, Sattler 1982), mentally retarded (Nagle, 1982), and emotionally disturbed children (Sattler 1982) have not found consistently significant differences.

An additional avenue of WISC-R research has involved the analysis of subtest scores for groups of children with various exceptionalities. For example, Kaufman (1979b) summarized the performance of learning-disabled children from existing research and found with some consistency that certain subtests tended to be more difficult for these children than others. The subtest rankings from easy to difficult were: (1) Object Assembly, (2) Picture Completion, (3) Picture Arrangement, (4) Block Design, (5) Comprehension, (6) Similarities, (7) Vocabulary, (8) Coding, (9) Arithmetic, and (10) Information. Using Bannatyne's (1974) classification system, Kaufman concluded that these groups of children exhibited strong "Spatial Ability" (Picture Completion, Object Assembly, Block Design), moderate "Verbal Comprehension Ability" (Similarities, Vocabulary, Comprehension), weak "Sequencing Ability" (Arithmetic, Coding, Digit Span), and very poor "Acquired Knowledge Ability" (Information, Arithmetic, Vocabulary).

Using a similar ranking system, Nagle (1982) examined WISC-R subtest differences for mentally retarded children from existing research. Nagle found the following rankings from easy to difficult: (1) Picture Completion, (2) Object Assembly, (3) Comprehension, (4) Coding, (5) Picture Arrangement, (6) Block Design, (7) Arithmetic, (8) Similarities, (9) Information, and (10) Vocabulary. Retarded children, like learning-disabled children, show relatively high Spatial Ability and low Acquired Knowledge. Sequencing Ability presents less of a problem than Verbal Comprehension Ability for retarded youngsters.

There are no subtest patterns which have been found to differentiate reliably between groups of emotionally disturbed children (Sattler, 1982); however, there is some evidence that these children tend to show more variability of subtest scores. Furthermore, juvenile delinquents have been found to show poorer Verbal IQ than Performance IQs, but these differences can be largely attributable to associated factors such as social class background, and level of academic achievement and self-control (Sattler 1982).

It should be kept in mind that this brief overview of characteristic profiles is based on group means, and therefore does not tell us about individuals within the group (Anastasi 1982, Kaufman 1979b). Profile interpretation is an individual, child-based process in which the psychologist must synthesize relevant background information as well as intra-test session behavior.

Interpretation of Intelligence Test Performance

The proper interpretation of a child's performance on an intelligence test requires that we try to understand *why* the youngster performed the way he or she did, and not just how well the child did (Kaufman 1979a). Interpretation first requires that we integrate the test findings with the child's educational and sociocultural background.

The test session provides the examining psychologist the opportunity to observe the child's behavior under a variety of different circumstances. Such aspects as the child's interpersonal skills with the examiner, motivation, verbal skills, distractibility, motor skills, approach to test items, problem-solving strategies, and reactions to success and failure can be readily observed in the test session. Since there are many behaviors which can affect a test performance besides the demands of the task itself, test interpretation must integrate behavioral observations of the child and his or her performance.

Several authors (Aliotti 1977, Kratochwill 1977) have advocated a more comprehensive mode of psychoeducational assessment which would include an evaluation of the "processes" used by different children during assessment. An example of this line of thought would be the "testing-the-limits" procedure. This procedure is used to understand more fully why a child experienced difficulty on a particular task. "Testing-the-limits" involves readministering a task under modified or unstandardized procedures after the task was given under standardized conditions. These modifications may involve changing directions, providing some clues to problem solutions, teaching task subskills, etc., to assess whether task performance would change. "Testing-the-limits" procedures are not included in our scoring since any deviation from standardized procedures invalidates the use of norms, which were established on the premise of uniformity of procedures. The value of "process" variables in the psychoeducational evaluation is to gain additional information about the child's learning style which later will be relevant to planning remedial interventions. In addition, "process" variables also help us interpret the child's profile and allow the examiner to generate hypotheses about the nature of the child's performance. Many of these hypotheses will need to be considered further through the use of supplemental testing. Psychologists have at their disposal a variety of supplemental tests assessing very specific behavioral domains, such as motor development, impulsivity, language development, visual-motor skills, auditory perception, basic concept development, and visual and auditory memory, which may be used to verify or disconfirm the hypotheses which were generated previously. For descriptions of these various tests, the reader is referred to Salvia and Ysseldyke (1981).

More recently, Brooks (1979) has emphasized that we expand "process" variables to include affective or emotional components. With knowledge of a child's coping style and ability to form alliances with the examiner, we may be able to glean information about the child which might be useful when instruction efforts aimed at helping the child are carried out.

Performance on IQ tests is invariably compared to the test

norms, so that the child's performance can be compared to those of his or her age-mates. Classification systems help us differentiate between various exceptionalities. As we previously discussed, the exceptionalities of mental retardation and learning disabilities place central importance on ability level. It should always be kept in mind that with IQ assessment, there is always a certain amount of error in our measurement which needs to be considered in the interpretation of individual test scores. Unfortunately, few definitional guidelines take this statistical phenomenon into account; thus it is necessary for the school psychologist to consider this during test interpretation. Based on the child's level of measured intellectual functioning, we can generate some level of expectancy of how well the child should be achieving in his or her academic skills.

ACHIEVEMENT TESTING

The most frequently used type of test in schools is the achievement test. The aim of achievement testing is to measure academic progress up to a particular point in time (Nunnally 1972). Although we may have information about the child's academic skills from his or her school records or the results of group achievement tests prior to referral, individual tests of academic achievement are most appropriate for individual educational planning. Nevertheless, data from group-administered tests should be considered in the assessment process, because they may provide a different sampling of content areas than some commonly used individual achievement tests. Test of individual academic achievement are usually comprised of at least the three basic skill areas of reading, spelling, and arithmetic. Despite the fact that many of the more popular individual achievement tests evaluate the same content areas, the manner and extent in which they are evaluated may vary somewhat. For example, when we compare the commonly used Wide Range Achievement Test (WRAT) and the Peabody Individual Achievement Test (PIAT), both include a spelling subtest. In both tests, the examiner says the word, reads the word in a sentence, and then says the word again. On the WRAT, the child is required to write the word correctly, whereas on the PIAT the child is asked to choose one of four words printed on a page which correctly corresponds to the stimulus word. It is obvious that the demand characteristics of both tasks vary, even though both are labeled spelling. It would be well, therefore, for the examining psychologist to consider both *what* is being assessed and *how* it is being assessed.

Individual achievement tests also vary in the extent to which they evaluate in given skill areas. Some individual achievement tests are best suited to appraise how well the child's general skill development compares to others at his or her age or grade level, whereas other individual tests, labeled diagnostic tests, provide a much more detailed and precise analysis of a child's strengths and weaknesses within a given subject area. The use of these two types of individual achievement tests are complementary. Standard achievement tests can detect general deficiencies in particular content areas, while diagnostic tests detect specific deficiencies in subskills within the content area. Obviously, diagnostic tests usually provide better information, which can more readily be adapted to remedial or intervention strategies. The precision of the standard achievement measures can be enhanced if the examiner analyzes and categorizes the types of errors the child makes during testing. For example, Wallace and Larsen (1978) provide examples of several systems designed to analyze oral reading errors. Such procedures can serve as a guide to remedial instruction, but they can also allow the school psychologist to choose the most appropriate diagnostic test, i.e., the instrument which will provide the best analysis, given the nature of the child's strengths and weaknesses. It is also useful sometimes to perform an analysis of errors during oral reading using the child's textbooks, which may give the examiner a more valid appraisal of the child's reading performance in the classroom.

Most achievement tests are norm-referenced, which means that an individual's performance is compared to others in some specified group (usually age or grade level) so that we are provided some index of the child's standing relative to the group. Norm-referenced testing is based on relative standards and answers the question, "How is this student doing in comparison to his or her peers?" In criterion-referenced testing, we are more interested in the pupil's level of mastery of specific skills; therefore, it is based on absolute standards and answers the question, "What can this child do?" In dealing with individual instructional programming, criterion-referenced testing is preferable if it is closely integrated with instruction. According to Salvia and Ysseldyke (1981), the essential point in evaluating individual progress is to determine the degree to which the student is meeting learning objectives that have been established. Norm-referenced tests, in general, sample too few behaviors to represent accurately a student's progress (Salvia and Ysseldyke 1981). Norm-referenced tests, however, appear to be best suited for some placement decisions, since the psychologist must determine, given a child's intellectual status, how deviant his achievement level is. Thus, decisions regarding individuals can be aided by both norm- and criterion-referenced testing.

THE APPRAISAL OF ADAPTIVE BEHAVIOR

Psychologists are increasingly using pluralistic methods in the assessment of children suspected of mental retardation. In accord with the current AAMD standards and many state placement guidelines, a child can be classified as mentally retarded only if he or she shows significant deficits in measures of both intellectual functioning and adaptive behavior. Adaptive behavior refers to the degree to which one meets standards of personal independence and social responsibility appropriate to one's age and sociocultural group. Although the importance of adaptive behavior has long been recognized in special educational programming, the impetus to include adaptive behavior formally in the assessment process has arisen from federal mandates and various litigations filed against school systems, which have challenged the placement of minority-group children in special classes solely on the basis of an IQ score (Lambert, Windmiller, Cole, and Figueroa 1975). The basic argument, according to Lambert et al., is that minority children are penalized by standardized IQ tests which provide estimates of how well the child will succeed academically but do not provide information about the child's ability to meet the societal and personal demands of everyday living. It is further argued that many minority children do poorly on intelligence tests because they lack opportunities to acquire the cognitive skills and knowledge necessary to perform well on such tests.

Arguments that advocate using both intelligence tests and a systematic appraisal of adaptive behavior in the evaluation process imply that adaptive behavior and intelligence are distinctively different constructs. One basic difference between adaptive behavior and intelligence constructs is the differing emphases they give to everyday behavior and thought processes (Meyers, Nihira, Zetlin 1979). The concept of measured intelligence was formulated from the need to make objective assessments of an individual's potential in the area of academic achievement, whereas adaptive behavior or social competency places emphasis on the individual's current ability to meet the demands of his or her environment, of which most are nonacademic in nature (Meyers et al. 1979). If IQ and adaptive behavior are separate constructs, then scores obtained in these areas should show little or no relationship to one another.

Among the most commonly used measures of adaptive behavior are the Vineland Social Maturity Scale (VSMS), the AAMD Adaptive Behavior Scale (ABS), and the Adaptive Behavior Inventory for Children (ABIC) of the System of Multicultural Pluralistic Assessment. All these scales have been shown to have low correlations with measures of intellectual ability (Meyers et al. 1979), thereby demonstrating that the construct of adaptive behavior is relatively independent of intellectual factors.

The most ambitious addition in nonbiased assessment has been the recently published System of Multicultural Pluralistic Assessment (SOMPA) by Mercer and Lewis (1978). The SOMPA is a system of tests designed to assess children of different sociocultural backgrounds from the perspective of a Medical Model, Social System Model, and a Pluralistic Model. (See Mercer [1979] for a full description of these three assessment models.) The most controversial aspect of the SOMPA involves the way WISC-R scores are interpreted. In the SOMPA, an IQ score is transformed into an Estimated Learning Potential (ELP) score, in which an individual child's performance on the WISC-R is compared to those of other children from similar sociocultural backgrounds as measured by the SOMPA's four sociocultural (SC) scales (Family Size, Family Structure, Socioeconomic Status, and Urban Acculturation). ELP distributions for each ethnic group, averaging 100, are based on regression equations derived from the SOMPA standardization sample. Brown (1979), in an excellent discussion, has voiced a cautious attitude toward the SOMPA in view of the paucity of validity studies of the proposed measures. This is particularly crucial to ELP's in which strong rational arguments can support its usage but empirical data cannot at the present time. The usefulness of the SOMPA will need to be demonstrated in future research and school psychological practice.

THE FINAL STAGES OF ASSESSMENT

Once the evaluation procedures are complete, the task of the school psychologist consists of the analysis, synthesis, and integration of all the relevant information gathered during the assessment process, including past histories, interviews, behavioral observations from the classroom setting, and test performances. These data are drawn together in a psychological report which generally serves as the main source of communication between the psychologist and other personnel who are involved in the educational planning of the child (Sattler 1974). The report should provide a qualitative and quantitative description of the child's performance, including such aspects as the child's strengths and weaknesses, the quality and style of cognitive and social functioning, inter-test comparisons (i.e., aptitude and achievement, intelligence, and adaptive behavior), behavioral determinants of test performance, and other related factors. Within this descriptive analysis, a major focus should be to clarify the nature of the referral and specify, if possible, factors contributing to the problem. Lastly, recommendations are made regarding possible ways to intervene with the referral problem.

A primary concern in report writing is to compose the psychological report in language which is lucid and readily comprehensible to its reader. The main consumer of psychological reports in schools is the teacher. In reviewing research on teacher evaluation of psychological reports, Sattler (1974) has indicated that the highest-rated reports were those that contained helpful suggestions, clear answers to the referral problem, specific and meaningful interpretations, and awareness of classroom procedures. The poorly rated reports were those that were brief, not well organized, and inadequate in the formulation of results and recommendations. Sattler concluded that the most important factor for teachers in evaluating the reports was the quality of recommendations.

The ability of the school psychologist to make relevant recommendations is contingent not only on being able to understand the nature of the child's learning problem but also to suggest procedures which will be able to ameliorate these problems. It is extremely important for school psychologists to have an understanding of interventive and remedial strategies (see Chapter 12 for descriptions of such strategies), and to know which of these strategies would be most practical or feasible given the child's educational environment. If several kinds of classroom interventions appear to be appropriate, it is generally desirable to discuss these alternatives with the teacher, who may be able to provide additional information and help in selecting the most appropriate intervention to adopt. The prior steps in the assessment process involving teacher interviews and classroom observations greatly facilitate intervention design.

One problem with some school psychological services is that appropriate follow-up is neglected. But assessment does not end once an intervention strategy has been implemented. Continuous follow-up is needed to determine the child's ongoing progress or lack of progress with the behavioral objectives of the intervention. The psychologist should serve as a consultant to the teacher, so that the necessary adjustments will be made in the intervention program.

Depending on the severity of the child's problem, placement in a special educational program may be recommended. It is usually beneficial to hold a feedback conference with the parents about their child's test results before the formal placement staffing or case conference. It is likewise important to hold similar sessions after assessment when special class placement is not a viable alternative. When communicating results to parents, there are two basic principles the psychologist should keep in mind. "First, parents have the right to know whatever the school knows about the abilities, the performance, and the problems of their children; and, second, the school has the obligation to communicate understandable and usable knowledge" (Psychological Corporation 1980, p. 1). The parents' right to know cannot be argued. It is the responsibility and right of parents to act as advocates in educational decision making affecting their child.

The school psychologist can do several things to prepare the parents so they more fully understand the child's test results (Losen and Diament 1978, Psychological Corporation 1980). First, parents need to understand what the test does and does not measure. Second, they need to know the extent to which the test information supplies information which is relevant to the child. And finally, the level of variability that is likely to be present in the test scores should be explained.

There is no single procedure that comprises the most appropriate means of reporting test results to parents. Nevertheless, it is important to (1) describe the tests' value and weaknesses, (2) explain reasons for specific test selection, and (3) present possible uses that are to be made with the test results (Psychological Corporation 1980). Many times, the school psychologist can facilitate parental understanding by qualitatively describing what the child has and has not mastered within a given subject or skill area.

When reporting achievement test results, it is best to express the child's performance through the use of percentile scores, since they are more easily understood than grade-level-equivalent scores. For example, if a test was given during the sixth month of the sixth grade, the student with a grade-level score of 6.6 would be described as achieving in accord with his or her grade level placement. If a child in the same class had a grade equivalent score of 8.3, this would mean that the child did as well as the average eighth grader in the third month of school on a *sixth grade test*. This does not mean that the child with a grade-level score of 8.3 has mastered eighth grade work, since there are many skills that eighth graders have acquired which are not assessed on the sixth grade test. Because of this potential for misunderstanding, grade equivalent scores probably should be avoided when reporting test results to parents. When test results are expressed in percentile scores, it is important (1) to tell the parents that percentile scores do not refer to the percent of questions answered correctly, but to the percent of children whose performance the child has equaled or exceeded, and (2) that the reference group used to compare the child's performance be specified (Psychological Corporation 1980). For example, depending on the census tract characteristics of the local population, the use of national, state, and local norms could portray a different set of percentile scores.

Percentile scores also provide a useful means of presenting intellectual test scores as well as IQ ranges (i.e., "Average", "Bright-Average") which are specified in the test manual. It is generally believed that statements regarding ability scores in isolation serve no constructive purpose (Psychological Corporation 1980). Perhaps the most sensible presentation of an intelligence test score is to compare it with the child's achievement level, which is perhaps the most basic use of an aptitude test score. It is also important to stress to parents that many factors influence intellectual functioning and that IQs are not a fixed or innate characteristic of the child.

When parent conferences are undertaken before a placement meeting, the school psychologist is in a position to serve as a facilitator of the parental advocate role. Turnbull and Leonard (1980) have argued that in order for parents to assume a constructive role in placement or IEP meetings, they must have adequate knowledge and decision making skills. By working with parents to assure active involvement in these meetings, the school psychologist also contributes to the well-being of the child.

CONCLUDING COMMENTS

The present chapter has outlined the multifaceted nature of the assessment process. Current assessment procedures emphasize the inextricable link between assessment and intervention. With increased pressures for accountability, educators are seeking increased assistance in implementing educational strategies which will meet the child's needs. In view of the importance of the link between assessment and intervention, we must continue to expand or modify our assessment proedures so that they may be more relevant to program planning. The incorporation of behavioral assessment and the evaluation of cognitive and affective "processes" are just a few examples of improving the assessment process.

The ability to select the most relevant test, given the nature of the referral problem, is of utmost importance. It is necessary for the school psychologist to ascertain the types of decisions that can be made with the greatest validity using particular types of test data.

School psychologists must be cognizant of the needs of parents and teachers. The establishment of relationships with these significant others during the assessment process will only serve to enhance later intervention efforts.

REFERENCES

Achenbach, T. Comparison of Stanford-Binet performance of nonretarded and retarded persons matched for MA and sex. *American Journal of Mental Deficiency,* 1970, *74,* 488–494.

Aliotti, N. C. Covert assessment in psychoeducational testing. *Psychology in the Schools,* 1977, *14,* 438–443.

American Psychological Association, American Educational Research Association, & National Council of Measurement in Education. *Standards for educational and psychological tests.* Washington, D.C.: American Psychological Association, 1974.

Anastasi, A. *Psychological testing* (4th ed.). New York: Macmillan, 1976.

Anastasi, A. *Psychological testing* (5th ed.). New York: Macmillan, 1982.

Bannatyne, A. Diagnosis: A note of recategorization of the WISC scaled scores, *Journal of Learning Disabilities,* 1974, *7,* 272–274.

Boehm, A. E. & Weinberg, R. *The classroom observer.* New York: Teachers College Press, 1977.

Brooks, R. Psychoeducational assessment: A broader perspective. *Professional Psychology,* 1979, *10,* 708–722.

Brown, F. The SOMPA: A system of measuring potential abilities. *School Psychology Digest,* 1979, *8,* 37–46.

Chase, C., & Sattler, T. M. Determining areas of strengths and weaknesses on the Stanford-Binet. *School Psychology Review,* 1980, *9,* 174–177.

Ciminero, A. R., & Drabman, R. S. Current developments in the behavioral assessment of children. In B. Lahey & A. E. Kazdin (Eds.), *Advances in clinical child psychology.* New York: Plenum Press, 1977.

Evans, P., & Richmond, B. A practitioner's comparison: The 1972 Stanford-Binet and the WISC-R. *Psychology in the Schools,* 1976, *13,* 9–14.

Federal Register, December 29, 1977.

Fischman, R., Proger, B., & Duffy, J. The Stanford-Binet revisited: A comparison of the 1960 and 1972 revisions of the Stanford-Binet Intelligence Scale. *Journal of Special Education,* 1976, *10,* 83–90.

Grossman, H. *Manual for terminology and classification in mental retardation* (1977 rev.). Washington, D.C.: American Association of Mental Deficiency, 1977.

Guilford, J. P. *The nature of human intelligence.* New York: McGraw-Hill, 1967.

Kaufman, A. S. *Intelligent testing with the WISC-R.* New York: Wiley, 1979. (a)

Kaufman, A. S. WISC-R research: Implications for interpretation. *School Psychology Digest,* 1979, *8,* 5–27. (b)

Kaufman, A. S., & Walterstreet, M. A. Determining a child's strong and weak areas of functioning on the Stanford-Binet: A simplification of Sattler's SD method. *Journal of School Psychology,* 1978, *16,* 72–78.

Kratochwill, T. R. The movement of psychological extras into ability testing. *Journal of Special Education,* 1977, *11,* 299–311.

Lambert, N., Windmiller, M., Cole, L., & Figueroa, R. *Manual of AAMD Adap-*

tive Behavior Scale, Public-school version (1974 rev.). Washington, D.C.: American Association on Mental Deficiency, 1975.

Lidz, C. S. *Improving assessment of school children.* San Francisco: Jossey-Bass, 1981.

Losen, S. M., & Diament, B. *Parent conferences in the schools: Procedures for developing effective partnership.* Boston: Allyn and Bacon, 1978.

Maloney, M. P., & Ward, M. P. *Psychological assessment: A conceptual approach.* New York: Oxford University Press, 1976.

Marholin, D., & Bijou, S. W. Behavioral assessment: Listen when the data speak. In D. Marholin (Ed.), *Child behavior therapy.* New York: Gardner Press, 1978.

Meeker, M. *The structure of intellect.* Columbus, Ohio: Charles E. Merrill, 1969.

Mercer, J. R. *SOMPA technical manual.* New York: Psychological Corporation, 1979.

Mercer, J. R., & Lewis, J. F. *System of Multicultural Pluralistic Assessment* (SOMPA). New York: The Psychology Corporation, 1978.

Mercer, J. R., & Richardson, J. C. Mental retardation as a social problem. In N. Hobbs (Ed.), *Issues in the classification of children* (Vol. II), San Francisco: Jossey-Bass, 1975.

Meyers, C. E., Nihira, K., & Zetlin, A. The measurement of adaptive behavior. In N. R. Ellis (Ed.), *Handbook of mental deficiency, psychological theory and research* (2nd ed.). Hillsdale, N.J.: Lawrence Erlbaum Associates, 1979.

Monroe, V. Roles and status of school psychology. In C. D. Phye & D. J. Reschly (Eds.), *School psychology: Perspectives and issues.* New York: Academic Press, 1979.

Nagle, R. J. The use of the WISC-R with mentally retarded children: Implications of research findings for interpretation. Unpublished manuscript, 1982.

Nunnally, J. *Educational measurement and evaluation.* New York: McGraw-Hill, 1972.

Psychological Corporation. *On telling parents about test results* (Test Service Notebook 154). New York: Psychological Corporation, 1980.

Salvia, J., & Ysseldyke, J. E. *Assessment in special and remedial education* (2nd ed.). Boston: Houghton Mifflin, 1981.

Salvia, J., Ysseldyke, J., & Lee, M. 1972 Revision of the Stanford-Binet: A farewell to mental age. *Psychology in the Schools,* 1975, *12,* 421–422.

Sarason, S. B. The unfortunate fate of Alfred Binet and school psychology. *Teachers College Record,* 1976, *77,* 579–592.

Sattler, J. M. Analysis of functions of the 1960 Stanford-Binet Intelligence Scale, Form L-M. *Journal of Clinical Psychology,* 1965, *21,* 173–179.

Sattler, J. M. *Assessment of children's intelligence* (rev. edn.). Philadelphia: J. B. Saunders, 1974.

Sattler, J. M. *The assessment of children's intelligence and special abilities.* Boston: Allyn and Bacon, 1982.

Shorr, D., McClelland, S., & Robinson, H. B. Corrected mental age scores for the

Stanford-Binet Intelligence Scale. *Measurement and Evaluation in Guidance,* 1977, *10,* 144–147.

Terman, L. M., & Merrill, M. A. *Stanford-Binet Intelligence Scale: 1972 norms edition.* Boston: Houghton-Mifflin, 1973.

Thompson, R. J. Consequences of using the 1972 Stanford-Binet Intelligence Scale Norms. *Psychology in the Schools,* 1977, *14,* 444–448.

Tindall, R. H. School psychology: The development of a profession. In C. D. Phye & D. J. Reschly (Eds.), *School Psychology: Perspectives and issues.* New York: Academic Press, 1979.

Turnbull, A. P., & Leonard, J. Parent involvement in special education: Emerging advocacy roles. *School Psychology Review,* 1981, *10,* 37–44.

Valett, R. A clinical profile for the Stanford-Binet. *Journal of School Psychology,* 1964, *2,* 49–54.

Waddell, D. D. The Stanford-Binet: An evaluation of the technical data available since the 1972 restandardization. *Journal of School Psychology,* 1980, *18,* 203–209.

Wallace, C., & Larsen, S. C. *Educational assessment of learning problems: Testing for teaching.* Boston: Allyn and Bacon, 1978.

Wechsler, D. *Manual for the Wechsler Intelligence Scale for Children – Revised (WISC-R).* New York: Psychological Corporation, 1974.

Wilson, R. *Criterion-referenced testing* (Test Service Notebook 37). New York: Psychological Corporation, 1980.

Ysseldyke, J. D. Issues in psychoeducational assessment. In G. D. Phye and D. J. Reschly (Eds.), *School Psychology: Perspectives and issues.* New York: Academic Press, 1979.

9

Projective Personality Assessment Techniques

JOHN E. OBRZUT AND STEVE ZUCKER

PROJECTIVE TECHNIQUES of personality assessment have achieved widespread clinical use. During the period from the 1930s through the early 1960s, there was a tremendous upsurge in the development and application of these techniques, as the major professional role of the clinician focused on assessment. These "tests" have been subjected to criticism and scrutinized by the scientific community since the inception of the Rorschach technique of personality assessment in 1921. Yet, not only have they weathered the storms of criticism, but now, in the sixth decade, the field is thriving, with techniques in various stages of development and with varying degrees of established validity and reliability. Their vigor and growth reflects the valuable tools they have proved themselves to be (Rabin and Haworth 1971).

In the present era, the role and function of the school psychologist has broadened to include focus on indirect, consultative service and a proactive emphasis on prevention as opposed to cure. However, assessment continues to be a major professional function, and projective techniques have become increasingly valuable tools to meet this need (Goh, Teslow, and Fuller 1980). Goh et al. (1980) reported on a national survey of psychological test use among school psychologists and found that approximately one half of a school psychologist's time is still devoted to assessment. Although substantial emphasis is placed on intellectual, academic, and perceptual-motor assessment, personality evaluation was found to be ranked fourth in importance. Among the personality assessment devices administered, behavioral measures accounted for only 8.6% of those used each year. This would suggest that school psychologists are "clinically" oriented and tend to use various types of projective tests in their approach to personality assessment.

In particular, the survey by Goh et al. found that school psychologists tend to prefer "quick, easy-to-use procedures (Bender-Gestalt, Sentence Completion, House-Tree-Person [HTP]) over more comprehensive, time-consuming techniques such as the TAT and Rorschach" (Goh, et al. 1980, p. 14). It was also noted that none of the objective measures was ranked among the most frequently used personality measures.

195

As Howes (1981) suggests, projective tests extend psychological testing beyond the routine collection of information and computation of IQs by providing insight into the dynamics of individual human personality. Projectives view personality in a global, holistic manner, rather than portraying it segmentally, as do objective personality inventories. In our judgment, projective tests can be viewed as the least nonbiased measures of personality functioning when they are not used in isolation.

HISTORICAL PERSPECTIVE

Piotrowski (1957) traces the ancestry of these techniques to ancient Greek artists who ruminated about the effect of stimulus ambiguity on the interpretation of objective reality, and to both Botticelli and Leonardo da Vinci, who specifically alluded to the usefulness of ambiguous stimuli in the process of creativity. It is known that da Vinci selected his students in part on the basis of their imaginative creations in response to ambiguous stimuli. The first formal projective technique was suggested by Sir Francis Galton in 1879, who discussed the possibility of using words to stimulate verbal associations. While it is unclear whether Galton's suggestions were ever carried out beyond mere pilot work, it is clear that Jung used the word-association technique better to understand the ideation of his patients (Exner 1976).

In 1895, Alfred Binet and Victor Henri proposed using inkblots to study visual imagination. In 1897 William Dearborn began to look at imaginative productions in the context of the individual's early life experiences, which is much of what one does today with projective techniques. Efforts at deriving normative data soon followed. Sharp, in 1899, attempted to develop typologies on the basis of imaginative responses, and Edwin Kirkpatrick in 1900 attempted the development of age norms, thereby relating quality of inkblot responses to the developmental process. In 1910, G. M. Whipple included inkblots to test "active imagination" in his battery of physical and mental tests, while Sir John Herbert Parsons in 1917 reported detailed age and sex differences in associations to a standard series of inkblots (Rabin 1968).

In 1910, Hermann Rorschach began his study of inkblot interpretations as a way to differentiate between various types of psychopathology. His important work in developing the Rorschach technique of personality assessment apparently began sometime after 1917 and was completed by 1920. The monograph *"Psychodiagnostik,"* published in 1921, reported the results of his "experiment" on various modes of perception and their relation to personality and psychopathology. The Rorschach technique was brought to the U.S. by David Levy, who introduced it to Samuel Beck, who in turn devised the first manual for the Rorschach method (Rabin 1968). However, the Rorschach was not readily accepted in the professional community, and it was not until the mid-1940s that extensive clinical use and empirical research with the instrument began.

In addition to the Rorschach technique, Henry Alexander Murray's Thematic Apperception Test (TAT) (1938) was an attempt to elicit meaningful responses to pictures. In 1905, Binet and Théodore Simon used such responses to assess intellectual development, and Brittain in 1907 wrote about his attempts at noting systematic sex differences in the stories told by his subjects and related these to the individual's broader social environment. In 1908, Libby used similar procedures with children and adolescents, and Schwartz in 1932 developed the Social Situation Test as an aid in interviewing delinquent boys (Rabin 1968, Bellak 1975). The TAT was first described by Morgan and Murray (1935); however, it was not until 1938 when Murray published *Exploration in Personality,* that the TAT gained its popularity. It was at this time that Murray introduced the term *projective test* to describe methods which attempt to "discover the covert (inhibited) and unconscious (partially repressed) tendencies of normal persons by stimulating the imaginative processes and facilitating their expression in words or in action" (Murray 1938).

The popularity and utility of the TAT led the way to the development of similar verbal and picture tests designed to meet the needs of various age groups, such as the Children's Apperception Test (CAT) (Bellak 1949), and the Picture Story Test (Symonds 1948) for use with adolescents.

Following the growth in popularity and use of the Rorschach and TAT, many new projective techniques were developed, accompanied by growing debate concerning their purpose, validity, and reliability.

In conjunction with the TAT, projective drawings appear to be the most frequent supplement to the Rorschach and have become a standard part of the test battery. Both the House-Tree-Person (Buck 1948) and Machover's Figure Drawing Technique (1949) developed out of experience using figure drawings as measures of intelligence. It became apparent that significant qualitative clues to the functioning of the total personality were evident in the symbolic speech of figure drawings, which seemed determined by the child's conscious and unconscious perception of self and the significant people in his or her environment.

While there has been a proliferation of methods which can serve to increase the understanding of a given individual, some are untested and therefore of tenuous validity. However, it is recognized that no projective test can be better, more valid, or more reliable than the psychologist's skill in the use of them in the clinical or school setting. The careful integration of several techniques, in conjunction with observations and historical data, can prove to be of great value towards understanding any given child.

Projective methods continue to flourish in clinical settings, as does the controversy which surrounds their use. Some of the controversy is related to the appropriate use of projective techniques. Their use requires a sound theoretical background in the psychodynamic approach to personality development. For example, it is imperative for the school psychologist to understand the assumptions underlying these techniques and to acknowledge the problems of reliability and validity. The following section will address several of these theoretical issues.

THEORETICAL AND EMPIRICAL ISSUES

Freud initially used the term *projection* to describe a defense mechanism of the ego, whereby the individual ascribes certain unacceptable and disturbing impulses or strivings to others in the outside world. While projection today is widely viewed in terms of its pathological or defensive function, Freud in his later writings extended the meaning of the term: "Projection is not specially created for the purpose of defense, it also comes into being where there are no conflicts . . . inner perception of ideational and emotional processes are projected outwardly like sense perceptions and are used to shape the outer world" (Freud 1938, p. 857). Freud's assumption, then, is that when an individual is asked to impose meaning or order on an ambiguous or unstructured stimulus or situation, his or her responses will be a projection (or reflection) of inner needs, desires, or conflicts. That all behavior manifestations are expressive of an individual's personality is inherent in this hypothesis. This fundamental assumption appears well supported in the literature (Lindzey 1952).

Several corollary assumptions have been derived from the projective hypothesis (Murstein 1961). One of the most widely held assumptions is that ambiguity of test items is directly related to the amount of subject projection. However, the relationship is more complex than it appears. In the case of Thematic Apperceptive Test techniques, there appears to be a curvilinear (rather than linear) relationship, with stimuli of moderate ambiguity eliciting the greatest amount of projective data (Murstein 1961).

Two other widely held assumptions are that: (1) the strength of a need is a function of its direct or symbolic manifestation on the projective technique, and (2) there is a parallel between projective test behavior and the individual's behavior in the environment. However, it appears there is no simple relationship between projective test responses and behavior, and the strength of a psychological need is only one of many variables which need consideration. Murstein (1961) has proposed a useful framework that considers the total situation in assessing need strength and making behavioral predictions. He contends that the individual's response is a function of the following variables: the projective stimulus properties, the perceived purpose of the testing, the individual's experiences, needs and expectations, and the examiner's instructions and his or her interpersonal influences or bias.

For example, Mussen and Naylor (1954) hypothesized that lower-class children who show a high amount of fantasy aggression and a low fear of punishment relative to their aggressive needs would display more overt aggression than those with few fantasy (projected) aggressive needs and a high fear of punishment relative to those needs. Their hypothesis was strongly supported ($p = < .003$) and thus indicates the need to consider variables other than the need strength itself.

Lesser (1957) examined environmental factors which would enhance the prediction from fantasy aggression to overt behavior. He found a greater degree of correspondence between fantasy and overt aggression in children for whom there was maternal encouragement of aggression than in cases where there was maternal disapproval.

Kagan (1956) found a significant positive relationship between fantasy and overt aggression in children when: (1) the stimulus material was suggestive of aggressive content; and (2) when the overt and fantasy behavior were similar in their mode of expression (i.e., predicting fighting behavior from fighting themes). Kagan further suggests that anxiety over expression of aggression may inhibit its expression, even if the stimulus is strongly cued in that direction.

Leary (1957) suggests a multilevel framework with which to view personality. Level I considers how the individual is perceived by others (observable behavior). Level II is essentially how the individual views him- or herself (the conscious-self concept). Level III, the level of private symbolization, considers unconscious processes and is said by Leary to be measured by projective techniques. Any projective technique, however, will likely tap several levels of personality simultaneously.

Using Leary's approach, one may be studying a child who is not viewed as aggressive by classmates or the teacher (Level I), who does not perceive him- or herself as aggressive (Level II), yet whose projective responses reveal a great deal of anger (Level III). A thorough understanding of the child would require consideration of all three levels. The child may be seething with anger, yet may repress and thus be unaware of these urges due to the anxiety or guilt which is aroused by their expression.

Murstein and Wolf (1970) report a significant correlation between amount of projection and the degree of psychopathology as rated by trained clinicians. It appears that normal subjects are able to censor their responses on more structured, Level I tests, but are less able to censor their responses and thus will project more "unconscious" material to highly ambiguous, Level III tests (such as the Rorschach). Psychiatric patients, on the other hand, expressed an equal degree of projection (and thus psychopathology), regardless of the level of stimulus structure.

It is quite clear that such factors as the individual's willingness to reveal self, ego involvement in the task, variables which serve to inhibit need expression, the specific stimulus properties of the projective materials, the setting of the test situation and examiner effects, and the theoretical framework are all factors which must be considered when interpreting a projective protocol.

Reliability, Validity, and Meaningfulness

The reliability, validity, and meaningfulness of a projective test battery are affected to a large extent by the examiner's experience with the tests, orientation to personality development, and familiarity with the subject's background. Many studies have shown various techniques to have considerable reliability and validity, particularly in the hands of a skilled clinician, while others have demonstrated projective techniques to have questionable validity. Part of the problem arises from the divergent definitions given to the concept of validity. Some authors look for a test's correlation with some criterion measure (psychiatric diagnosis or performance on another "validated" instrument) and others look for correlation coefficients between raw and "true" (error-free) scores. For some, validity means utility and others stress the interpretability of test scores (Ebel 1961).

Projective techniques are intended to measure and describe psychological constructs and to allow psychologists to make appropriate inferences about an individual's personality and behavior. The APA *Standards for Educational and Psychological Tests* (APA 1974) describes a psychological construct as "a dimension understood or inferred from its network of interrelationships" (p. 29). Construct validity is appropriate when the examiner has no single alternative criterion which is known to measure a specific trait. "Evidence of construct validity is not found in a single study; rather, judgments of construct validity are based upon an accumulation of research results" (p. 30).

The process of validation of projective techniques seems more similar to validating an experimental hypothesis than to validating a more traditional psychological/educational test (Ainsworth 1951). No single coefficient can be provided to demonstrate the validity of a particular projective technique. Validity coefficients are situation specific and may provide support for a specific hypothesis about a particular technique and/or the underlying trait or process it is presumed to measure. It is reasonable to view the accumulated research as an interrelated network of data which, when viewed collectively, lends support to the construct of projective testing.

Singer (1968) provided an extensive review of the literature on the research applications of projective methods, citing a multitude of studies which provide considerable support for the validity of projective interpretations and the continued use of these techniques. When one considers the growing popularity and continued use of projective techniques (Howes 1981), there is surprisingly little recent research on the validity and reliability of these methods in general. A computer search for the years 1975–81 turned up only a handful of studies which primarily and specifically address these issues as applied to children and adolescents. Some of these studies are worth noting.

Miller and Hutt (1975) demonstrated a high retest reliability (.87 for males and .83 for females) as well as a high interjudge reliability (.89) for the psychopathology scale of the Hutt adaptation of the Bender-Gestalt Test over a two-week interval. Raskin and Pitcher (1977) provide support for projective interpretations of the Kinetic Family Drawing with kindergarten and first grade learning-disabled children. Schroth (1977) reports a high interscorer reliability for specific CAT scoring categories and suggests that interscorer reliability may increase as the age of the child increases. Kelly and Berg (1978) report test-retest reliability and internal consistency coefficients in the .70s for a group of 488 fourth and eighth grade children using the Family Story Test.

Examining the temporal stability of specific Rorschach scoring features over a three-year period, Exner, Armbruster and Viglione (1978) report coefficients of stability ranging from .66 to .90, with nine of the correlations in excess of .80. Fallstrom and Vegelius (1978) demonstrated the utility/validity of the Rorschach in differentiating diabetic from non-diabetic girls (ages 7–15). Kendra (1979) reports on the use of Rorschach protocols (scored blindly) in predicting which individuals would attempt suicide. Prediction levels were significantly above chance.

Hayden (1981), in a study using 67 emotionally disturbed children and adolescents, provided support for the interpretive view that responses to cards IV and VII on the Rorschach are representative of the child's relationship with his or her father and mother respectively. Howes (1981) provides a historical review of research on the Rorschach, citing many recent studies which support the reliability of the Rorschach as well as its predictive utility.

Criterion-related validity is an evaluation of the validity of the test based on its agreement with some other measure (criterion). However, while projective tests often fare poorly in predicting psychiatric diagnosis, studies have shown that the failure is related to the criterion measure rather than to the adequacy of the projective instrument. Not only does psychiatric diagnosis differ from setting to setting, but it varies considerably between clinicians within the same setting. While Schmidt and Fonda report nearly 80 percent agreement between pairs of psychiatrists on three major diagnostic categories (organic, psychotic, and characterological), "agreement with respect to diagnosis of the specific subtype of a disorder occurred in only about half of the cases and was almost absent in cases involving personality patterns, trait disorders and the psychoneuroses" (Schmidt and Fonda 1956, p. 266).

Predictive validity is also a questionable criterion because of the erroneous assumption that projective methods should have special predictive capabilities. However, the value of using projectives is to understand the person "as he or she is," not how "he or she will be." The overall aim in projective testing is to gain an understanding of the total personality, assessment of the strengths, weaknesses, and defenses, and an understanding of the individual's primary needs and desires and degree of satisfaction or frustration in meeting those needs (Exner 1976). When evaluating the reliability of projective techniques, one must consider the nature of the variable being measured. Test-retest reliability or consistency over time can only be considered relevant if the variable being measured is also consistent over time. Most of the traits and characteristics that are measured with projective devices are motivational and emotional in nature, and there is no reason to assume that these characteristics are temporally stable. However, numerous studies demonstrate substantial reliability for both the Rorschach and the TAT and for specific variables, even when lengthy periods exist between testings (Exner 1976).

Regarding internal consistency (split-half reliability), the questions of motivation, ego defense, and control must be considered. An emotional, cathartic release on Card 1 of the TAT may very likely be followed by a more controlled and benign story. Individuals must often pull back and regroup in the face of emotionally provocative stimuli. If the instrument is valid and reflects these changes, then reliability is essentially an irrelevant matter. While critics may cite poor split-half reliabilities as a shortcoming of projective techniques, the fact is that none of these methods was designed with equivalence of the stimuli as a goal! Rather, each specific part is expected to contribute to the whole, but not necessarily with the same weight or with the same impact for each subject (Exner 1976).

To add to the meaningfulness of a test, Ebel (1961) suggests the use of a battery of tests, in which the intercorrelations among the test results add to the meaningfulness of each test. Other factors which contribute to a test's meaningfulness are: operational definitions, reliability, norms, the importance or usefulness of the information the test provides, and its convenience in administration and use. Ebel is not suggesting we ignore traditional concepts of validity, but rather that we move away from the philosophical belief that quantifiable human traits and characteristics exist, independent of any operation used to measure them. The more information from a variety of sources that can be gathered and integrated to make inferences and draw conclusions, the more meaningful and valid those descriptions are likely to be.

Projection in Children

While the purposes of testing and the techniques employed may be similar in the evaluation of both children and adults, there are special considerations when evaluating young children. The child's perception of the test situation and ease of interaction with the examiner will likely affect, in varying degrees, the nature and content of the responses, as well as the overall productivity of the procedure. Therefore, while the child's age, developmental status, and verbal ability are factors which will influence the quantity and quality (or richness) of responses, the child's desire or willingness to reveal his or her personality may be to a large extent dependent on his or her overall mood and ease with the examiner and the test situation (Rabin and Haworth 1971).

The child and the projective responses obtained must each be evaluated from both a developmental and a normative perspective. Problems in distinguishing what is immature from what is aberrant are more acute in work with children than in work with adults (Altman 1971). What would be considered distorted responses and indications of pathology in adults may be merely signs of developmental immaturity in children. Due to their limited experience with, and knowledge of, the social and physical reality around them, as well as their limited verbal and abstract reasoning skills, their "distorted responses" cannot necessarily be taken to mean defensiveness, regression, or ego disintegration. The young child's Rorschach record, for example, may be more indicative of developmental status than of personality organization per se. For example, impulsive responses reflecting poor judgment and tenuous controls may be expected from a child of four or five who is just beginning to exercise control over his or her impulses. It is not until the age of six or seven that one begins to see patterns which reflect the child's general coping style (constriction, withdrawal, aggression, etc.).

In summary, the social setting of the test situation, the examiner's effects upon the child (and vice-versa), the child's shortened attention span and limited verbal skills, as well as his or her spontaneous and often revealing conversation are all factors that deserve special consideration in the testing of children and interpretation of results.

The following case illustrates the significance of the child's spontaneous verbalizations.

> Bobby was 7 years and 3 months old at the time of the psychological evaluation. His mother deserted the family when he was 4 years old and his father had placed him in residential care due to Bobby's uncontrollable outbursts of aggression. Bobby was keenly aware of and distressed by his deficits, particularly his visual-motor integrative difficulties, as evidenced in his poor Bender-Gestalt reproductions.
>
> In the middle of the WISC-R administration, with the increasing pressure of more difficult items, Bobby began shifting in his chair until he was lying down on it and said he didn't want to do any more. He finally withdrew to sitting on the floor, peering out from behind his chair. Even in this silent and frightened state, he could be gently coaxed to continue. From this frozen position he commented, while pointing to a toy (a small toy man inside a plastic container), "This guy's all locked up; he can't get out." It was clear that Bobby was vividly describing his own feelings at that moment. His final TAT story revealed his wishes and needs and his ability to experience great satisfaction from very basic pleasures. His face lit up as he told a story (to TAT Card 10) of "a man and a woman, going out on a date, happy, eating ice cream, cake, and soda and going home to sleep."

The following case illustrates the concept of projection in children and the importance of integrating historical, observational, and test data in drawing inferences and making predictions.

> At the time of testing, Sally was 10 years, 9 months of age. She was removed from her family six months prior to testing by the state Children's Protective Agency following an incident of severe maternal abuse. (While in a "trance-like" state, her mother attacked her with a knife,

leaving a deep scar around the entire front portion of her neck.) Following her discharge from the hospital (where she came close to death), her father's suggestion to the child was to "forget the whole thing," while her older sister advised, "just don't look in the mirror." Sally's family drawing (see Figure 9.1) is quite revealing of the trauma she experienced.

The absence of pupils in the eyes of her father and sister (third figure from left) may be interpreted as representative of their instructions to Sally to "forget the whole thing" and "just don't look in the mirror." The talon-like fingers symbolize the danger and aggression inherent in contact. Also revealing is the absence of a neck in both her mother and father, while present in her sister and herself. As the neck is often considered the link between the body (impulse life) and the head (intellect, rational control), one may conjecture about Sally's perception of her mother and father and their inability to control their impulses. Most revealing of her self-projection are the last two items included in the drawing. The little "devil's horns" on her head were followed by the drawing of the scarf around her neck, which in fact she always wore to hide the visible scar on her neck.

The interpretation of "devil's horns" is supported by one of her TAT

Figure 9.1

stories, which indicates her self-blame and guilt over her mother's assault. (Looking at Card 13 B): "This boy is thinking about his parents; they ran away." Interviewer: *What happened?* "They ran away. Maybe they want to live together, but they don't want to live with the little boy." *How does the boy feel?* "He feels bad. He'll call the police and they'll find them and ask them why they ran away and they'll say, "cause they don't want to live with him and he'll have to get another mother."

As the courts were to decide if the child should be placed back in her own home or if parental rights were to be severed and adoptive placement pursued, this story reflects Sally's dominant and realistic concern.

FREQUENTLY USED PROJECTIVE METHODS

The purpose of this section is to review projective assessment techniques used with children. It is an effort to compare the clinical utility and the empirical reliability/validity of the instruments. The instruments are divided into four groups: picture techniques, completion techniques—verbal, drawing techniques—nonverbal, and kinesthetic methods. Since the Rorschach method is not inclusive of the above categories, it will be discussed independently.

Rorschach Technique

The Rorschach was the first projective method to be used widely by the majority of clinicians interested in studying personality dynamics. The availability of this technique began to change the orientation of clinicians from making nomothetic comparisons to making idiographic comparisons of the individual. This change emphasized the unique needs, interests, pressures, conflicts, affective and cognitive styles, and coping strategies that characterize each person. Thus, the value of the Rorschach technique lies in its ability to provide a more concise and unique description of the person than that of other devices. The development of the test can be attributed primarily to the efforts of five scholars, each of whom approached the Rorschach from a unique theoretical and/or methodological point of view (Beck 1944, Klopfer and Davidson 1962, Hertz 1970, Piotrowski 1964, Rapaport 1946).

The administration of the test requires that the subject be given each of the ten inkblots twice. The first response to the cards is called the "free association period," while the second response is considered the "inquiry." All responses of the subject are recorded verbatim and scored for location of the perception, the determinant for the response, and content of the response. The psychological significance of these scorings is related to intellectual processes, emotional functioning, and avenues for coping with stress. Once responses are scored, frequency tallies are developed for each kind of score. In addition, ratios and percentages are calculated to provide a structural summary. Interpretation involves both the quantified data and quality of subject's responses. In the structural summary, the focus is on profile configuration, which are characteristics that occur significantly more or less frequently than expected. Norms have been developed for a variety of populations and have even been reported for children as young as two years of age (Ames, Métraux, Rodell, and Walker 1974).

There is controversy surrounding the empirical validity and reliability of this technique. The responses recorded are not predictive in nature, nor do they provide a complete description of the subject (Exner 1976). Rather, the Rorschach is an attempt to describe present intrapersonal needs, fears, conflicts, and general style of response in a given situation. Unlike in a traditional psychometric approach, interpretation is based on the extent to which a summation of responses agrees with or deviates from an established norm. The primary purpose of this method is to facilitate description and understanding of the person (Exner 1976).

Picture Techniques

One of the most widely used picture techniques in clinical work today is the *Thematic Apperception Test* (TAT) (Morgan and Murray 1935). This technique was devised on the premise that people reveal aspects of their personalities when confronted with ambiguous social situations. Murray (1938) actually described how the process of projection operates in an ambiguous stimulus situation and is responsible for clarifying the process underlying projective instruments.

The TAT consists of thirty pictures, most of which show people in implied action. The number of cards allows the examiner to create specific groupings for sex and developmental age. Ten cards are recommended to be given to a subject. The subjects are instructed to create a story about each stimulus picture, including what is happening, what led to the event, what the characters are feeling and thinking, and what the outcome will be. The assumption is that the subjects will become so engrossed in the test that they will employ fewer defenses and project qualities of self onto the characters. In addition, the elements that are most important to subjects will be alluded to most frequently.

This procedure, unlike the Rorschach, focuses on describing the interpersonal needs, pressures, and themes for an individual. The technique is not used to make a diagnosis per se, but rather to explore personality dynamics. Although scoring focuses on both content and quantitative analysis, most clinicians do not attempt to score the TAT, but use a qualitative approach to interpretation.

Researchers do not make strong claims regarding empirical validity or reliability but rather focus on clinical utility. As Murstein (1965) states, the TAT has not demonstrated much utility with respect to specific issues of psychiatric diagnosis. Most literature confirms the usefulness of the TAT in differentiating the stories of neurotics, schizophrenics, and some types of characterological problems (Harrison 1965). In this regard clinicians would tend to agree that stories offered by people with identified psychiatric problems are generally much different from the stories provided by nonpatients.

One of the major limitations of TAT research is that it has been trait-specific and of minimal use to the practitioner in a clinical setting (Exner 1976). This is the probable reason that most clinicians avoid scoring each story and instead use a qualitative approach to interpretation, as suggested earlier. It has been in this context that the TAT has flourished as a clinical assessment technique.

The *Children's Apperception Test (CAT)* (Bellak and Bellak 1952) presents animals depicted in human-like actions. The assumption is that young children will respond with stories about animal characters more readily than they will to scenes depicting people. The test has been found useful in the study of twins (Magnusson 1960) and for clinical groups such as schizophrenics (Gurevitz and Klapper 1951), the emotionally disturbed (Kanehira 1958), and the speech-handicapped (Fitzsimmons 1958). The focus for interpretation is mainly on content analysis—the status of the hero, conflicts, and outcome as it relates to the status of the hero. There is as much controversy about the empirical validity and reliability of this procedure as with the TAT, especially when the verbal abilities of children are taken into consideration. Since young children's verbal expressive abilities are still developing, it is difficult to know if an impoverished response indicates the expression of a defense mechanism or simply poor verbal skills.

The *Blacky Pictures Test* (Blum 1950) was developed to investigate and validate the psychoanalytic theory of psychosexual development and defense mechanisms by having subjects chronicle the events in the life of a small dog. The test is designed for use with subjects five years of age

to adulthood. The administration of the Blacky is divided into three seg-
ments: spontaneous stories or free association, an inquiry composed of
questions that pertain to the psychoanalytic dimension measured by the
card, and cartoon preferences indicating cards most liked and disliked.
The test is considered a qualitative one in which interpretation is based on
knowledge of psychoanalytic theory and projective techniques. Research
does indicate good interjudge, test-retest, and split-half reliability (Granick
and Scheflin 1958).

The *Make-A-Picture Story Test (MAPS)* (Shneidman 1952) is essentially a variation of the TAT in which the backgrounds and figures are
separated, so that the subject is faced with the task of selecting one or
more cutout, human-like or animal figures from among many such figures, and placing it or them on background pictures selected by the examiner. One of the basic assumptions is that the variety of combinations of
cutouts and backgrounds offers more extensive stimulus variability than
the TAT. But because of this variability, attempts to standardize the test or
assess its validity are very difficult. The MAPS has gained the greatest
clinical use with young clients who are hyperactive or resistive to producing data on the TAT. The technique allows for many variations, such as
the use of plastic or wooden figures, and resembles some of the techniques used in play therapy.

Completion Techniques—Verbal

The *word association* technique has a long history in psychology.
Both Wundt and Galton experimented with the approach (Forer 1960),
and Jung recognized it as an efficient means of investigating complexes,
i.e. the combination of an idea with its strong affect (Alexander and Sel-
nick 1966). Word association techniques flourished during the early years
of psychoanalysis and were useful means of understanding the unconscious. Rapaport, Gill, and Schafer (1946) demonstrated its value as a
clinical and research tool, although relatively few current contributions
are being made.

The administration of word association tests is easy, and the subject's responses are limited to just a single word. The major assumption
underlying these instruments is that verbalizations reflect ideation, and
the study of associative thought under controlled conditions can provide
information about personal dynamics and defense systems. The responses can be categorized in a qualitative rather than quantitative
scheme. Norms have been developed that address the most common and
acceptable responses. These responses have been shown to differentiate

among brain-damaged, psychiatric, and normal populations (Appelbaum 1963). The major problems in using these techniques in research include predilection to response in general and socially desirable responses in particular. Also, appropriateness of norms is a concern, as norms need to be directed at specific populations and also become quickly outdated.

The *Sentence Completion Method (SCM)* also has a long history in psychology. Ebbinghaus and Galton both used this method to study memory (Rohde 1957). However, the first systematic use of these methods in the area of personality assessment was in the 1920s and early 1930s. Researchers found them of value as indices of response styles and emotional reactions with diverse populations (Forer 1960, Rotter 1951). The popularity of these methods today can be attributed to their clinical utility, ease of administration to both individuals and groups, acceptance by those who advocate projective techniques and by those who prefer a psychometric approach, and the relative ease with which they can be studied empirically (Exner 1976). These methods tap broad issues in both assessment and psychodiagnosis. They can be easily developed for specific subject populations by choosing sentence stubs that are pertinent to the subject area or population being studied. These methods can also be administered in either written or oral form.

Few of these methods are considered objective or standardized. In clinical practice, most investigators rely on the interpretation of the content and interpretive methods range from the rather rigorous to the intuitive-impressionistic. In most instances, the responses are grouped into clusters and hypotheses are subsequently generated. Consequently, these methods are more clinical-descriptive than quantitative. Empirically, Rotter (1951) has described split-half reliability as high as .85. Concurrent validity as well as predictive validity is also high (Murstein 1965). However, a major concern is the extent to which a subject can control his or her response, so that the investigator is certain of actually studying underlying issues and not just the material the subject is willing to provide. These methods, in and of themselves, do not provide a significant amount of information about subjects, but are useful as a clinical tool within a battery of tests.

The *Story Completion Methods* also have a long history which has come full circle. These methods began with research efforts arising from theoretical concerns about complex facets of personality. Considerable care was used in designing stories that would elicit special types of responses. At present, there is a revitalized interest in cognitive styles, creativity, and imagination in the study of personality and its development through transactions with the environment. Story completion methods seem well suited to these theoretical interests. They can be administered either orally or in written form. The assumption underlying these methods is that subjects identify with the hero, and in doing so reveal aspects of their personality.

As with most projective techniques, there is criticism concerned with the validity of these methods. It is generally argued that the story completion methods measure more of the clinicians' theoretical biases than they do the underlying issues, problems, or personalities of subjects. Although empirical studies that investigate the relationship between subjects' responses and overt behavior have yielded negative results (Grinder and McMichael 1963), reliability of these measures is quite good. It is concluded that these methods have little value in regards to differential diagnoses and that normative studies are needed.

Drawing Techniques — Nonverbal

Compared to the former verbal techniques, considerable controversy has surrounded the projective drawings approach. One of the most widely used drawing techniques is the *Draw-A-Person* (D-A-P) technique adapted by Karen Machover (1949) to provide clinical information about personality and adjustment. Compared to other projective instruments it is easy to administer, especially to children. Clinicians interpret various features of the drawing, including symmetry, stance, perspective, size, placement, line quality, and shading. The basic assumption underlying the technique is that the subject's drawing of a person represents an expression of the self in the environment (self concept). The details convey information about children's preoccupations, conflicts, and self attitudes. Global ratings of this technique appear to be more reliable than specific "signs" (Swensen 1968). One consistent finding is that "well adjusted" subjects' drawings have better artistic quality and show more detail; yet the more detail they contain, the more conflict indicators the drawing is likely to include. Overall, there has not been convincing empirical evidence to support Machover's (1965) hypotheses, and more well-designed validity studies are needed.

A variant of the D-A-P is the *Draw-A-Family Test* (D-A-F), which was first reported in the literature by Hulse (1951, 1952). Affective attitudes toward various family members are often clearly revealed. The child's perception of his or her own role in the family and his or her concept of self are reflected in these drawings. These drawings can be a clue to the child's interpersonal relationships with family members. The child's conscious and unconscious perception of self and significant people in the environment determine the content of the drawing.

As with the D-A-P, it is important in the D-A-F to examine the size of the figures, their placement on the page, and distances between various figures. In addition, observations about exaggerations of figures, omission of family members, erasures, and shading oftentimes are of clinical significance. For example, the child's concept of self may be inferred from the size of the self figure or in the absence of the self figure from the drawing. Hulse (1951) found that rejected children tend to draw parents as dominating the family group. Cases in which parents are known to be seductive are represented in children's drawings by the posture or facial expression of the drawn parent. As pointed out by Hammer (1958), this technique taps social and interpersonal variables similar to those obtained verbally with the TAT.

The *Kinetic-Family-Drawing* (K-F-D) (Burns and Kaufman 1972) is yet another variation of the D-A-P and the D-A-F. Subjects are simply asked to draw the members of their families doing things. The assumption is that by adding movement to the akinetic drawings, mobilization of a child's feelings regarding self concept and interpersonal relations will be encouraged. The authors suggest that this technique often reflects primary disturbances much more quickly and adequately than interviews or other probing techniques.

The *House-Tree-Person* (H-T-P) technique (Buck 1970 revised manual) was "designed to aid the clinician in obtaining information concerning an individual's sensitivity, maturity, flexibility, efficiency, degree of personality integration, and interaction with the environment" (p. 1). Simply, the child is asked to draw a house, a tree, and a person. For children, the house has been found to tap attitudes concerning the home situation and their relationships to parents and siblings. The drawing of the tree appears to reflect the subject's deeper and more unconscious feelings about self, whereas the drawn person becomes the vehicle for conveying the subject's closer-to-conscious view of self in relation to the environment. The person tends to elicit a self portrait, an ideal self, and a depiction of one's perception of significant others (Hammer 1960). The self portrait represents the projection of the child's physical and psychological self, while the ego ideal represents what the child would rather be. The child's perception of significant others is often represented by his or her depiction of another person with whom the child has had strong positive or negative valences. As with other drawing devices, the H-T-P is useful in working with children who may find it easier to communicate through drawings than through the verbal projective techniques. The child may project his or her traits and attitudes, behavioral characteristics, and personality strengths and weaknesses. Children tend to draw elements that they consider significant and eliminate those features which do not concern them.

The *Bender Visual-Motor Gestalt Test (BV-GT)* (Bender 1938) was originally devised as a method to assess disturbance in perceptual-motor behavior. The child is asked to copy a series of drawings, each presented individually. However, clinicians following the work of Bell (1948) have employed the test as a projective technique to assess various aspects of personality functioning. Several attempts to establish an objective scoring method for this technique with adults have been made (Billingslea 1948, Pascal and Suttell 1951). A number of other authors devised methods of scoring and norms for the evaluation of children's records (Byrd 1956, Clawson 1959, Koppitz 1963). The test is useful in detecting some types of organic pathology, psychotic conditions of a schizophrenic nature, and perceptual-motoric immaturity (Tolor and Schulberg 1963). For example, Byrd (1956) reported results of a comparison of 200 children recommended for psychotherapy with 200 who were judged to be "well adjusted." He found that the well-adjusted children showed more use of orderly sequence, and less change in curvature, closure difficulty, and rotation than the children in need of psychotherapy. Clawson (1959), comparing eighty children who were clients in a child guidance clinic with a like number of controls, found a positive relationship between "expansive organization" and acting-out behavior, as well as between "compressed organization" and "decreased figure size" and the symptom of withdrawal.

Hutt (1968) has outlined three approaches to test protocol analysis: (1) the clinical-intuitive method, which relies on the meaning of perceptual-motoric behavior; (2) the configurational method, which relies on clusters of signs, scores, or traits that discriminate among psychoneurosis, intracranial damage, schizophrenia, mental retardation, and manic states; and (3) the objective method, which measures the degree of approach-avoidance behavior, which in turn is related to an individual's preferred stimulation.

Although it may be stated that many BV-GT scoring factors differentiate between clinical and nonclinical groups of adults and children, the most reliable and valid use of the test is in differentiating cases of brain damage.

Animal drawings of children are yet another clinical method for gaining insight into personality dynamics. Children readily respond to the task of drawing the animals they would most like to be and least like to be. Animal drawings reveal the subject's primary impulses (e.g., fear, rage, etc.), and insight into specific symbolism can be derived from the features of the drawings. For example, animal symbolism may reveal disposition and temperament, role function, and ascribed status. (Schwartz and Rosenberg 1955). Further, the symbolic significance of various species of animals and types (aggressive, non-aggressive, birds in flight, etc.) has been reported (Bender and Rapoport 1944, Hammer 1958, Levy and Levy 1958). In essence, animal drawings tend to reveal deeper aspects of personality for children. More contemporary research needs to be completed with these techniques. Cross-cultural studies could be particularly meaningful.

Kinesthetic Methods

Free play is one kinesthetic method that provides data on the child's relationships to and ways of dealing with people. It reveals a child's concepts about the world and human experiences, style of expression, methods of coping with conflicts and anxieties, creativity and capacity to restructure situations, and his or her perceptions, preferences, and needs (Murphy and Krall 1971). In general, free play can sort out a child's cognitive, affective, and motor responses, without having to rely on verbal communication. In evaluating a child's free play, it is important to make inferences consonant with developmental level and environmental situation. Observations are made regarding the child's control over emotional and physical behavior and how he or she copes with frustration and the structural aspects of the play (i.e. concern for order or tendency towards disorganization, spontaneous qualities of clarity as contrasted with tendencies toward confusion), responses that may be evidence of problems which interfere with the child's capacity for integration and handling of emotions.

In addition, play also provides data on factors such as perception, memory, communication, social interaction and reality testing, the extent of fine and gross motor control, and a variety of integrative and executive functions of the ego (Murphy and Krall 1971). Finally, the process of play may reveal the value play has for a particular child, or with what difficulties the child may need help. This process analysis indicates what the child is doing with his or her play. Thus a discharge of aggression can be followed by relaxation and constructive activity, fear, or by more aggression.

Doll play techniques have been utilized most frequently with preschool children as a means of eliciting projective responses independent of verbal ability. The underlying assumption is that the child's constructions will reproduce his or her reality situations. It is believed that children will recreate experiences as they exist in their own homes with respect to their own family members. Also, their fears, anxieties, rivalries, and aggressive impulses will be revealed. As Levin and Wardwell (1962) point out, the child's products may also represent fantasy and wish-fulfillment.

Most of the experimental studies have used children in the age range from 5–13 years. The studies have focused on punishment fantasies (Bookbinder 1955), accident repeaters (Krall 1953), predelinquents (Bach and Bremer 1947), and children with chronic illnesses, such as rheumatic fever (Lynn, Glazer and Harrison 1962) and asthma (Peixotto and Hill 1965). Observer reliabilities have ranged from the .70s to the .90s. Test-retest findings suggest that a single session may yield as reliable a picture as multiple ones. Sears (1951) found session-to-session correlations of .73 for boys and .49 for girls. The major problem in establishing validity centers around whether or not doll play represents a replication of real life experiences or a means of wish-fulfillment. Although little relationship has been found between teacher ratings of overt behavior and doll play fantasy (Bach 1945), some association has been found between high stereotypy and high behavioral compliance, and between low stereotypy and highly emotional outbursts.

Doll play has been researched in a variety of areas, such as in the manipulation of environmental variables, personality assessment, parent-child interactions, emotional disturbances, and the influence of situational factors, such as the absence of a parent, and illness or physical handicaps.

Puppetry is also used as a means by which children can project conflicts and emotions. This technique appears to be better suited for older children than doll-house play. Most clinicians utilize the "half-show" procedure, where the child is stopped at a critical point in the drama and asked what will happen next (Woltmann 1951). Clinicians use an analysis sheet for personality assessment to measure indices of identification, aggression, guilt, and anxiety. Inter-scorer reliabilities have been reported ranging from .83 to .94. Norms have also been established for comparison purposes (Haworth 1957).

The *Family Relations Test* (Bene and Anthony 1957) was devised to assess children's feelings toward members of their families and their perceptions of family member attitudes toward them. This technique does not require verbalization and thus may be useful for eliciting emotional variables from very young children. The test materials consist of twenty drawn cardboard people of both sexes and various ages. The child selects figures which represent self and family members. Two sets of cards containing printed messages are also used. The examiner reads the message to the child, who then drops the card in the slot of the person it characterizes best. Test items describe both negative and positive feelings toward family members. Feelings of affiliation, dependency, need for affection, unfriendliness, hostility, independence, overindulgence, and overprotection are being tapped.

The *Kahn Test of Symbol Arrangement (KTSA)* (Kahn 1956) was devised as a projective tool to reveal unconscious symbolization of objects. The subject is required to place fifteen objects on a strip of felt segmented into fifteen consecutively numbered spaces. This procedure is repeated five times. Subjects can arrange symbols in any desired order on three of the five trials. On one of the final two trials the subject must duplicate one of the original three trials. The remaining trial requires the subject to arrange the objects along a like-dislike continuum. Subjects must name objects in one instance, and in another must arrange the symbols into categories labeled *love, hate, bad, good, living, dead, small, and large.* Subjects responses are recorded with special attention to the direction of object placement, time, and position of objects.

The standardization data for adults (see 1962 manual) are based on studies conducted over a seven-year period including 453 men and 47 women ranging in age from 18–87 years. Test-retest reliability correlations vary from .66 to .95. Interscorer reliability coefficients range from .97 to .99. Most of the research with this test has been done with normal adults, psychotics, and brain-damaged adults. The procedure seems to be particularly discriminative of organics, who are more readily identifiable by symbol patterns, show more concrete associations to symbols, and perform more slowly than do normal adults. The procedure lacks norms on women and children and could benefit from a briefer form for children.

As one can see, a wide variety of techniques are encompassed under the rubric of projective assessment. Some of these techniques are categorized as constitutive methods, such as the Rorschach, whereby individuals are asked to impose a structure on a relatively unstructured stimulus situation; picture techniques (e.g., TAT, CAT, etc.), which call for interpretive statements to be made regarding structured stimulus material; constructive methods (e.g., completion and drawing techniques); and kinesthetic methods, which stimulate emotional reaction, such as free play, doll play, and puppetry. While the techniques are varied, all are based upon the projective hypothesis.

Despite criticism concerning the lack of definitive evidence of the reliability and validity of many of the projective techniques, it appears that many clinicians and school psychologists have not reduced their use. In fact, a number of surveys of clinicians and mental health agencies (e.g., Wade, Baker, Morton, and Baker 1978) and surveys of school psychologists (e.g., Goh et al., 1980) have shown that the use of projective techniques has not significantly diminished over time, and that most employment agencies and academic training programs continue to view skills in administering these techniques as important prerequisites for future employment.

Realistically, many clinicians and school psychologists place much emphasis on their intuitive judgments when working in clinical and school settings. Thus these professionals tend to consider projective tests to be more valuable than might be suggested by the reliability and validity studies. In particular, the Rorschach technique has remained one of the most frequently used psychological tests, and according to Wade, et al. (1978), it is the test which most clinicians advised clinical psychology students to learn.

Projective tests in general may be most valid when used as a type of structured clinical interview. It is in this context that projective tests are useful as a means of understanding the unique needs, interests, pressures, conflicts, affective and cognitive styles, and coping strategies that characterize individual adults or children. Therefore, in light of the fact that there are few practical alternatives to tests, and that many clinicians and school psychologists prefer to rely on their clinical experience over empirical evidence when these are at odds, it seems that projective tests will continue to flourish and may be, in the hands of an experienced user, our best nonbiased assessment device.

INTEGRATION AND APPLICATION OF TEST RESULTS

The purpose of the evaluation, the child's background, and his or her current test behaviors and the test results themselves should all be considered when providing personality descriptions, psychodynamic interpretations, diagnostic formulations, or prognoses and recommendations for any given child. The psychological evaluation should be an integration of the available information about the child and should be geared towards a better understanding of the child's present adjustment, behavior, conflicts, strengths, and limitations. The referral problem should guide the selection of instruments, the specific questions to be answered, and the nature of the recommendations.

The following case material exemplifies the integration and application of all relevant data. Both children were seen by the authors.

Case 1

At the time of testing Billy was almost nine years of age. He was living outside his home due to difficulty adjusting to recent changes in his family. His father committed suicide several years earlier while in a prison hospital, and his mother was planning to be remarried in a few months. Referral concerns centered on Billy's ability to return to his family and the behavioral problems he exhibited in his classroom.

Test behavior revealed a preoccupation with religious concerns, as Billy made frequent references to God and stated that although he felt he had misbehaved, "it was o.k., for God gave you more than one chance." Sexual preoccupations were also evident in his comment (while completing a figure drawing), "My lady has a cigarette and high heels. I'm gonna color her [because] she can't be naked . . . she's going to dance with tight clothes on." On completing the drawing he commented, "My mother is so pretty when she gets all dressed up."

On the WISC-R, Billy's highest score was on a task involving attention to detail (Picture Completion — Scaled Score = 12), which was consistent with his cautious and watchful attitude overall. His lowest score was on a task involving the ability to plan and anticipate in social situations. While Billy understood social situations in the abstract, once involved in them, he was unsure of their meaning.

Several themes became evident as testing continued. His perception of his mother as seductive and alluring on the one hand, yet unavailable and forbidding on the other, was seen in a TAT story in which "the lady hugs the man, but she doesn't want to be kissed . . . she pushes the man away and was laughing, because probably in her mind she knew she could run away and not see the guy any more." His evasive and cautious style may have resulted largely from the maternal relationship, as Billy tends to look for hidden or covert meanings in other people's behavior. This speculation is based on the examiners' impressions from several different sources. Consistent with this orientation was his response to Card VII on the Rorschach. His initial response to this card was "a lady bug." However, during the detailed inquiry, Billy thought for quite some time and decided "it's really a crab . . . with these two things opening [as he pointed to a very tiny detail on the card] . . . it's a mouth."

Considering his preoccupation with heaven and hell, his father's suicide, and his mother's plans to remarry, his last TAT story, in which the heroine "fainted, fell down, and accidentally stabbed herself in the stomach and died," is quite revealing. These test results suggest that the therapist be sensitive to Billy's feelings of anger and depression and possibly self-destructive behavior, in reaction to his perceived loss of his mother.

Case 2

Psychological reassessment will often provide a good measure of a subject's improvement in both perceptual-motor/developmental and emotional/psychodynamic areas of functioning.

Figure 9.2

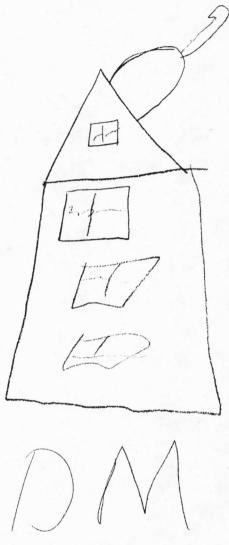

Figure 9.3

Figure 9.4

Figure 9.5

Donna was first evaluated when she was ten years, seven months old, following her removal from a family in which she was exposed to considerable sexual abuse. The evaluation revealed limited intellectual skills, rather tenuous ego controls, and significant conflict and ambivalence regarding physical contact. Figures 9.2, 9.3, and 9.4 represent House-Tree-Person drawings made when Donna was 10.7 years of age. The drawings lack contact features. (The figure has no hands or feet). The disproportionately large head may be a reflection of her felt intellectual deficits and her apparent sadness, as tears are rolling down the cheeks. Her initials on the drawings are an immature sign, more commonly seen in the productions of younger children. Her "house" lacks an entrance, and the phallic chimney may reflect early sexual abuse, which is consistent with

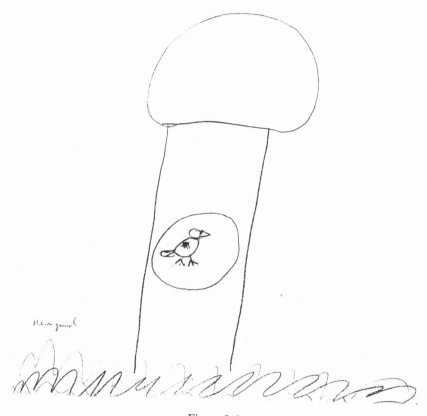

Figure 9.6

her early home experiences. She insisted on covering up the bottom of her tree with "dirt . . . to bury it," and this may be interpreted as a reflection of her attempt to repress very painful early memories.

Donna had lived in a residential treatment facility for about three years by the time of her reevaluation (chronological age 11 years, 11 months). Figures 9.5, 9.6, and 9.7 reveal considerable gains in both her perceptual-motor and her emotional development. Sex-role identity is more clearly established. Her overall rebelliousness (reported by her therapist) is evident in her inclusion of a cigarette lighter in the figure's hand.

The full trunk of the tree is now clearly visible and may reveal an increased capacity to examine and attempt to resolve her early memories

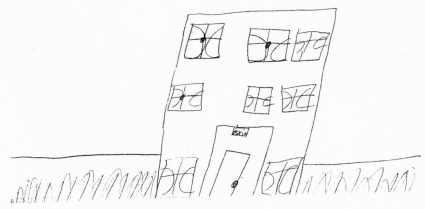

Figure 9.7

and conflicts. The bird which rests on the tree appears wounded, as Donna feels scarred by traumatic experiences.

The house provides an indication of her identification as a "residential" child, as she stated this was a picture of her treatment center. The presence of a door indicates an increased accessibility. The referral question centered around her readiness to leave the treatment center and enter a foster family. Donna provided an indication of her feelings on this matter in the last detail she added to the drawing—the "exit" sign over the door.

REFERENCES

Ainsworth, M. G. Some problems of validation of projective techniques. *British Journal of Medical Psychology, 1951, 24,* 151–161.

Alexander, F. G., & Selsnick, S. T. *The history of psychiatry.* New York: Harper and Row, 1966.

Altman, C. H. Projective techniques in the clinical setting. In A. I. Rabin and M. R. Haworth (Eds.), *Projective techniques with children.* New York: Grune & Stratton, 1971.

American Psychological Association. *Standards for education and psychological tests.* Washington, D.C.: Author, 1974.

Ames, L. B., Métraux, R. W., Rodell, J. L., & Walker, R. N. *Child Rorschach responses: Developmental trends from two to ten years.* New York: Brunner/Mazel Publishers, 1974.

Appelbaum, S. A. The expanded word association test as a measure of psychological deficit associated with brain-damage. *Journal of Clinical Psychology,* 1963, *19,* 78–84.

Bach, G. R. Young children's play fantasies. *Psychological Monographs,* 1945, *59,* No. 2.

Bach, G. R., & Bremer, G. Projective father fantasies of preadolescent, delinquent children. *Journal of Psychology,* 1947, *24,* 3–17.

Beck, S. J. *Rorschach's Test I. Basic processes.* New York: Grune & Stratton, 1944.

Beck, S. J. The Blacky Pictures. In O. K. Buros (Ed.), *The fifth mental measurements yearbook.* Highland Park, N.J.: Gryphon Press, 1959.

Bell, J. E. *Projective techniques.* New York: Longmans, Green, 1948.

Bellak, L. *The Children's Apperception Test.* New York: C.P.S. Company, 1949.

Bellak, L. *The Thematic Apperception Test, The Children's Apperception Test, and The Senior Apperception Test in clinical use.* New York: Grune & Stratton, 1975.

Bellak, L., & Bellak, S. *Children's Apperception Test.* New York: C.P.S. Company, 1952.

Bender, L. A visual-motor gestalt test and its clinical use. *Research Monograph of the American Orthopsychiatric Association.* 1938, #3.

Bender, L., & Rapaport, J. Animal drawings of children. *American Journal of Orthopsychiatry,* 1944, *14,* 521–527.

Bene, E., & Anthony, J. *Manual for the Family Relations Test.* London: National Foundation for Educational Research in England and Wales, 1957.

Billingslea, F. Y. The Bender-Gestalt: An objective scoring method and validating data. *Journal of Clinical Psychology,* 1948, *4,* 1–27.

Blum, G. S. *The Blacky Pictures: Manual of instructions.* New York: Psychological Corporation, 1950.

Bookbinder, K. F. The relation of social status and punishment as observed in stories obtained with the Driscoll Play Kit. *Dissertation Abstracts,* 1955, *15,* 1252–1253.

Buck, J. N. The H-T-P Technique: A qualitative and quantitative scoring manual. *Archives of the Behavioral Sciences,* 1948, No. 5, 1–120.

Buck, J. N. *The House-Tree-Person Technique: Revised manual.* Beverly Hills: Western Psychological Services, 1970.

Burns, R. C., & Kaufman, S. H. *Actions, Styles and Symbols in Kinetic Family Drawings (K-F-D).* New York: Brunner/Mazel, 1972.

Byrd, E. The clinical validity of the Bender-Gestalt Test with children: A developmental comparison of children in need of psychotherapy and children judged well adjusted. *Journal of Projective Techniques,* 1956, *20,* 127–136.

Clawson, A. The Bender Visual Motor Gestalt Test as an index of emotional disturbance in children. *Journal of Projective Techniques,* 1959, *23,* 198–206.

Ebel, E. L. Must all tests be valid? *American Psychologist,* 1961, *16,* 640–647.

Exner, J. E. Projective techniques. In I. B. Weiner (Ed.), *Clinical methods in psychology.* New York: John Wiley and Sons, 1976.

Exner, J. E. Jr., Armbruster, G. I., & Viglione, D. The temporal stability of some Rorschach features. *Journal of Personality Assessment,* 1978, *42,* 474–481.

Fallstrom, K., & Vegelius, J. A discriminatory analysis based on dichotomized Rorschach scores of diabetic children. *International Journal of Rehabilitation Research,* 1978, *1,* 321–327.

Fitzsimmons, R. Developmental, psychosocial, and educational factors in children with nonorganic articulation problems. *Child Development,* 1958, *24,* 481–489.

Forer, B. R. Word Association and Sentence Completion methods. In A. I. Rabin, and M. R. Haworth (Eds.), *Projective techniques with children.* New York: Grune & Stratton, 1960.

Freud, S. Totem and Taboo. In A. A. Brill (Ed.), *Basic Writings of Sigmund Freud.* New York: Modern Library, 1938.

Goh, D. S., Teslow, C. J., & Fuller, G. B. *The practice of psychological assessment among school psychologists.* Paper presented at the Twelfth Annual Convention of the National Association of School Psychologists, Washington, D.C., April 1980.

Granick, S., & Scheflen, N. A. Approaches to reliability of projective tests with special reference to the Blacky Pictures Test. *Journal of Consulting Psychology,* 1958, *22,* 137–141.

Grinder, R., & McMichael, R. Cultural influences on conscience development: Resistance to temptation and guilt among Samoans and American Caucasians. *Journal of Abnormal and Social Psychology,* 1963, *66,* 503–507.

Gurevitz, S., & Klapper, Z. S. Techniques for and evaluation of the responses of schizophrenic and cerebral palsied children to the Children's Apperception Test. *Quarterly Journal of Child Behavior,* 1951, *3,* 38–65.

Hammer, E. F. *The clinical application of projective drawings.* Springfield, Ill.: Charles C. Thomas, 1958.

Hammer, E. F. The House-Tree-Person (H-T-P) Drawings as a projective technique with children. In A. I. Rabin & M. R. Haworth, *Projective Techniques with Children.* New York: Grune & Stratton, 1960.

Harrison, R. Thematic apperceptive methods. In B. Wolman (Ed.), *Handbook of clinical psychology.* New York: McGraw-Hill, 1965.

Haworth, M. R. The use of a filmed puppet show as a group projective technique for children. *Genetic Psychology Monographs,* 1957, *56,* 257–296.

Hayden, B. C. Rorschach cards IV and VII revisited. *Journal of Personality Assessment,* 1981, *45,* 226–229.

Hertz, M. R. *Frequency tables for scoring Rorschach responses* (5th ed.). Cleveland: Case Western Reserve University Press, 1970.

Howes, R. J. The Rorschach: Does it have a future? *Journal of Personality Assessment,* 1981, *45,* 339–351.

Hulse, W. C. Child conflict expressed through family drawings. *Journal of Projective Techniques,* 1952, *16,* 66–79.

Hulse, W. C. The emotionally disturbed child draws his family. *Quarterly Journal of Child Behavior,* 1951, *3,* 152–174.

Hutt, M. L. The projective use of the Bender-Gestalt test. In A. I. Rabin (Ed.), *Projective techniques in personality assessment.* New York: Springer Publishing Company, 1968.

Kagan, J. The measurement of overt aggression from fantasy. *Journal of Abnormal and Social Psychology,* 1956, *52,* 390–393.

Kahn, T. C. Kahn Test of Symbol Arrangement: Administration and scoring. *Perceptual and Motor Skills Monograph Supplement,* 1956, *6,* No. 4.

Kanehira, T. Diagnosis of parent-child relationships by CAT. *Japanese Journal of Case Studies,* 1958, *3,* 49–63.

Keily, R., & Berg, B. Measuring children's reactions to divorce. *Journal of Clinical Psychology,* 1978, *34,* 215–221.

Kendra, J. M. Predicting suicide using the Rorschach inkblot test. *Journal of Personality Assessment,* 1979, *43,* 452–456.

Klopfer, B., & Davidson, H. H. *The Rorschach Technique: An introductory manual.* New York: Harcourt, Brace and World, 1962.

Koppitz, E. M. *The Bender Gestalt Test for young children.* New York: Grune & Stratton, 1963.

Krall, V. Personality characteristics of accident repeating children. *Journal of Abnormal Social Psychology,* 1953, *48,* 99–107.

Leary, T. F. *The interpersonal diagnosis of personality.* New York: Ronald Press, 1957.

Lesser, G. S. The relationship between overt and fantasy aggression as a function of maternal response to aggression. *Journal of Abnormal and Social Psychology,* 1957, *55,* 218–221.

Levin, H., & Wardwell, E. The research uses of doll play. *Psychological Bulletin,* 1962, *59,* 27–56.

Levy, S., & Levy, R. A. Symbolism in animal drawings, In E. F. Hammer (Ed.), *The clinical application of projective drawings.* Springfield, Ill.: Charles C. Thomas, 1958.

Lindzey, G. Thematic Apperception Test: Interpretive assumptions and related empirical evidence. *Psychological Bulletin,* 1952, *49,* 1–25.

Lynn, D. B., Glazer, H. H., & Harrison, G. S. Comprehensive medical care for handicapped children: III. Concepts of illness in children with rheumatic fever. *American Journal of Disabled Children,* 1962, *103,* 120–128.

Machover, K. *Personality projection in the drawing of the human figure.* Springfield, Ill.: Charles C. Thomas, 1949.

Magnusson, D. Some personality tests applied on identical twins. *Scandanavian Journal of Psychology,* 1960, *1,* 55–61.

Miller, L. J., & Hutt, M. L. Psychopathology scale of the Hutt adaptation of the Bender-Gestalt Test: Reliability. *Journal of Personality Assessment,* 1975, *39,* 129–131.

Morgan, C. D., & Murray, H. A. A method for investigating phantasies: The Thematic Apperception Test. *Archives of Neurology and Psychiatry,* 1935, *34,* 289–306.

Murphy, L. B., & Krall, V. Free play as a projective tool. An A. I. Rabin and M. R. Haworth (Eds.), *Projective techniques with children*. New York: Grune & Stratton, 1971.

Murray, H. A. *Exploration in personality*. New York: Oxford University Press, 1938.

Murstein, B. Assumptions, adaptation level and projective techniques. *Perceptual and Motor Skills*, 1961, *12*, 107–125.

Murstein, B. (Ed.), *Handbook of projective techniques*. New York: Basic Books, 1965.

Murstein, B. I., & Wolf, S. R. Empirical test of the "levels" hypothesis with five projective techniques. *Journal of Abnormal Psychology*, 1970, *75*, 38–44.

Mussen, P. H., & Naylor, K. The relationships between overt and fantasy aggression. *The Journal of Abnormal and Social Psychology*, 1954, *49*, 235–240.

Newton, K. R. The Blacky Pictures. In O. K. Buros (Ed.), *The fifth mental measurements yearbook*. Highland Park, N.J.: Gryphon Press, 1959.

Pascal, G. R., & Suttell, B. J. *The Bender-Gestalt Test: Quantification and validity for adults*. New York: Grune & Stratton, 1951.

Peixotto, H. E., & Hill, E. F. Phantasy in asthmatic children with special reference to Driscoll Doll Play. *Journal of Asthma Research*, 1965, *2*, 199–204.

Piotrowski, Z. A. *Perceptanalysis*. New York: Macmillan, 1957.

Piotrowski, Z. A. Digital computer interpretation of ink-blot test data. Psychiatric Quarterly, 1964, *38*, 1–26.

Rabin, A. I. Projective methods and projection in children. In A. I. Rabin and M. R. Haworth (Eds.), *Projective techniques with children*. New York: Grune & Stratton, 1960.

Rabin, A. I. Projective methods: An historical introduction. In A. I. Rabin (Ed.), *Projective techniques in personality assessment*. New York: Springer, 1968.

Rabin, A. I., & Haworth, M. R. (Eds.). *Projective techniques with children*. New York: Grune & Stratton, 1971.

Rapaport, D. *Diagnostic psychological testing* (Vol. II). Chicago: Year Book Publishers, 1946.

Raskin, L., & Pitcher, G. B. Kinetic Family Drawings by children with perceptual-motor delays. *Journal of Learning Disabilities*. 1977, *10*, 370–374.

Rohde, A. R. *The Sentence Completion Method*. New York: Ronald Press, 1957.

Rotter, J. B. Word Association and Sentence Completion methods. In H. H. Anderson and G. L. Anderson (Eds.), *An introduction to projective techniques*. (Englewood Cliffs, N.J.: Prentice-Hall, 1951.

Schmidt, H. O., & Fonda, C. P. The reliability of psychiatric diagnosis: A new look. *The Journal of Abnormal and Social Psychology*, 1956, *52*, 262–267.

Schroth, M. L. The use of the associative elaboration and integration scales for evaluating CAT protocols. *Journal of Psychology*, 1977, *97*, 29–35.

Schwartz, A. A. & Rosenberg, I. H. Observations on the significance of animal drawings. *American Journal of Orthopsychiatry,* 1955, *25,* 729–746.

Sears, P. S. Dollplay aggression in normal young children: Influence of sex, age, sibling status, father's absence. *Psychological Monographs,* 1951, *65,* No. 6.

Shneidman, E. S. Manual for the MAPS Method. *Projective Techniques and Monographs,* 1952, *1,* No. 2.

Singer, J. L. Research applications of projective methods. In A. I. Rabin (Ed.), *Projective techniques in personality assessment.* New York: Springer Publishing Co., 1968.

Swensen, C. H. Empirical evaluations of human figure drawings: 1957–1966. *Psychological Bulletin,* 1968, *70,* 20–44.

Symonds, P. M. *Manual for Symonds' Picture-Story Test.* New York: Columbia University Press, 1948.

Tolor, A., & Schulberg, H. *An evaluation of the Bender-Gestalt Test.* Springfield, Ill.: Charles C. Thomas, 1963.

Wade, T., Baker, T., Morton, T., & Baker, L. The status of psychological testing in clinical psychology. *Journal of Personality Assessment, 1978, 42,* 3–9.

Woltmann, A. G. The use of puppetry as a projective method in therapy. In H. H. Anderson and G. L. Anderson (Eds.), *An introduction to projective techniques.* Englewood Cliffs, N.J.: Prentice-Hall, 1951.

10

Brain-Behavior Relationships in Children
Neuropsychological Assessment in the Schools
GEORGE W. HYND AND LAWRENCE C. HARTLAGE

WITHIN THE PAST several decades, remarkable progress has been made in expanding our understanding of how the brain perceives, stores, and makes use of information (Wittrock 1978). The interaction between environment and cortical development is just now being understood in sufficient depth that educational implications are emerging for both special education students (Gaddes 1980, Gaddes 1981a, b) and students without learning or behavioral problems (Toepfer 1982). Recognition and respect for a neuropsychological perspective in educational matters have been a long time in development. Working relationships between those with behavioral or medical perspectives can be strengthened by mutual understanding of what each perspective can contribute in working with children in need of school psychological services (Horton 1981). This chapter will outline the reasons for such an approach in school psychology, discuss basic brain-behavior relationships as presently conceived, and attempt to provide examples of how such a neuropsychological approach can contribute in differential diagnosis and in developing intervention strategies.

It should be stressed that by advocating the development of an understanding of brain-behavior relationships among school psychologists, we do not intend to ignore or reject other traditional approaches; rather, all these approaches are seen as complementary. The properly trained school psychologist should have a solid foundation in psychology and education, and he or she should be able to make optimal use of a variety of approaches, as appropriate, in helping children, teachers, parents, or schools in need of psychological services. This view is consistent with the model of school psychology originally proposed by Lightner Witmer in 1896 (Brothmarkle 1931) and fits well with the demand for school psychology services today (Hynd 1981).

It has been suggested by some psychologists and educators that a neuropsychological model of behavior has little relevance to the educational process of normal or exceptional children (e.g., Coles 1978, Gallagher 1966, Sandoval and Haapanen 1981). This is despite the best efforts of advocates such as Cruickshank (1981) who argue strongly that we should be preparing "neuroeducators" to work with exceptional children. Objections to the integration of educational, psychological, and neurological practice have been encouraged by psychologists who see no need even to consider such a perspective. B. F. Skinner, for example, argued, "There are two independent subject matters (behavior and the nervous system) which must have their own techniques and methods and yield their own respective data. . . . I am asserting, then, not only that a science of behavior is independent of neurology but that it must be established as a separate discipline whether or not a rapprochement with neurology is ever attempted" (Skinner 1938).

Other more practical objections to conceptualizing behavior as a natural extension of brain function have been: (1) that it is pessimistic because it stresses disease and chronicity; (2) that it encourages pharmacologic intervention and places little value on psychoeducational intervention; (3) that our conceptualization of brain-behavior relationships is inadequate in explaining all behavior; and (4) that labels are used (e.g., brain damaged) which are pessimistic and offer little hope of reversibility (Gaddes 1980, Sandoval and Haapanen 1981).

In many respects these criticisms and concerns are a response to early attempts to make use of limited knowledge about the neurological basis of behavior. The poor results of intervention strategies based on inadequate theory are reviewed by Kaufman and Kaufman in this volume. The widespread failure of these neurologically based programs has done much to discredit the application of neuropsychological knowledge in the schools. Other problems have arisen because of the premature claims of early researchers. It was Franz Josef Gall (1758–1828), for instance, who first proposed that function was differentially localized in the brain. Gall had observed that his brightest students frequently had protruding eyes. He hypothesized that the frontal lobes were enhanced or enlarged in these students and thus, the frontal lobes must be responsible for superior speech and language functions (Pirozzolo 1978). He also correctly proposed that the brain stem was vital for life-sustaining functions and that intellectual or cognitive functions were housed in the two cerebral hemispheres. Unfortunately, Gall became enamored with the idea that variations in skull size could reveal underlying cognitive abilities. This notion was based on the belief that protuberances on the skull directly correlated with areas in the brain which were neurally more developed. This notion was indeed nonsense, but in many circles the validation of his localizationist theory by Paul Broca (1861) and Carl Wernicke (1874) went unnoticed in favor of his ideas regarding phrenology. The research conducted by Lashley (1938) and others who argued against localizationist theory (e.g., Conrad 1948, Goldstein 1948, Leishner 1957) did much to reduce the application and impact of more recent medical knowledge with school-age children. It has only been recently that educators again seem willing to consider brain-behavior relationships in children.

A RATIONALE

While the objections which were stated above to a neuropsychological approach in education were made sincerely, a careful consideration of the research literature will demonstrate that this approach has as much validity as other conceptualizations of behavior (e.g., learning theory and information-processing models). The interested reader is referred to discussions of the validity of the neuropsychological model where these and other points are addressed (Gaddes 1980, Gaddes 1981, Hynd and Obrzut 1981a, Hynd 1981). Suffice it to say that educators have typically considered children only at a behavioral level and have not acknowledged the obvious contribution of the central nervous system to all behavior. The seminal work of John Hughlings Jackson (1872), William James (1890), and S. T. Orton (1937), and the more recent work of Reitan (1966) and Luria (1966, 1970) has led many psychologists to an appreciation of the physiological basis of behavior and to develop appropriate clinical assessment and intervention techniques. In fact, it is probably in the area of assessment where such an approach can potentially have its greatest impact. The case studies presented later in this chapter will serve to illustrate this point.

In presenting the argument for studying brain-behavior relationships in school-age children, we should point out that specific coursework in the physiological aspects of behavior is required in the APA standards for training, and neuropsychological training standards and proposed rules for certification of doctoral-level school psychologists have already been outlined (Hynd 1981, Hynd and Obrzut 1981a). Furthermore, as the public schools become responsible for *all* handicapped children between the ages of three and twenty-one, it is likely that many more unique cases of neurological handicaps will be seen by the school psychologist. Some programs already offer specialized training to their students to serve these children (Hynd, Quackenbush, and Obrzut 1980).

It has been suggested that two factors have contributed to the increased interest by school psychologists in physiological determinants of behavior in children (Hynd and Obrzut 1981a). First, it has been recognized that the neuropsychological literature has much to offer the school psychologist in terms of procedures and assessment techniques valuable in differential diagnosis (Mowder and DeMartino 1980, Rourke 1975, Rourke and Gates 1981). Recognized subtypes of learning disabilities can now be identified with the more refined neuropsychological test batteries developed within the past decade. A second factor which has helped increase the interest in brain-behavior relationships in children is federal legislation (e.g., PL 94-142) that directly ties the receipt of funds to the number of differentially diagnosed children with handicapping conditions. As the number of referrals to outside agencies decreased over the past ten years (Ramage 1979), more school psychologists seemed to be assuming a more active role in differential diagnoses of potentially difficult cases. Recent changes in federal funding procedures may change this focus, but past funding regulations have certainly had an impact on assessment procedures by school psychologists.

This need has prompted the publication of a number of articles discussing promising clinical procedures (e.g., Obrzut 1981, Reynolds and Gutkin 1979), debating important theoretical issues of relevance to school psychologists (e.g., Dean 1979, Hynd, Obrzut, Weed, and Hynd 1979, Hynd and Obrzut 1981c; Kaufman 1979, Ullman 1977), and reviewing neuropsychologically based intervention procedures (e.g., Bakker, Moerland, and Goekoop-Hoefkens 1981, Horton 1981, Van den Honert 1977).

So that a better understanding can be developed of how brain-behavior relationships affect the school psychologist's work with children, a brief overview of functional neuroanatomy is in order. The following section presents a very basic discussion of how the brain and the nervous system are thought to relate to behavior. For the sake of organization, the presentation outlines areas of the brain and nervous system in isolation. An overly simplistic view could result if the reader fails to realize that all areas of the brain interact with each other and that the system is *significantly* more complex than presented in this brief introduction. However, as an introduction and with these cautions in mind the following should serve reasonably well in building a foundation for further study.

FUNCTIONAL ORGANIZATION OF THE BRAIN

Neural differentiation in the human embryo begins at the end of the second week of gestation and continues until the brain is fully evolved, weighing in at about 1200–1500 grams. It is believed to consist of about 10–25 billion nerve cells (Jacobson 1972). One of the early notions of how the nervous system operated speculated that some sort of fluid flowed through the nerves carrying messages from one region to another. Although cell theory was developed much earlier, it was not until Otto Frederick Karl Deiters (1834–63) demonstrated that neurons existed did the "neuron doctrine" become accepted (see Figure 10.1). Through the work of Santiago Ramón y Cajal (1852–1934) and Wilhelm von Waldeyer (1836–1921), our knowledge has increased significantly about how neurons function (Gardner 1975). Not only have they been photographed, but in some

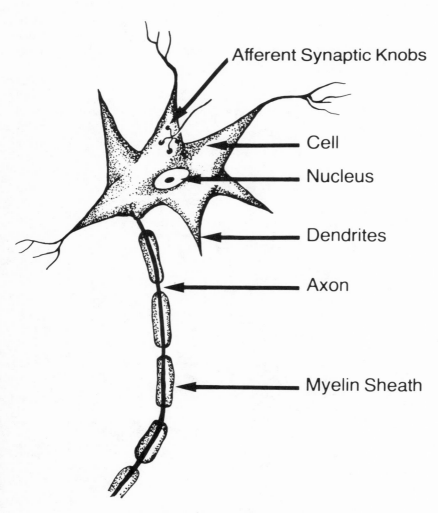

Figure 10.1 A prototype neuron.

cases we have actually been able to isolate and individually record neurons as they interact and contribute to various functional systems (Furster and Jervey 1981).

By the time the brain is fully mature, it is marked by prominent fissures and sulci, with the various lobes reasonably differentiated. The fact that the brain is characterized by so many sulci is important, since more than 70 percent of the cortical surface is hidden from view in the brain's attempt to gain precious more cortical surface area in the limited space of the skull. If the brain were not so "wrinkled," it has been estimated that our brains would need to be the size of basketballs in order to accommodate the same amount of surface area (Gaddes 1980)! The following discussion will briefly focus on the lower and midbrain structures,

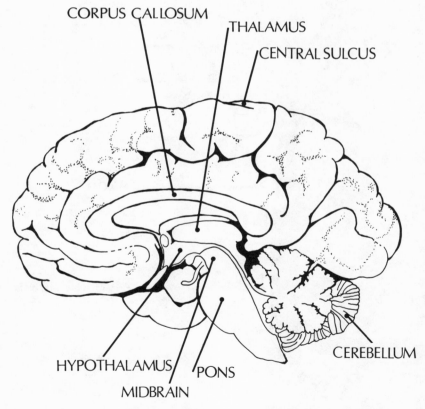

Figure 10.2 A sectioned brain showing the brain stem and associated structures.

and more space will be devoted to the cerebrum, as most neurologically based disorders of learning are related to deficits in the cortical areas of the brain.

The Hindbrain

The hindbrain is the lowest recognizable part of the brain and generally is thought to consist of the medulla, reticular activating system (RAS), pons, and cerebellum. The medulla (bulb) is the lowest part of the brain stem and is critical as a life-support system (see Figure 10.2). It is responsible for respiration, blood pressure, and heartbeat. Significant injury results in death. The RAS is located in the bulb and extends upwards through the thalamus and hypothalamus. The RAS is a cluster of functionally related cells which moderate posture, muscle tone, and most importantly, cortical arousal (French 1966). Consequently, damage to the RAS may result in various types of hyperactivity (see Golden 1981), stupor, coma, and possibly sleep apnea. The pons and cerebellum coordinate posture and kinesthetic (muscle-movement sense) abilities, and compute and refine muscle impulses received from the cerebrum. Damage to the pons and cerebellum may result in problems in fine or gross motor abilities or in subtle deficits in coordination (Lezak 1976).

The Midbrain

Above the hindbrain is the midbrain area including the structures between the thalamus and pons. Basically, the midbrain area is responsible for the cranial nerve reflexes such as the startle, blinking, gag reflex, etc. Damage may manifest itself in disorders related to the control of basic neurological functioning such as visual-tracking abilities.

The Forebrain

The forebrain consists of two major divisions, the diencephalon and the telencephalon. The diencephalon includes the thalamus and hypothalamus. The thalamus is a way station for all impulses traveling between the cortex and other neural centers. A thalamic lesion could manifest itself in the disturbance of any sensory tract. Also, "withering" of speech abilities and some cases of mutism seem to be associated with thalamic lesions. The hypothalamus is in front (anterior) of and below the thalamus and seems important in regulating appetite, sexual arousal, and thirst and may be associated with rage and fear reactions. Damage to the hypothalamus could result in obesity, socially obnoxious behavior, and disorders of temperature control and mood (Gaddes 1980, Lezak 1976).

The telencephalon or cerebrum constitutes the end of the neural tube and is the most recently evolved part of our nervous system. It consists of two nearly alike cerebral hemispheres. The internal cellular matter consists of three types of conduction fibers: (1) association fibers which transmit impulses between cortical points within a hemisphere; (2) commisural fibers which cross between and connect the two cerebral hemispheres; and (3) projection fibers which transmit impulses between the cortex and the lower neural centers (Lezak 1976). The cortex is the outer convoluted layer which is that part of the brain most relevant to our discussion.

The Cerebral Cortex

The cerebral cortex is asymmetrical in nature, with the left temporal lobe being slightly larger than the right (Geschwind and Levitsky 1968). Despite this asymmetry, the two hemispheres are remarkably alike in structure and uniquely different in function. Generally, the left hemisphere is associated with speech and language functions as well as sequential processing. The right hemisphere seems preprogrammed to subserve visual-spatial functions, native musical ability, perceptual orientation, some rudimentary verbal skills, and gestalt processing. See Table 10.1 for a summary of abilities believed to be associated with each hemisphere. Generalizations can also be made regarding the behavior elicited by hemi-

TABLE 10.1

Cognitive Abilities Generally Associated with
the Left and Right Cerebral Hemispheres

Left Hemisphere	Right Hemisphere
Language	Spatial orientation
Expressive	Nonverbal processing
Receptive	Gestalt perception
Sequential processing	Simultaneous processing
Arithmetic	Spatial integration
Temporal processing	Facial recognition
Complex motor functions	Sound recognition
Ideation	Tactile recognition
Writing	Intuitive problem solving

spheric damage. Damage or lesions to the left hemisphere can result in severe anxiety, including catastrophic reactions. Agitation and tearfulness may also be manifested. These behaviors seem more amenable to therapy than those behaviors associated with damage to the right hemisphere. Right hemisphere damage typically results in a denial of difficulty, where the child or adult tends to ignore or be unaware of the damage or impairment. The lack of anxiety can result in irresponsible and seemingly self-destructive behavior that is complicated by the fact that the child may be unable to learn from past mistakes (Lezak 1976). While these generalized patterns of behavior seem to be evident according to hemispheric disability, each area in the cerebrum seems also to subserve different functions. The areas most important to our discussion will be covered. See Figure 10.3 for a representation of important cortical areas.

Prior to examining the functional asymmetry of the cortex, a word of caution is warranted. It used to be believed that we could develop cytoarchitectonic maps of the brain where each specific behavior could be localized. Based on the work of Lashley (1920, 1929) and others, the notion that the brain acted as a whole unit (mass action) became popular. In

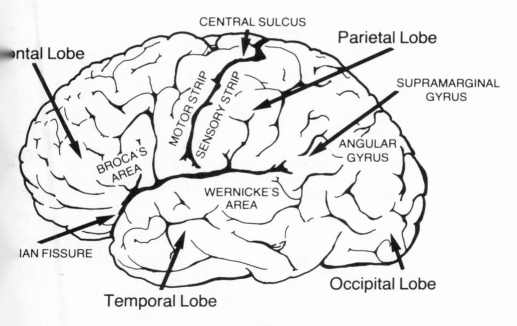

Figure 10.3 The cerebral cortex.

reality, both positions are evidently correct, as there seem to be highly localized functions (e.g., primarily sensory or motor functions) and those
which require a cooperative effort involving many areas of the brain
(e.g., reading aloud). The reader should also be aware that most motor
and sensory abilities operate on the principle of contralaterality. That is,
the right hand is coordinated by neurons in the left motor cortex, while
the opposite is true for the left hand.

The Occipital Lobe

The most posterior portion of the cerebral cortex comprises the
occipital lobe. Deficits or damage to neurons in the occipital lobe may
cause "cortical blindness" or discrete blind spots in the visual field. The
areas immediately anterior (in front of) the occipital pole comprise the
visual association zone, where meaning is attached to visual stimuli. Laterality effects are manifested here with verbal stimuli (words) being recognized more reliably in the left hemisphere, and visual-spatial stimuli
(designs) showing a right-sided effect (Pirozzolo and Rayner 1979). Any
time damage occurs in the association areas, one must consider the possibility of difficulties in visual-form recognition, building sight-word vo-
cabularies, and facial recognition (to name only a few areas of concern).

The Temporal Lobe

The temporal lobe is below the Sylvian fissure and is typically enlarged on the left side—theoretically to assume language functions. It is
interesting to note that Neanderthal man had an enlarged temporal lobe,
suggesting the existence of language abilities. Audition is generally associated with the temporal lobe. When damage occurs in Wernicke's area, receptive aphasia (language comprehension) results. Lateralization of function also occurs in the temporal lobe, as left temporal lobe lesions result
in language disorders, while right temporal lobe lesions may result in deficits in picture comprehension.

The Angular Gyrus

The angular gyrus is believed to be critically important, and an
inspection of its strategic location may reveal why. Localized in the terti-
ary area of the temporal, occipital, and parietal lobes, it is thought to be
the latest in neural evolution and is known to be one of the last areas of
the brain to myelinate (Geschwind 1965). This gyrus does not appear in
subprimates and is not well developed in apes. Luria (1970) and others

(e.g., Pirozzolo and Hansch 1982) have implicated this area of the brain as critical to the reading process. Bordering on the association zones (where meaning is attached to sensory stimuli), the angular gyrus is in a perfect location to perform the task of cross-modal integration so critical to a number of complex cognitive tasks, especially reading. In fact, it is interesting to note that much of the neuropsychological research on dyslexia has specifically implicated cross-modal deficits as one of the primary problems in developmental dyslexia (see Hynd and Cohen 1983 for a review). This finding is consistent with the theory of Geschwind (1962, 1972) as to the function of this relatively newly evolved region of the brain.

The Frontal Lobes

Generally, the frontal lobes include the cortical area directly anterior to the central sulcus (including the motor strip) and rostral to the Sylvian fissure. This region includes about 40 percent of the total cortical area (Filskov, Grimm, and Lewis 1981). Broca's area is included in the prefrontal region, and damage to this area in the left hemisphere usually results in deficits in expressive speech. Broca's and Wernicke's area are connected by the arcuate fasciculus, and a lesion to this important neural pathway can result in a disconnection between the ability to understand speech and the ability to repeat what was heard. Returning to the frontal lobe, however, it is important to realize that lateralization of function is not nearly so evident in the frontal area. Also, important developmental considerations enter into the picture here. The frontal lobes are thought not to assert real control over behavior until a child reaches 7 or 8 or even later. At that point, the frontal lobes seem to assert an ever-increasing control over the planning, organization, and execution of behavior (Luria 1966, 1969). If damage occurs early in development, its behavioral manifestation may be delayed until that time when the frontal lobes should assert their control over behavior. On the other hand, the "disappearance" of hyperactive behavior in early adolescence may simply reflect the development of frontal-lobe function, so that previously problematical behavior is brought under control by the now active frontal cortex (Golden 1981). Generalized damage to the frontal lobes can result in a "slowing" of the thought process, a loss of initiative or motivation, and problems in conceptual set shifting (resulting in perseveration). According to Lezak (1976), other deficits arising from frontal lobe lesions may include problems in emotional and social adjustment as well as more generalized cognitive deficits.

With this very brief overview of functional brain organization in mind (and realizing there may be some individual structural and functional variation), it is now appropriate to direct our attention toward some of the research which has advanced our conceptual understanding of how the brain and its functional organization relate to disorders of learning seen by school psychologists.

RELEVANCE OF NEUROPSYCHOLOGICAL RESEARCH

It is interesting to note that some contemporary educators and psychologists consider a neurological perspective on learning disorders to be a relatively recent development. It is interesting because the first known attempts to understand children and adults with learning problems came from clinical studies of brain-damaged patients (e.g., Hinshelwood 1895). Morgan (1896) studied a boy under his care who evidenced reading problems similar to those shown by the brain-damaged patients of Hinshelwood. Based on his study of this child, Morgan suggested that the cortical area, recognized as important in reading, was delayed in its development in his patient.

Some decades later, Samuel Orton (1937) adopted the notion of developmental delay in explaining why reversals of letters or words (e.g., *was* for *saw* or *d* for *b*) were so common in the reading and writing of young children. He suggested that one hemisphere failed to develop dominance over the other for language functions. It was thought that for effective reading, the left hemisphere had to establish a "dominance" over the minor, or right cerebral hemisphere. Otherwise, both hemispheres would struggle to establish a memory representation for the word or letter. The image in the right hemisphere was thought to be the mirror image of the correct, left hemisphere image. This idea gained quick and unquestioning acceptance among educators because in Orton's (1937) concept, this imbalance in cerebral dominance was attributed to a developmental *delay* and was not due to cerebral insult or dysfunction. This theory gave educators hope that the developmental delay could be directly remediated, and as a result, reading would be enhanced. As indicated previously, the chapter by Kaufman and Kaufman on remedial intervention reviews the research on the programs based on Orton's theory.

Deficit or Delay

Despite the general failure of these programs of intervention, educators and psychologists have been slow to question the idea that learning-disabled children suffer a developmental delay. Recently, however, investigations by one of the authors (Hynd and Obrzut 1977, Hynd, et al. 1979, Hynd and Obrzut 1981b, Obrzut, Hynd, Obrzut, and Pirozzolo 1981) and others (e.g., Hiscock and Kinsbourne 1978, Kinsbourne and Hiscock 1978, Molfese and Molfese 1979) provide evidence for two tentative conclusions. First, cerebral lateralization for function does not develop and is present at birth. Second, children with learning disabilities seem to show the same "degree" of cerebral dominance as normal children, but they perform at a degraded level due to their well-documented deficits in attention (e.g., Dykman, Ackerman, Clements, and Peters 1971, Hynd, Obrzut, Hynd, and Connor 1978). It may well be that the deficits in attention have been misinterpreted as evidence for incomplete cerebral dominance. As previously noted, the frontal lobes may take more command in organizing sequential behavior as children get older and may assert control over distractible behavior, thus giving the wrong impression that learning-disabled children have "caught up" in a developmental sense.

Others have criticized this line of research because it typically used an analysis of data derived from groups of children at different age levels to support the conclusion that developmental delays do not exist. Needless to say, such a criticism may be well founded. For instance, Satz and his colleagues followed 442 boys from kindergarten through fifth grade, using a variety of neuropsychological measures. Satz advances a theory of maturational lag which assumes that children develop reading or learning problems because they are delayed in functional brain development (Satz, Rardin and Ross 1971, Satz and Sparrow 1970, Satz and Van Nostrand 1973). Satz argues that deficits in cognitive function do not necessarily mean brain damage, but simply that the involved region of the brain is slow to develop to its fullest capacity. But if the child is never able to "catch up" on cognitive tasks even over time, then the possibility of brain damage or tissue impairment becomes more real.

Of special interest to school psychologists, Satz found that on the basis of a brief neuropsychological test battery administered in kindergarten, he could accurately predict reading achievement in second grade quite well. Based on a discriminant analysis of sixteen possible predictor variables, 89 percent of the severely disabled readers could be classified, 94 percent of the superior readers, and for the whole group of children, the predicted reading achievement was correct in 78 percent of the cases. Similar rates were achieved when the children were reexamined at the end of grade 5. The important point, however, is that Satz reports data in support of the developmental lag hypothesis.

What is one to make of such conflicting reports regarding such an important area of research? It seems reasonable (as is typical in such cases) to suspect that both perspectives are probably correct, depending on the case in point. Generally, it would be reasonable to conclude that children with learning problems who *demonstrate neuropsychologically based deficits* may indeed suffer some developmental delay. If direct intervention in the area of deficit does not prove successful or at least offer some hope of being so, then the learning problem is probably due to neurological dysfunction and not delay. In this case it would seem most prudent to circumvent the deficit and teach to available areas of strength. Again, the chapter by Kaufman and Kaufman elaborates on these ideas with respect to intervention.

It should be stressed that the neuropsychological research, while not answering the question of the etiology of learning problems, has at least clarified the issues, thereby allowing reasonable strategies of intervention to be formulated. Also, the research in this area has led us to conclude that measures of perceptual and manual asymmetry (such as handedness and footedness) are not necessarily correlated with learning deficit, as they were once thought to be (Hynd, Obrzut and Obrzut 1981). If anything, the neuropsychological research has taught school psychologists to be *more* cautious than ever before in applying theory to practice. This is indeed progress if one considers that it was only about forty-five years ago that the now infamous Cyril Burt (1937) stated with absolute assurance that left handers (thought to be deficient in terms of cerebral dominance), ". . . squint, they stammer, they shuffle, and shamble, they flounder about like seals out of water. Awkward in the house, and clumsy in their games, they are fumblers and bunglers at whatever they do" (p. 287, quoted by Corballis 1980).

Subtypes of Learning Disabilities

For those children who evidence neuropsychologically based learning problems, it now seems apparent that among this group several rather consistent subtypes of disabled learners exist (Fisk and Rourke 1979). As psychological and neurological measures become more refined, so does the ability to make finer discriminations between intraindividual abilities and disabilities. Some of the research has been conducted with learning-disabled children suffering spelling (e.g., Sweeney and Rourke 1978) and arithmetic (e.g., Rourke and Finlayson 1978, Rourke and Strang 1981) disorders. However, the vast majority of the subtype research has focused on differentiating categories of reading disability (e.g., Boder 1971, 1973; Mattis, French, and Rapin 1975, Obrzut 1979, Pirozzolo 1979, 1981).

Generally, it can be said that at least two and quite possibly more subtypes of disabled readers exist. One subtype has difficulty with sound-symbol relationships, suffers language delay, evidences speech deficits, anomia (object-naming deficit), and may evidence a lower verbal IQ compared to a performance IQ. A second, less prevalent group experiences difficulty with the visual-spatial qualities of reading, has faulty eye movements, may evidence spatial disorientation, and has a lower performance IQ than verbal IQ (Pirozzolo 1979, 1981). Most of these characteristics can easily be identified through behavioral assessment procedures (see Keller 1980, Smith 1980). Consequently, the question arises about what, exactly, our knowledge of brain-behavior relationships has contributed to understanding these subtypes.

This question can be answered by examining the neuropsychological research with these children. For instance, Obrzut (1979) found in examining these subtypes that recognized measures of cortical integrity related to auditory functioning showed deficits only in the dysphonetic group. This finding suggested that the auditory cortex (roughly equiva-

TABLE 10.2

Neuropsychological Criteria for the Differential Diagnosis
of Two Subtypes of Developmental Dyslexia*

Subtype	
Auditory-Linguistic	Visual-Spatial
1. At least 1½–2 yrs. delay in reading	1. 1½–2 yrs. delay in reading acquisition after year eight
2. Delayed language onset	2. Right-left disorientation
3. Expressive speech deficits	3. Poor handwriting
4. Anomia, object and color-naming deficits	4. Finger agnosia
5. Spelling errors suggesting deficits in phoneme-to-grapheme translation	5. Letter and word reversals in spelling
6. Phonetic reading errors	6. Reading errors involving the visual aspects of word decoding
7. Low verbal IQ (relative to performance IQ)	7. Faulty eye movements
8. Average to above average performance IQ	8. Early evidence for a preference for mirror-writing
9. Relatively intact visual-spatial abilities	9. Low performance IQ (relative to verbal IQ)
10. Normal eye movements	10. Average to above average verbal IQ
11. Letter-by-letter decoding strategy	11. Relatively intact oral language abilities
12. Agrammatism	12. Phonetic decoding strategy

*Adopted from Pirozzolo, F. J. Neuropsychological aspects of developmental reading disability. *School Psychology Review*, 1981, *10*, 350–355 (with permission).

lent to Wernicke's region) was dysfunctional. In another study, Fried, Tanguay, Boder, Doubleday and Greensite (1981) used EEG and measures of electrical processing during cognition to examine cortical functioning in subtypes of disabled readers. When compared to findings on control children, the results were consistent with the theory that those children who had visual-spatial deficits evidenced right hemisphere dysfunction, and those with left hemisphere dysfunction had difficulty with auditory-linguistic aspects of fluent reading. Other studies seem to support these conclusions regarding subtypes of disabled readers (e.g., Pirozzolo and Rayner 1979).

It seems that the subtype research, which generally includes carefully screened subjects, supports the notion that neurological deficit, or at least dysfunction, is the basis of some severe learning problems. However, there is an important issue here that cannot and should not be overlooked. It is well known that a correlation exists between environmental stimulation, socioeconomic factors, and other important factors and brain weight (Khang-cheng, Roessmann, Hause, and Monroe 1981, Soto-Moyano, Perez, Carrillo, and Hernandez, 1981; Walsh, 1981). It is entirely possible that learning deficits are not due to damage or abnormal development but merely to a failure of normal development in a given cortical region. EEG differences or other neuropsychological evidence of differences between normal and learning-disabled children tell us little about how the brain actually *looks*. School psychologists could feel more secure in their assumptions if direct evidence of the neurological nature of learning disabilities existed. Some limited evidence exists at this point in time.

Cytoarchitectonic (Neuropathological) Studies

Only two published neuropathological studies of the brains of children with reading disorders exist. As Pirozzolo and Hansch (1982) note, reading or learning disabilities are not life threatening and thus, systematic neurological studies have not been carried out for them as they have with neurological diseases. However, due to increasing interest in the neurological deficit theory, two cytoarchitectonic studies have been completed, and they lend important support to this notion as to the basis of some learning problems.

Drake (1968) examined a twelve-year-old dyslexic boy who died from a hemorrhage in the cerebellar region. He had normal intelligence and evidenced no developmental delay in reaching any important motor or cognitive milestones. The brain at autopsy revealed atypical gyrial organization in both parietal lobes. The gyri were unusually wide and the corpus callosum was atrophied. The cortex was equally atypical. It can be speculated that the corpus callosum (which connects both cerebral hemispheres) allowed for less efficient transfer of information (see Hynd, et al. 1979), and that the abnormalities noted in the parietal lobes were probably associated with the failures of this boy in learning to read, write, or carry out arithmetical calculations. It will be recalled from the previous discussion that the parietal lobes are especially important in drawing meaning from all sensory stimuli and in integrating cross-modal information (angular gyrus) — a task critical to reading.

Eleven years later, Galaburda and Kemper (1979) published a comprehensive study of a twenty-year-old dyslexic who died from a fall at his first employment as a construction worker. Interestingly, this young man had a history of familial dyslexia and was left handed. At autopsy the brain looked normal, with the exception that the cortex around Wernicke's area was not enlarged over the homologous area in the right hemisphere as it is in most normal brains (Geschwind and Levitsky 1968). Microscopic examination revealed that the layers of the cortex were not well differentiated, and abnormal tissue was noted in the auditory association cortex. The right cerebral hemisphere was without pathology. The fact that the left hemisphere and especially the auditory association cortex were pathological could be very important as a correlate of the dyslexia. This study supports others who suggest that the language area of the brain may be small and malformed in the reading disabled or dyslexic (e.g., Galaburda, LeMay, Kemper and Geschwind 1978, Galaburda, Sanides, and Geschwind 1978, Hier, LeMay, Rosenberger, and Perlo 1978).

While it may seem risky to draw the conclusion that the brains of dyslexics may be abnormal in structure as a result of two cytoarchitectonic studies, it should be realized that there are numerous electrophysiological studies in support of these conclusions. Duffy, Denckla, Bartels, and Sandini (1980) found aberrant electrophysiology in the areas typically involved in reading and speech using an examination of regional differences in electrical brain activity. Based on this study, electrophysiological methods are now being advocated for the diagnosis of dyslexia (Duffy, Denckla, Bartels, Sandini, and Kiessling 1980). One can hypothesize that it will not be too distant in the future when other cytoarchitectonic and electrophysiological studies will appear investigating other learning disabilities (e.g., difficulties in arithmetic, sensory processing, etc.).

Based on this brief review of selected areas of neuropsychological research, it is reasonable to conclude that a basic knowledge of functional neuroanatomy and conceptualization of brain-behavior relationships may shed some light on the often complex problems manifested by some learning-disabled children. Not even mentioned is the considerable literature regarding children with cerebral palsy, brain damage, neuro-muscular disorders, and other medical disorders which may affect learning or classroom behavior (see Obrzut and Hynd, 1983, for a review). While not all school psychologists need to pursue advanced study in the physiological basis of behavior, some basic understanding should be of benefit in working with this population of school children.

The following section will provide a more concrete discussion of how a neuropsychological perspective can be of value in conceptualizing a child's difficulty and in formulating educational intervention. Two case studies will be provided which should serve to underscore the points made in this chapter.

NEUROPSYCHOLOGICAL EVALUATION OF THE SCHOOL-AGE CHILD

Since different sorts of mental functions of consequence for school performance depend on various areas of the brain, it is of considerable importance that any approach to neuropsychological evaluation of the school-age child provide for measurement of all cortical areas which mediate cognitive functions of educational relevance. A question logically arises about the general utility of cortical assessment, as opposed to the assessment of cognitive processes more or less independent of their cortical substrates. There are two reasons why assessment of cortical integrity is a more sensitive and generalizable approach than an assessment of simple processing facility. Since multiple, discrete cortical areas are involved in simple processes such as "short-term memory," a process-model approach cannot identify the specific, cortically mediated components of problems with memory. Differential cortical involvement is required for processing such educationally relevant, short-term memory functions as verbal memory versus pictorial memory; type of language functions (e.g., recognition versus expression); and the unique quality of items to be remembered. By a systematic assessment of cortical areas with which each of these facets of short-term memory is involved, it is possible to develop instructional and test-taking strategies for an individual child with much greater precision than that provided by a process model.

Of more importance from a longer-term educational perspective, however, is the increased generalizability of data derived from cortical function assessment as compared to process assessment. Since there are changes in the processes involved in the performance of a single task both over time and at increasing levels of complexity, the assessment of cortical substrates of given behaviors permits extrapolation of current findings to future educational contexts much more efficiently than the analysis of the process involved at a given time in the performance of a given task. In the case of reading, for example, it has been demonstrated that there is a shift in the processes involved in reading during the first three years of school (Hartlage 1975a), possibly reflecting what Rourke (1982) has postulated as a shift from right to left hemisphere involvement in reading. This may reflect a development shift from spatial cues in word recognition to a phonetic-linguistic analysis of words. There is evidence that the acquisition of reading ability is dependent on quite different cortical substrates than those involved in comprehending what one is reading (Hartlage 1975b) — a further argument against the limitations of a simple process-analysis approach for any longer-term educational programming.

APPROACHES TO NEUROPSYCHOLOGICAL ASSESSMENT

There are essentially two major approaches to conducting a systematic evaluation of cortical function. One approach, which has been available for more than two decades, grew out of research using Ward Halstead's approach to the measurement of biological intelligence. Perhaps best known through the work of Halstead's student, Ralph Reitan, this approach systematically samples a very comprehensive range of cognitive and psychomotor abilities in such a way as to permit an assessment of the functional integrity of essentially all cortical areas. The battery used in this approach, typically referred to as the Halstead-Reitan Battery, or the Reitan-Indiana Battery, includes many individual tests, including the Categories Test, the Aphasia Test, the Tactile Performance Test, the Trail Making Test, the Sensory-Perceptual Examination, the Finger Oscillation Test, and a number of other tests and scales which can require up to eight hours to administer (Hartlage and Hartlage 1982). Because of the way in which the battery is constructed, it is not considered feasible to give only portions of the battery without compromising the battery's validity.

In the hands of a neuropsychologist trained in its use and well versed in brain-behavior relationships, the validity of this battery has been repeatedly demonstrated, and there is virtually no disagreement that it is both valid and sensitive as a measure of the functional integrity of most areas of the cerebral cortex in children (Reitan 1974). Its main disadvantages lie in the time required to learn its administration, the considerable neuropsychological sophistication required for its interpretation, and the lengthy time needed for administration to each individual. Another disadvantage for its use by school psychologists is the relatively extensive amount of test apparatus and equipment involved which, in addition to its expense, make it impractical for use where portability is required.

Another type of test battery, still in the experimental stage of development for use with children, grew out of Golden's development (from the work of Luria) of a reasonably objective, quantified neuropsychological assessment battery for adults, known as the Luria-Nebraska. This battery, consisting of a large number of fairly simple tests, each scored on a three point scale, can be plotted onto a summary sheet on which the scores measure possible areas of dysfunction. Separate scores are provided for such items as expression, memory, motor, and rhythm, with a separate scale for determining whether the global configuration is pathognomonic. Additional scale configurations can be used to indicate whether dysfunctions are chronic or acute (Golden, Hammeke and Purisch 1978). The administration of the Luria-Nebraska does not require a great deal of time to learn, and the battery can generally be completed in well under three hours. The scoring system is fairly simple, and the interpretation can be inferred from the summary sheet without much neuropsychological sophistication. There is relatively little apparatus involved, and the battery is readily portable.

Extensive research with the adult version has documented its validity for neuropsychological diagnosis (Golden 1979, Golden, Hammeke, Osmon, Sweet, Purisch, and Graber 1981, Hammeke, Golden, and Purisch 1978, Lewis, Golden, Moses, Osmon, Purisch, and Hammeke 1979, Moses and Golden 1979, Osmon, Golden, Purisch, and Hammeke 1979), and there is good likelihood that the children's version will approach the validity of the adult version (Wilkening, Golden, MacInnes, Plaistead, and Hermann 1981). One disadvantage of this approach for school neuropsychological assessment is that it does not include measures commonly required by school administrations, and so must be augmented by individual assessment of intellectual ability, etc., thus extending the time potentially required for evaluation of a given child to well in excess of four hours. Another possible problem against which Golden cautions is the use of the test by individuals untrained in neuropsychology for purposes of neurodiagnosis which may exceed their levels of sophistication in the interpretation of data.

Another approach, both operationally and conceptually different from the formal neuropsychological test battery approach, involves the use of psychometric tests generally familiar to and in common use by school psychologists, with augmentation by a few specialized measures to provide a global survey of all major cortical areas of relevance to school performance (Hartlage 1981). An evaluation using such an approach would typically include such common instruments as WISC-R, PPVT, WRAT, and VMI, and add further tests, such as finger-tapping rate and recognition of numbers written on fingertips. The rationale for the use of such tests for measurement of neuropsychological function is based on principles discussed earlier in this chapter — for example, it is important to have data involving the comparison of cognitive abilities known to be localized to the left and right cerebral hemispheres; differential right and left hand tapping rates as measures of motor performance; and number recognition on right and left hand fingertips to assess sensory-parietal abilities. Data relative to anterior-posterior functions are derived from comparisons of receptive language functions (e.g., PPVT) with language functions involving expressive components (e.g., Vocabulary); spatial functions having executory components (e.g., VMI, Block Design) with those not involving significant motor components (e.g., Picture Completion); and comparison of purely perceptual (e.g., fingertip number writing) and more purely motor functions (e.g., tapping rate) (Hartlage and Reynolds 1981).

Advantages of this approach involve the comparative familiarity of test procedures to psychologists typically involved in the evaluation of school-age children, and the fairly direct transferability of data to answer questions commonly at issue in the development of an individual educational profile, as well as the comparative brevity of administration time and lack of involved apparatus. Like all approaches to neuropsychological assessment of school-age children, it contains potential for misinterpretation by neuropsychologically unsophisticated users. This approach, using familiar tests which are in common use for educational evaluation, probably contains less potential for problems of interpretation by naive examiners, since it provides no ready labels relating poor performance on given scales to specific lobes or cortical areas. For a more thorough coverage of neuropsychological assessment procedures with school-age children, the interested reader is referred to Hynd and Obrzut's (1981) volume.

To illustrate how the data from psychometric tests in common use, when augmented by simple neuropsychological measures of motor and perceptual performance, can be applied to neuropsychological assessment of the school-age child, the following sample cases — seen by the second author provide models for such data interpretation.

CASE REPORTS

Case 1

Felicity, a thirteen-year-old, right-handed, eighth-grade girl, was referred for evaluation of school difficulties of an apparently emotional nature. She was reported to "break down and cry" in class, and had been removed from public school and placed in a private school because of this problem. Felicity was unsuccessful in private school, and returned to public school, where her attendance had become so infrequent that a homebound teacher was recommended.

She reportedly had formerly been a good student, and copies of her school grades until two years ago had shown her to be an A and B student. Over the past two years, her grades had become mostly Cs, with no As in any subject and a D in conduct. No prior individual testing had been done, but group testing (Otis-Lennon) four years earlier had resulted in a standard score of 93. Felicity's mother reported that two years ago she had begun to awake at night screaming and complaining of headaches. This had resolved over the past year, but she continued to be extremely anxious and to become agitated in crowds. Felicity became especially anxious in school, and had been described as school phobic by one physician who examined her.

Teachers noted that she often seemed to be in a world of her own and startled easily when called. Despite her very poor school attendance, teachers generally described her as a good student.

Just prior to beginning school two years ago, she was in a minor accident, being struck by a car while crossing the street. She suffered bruises to her right thigh, fingers on her left hand, and over the left parietal area, and reportedly was unconscious for five minutes. A complete neurological examination was done and was entirely within normal limits. Because of her headaches she was examined by a neurosurgeon, who similarly found no evidence of damage. Because of persistent emotional problems, she again saw a neurologist, who performed an EEG and a CT scan. Both these tests were normal, and her problem was considered to be emotional, with a diagnosis of adolescent adjustment problems.

Felicity was a physically mature, well-dressed black girl of average size and weight, who was described as a "friendly, relaxed, cute girl." Her activity level during testing was normal, and she was described as having excellent motivation and as being "perfectionistic" on the Beery and the Draw-A-Person.

WISC-R full-scale IQ was 75, with verbal IQ at 86 and performance IQ at 68 (Table 10.3). All designs on the Beery were correctly reproduced, but her PPVT was at the 9-5 mental age level, corresponding to a standard score of 77. WRAT arithmetic was at the fifth grade, seventh month level (Scaled Score of 86), with WRAT reading at the fifth grade, sixth month level (SS 86). Felicity's D-A-P was small (less than 2½ inches high), displaced to the upper left portion of the paper, and carefully done with many erasures, with a mental age of eight to nine. Her grip strength was 29 kg. on the right hand and 24 kg. on the left hand; tapping rates at ten seconds were 50.7 for the right hand and 38.0 for the left hand. Felicity correctly identified 19 of 20 numbers written on the fingertips of her left hand, and 18 of 20 written on her right hand.

TABLE 10.3

Felicity's Test Results (CA = 13-4)

WISC-R RESULTS		
Verbal Tests	Raw Score	Scaled Score
Information	15	8
Similarities	11	6
Arithmetic	13	9
Vocabulary	33	8
Comprehension	19	8
Digit Span	(12)	(9)
Performance Tests		
Picture Completion	18	7
Picture Arrangement	11	4
Block Design	6	1
Object Assembly	14	4
Coding	48	9
Verbal IQ	86	
Performance IQ	68	
Full Scale IQ	75	

Peabody Picture Vocabulary Test

MA = 9-5

IQ = 77

Wide Range Achievement Test	Grade Equivalent	Scaled Score
Reading (Word Recognition)	5.6	86
Arithmetic	5.7	86

Grip Strength

R. H. = 29 kg.
L. H. = 24 kg.

Finger Tapping (10")

R. H. = 50.7
L. H. = 38.0

Finger-Tip Number Writing (# correct)

R. H. = 18/20
L. H. = 19/20

NOTE: The reader should realize that a comprehensive neuropsychological evaluation incorporates a much more extensive battery than the one reported here. These brief results are presented for illustrative purposes only.

Most striking, of course, is the discrepancy both between her verbal and performance IQ and between her previous group IQ scores and school grades and her current full-scale Wechsler IQ, PPVT, and WRAT achievement levels. These discrepancies, when interpreted from a fairly straightforward school psychological perspective, suggest several hypotheses:

1. Although there were no signs of damage on comprehensive neurological examination, Felicity appears to have sustained a rather considerable decline in her level of intellectual functioning.

2. Although the decline in mental functioning appears to involve mainly nonverbal IQ, the low PPVT suggests that there may be a decline in at least some aspects of language function.

3. There is some disparity between reports of her school-phobic type of behavior and her self-report of liking school, thinking she is doing well, and looking forward to high school.

Although the ability and achievement scores provide ample documentation that Felicity is at considerable risk for academic problems, the examiner's reports of her relaxed, friendly, apparently task-oriented behavior do not yield any clues to the cause of these school problems. Examination of these findings from a neuropsychological perspective would suggest several hypotheses of a slightly different nature from those of the straightforward school psychological perspective.

1. The verbal-performance discrepancy, combined with current mild retardation level IQ and previous school grades, suggest significant involvement of the right cerebral hemisphere. The unique depression on Block Design suggests major involvement of the right temporal area. This area was most likely damaged by a centra-coup injury, caused by a blow to the left side of the head, causing the brain on the contralateral (right) side to sustain damage by striking against the skull on a rebound from the side of injury. Such injuries often result in damage more severe than that sustained by the cortical area on the original side of injury.

2. There was some milder impairment of parietal areas of the left hemisphere (corresponding to her site of injury), reflected in the depressed PPVT score and the slight superiority of identification of numbers written on her left hand fingertips.

3. The damage to the right temporal lobe also extended anteriorly across the Sylvian Fissure to the motor cortex of the right cerebral hemisphere, as reflected in the marked inferiority of the left hand on finger tapping and the slight superiority of right hand grip strength.

4. From a comparison of her previous school grades and current WRAT levels, data suggest that there has been very little acquisition of new learning during the past two-year period.

5. The apparent mechanism of denial reflected in Felicity's self-report of liking school and doing well is a fairly prototypical sequel to damage to the right cerebral hemisphere, often described in the neurologic literature as *la belle indifference* reaction.

Educational Implications Interpretation of data from a conventional psychological perspective, while clearly documenting the likelihood of considerable decline in level of intellectual functioning, does not provide any etiologic basis for the apparent decline, and of more consequence, does not suggest any specific educational implications. Using a neuro-psychological interpretation of the data, the educational implications could take the form of the following recommendations:

1. The cortical area involved in constructional apraxic functions are damaged. So emphasis on remediation of functions subserved by these cortical areas will most likely not provide much improvement in the level of functioning and would likely result in increasing Felicity's frustration.

2. Attempting to alleviate the educationally handicapping conditions resultant from her right temporal area damage could be accomplished by focusing on the comparatively intact visual-spatial, right hemisphere function (e.g., Picture Completion SS of 7), and relatively strong abilities in both visual and auditory sequencing (e.g., both Coding and Digit Span scaled scores of 9), while deemphasizing language recognition approaches.

3. Her global cognitive ability is rather markedly reduced, and academic achievement expectancies should be modified to match this reduction.

4. The apparent denial mechanism reflected in her handling of school problems is attributable to her neurological impairment and thus is not a primary precipitating cause of her general adjustment problems.

5. In light of the fact that her closed head injury occurred more than two and a half years ago, it is extremely unlikely that much recovery of function over present levels should be anticipated, so that future educational plans should be developed on the basis of her current intellectual abilities rather than prior school grade or test scores.

6. Much of her unhappiness in the school setting and her apparent school phobia may be attributable to her reduced cognitive ability, rather than to more functional causes; thus lowering of expectation rather than symptom-focused psychotherapy or behavioral intervention may represent the more appropriate approach to these problems.

Although Felicity was evaluated shortly before this chapter was written, so that no follow-up data are available, her situation is not unlike that of a surprisingly large number of children who have sustained apparently very minor head injuries and for whom follow-up data are available (e.g., Rimel, Giordani, Barth, Boll, and Jane 1981). In general, the prognosis for eventual outcome depends to a significant extent on the educational interventions which are implemented. Focus on the deficit areas rather than leading to specific improvement will more commonly evoke negative behavioral reactions. An intervention strategy which utilizes residual strengths can enhance both academic performance and self concept, since the focus will be on tasks which the child can (as opposed to cannot, as might be proposed by a process model) perform (Hartlage 1979).

Of considerably more consequence for school psychology, however, is the utility of neuropsychological procedures in providing a structure for data interpretation of the sort provided by psychometric instruments in common use by school psychologists. Examples of such use involve the differentiated academic processing styles of children with comparatively more efficient functioning of one cerebral hemisphere. It has been demonstrated, for example, that there is a significant discrepancy in the size of the cerebral hemisphere in approximately 77 percent of most presumably normal children and adults, with the left cerebral hemisphere larger in 65 percent and the right cerebral hemisphere larger in 12 percent (Geschwind and Levitsky 1968, Galaburda, et al. 1978, Chi, Dooling and Gilles 1977). The consequences of such anatomic asymmetry have been described in terms of their relevance for both academic and behavioral management strategies, taking into account the neuropsychological processes differentially mediated by each hemisphere (Hartlage and Hartlage 1977). In general, children with superiority of left hemisphere functioning have been found to profit from greater emphasis on linguistic-phonetic approaches to reading and instruction which focuses on understanding principles rather than on workbook exercises, while children with right hemisphere superiority profit more from traditional orthographic approaches to reading and instruction which focuses on gestalt rather than sequential learning (Hartlage 1979). In light of the fact that more than three out of every four children can be expected to be asymmetrical in their cortical organization, attention to such neuropsychological considerations in the development of individual educational programs for given children is likely to enhance the relevance of a given child's program to his or her optimal learning modalities and most efficient strategies for information processing.

The following sample case describes a child with an educational problem that occurs with considerable frequency among school-age children and demonstrates how a neuropsychological approach to interpretation of data from fairly commonly available tests can be applied toward developing optimal educational approaches.

Case 2

Jerry, a nine-year-six-month-old, right-handed, fourth grader, was referred for school psychological evaluation of a specific reading problem. He had not experienced previous reading or other academic problems and was described by all his former teachers as a conscientious student. His first grade teacher had, in fact, considered him to be a good student, although no specific letter grades were used in first grade. Jerry's second and third grade teachers both described him as a fairly good student, and his grades during these two years had been in the B and C grade range. His current (fourth grade) teacher felt he had problems with both word attack and reading comprehension, and had recommended some phonics exercises for him to his parents.

Jerry's development and medical history were unremarkable. The family pediatrician had been asked whether there were any medical or neurological factors in Jerry's reading problems, and had in response described Jerry as a perfectly normal boy in every way, except perhaps just a bit on the shy and quiet side. Both parents denied any school problems. The father, a sales representative, was a high school graduate with one and a half years of college. Although Jerry's mother had dropped out of school after the tenth grade, she reported that she had earned passing grades in all subjects.

Jerry was described as very neat, extremely well behaved, and apparently putting forth a good degree of effort on all test items. He did not initiate any conversation and tended to respond with brief answers, but did not demonstrate signs of depression. When he was uncertain of an answer, he was reluctant to give one and frequently responded, "I don't know," requiring prompting to venture a more substantive response. He was extremely involved in the Block Design subtest and wanted to continue on the more difficult items even after time had run out. Jerry's responses to Vocabulary and Comprehension subtests required the examiner to request him to elaborate, as he tended to make one or two-word responses. Wechsler (WISC-R) testing by the school psychologist a month previously revealed a verbal IQ of 84, performance IQ of 98, and full scale IQ of 89 (Table 10.4). Bender-Gestalt was appropriate for this age, and Draw-A-Person was slightly above age expectancy. Wide Range Achievement Test scores were reported at the second grade-ninth month, second grade-eighth month, and beginning fourth grade on reading, spelling, and arithmetic respectively, corresponding to standard scores of 84, 84, and 94 (1965 norms). The school psychological report had indicated the possibility of a learning disability on the basis of the discrepancy between his verbal and performance IQ and the subtest scatter on the WISC-R. The parents had brought Jerry to the medical center on the recommendation of the family pediatrician, who doubted that Jerry was learning disabled and had requested a second opinion. Neuropsychological examination included only the PPVT, finger tapping rate, and fingertip writing, since the data from the school psychological evaluation done one month previously was provided before the time of his visit. These tests resulted in a PPVT IQ equivalent of 84; finger tapping of 30 and 31 taps per ten seconds with right and left hand respectively; and 17 of 20 numbers correctly identified on right hand fingertips and 19 of 20 numbers correctly identified on left hand fingertips. When combined with data from the school psychological examination, the following conclusions were felt to be substantiated by the data:

TABLE 10.4

Jerry's Test Results (CA = 9-6)

WISC-R RESULTS	Raw Score	Scaled Score
Verbal Tests		
Information	12	8
Similarities	8	7
Arithmetic	8	6
Vocabulary	19	7
Comprehension	14	9
Performance Tests		
Picture Completion	18	11
Picture Arrangement	26	11
Block Design	22	10
Object Assembly	18	9
Coding	32	8
Verbal IQ	84	
Performance IQ	98	
Full Scale IQ	89	

Peabody Picture Vocabulary Test

IQ = 84

Wide Range Achievement Test	Grade Equivalent	Scaled Score
Reading (Word Recognition)	2.9	84
Spelling	2.8	84
Arithmetic	4.0	94

Finger Tapping (10")

R. H. = 30
L. H. = 31

Finger-Tip Number Writing (# correct)

R. H. = 17/20
L. H. = 19/20

NOTE: The reader should realize that a comprehensive neuropsychological evaluation incorporates a much more extensive battery than the one reported here. These brief results are presented for illustrative purposes only.

1. There is test evidence of fairly generalized and quite consistent superiority of right over left cortical hemisphere function, as reflected in such discrepancies as performance higher than verbal IQ; VMI and D-A-P standard scores higher than PPVT; superiority of left over right hand tapping rate (even though he was right-handed); more accurate recogni-

tion of numbers written on left hand fingertips; and somewhat higher arithmetic score than WISC-R arithmetic levels.

2. Academic history is compatible with chronic superiority of right hemisphere function, to some extent reflected in his declining academic performance as the educational curriculum progressively depended less on right hemisphere-mediated abilities and progressively more on left hemisphere abilities.

3. The behaviors reported by teachers, the school psychological examiner, and the family pediatrician are all consistent with what might be expected of a youngster with chronic deficiency of the left cerebral hemisphere. This profile of abilities and disabilities is also consistent with the model of the auditory-linguistic dyslexic child as conceived by Pirozzolo (1979, 1981) and discussed earlier in the chapter. Although this child's pattern of disabilities would not yet qualify him as being dyslexic, it can be postulated that his cognitive profile is similar to but not as severe as the true auditory-linguistic dyslexic child. In this regard, this case is a good example that brain *damage* need not exist to produce neuropsychologically based learning disorders. Consistent with Galaburda and Kemper's (1979) report, learning disabilities may simply evidence a failure of given cortical areas of the brain to develop normally. This may not be true in all cases, but the data provided in Jerry's case seem to support this conclusion for him.

CONCLUSION

The application of neuropsychological knowledge to problems of learning and behavior encountered in the school environment offers an exciting and promising alternative in conceptualizing the possible etiology of disorders and appropriate intervention strategies. Neuropsychological perspectives differ significantly from behavioral, psychoeducational, and other more traditional viewpoints encountered in educational circles. It is recognized that neuropsychological assessment of children experiencing learning or behavioral difficulties will not be needed in the majority of cases, for which more traditional approaches may determine the nature of the difficulty and its treatment. However, the manifestation of cortical function in behavior must be recognized, so that in appropriate instances a neuropsychological approach to diagnosis and treatment can be provided.

Training standards for school psychologists developed by the American Psychological Association and the National Association of School Psychologists insure that most sixth-year and doctoral-level programs produce psychologists capable of meeting the demands for professional services placed on them. However, training in the area of neuropsychology for school psychologists has just recently been proposed (see Hynd 1981). Roles for sixth year as well as doctoral-level school psychologists are envisioned. However, the time required to obtain appropriate additional training in this area could extend most graduate study by a minimum of a year or two. Since the need for those able to provide neuropsychological services is relatively small, although increasing, those willing and able to pursue advanced training in this area will surely find their services sought in the public schools.

It was the intention of this chapter to paint in broad strokes the rationale for studying brain-behavior relationships in school-age children, some basic principles regarding functional neuroanatomy, and areas of exciting new research efforts, and to suggest what a neuropsychological perspective means in the realm of differential clinical diagnosis with school children. School psychology students interested in pursuing advanced study in neuropsychology, in addition to more traditional academic preparation, will very probably be able to meet a significant area of need in providing school children appropriate and much needed psychological services.

REFERENCES

Bakker, D. J., Moerland, R., & Goekoop-Hoefkens, M. Effects of hemisphere-specific stimulation on the reading performance of dyslexic boys: A pilot study. *Journal of Clinical Neuropsychology,* 1981, *3,* 155–160.

Boder, E. Developmental dyslexia: Prevailing diagnostic concepts and a new diagnostic approach. In H. Myklebust (Ed.), *Progress in learning disabilities.* New York: Grune & Stratton, 1971.

Boder, E. Developmental dyslexia: A diagnostic approach based on three atypical reading-spelling patterns. *Developmental Medicine and Child Neurology,* 1973, *15,* 663–687.

Broca, P. Nouvelle observation d'aphemie produite par une lesion de la moite posterieure des deuxieme et troisieme circonvolutions frontales. *Bulletin de la Society Anatomique de Paris,* 1861, *36,* 398–407.

Brothmarkle, R. A. (Ed.). *Clinical psychology: Studies in honor of Lightner Witmer to commemorate the thirty-fifth anniversary of the founding of the first psychological clinic.* Philadelphia: University of Pennsylvania Press, 1931.

Chi, J. G., Dooling, E. C., & Gilles, F. H. Gyral development of the human brain. *Annals of Neurology,* 1977, *1,* 86.

Coles, G. S. The learning-disabilities test batteries: Empirical and social issues. *Harvard Educational Review,* 1978, *48,* 313–340.

Conrad, K. Beitrag sum problem dor parietalen alexia. *Archives Psychologie,* 1948, *181,* 398–420.

Corballis, M. C. Laterality and myth. *American Psychologist,* 1980, *35,* 284–295.

Cruickshank, W. M. A new perspective in teacher education: The neuroeducator. *Journal of Learning Disabilities,* 1981, *14,* 337–341, 367.

Dean, R. S. Cerebral laterality and verbal-performance discrepancies in intelligence. *Journal of School Psychology,* 1979, *17,* 145–150.

Drake, W. Clinical and pathological findings in a child with developmental learning disability. *Journal of Learning Disabilities,* 1968, *1,* 468–475.

Duffy, F. H., Denckla, M. D., Bartels, P. H., & Sandini, G. Dyslexia: Regional differences in brain electrical activity by topographic mapping. *Annals of Neurology,* 1980, *7,* 412–420.

Duffy, F. H., Denckla, M. D., Bartels, P. H., Sandini, G., & Kiessling, L. S. Dyslexia: Automated diagnosis of computerized classification of brain electrical activity. *Annals of Neurology,* 1980, *7,* 421–428.

Dykman, R. A., Ackerman, P. T., Clements, S. D., & Peters, J. E. Specific learning disabilities: An attentional deficit syndrome. In H. D. Myklebust (Ed.), *Progress in learning disabilities* (Vol. III). New York: Grune & Stratton, 1971.

Filskov, S. B., Grimm, B. H., & Lewis, J. A. Brain-behavior relationships. In S. B. Filskov & T. J. Bell (Eds.), *Handbook of Clinical Neuropsychology.* New York: John Wiley & Sons, 1980.

Fisk, J. L., & Rourke, B. P. Identification of subtypes of learning disabled children at three age levels: A neuropsychological, multivariate approach. *Journal of Clinical Neuropsychology,* 1979, *1,* 289–310.

French, J. D. The reticular formation. In J. L. McGaugh, N. M. Weinberger, and R. E. Whalen (Eds.), *Psychobiology: The biological basis of behavior.* San Francisco: W. H. Freeman, 1966.

Fried, I., Tanguay, P. E., Boder, E., Doubleday, C., & Greensite, M. Developmental dyslexia: Electrophysiological evidence of clinical subgroups. *Brain and Language,* 1981, *12,* 14–22.

Fuster, J. M., & Jervey, J. P. Inferotemporal neurons distinguish and retain behaviorally relevant features of visual stimuli. *Science,* 1981, *212,* 952–955.

Gaddes, W. H. *Learning disabilities and brain function: A neuropsychological approach.* New York: Springer-Verlag, 1980.

Gaddes, W. H. An examination of the validity of neuropsychological knowledge in educational diagnosis and remediation. In G. W. Hynd & J. E. Obrzut (Eds.), *Neuropsychological assessment of the school-age child: Issues and procedures.* New York: Grune & Stratton, 1981. (a)

Gaddes, W. H. Neuropsychology, fact or mythology, educational help or hindrance? *School Psychology Review,* 1981, *10,* 322–330. (b)

Galaburda, A., & Kemper, T. Cytoarchitectonic abnormalities in developmental dyslexia: A case study. *Annals of Neurology,* 1979, *6,* 94–100.

Galaburda, A. M., LeMay, M., Kemper, T. L., & Geschwind, M. Right-left asymmetries in the brain. *Science,* 1979, *199,* 852–856.

Galaburda, A. M., Sandies, F., & Geschwind, N. Human brain: Cytoarchitectonic left-right asymmetries in temporal speech region. *Archives of Neurology,* 1978, *35,* 812.

Gallagher, J. J. Children with developmental imbalances: A psychoeducational definition. In W. M. Cruickshank (Ed.), *The teacher of brain-injured children.* Syracuse: Syracuse University Press, 1966.

Gardner, E. *Fundamentals of Neurology.* Philadelphia: W. B. Saunders, 1975.

Geschwind, N. In J. Money (Ed.), *Reading Disability.* Baltimore: Johns Hopkins Press, 1962.

Geschwind, N. Disconnection syndromes in animals and man. *Brain,* 1965, *88,* 237–294.

Geschwind, N., & Levitsky, W. Human brain: Left-right asymmetries in temporal speech region. *Science,* 1968, *161,* 186–187.

Golden, C. J. Identification of specific neurological disorders using double discrimination scale derived from the standardized Luria Neuropsychological Battery. *International Journal of Neuroscience,* 1979, *10,* 51–56.

Golden, C. J. The Luria-Nebraska Children's Battery: Theory and formulation. In G. W. Hynd & J. E. Obrzut (Eds.), *Neuropsychological assessment and the school-age child: Issues and procedures.* New York: Grune & Stratton, 1981.

Golden, C. J., Hammeke, T. A., Osmon, D. C., Sweet, J., Purisch, A. D., & Graber, B. Factor analysis of the Luria-Nebraska Neuropsychological Battery: IV Intelligence and Pathognomic Scale. *International Journal of Neuroscience,* 1981, *15,* 87–92.

Golden C. J., Hammeke, T. A., & Purisch, A. D. Diagnostic validity of a standardized neuropsychological battery derived from Luria's Neuropsychological Tests. *Journal of Consulting and Clinical Psychology,* 1975, *46,* 1256–1265.

Goldstein, K. *Language and language disturbances.* New York: Grune & Stratton, 1948.

Hammeke, T. A., Golden, C. J., & Pursich, A. D. A standardized, short and comprehensive neuropsychological test battery based on the Luria Neuropsychological evaluation. *International Journal of Neuroscience,* 1978, *8,* 135–141.

Hartlage, L. C. Neuropsychological approaches to predicting outcome of remedial educational strategies for learning disabled children. *Pediatric Psychology,* 1975, *3,* 23. (a)

Hartlage, L. C. Differential age correlates of reading ability. *Perceptual and Motor Skills,* 1975, *41.* 968–970. (b)

Hartlage, L. C. Management of common clinical problems: Learning disabilities. *School Related Health Care* (Ross Laboratories Monograph # 9), 1979, 28–33.

Hartlage, L. C. Neuropsychological assessment techniques. In C. R. Reynolds &

T. Gutkin (Eds.), *Handbook of School Psychology.* New York: J. Wiley, 1981.

Hartlage, L. C., & Hartlage, P. L. The application of neuropsychological principles in the diagnosis of learning disabilities. In L. Tarnopol (Ed.), *Brain Function and Reading Disability.* Baltimore: University Park Press, 1977.

Hartlage, L. C., & Hartlage, P. L. Psychological testing in neurological diagnosis. In J. Youmans (Ed.), *Neurological Surgery.* New York: Saunders, 1982.

Hartlage, L. C., & Reynolds, C. R. Individual educational program (IEP's) and neuropsychological differentiation. In G. W. Hynd and J. E. Obrzut (Eds.), *Neuropsychological assessment and the school-age child: Issues and procedures.* New York: Grune & Stratton, 1981.

Hier, D. B., LeMay, M., Rosenberger, P. B., & Perlo, V. P. Developmental dyslexia: Evidence for a subgroup with a reversal of cerebral asymmetry. *Archives of Neurology,* 1978, *35,* 90–92.

Hinshelwood, J. Wordblindness and visual memory. *Lancet,* 1895, *2,* 1564–1570.

Hiscock, M., & Kinsbourne, M. Ontogeny of cerebral dominance: Evidence from time-sharing asymmetry in children. *Developmental Psychology,* 1978, *14,* 321–329.

Horton, A. M., Jr. Behavioral neuropsychology in the schools. *School Psychology Review,* 1981, *10,* 367–372.

Hynd, G. W. Training the school psychologist in neuropsychology: Perspectives, issues, and models. In G. W. Hynd & J. E. Obrzut (eds.), *Neuropsychological assessment and the school-age child: Issues and procedures.* New York: Grune & Stratton, 1981.

Hynd, G. W., & Cohen, M. *Dyslexia: Neuropsychological theory, research, and clinical differentiation.* New York: Grune & Stratton, 1983.

Hynd, G. W., & Obrzut, J. E. The effects of grade level and sex on the magnitude of the dichotic ear advantage. *Neuropsychologia,* 1977, *15,* 689–692.

Hynd, G. W., & Obrzut, J. E. School neuropsychology. *Journal of School Psychology,* 1981 *19,* 45–50. (a)

Hynd, G. W., & Obrzut, J. E. (Eds.). *Neuropsychological assessment and the school-age child: Issues and procedures.* New York: Grune & Stratton, 1981. (b)

Hynd, G. W., & Obrzut, J. E. Reconceptualizing cerebral dominance: Implications for reading and learning disabled children. *Journal of Special Education,* 1981, *15,* 447–457. (c)

Hynd, G. W., Obrzut, J. E., Hynd, C. R., & Conner, R. T. Attentional deficits and word attributes preferred by learning disabled children in grades 2, 4, and 6. *Perceptual and Motor Skills,* 1978, *47,* 643–652.

Hynd, G. W., Obrzut, J. E., & Obrzut, A. Are lateral and perceptual asymmetries related to WISC-R and achievement test performance in normal and learning disabled children? *Journal of Consulting and Clinical Psychology,* 1981, *49,* 977–979.

Hynd, G. W., Obrzut, J. E., Weed, W., & Hynd, C. R. Development of cerebral dominance: Dichotic listening asymmetry in normal and learning disabled children. *Journal of Experimental Child Psychology,* 1979, *28,* 445–454.

Hynd, G. W., Quackenbush, R., & Obrzut, J. E. Training school psychologists in neuropsychological assessment: Current practices and trends. *Journal of School Psychology,* 1980, *18,* 148–153.

Jackson, J. H. The Hunterian oration at Oxford University in 1872. *Selected writings of John Hughlings Jackson* (Vol. II). London: Staples Press, 1958.

Jacobson, S. Neuroembryology. In B. A. Curtis, S. Jacobson, & E. M. Marcus (Eds.), *An introduction to the neurosciences.* Philadelphia: W. B. Saunders Company, 1972.

James, W. *Principles of psychology.* New York: Holt Press, 1890.

Kaufman, A. S. *Intelligent testing with the WISC-R.* New York: Wiley Interscience, 1979.

Keller, H. R. Issues in the use of observational assessment. *School Psychology Review,* 1980, *9,* 21–30.

Khang-cheng, H., Roessman, U., Hause, L., & Monroe, G. Newborn brain weight in relation to maturity, sex, and race. *Annals of Neurology,* 1981, 19, 243–246.

Kinsbourne, M., & Hiscock, M. Cerebral lateralization and cognitive development. In M. Grady and E. Luecke (Eds.), *Education and the brain.* Chicago: University of Chicago Press, 1978.

Lashley, K. S. Studies in cerebral function in learning. *Psychobiology,* 1920, *2,* 55–136.

Lashley, K. S. *Brain mechanisms and intelligence: A quantitative study of injuries to the brain.* Chicago: University of Chicago Press, 1929.

Lashley, K. S. Factors limiting recovery after central nervous lesions. *Journal of Nervous and Mental Diseases,* 1938, *88,* 733–755.

Leischner, A. *Die Storunger der schriftspracke (Agraphie und Alexie).* Stuttgart: Georg Thieme Verlag, 1957.

Lewis, G. P., Golden, C. J., Moses, J. A., Osmon, D. C., Purisch, J. A., & Hammeke, T. A. Localization of cerebral dysfunction with a standardized version of Luria's Neuropsychological Battery. *Journal of Consulting and Clinical Psychology,* 1979, *47,* 1003–1019.

Lezak, M. D. *Neuropsychological assessment.* New York: Oxford University Press, 1976.

Luria, A. R. *Higher cortical functions in man.* New York: Basic Books, 1966.

Luria, A. R. Frontal lobe syndromes. In P. J. Vicken & G. W. Bruyn (Eds.), *Handbook of clinical neurology* (Vol. II). Amsterdam: North Holland Publishing Company, 1969.

Luria, A. R. *Traumatic aphasia, its syndromes, psychology, and treatment.* The Hague: Mouton, 1970.

Mattis, S., French, J., & Rapin, I. Dyslexia in children and young adults: Three independent neuropsychological syndromes. *Developmental Medicine and Child Neurology,* 1975, *17,* 150–163.

Molfese, D. C., & Molfese, V. J. Hemisphere and stimulus differences as reflected in the cortical responses of newborn infants to speech stimulus. *Developmental Psychology,* 1979, *15,* 505–511.

Morgan, W. P. A case of congenital word-blindness. *British Medical Journal,* 1896, *2,* 1378.

Moses, J. A., & Golden, C. J. Cross validation of the discriminative effectiveness of the standardized Luria Neuropsychological Battery. *International Journal of Neuroscience,* 1979, *9,* 149–155.

Mowder, B., & DeMartino, R. A. Continuing education needs in school psychology. *Professional Psychology,* 1979, *10,* 827–833.

Obrzut, J. E. Dichotic listening and bisensory memory skills in qualitatively diverse dyslexic readers. *Journal of Learning Disabilities,* 1979, *12,* 304–314.

Obrzut, J. E. Neuropsychological procedure with school-age children. In G. W. Hynd & J. E. Obrzut (Eds.), *Neuropsychological assessment and the school-age child: Issues and procedures.* New York: Grune & Stratton, 1981.

Obrzut, J. E., Hynd, G. W., Obrzut, J. A., & Pirozzolo, F. J. Effect of directed attention on cerebral asymmetries in normal and learning disabled children. *Developmental Psychology,* 1981, *17,* 118–125.

Orton, S. T. *Reading, writing, and speech problems in children.* New York: Norton, 1937.

Osmon, D. C., Golden, C. J., Purisch, A. D., Hammeke, T. A., & Blume, H. G. The use of a standardized battery of Luria's tests in the diagnosis of lateralized cerebral dysfunction. *International Journal of Neuroscience,* 1979, *9,* 1–9.

Pirozzolo, F. J. Cerebral asymmetries and reading acquisition. *Academic Therapy,* 1978, *13,* 261–266.

Pirozzolo, F. J. *The neuropsychology of developmental reading disorders.* New York: Praeger Press, 1979.

Pirozzolo, F. J. Language and brain: Neuropsychological aspects of developmental reading disability. *School Psychology Review,* 1981, *10,* 350–355.

Pirozzolo, F. J., & Hansch, E. C. The neurobiology of developmental reading disorders. In R. N. Malatesha & P. G. Aaron (Eds.), *Neuropsychological and neurolinguistic aspects of reading disorders.* New York: Academic Press, in press.

Pirozzolo, F. J., & Rayner, K. Cerebral organization and reading disability. *Neuropsychologia,* 1979, *17,* 485–491.

Ramage, J. C. National survey of school psychologists: Update. *School Psychology Digest,* 1979, *8,* 153–161.

Reitan, R. M. Diagnostic inferences of brain lesions based on psychological test results. *Canadian Psychologist,* 1966, *7,* 336–392.

Reitan, R. M. Psychological effects of cerebral lesions in children of early school-age. In R. M. Reitan & L. Davidson (Eds.), *Clinical neuropsychology: Current status and applications.* New York: V. H. Winston, 1974.

Reynolds, C. R., & Gutkin, T. B. Predicting premorbid intellectual status of children using demographic data. *Clinical Neuropsychology,* 1979, *1,* 36–38.

Rimel, R. W., Giordani, B., Barth, J. T., Boll, T. J., & Jane, J. A. Disability caused by minor head injury. *Neurosurgery,* 1981, *9,* 221–228.

Rourke, B. P. Brain-behavior relationships in children with learning disabilities: A research program. *American Psychologist,* 1975, *30,* 911–920.

Rourke, B. P. *Central processing deficiencies in children: A developmental neuropsychological model.* Presidential address: International Neuropsychological Society, Pittsburgh, February, 1982.

Rourke, B. P., & Finlayson, M. A. Neuropsychological significance of variance in patterns of academic performance: Verbal and visual-spatial abilities. *Journal of Abnormal Child Psychology,* 1978, *6,* 121–133.

Rourke, B., & Gates, R. D. Neuropsychological research and school psychology. In G. W. Hynd & J. E. Obrzut (Eds.), *Neuropsychological assessment and the school-age child: Issues and procedures.* New York: Grune & Stratton, 1981.

Rourke, B. P., & Strang, J. D. Subtypes of reading and arithmetic disabilities: A neuropsychological analysis. In M. Rutter (Ed.), *Behavioral syndromes of brain dysfunction in children.* New York: Guilford, 1981.

Sandoval, J., & Haapanen, R. M. A critical commentary on neuropsychology in the schools: Are we ready? *School Psychology Review,* 1981, *10,* 381–388.

Satz, P., Rardin, D., & Ross, J. An evaluation of a theory of specific developmental dyslexia. *Child Development,* 1971, *42,* 2009–2021.

Satz, P., & Sparrow, S. Specific developmental dyslexia: A theoretical formulation. In D. J. Bakker and P. Satz (Eds.), *Specific reading disability: Advances in theory and method.* Rotterdam: Rotterdam University Press, 1970.

Satz, P., & Van Nostrand, G. K. Developmental dyslexia: An evaluation of a theory. In P. S. Ross & J. Ross (Eds.), *The disabled learner: Early detection and intervention.* Rotterdam: Rotterdam University Press, 1973.

Skinner, B. F. *The behavior of organisms.* New York: Appleton-Century, 1938.

Smith, C. R. Assessment alternatives: Non-standardized procedures. *School Psychology Review,* 1980, *9,* 46–57.

Soto-Moyano, R., Perez, R., Carrillo, R., & Hernandez, A. Effect of prenatal malnutrition on cortical reactivity of the RAT parietal association area. *International Journal of Neuroscience,* 1981, *13,* 99–102.

Sweeney, J. E., & Rourke, B. A. Neuropsychological significance of phonetically accurate and phonetically inaccurate spelling errors in younger and older retarded spellers. *Brain and Language,* 1978, *6,* 212–225.

Toepfer, C. Curriculum design and neuropsychology. *Journal of Educational Research and Development,* 1982, *15,* 1–11.

Ullman, D. G. Children's lateral preference patterns: Frequency and relationships with achievement and intelligence. *Journal of School Psychology,* 1977, *15,* 36–43.

Van den Honert, D. A neuropsychological technique for training dyslexics. *Journal of Learning Disabilities,* 1977, *10,* 21–27.

Walsh, R. N. Effects of environmental complexity and deprivation on brain anatomy and histology: A review. *International Journal of Neuroscience,* 1981, *12,* 33–51.

Wernicke, C. *Der aphasiche symptomenkomplex.* Breslau: Cohn and Weigert, 1874.

Wilkening, G. N., Golden, C. J., MacInnes, W. D., Plaistead, J. R., & Herman, B. *The Luria-Nebraska Neuropsychological Battery,* 1981.

Wittrock, M. C. Education and the cognitive processes of the brain. In J. S. Chall & A. F. Mirsky (Eds.), *Education and the brain.* Chicago: University of Chicago Press, 1978.

11

Consultation in the Schools

ROY P. MARTIN

SCHOOL PSYCHOLOGISTS spend much of their working time talking to other professionals. A teacher may be seeking the psychologist's opinion of a child's behavior, or a psychologist may ask a physician about a child's medical condition and how that condition may affect classroom learning. Often the interaction between the school psychologist and the other professional has a problem-solving quality. For example, a counselor may discuss with the psychologist methods of helping emotionally disturbed children to improve their social skills. Since there is no single technique that has proven universally effective in fostering such skills, the school psychologist and the counselor must put their heads together in order to agree on an approach to the specific situation.

Interprofessional interactions such as these have elements in common with other types of interpersonal interactions engaged in by psychologists, such as teaching, supervision, and therapy. Yet the spirit, form, and process of this type of interaction is unique. For this reason a specific term has come into use to denote this process; that term is *consultation*.

Formal definitions of consultation have been provided by several authorities in the field (Bergan 1977, Caplan 1970, Lippitt 1959). However, the definitions are not always similar, due to the variety of theoretical predilections of the writers. However, Meyers, Parsons, and Martin (1979) have listed six characteristics which describe the essential aspects of the process:

1. Consultation is a helping or problem-solving process.
2. It occurs between a professional help giver (referred to as the *consultant*) and a help seeker (referred to as the *consultee*), the latter of whom has primary responsibility for the care of another person (referred to as the *client*).
3. It is a relationship entered into voluntarily by both parties.
4. It is a relationship in which both parties share responsibility for solving the problem.

5. The short-term goal of the interaction is to help the consultee solve a current work problem, and this problem usually involves interaction between the consultee and a client.
6. The long-term goal of the interaction is to help the consultee handle similar problems in the future more skillfully.

These characteristics of the consultation process help differentiate it from other processes such as therapy, counseling, supervision, and teaching. For example, consultation differs from therapy in that therapy is primarily a remedial activity, while consultation is primarily a prevention-oriented activity. Further, in most therapies the therapist has primary responsibility for solving the problem. (Although some therapists conceptualize therapy as mutual problem solving, usually the roles of the client and the therapist are not given equal consideration in problem solution.) Perhaps the greatest distinction between consultation and therapy, however, is that consultation focuses only on the behavior of the consultee in the work place and particularly that behavior which has direct impact on the client, while therapy deals with a much wider range of behaviors.

The primary distinction between consultation and supervision is that supervision takes place between professionals in the same field (e.g., a chief psychologist supervises the work of another psychologist), while consultation explicitly involves persons with different professional identifications. Further, supervision is explicitly not a process of sharing expertise. The supervisor is assumed to have higher levels of professional expertise than the supervisee, and problem solving in this context involves a disproportionate application of the supervisor's expertise. Finally, supervision may not be a process entered voluntarily by the supervisee; in many settings supervision is an integral part of a particular job function.

The reader can, no doubt, make distinctions between teaching and consultation along lines similar to those listed above.

A LITTLE HISTORY

In order to understand the importance placed on interprofessional consultation, one must understand how current practices have evolved. Consultation is one of several elements in a new approach to professional psychological service delivery that began in the late 1950s. The movement is identified by several names, including *community mental health, preventive mental health, community psychology, and community psychia-*

try. The community mental health movement was a reaction against the clinical or medical model of service delivery that had dominated psychological practice for the preceding thirty years.

The primary characterstics of the clinical model of service delivery are:

1. Professional practitioners focus their primary attention on remediation of currently manifested problems. Prevention is a secondary goal.
2. Service is provided by highly trained, medically oriented professionals.
3. Services provided often require extended periods of direct practitioner-client interaction, both in the diagnostic and remedial phases.
4. These services are aimed at restructuring the general personality or behavior of the client.
5. Service providers see clients in centrally located facilities which are organized to conserve the practitioner's valuable time.
6. Interaction between the service provider and the client in the clinical setting is assumed to be representative of the behavior of the client outside the clinic. Relatively little emphasis, then, is placed on observing the client's behavior in the "natural" environment or on reports of caretakers or peers in that environment.
7. Therapy is the principal and most prestigious activity of the professional service provider.

This model of service delivery has many problems associated with it. First, even the most advanced industrial societies cannot afford the number of practitioners required by this model to provide services for all the clients who could profit from them. The difficulties faced by the medical and health establishment in this country in dealing with the needs of the poor are a case in point. The fact that school psychology practice has come to be seen as focusing on only the most acute psychoeducational problems is another example. There are simply not enough psychologists to deal with the less severe problems, and the realities of school financing make the future look no more positive.

Second, the medical or clinical model is designed to deal with acute problems or at least problems that are currently active. Because of the cost of training the personnel needed to cope with medical and psychological emergencies, society can only afford sufficient personnel to deal with the most serious problems. Consequently, this system of service delivery is always on the brink of being overwhelmed with the current case load. This means that the secondary goal of the clinical model—prevention—is given lip service only. Many school psychologists for example, spend so much of their time dealing with the special-education population that they have little time to develop programs for parents and children in the regular school population. Prevention programs, such as parent education about the typical developmental problems of school-age children and ways of coping with them, are seldom systematically or consistently implemented. Such prevention programs are often given little support by school administrators; they are considered unnecessary, unproven, or unaffordable "luxuries."

Not only is the clinical model often unable to accomplish its secondary goal of prevention, but the logic of setting prevention as a secondary goal can be questioned. In psychology as in medicine, once a pathology is established, the costs of intervention are very high, both in terms of human suffering and in terms of societal and economic costs. The logic of emphasizing remediation has been likened to attempting to dam the Mississippi at New Orleans. Damming the flow of pathology upstream is a much more appealing alternative.

The practice of making a diagnosis in a clinic environment assumes that behavior seen in the clinic is the same behavior, or is similar in fundamental ways, to that manifested outside the clinic. However, much research shows that people behave differently in different environments. Further, the medical-psychodiagnostic-therapeutic environment is a particularly strong and unique environment which undoubtedly affects behavior in a variety of specific ways. Thus, there is much evidence to contradict one of the basic assumptions of the medical model. Notice that in clinical medicine the assumption that the pathology seen in the clinic is the same as that manifest on the outside is generally sound. That is, the essential signs of pneumonia are present no matter what environment the patient is in. However, a seven-year-old child may be aggressive and hostile toward his or her peers in the classroom and exhibit no signs of aggression or hostility during a psychological evaluation.

The major shortcomings, then, of the clinical model of service delivery, as applied by school psychologists and related professional groups, are that society is unlikely to underwrite the costs of sufficient numbers of professionals to implement the model fully, and the model's secondary goal of prevention is seldom effectively met. Further, emphasizing remediation over prevention is illogical on several grounds, and the situational specificity of behavior contradicts a major assumption of the clinical model, i.e., that accurate diagnoses can be made in a centralized, artificial environment.

The community mental health movement reacted to these shortcomings by offering an alternative model of service delivery. The major characteristics of the alternative delivery system are as follows:

1. The primary focus of psychoeducational service is on prevention.
2. Service is provided by practitioners at several levels of training. In the simplest form, direct service is provided predominantly by community workers under the supervision of professional mental health workers.
3. Emphasis is on short-term interventions.
4. Services are aimed at specific problems, not a general restructuring of the personality.
5. Services are provided in the community, that is, in the location in which problem behaviors have occurred or are most likely to occur.
6. Diagnostic emphasis is on behavior as manifested in the real-life situation.
7. Consultation is the dominant professional activity.

The reordering and redefinition of service offerings in this model carry numerous implications for mental health practice in general, and the practice of the school psychologist specifically. However, to keep the discussion focused on the central concern of this chapter, only those facets of this service delivery system with direct implications for consultation will be presented.

In the community mental health model of service delivery, consultation becomes the dominant professional activity. Consultation is given this pivotal position because this service is consistent with the preventive focus of the model. Consultation is conceived as an intervention with professionals who have responsibility for a number of other persons. If the behavior, attitudes, and opinions of these persons (consultees) can be appropriately guided or influenced, individuals in the future care of this person will be positively affected. Consultation is also a partial solution to the personnel problem so often characteristic of psychoeducational services. The consultant who can positively affect the student-teacher interactions of one teacher can have a salutary effect on the lives of hundreds of children. The same is true of the consultant who works with physicians, nurses, police officers, the clergy, and school administrators. In this way, the professional multiplies his or her effect many times, thereby reducing overall staffing requirements.

One of the major tenets of the community mental health movement is that service should be provided in the environment in which problem behavior is likely to occur or has occurred. Consultation nicely fits this principle, because it is directed at community agents, who then carry out the recommendations made in consultation in their work place. Consultation is also highly compatible with the short-term intervention provision of the model, as well as the provision for a highly focused intervention. Consultation, by definition, is not aimed at a restructuring of the personality. All writers on consultation that I am aware of agree that the emphasis in consultation must be on the caretaker behavior of the consultee only, and adjustments in this behavior are emphasized, as opposed to adjustments in basic life goals, world views, or behavioral styles.

It is perhaps worthy of note that the community mental health movement was most visible during the late 1960s and early 1970s. Like all new movements, it stood out in a figure-ground relationship to the service delivery system that preceded it. In the 1980s, the basic tenets of the movement have been absorbed into the mainstream of thinking about service delivery. Thus the movement itself has become less visible, but only because it has become an integral part of all professional thinking about mental health delivery systems. One manifestation of this integration of the preventive ideology into traditional practice is that the importance of consultation does not now have to be argued. The only disagreement that remains is how best to carry out this function.

TYPES OF CONSULTATION

Any set of activities as complex and varied as interprofessional consultation can be analyzed and categorized in numerous ways. In the beginning phases of the study of any new topic, categorization is a primary activity and this has been the case for consultation. The following variables have been considered important by writers in making distinctions between forms of consultation.

The Emphasis Placed on the Goal of Prevention

All consultation in the schools has a preventive goal. However, for some consultation interventions, prevention is the primary concern, while for others it is secondary. Consider a teacher who is having a very difficult time managing the behavior of one child. It is the consultant's hope that the techniques that he or she and the teacher generate will generalize to other, similar problems this teacher may face in the future. However, the primary goal in this case must be to remedy the immediate problem. Prevention is secondary. It is a different matter when a teacher approaches a consultant to discuss some general concerns about his or her teaching style. In this case, the consultee may feel that the teacher needs objective feedback regarding the quality and quantity of interactions with students. In such a case there is no immediate crisis, but rather a vague feeling of inadequacy or a simple desire for self improvement. Consultation in this case has a remedial component, but it is secondary to the main goal of preventing teacher-student interaction problems in the future.

Individual versus Organizational Focus

The two examples presented above involved requests for consultation made by individuals who felt their own behavior or that of a client should be the focus of consultation. Sometimes a consultee, usually a department head or the chief executive of an organization, seeks consultation regarding broad organizational problems. Perhaps, for example, a superintendent of a school system feels that the relationship between special education teachers and other teachers is deteriorating due to the perception by "regular" education personnel that special educators get an unfair share of new materials, teacher aides, and specialized staff support (e.g., speech therapy help, psychological consultation, etc.). The consultant in such situations would be careful to keep the problem defined as a problem of the system and not as a personal problem of individual teachers; thus the focus would be on organizational variables like improvement in communication between the special and regular teaching staffs.

Note that the individual/organizational dimension is independent of the emphasis on prevention. That is, in either individual or organizational consultation, the emphasis may be primarily remedial or preventive.

Gerald Caplan (1970) has developed from these first two dimensions a useful categorization schema widely accepted in the consultation literature. His schema is represented below:

	INDIVIDUAL FOCUS	ORGANIZATIONAL FOCUS
REMEDIAL EMPHASIS	CLIENT–CENTERED CASE CONSULTATION	PROGRAM–CENTERED ADMINISTRATIVE CONSULTATION
PREVENTIVE EMPHASIS	CONSULTEE–CENTERED CASE CONSULTATION	CONSULTEE–CENTERED ADMINISTRATIVE CONSULTATION

Figure 11.1 Caplan's (1970) schema for consultation.

The Content of the Consultation

Content in this context denotes the subject matter discussed by the consultant and consultee. An individual may seek consultation regarding the behavior management of a child, appropriate testing materials to be used in screening children for perceptually based learning problems, or better techniques to use in conferences with parents. These three problems all involve different content. The student of the consultation literature will find references to "mental health consultation," for example (Caplan 1970). Mental health consultation encompasses all those problems which have direct effects on the mental health of consultee and client. This could be contrasted to curricular consultation, which would focus on the materials used in instruction and the design of instructional sequences.

Nature of the Consultation Problem

A dimension mentioned in the consultation literature and related to the content dimension is the nature of the problem. Blake and Mouton (1976), for example, feel that the problems with which consultants are most often asked to help can be divided into four different categories:

1. Power/authority problems (e.g., teachers resent the manner in which an administrator exercises his or her authority);
2. Morale/cohesion problems (e.g., a person or group feels they make no worthwhile contribution to an organization; thus they experience negative feelings about the organization and a lack of commitment to the goals of the organization);
3. Goals/objectives problems (e.g., teachers cannot agree whether social adjustment or pre-academic skills are most important in kindergarten);
4. Norms/standards problems (e.g., a school has an unspoken norm or expectation that its top administrators will be males. This norm is frustrating to the upwardly striving women who aspire to these positions).

Caplan (1970) discusses a different list of consultee problems. The problems focused on by Caplan are those he believes are most often encountered in consultation with individuals (in "consultee-centered case consultation," to use his terminology). Caplan's list of consultee problems includes (*a*) lack of confidence in dealing with the client, (*b*) lack of knowledge, (*c*) lack of skill, and (*d*) lack of professional objectivity.

We can see from these two examples that while there is little agreement about the nature of the problems presented to the consultant, there is agreement that the nature of the consultation problem is an essential element in determining how the consultation will take place.

The Process of Consultation

Consultation can also be categorized according to the theoretical predilection of the consultant and the consultative techniques used, which are derived from the consultant's theoretical orientation. For example, a behavioral consultant (see Bergan 1977) would operate in a different manner from an Alderian consultant (Dinkmeyer and Carlson 1973); a consultant basing his or her approach on social-psychological principles of interpersonal influence (Martin 1978) would conceptualize the relationship with the consultee in a different manner than would a consultant working from a Rogerian-Carcuffian model. Blake and Mouton (1976) present a list of interventions categorized by process types:

1. Acceptance interventions (use of sympathetic listening and emphathic support);
2. Catalytic interventions (use of the consultant to hasten a change in interpersonal process, often through the analysis of interpersonal processes in T-group-like activities);
3. Prescriptive interventions (a consultant diagnoses a consultee's problem and confidently outlines the best solution);
4. Confrontational interventions (through challenges, probes, direct questions, etc., the consultant cuts through the rationalizations or self justifications of an individual or group);
5. Theory-principles interventions (the consultant carries out his or her consultation activities following one well-rationalized theoretical position).

The process dimension is one of the most difficult to conceptualize and categorize precisely. For example, it is probably obvious to the reader that the five categories of intervention just mentioned are not mutually exclusive. A confrontation intervention could be based on a well-established theory, as could an acceptance intervention. One of the problems in this regard is that some writers refer to the consultant's process as the ideas about consultation that the consultant "carries around in his or her head." Others use the term to indicate an observer's "objective" view of the ways the consultant deals with the consultee. A consultant working from the acceptance-empathy framework (his or her internal model) might be seen by an observer to be reinforcing certain types of consultee statements more than others with verbal acceptance utterances, and thus the observer could categorize the process as an intervention based on behavioral principles.

Although many more distinguishing dimensions in consultation may be discussed by future writers and practitioners, these five dimensions — emphasis placed on prevention, individual versus group focus, content, nature of the problem, and process — serve as the primary structure for classification of consultation types. Unfortunately, many current writers in consultation have not consistently utilized the dimensions just described, or have used descriptive terms whose meaning was not clear.

STAGES OF CONSULTATION

To this point, the chapter has talked in the abstract about consultation, discussing definitions, historical antecedents, the rationale for the process, and categorization schemes. The reader is no doubt becoming impatient to know what consultants actually do. It is the purpose of the following section to begin to orient the reader to the process of consultation. This section will incorporate a scattering of "how-to-do-it" principles, but they should serve only as an introduction to entice the reader to study more complete descriptions of the consultation process.

Discussions of consultation process are often presented in terms of the stages of consultation. This discussion will utilize that approach. For present purposes, consultation will be divided into six stages: (1) entry into the system, (2) orientation to consultation, (3) problem identification, (4) developing an intervention plan, (5) assessing the impact of the consultation intervention, and (6) ending the consultation.

Stage 1—Entry into the System

Entry into consultation relationships involves two distinct phases. First, the consultant must gain the respect of one or more persons in order to be invited to consult. As outlined by Martin (1978), a psychologist (or indeed any other type of advisor) is chosen primarily because of two qualities — expertise and likeability. With respect to expertise, it is the consultee's perception of the level of skill possessed by the consultant that is central, not some absolute level of ability. Further, it is primarily the expertise of the consultant relative to that of the consultee that determines how much expertise is attributed to the former.

The second variable, here referred to as likeability, has been described in a variety of ways, including the ease with which the consultee can identify with the consultant, the interpersonal process skill of the consultant, "referent power," or simply "bedside manner." This characteristic involves a perception on the part of the consultee that the consultant is easy to talk to or confide in, is trustworthy, and "understands what I am saying." When this feeling of rapport is analyzed more closely, it is usually found to be a function of perceived similarity between consultant and consultee, as viewed by the consultee.

Whether expertise or likeability is the primary factor in consultant selection depends on several things. If, for example, the problem is acute and causing great stress, expertise is the primary consideration. If one's appendix is infected and needs to be removed, it does not much matter whether the surgeon is a nice person but it does matter how skilled he or she is. The same may be true of a teacher who daily faces a severe behavior problem in the classroom, or a school district anticipating that irate parents may express disapproval of a district policy in a public meeting. The balance between expertise and likeability is also affected by whether the consultant comes from inside the consultee organization or outside. Inside consultants are often limited in the amount of expertise that is attributed to them, since daily contact with someone tends to diminish perceptions of expertise. Thus, inside consultants, while considered expert, are always evaluated on their trustworthiness and general interpersonal style. Outside consultants, on the other hand, tend to be chosen predominantly on the basis of expertise.

The most important point to be made about the criteria used in selection of a consultant is that both expertise and likeability must be present. Studies have shown (Aronson, Willerman, and Floyd 1966) that both are essential, and some balance between these characteristics is desirable.

Once a consultant has been approached by a potential consultee and is asked to provide a service, the second phase of the entry process begins. This phase involves negotiating a contract with the consultee and with the administrative personnel in charge of the work behavior of the consultee. Many inexperienced consultants, being flattered that they have been asked to provide advice or help solve a problem, skip the contract-negotiating process and jump immediately into stage two (orientation to consultation), stage three (problem identification), or worse, into stage four (development of the intervention). This almost always guarantees consultation failure due to misunderstandings between consultant and consultee.

The contract negotiated by the consultant may be formal or informal, written or verbal. It must, however, be explicit. Some of the points to be covered in such a contract are:

1. What kinds of data will the consultant have access to?
2. With whom is the consultant expected to meet or restricted from meeting with?
3. How much time does the consultee and the consultee organization expect to devote to the solution of the problem?
4. What types of feedback are desired (e.g., written formal report, verbal report, group-process feedback, etc.)?
5. To whom is feedback to be given?
6. What kinds of limits are placed on the confidentiality of informants (e.g., does the principal of the school expect the consultant to reveal the content of conversations with teachers who are consultees)?
7. When will the consultant meet with consultees and others in the organization?
8. What kinds of "homework" (such as data collection) will be expected of the consultee?
9. What are the financial arrangements for the consultant—that is, how much will he or she be paid and when will payment be received?

Different types of consultation situations require the resolution of different questions, so the above list is only suggestive. However, no matter what issues are negotiated at the outset of consultation, a provision should be made for reevaluation of the contract on a regular basis throughout the consultation period. This is necessary because many contingencies, which cannot be anticipated, may alter the emphasis needed for various aspects of the process.

Stage 2—Orientation to Consultation

Stage two has much in common with the contract-negotiation phase of stage one. However, they are discussed separately here in order to emphasize the importance of making sure that the consultee and the consultee organization have a sound understanding of what to expect from the consultation process.

Many consultees ask for help expecting that some expert can solve their problems relatively quickly. Experienced consultants know, however, that at best they have access to general principles that may apply to the problem at hand; ready-made formulas for problem solving simply don't exist. These general principles, however, must always be adapted to meet the specific circumstances of the consultee's situation. This adaptation function must be carried out primarily by the consultee with the aid of the consultant. This means that the consultee must play a significant part in problem resolution. The part played by the consultee often requires much more time, effort, and ingenuity than he or she expects, so appropriate expectations must be established early in the consultation process.

Consider the example of a teacher who needs help in handling a small group of disruptive boys in her third grade class. The consultant will approach the problem from one of several theoretical positions, using Adlerian principles, operant behavior management principles, or some other systematic body of knowledge. The consultant's job is to convince the consultee that particular principles from this body of knowledge are applicable to the problem; for example, she should attempt to reinforce more appropriate behavior and overlook minor transgressions, because her attention is reinforcing the attention-getting antics of the group. Although the teacher may readily accept this line of reasoning, a number of questions remain to be dealt with. Exactly what reinforcement will the teacher utilize? What kind of data collection procedure will be used to determine if the program is indeed reducing the disruptive behavior? Exactly what kinds of behaviors will and will not be ignored? These and many other questions will have to be resolved in interaction between consultant and consultee. However, in all cases, as long as the general principles are not violated, these matters should be adjusted so that they fit the particular teacher's skills, knowledge, and attitudes. What is the teacher willing and able to do with regard to each of these matters? What does the teacher think will be most effective with her class? These are the determining factors in engineering the consultant's general recommendations. Not only must the consultee make a lot of decisions and discuss at length a variety of issues regarding the intervention, the consultee may have to make difficult changes in behavior and engage in additional behaviors that are time consuming and add to an already busy schedule. When consultees realize how much they must do to create a change, they sometimes decide the problem is not worth the effort. They wanted an easy solution carried out by someone else. Therefore, the consultant must make the consultee's responsibilities clear as soon as these responsibilities can reasonably be outlined.

Another expectation which often cannot be met by the consultant is that of a speedy solution. Organizations seeking consultation often fail to understand the extensive amount of data collection that is necessary for a consultant to have even a rudimentary understanding of a problem. If this need for data collection is not made clear early in the process of consultation, the consultees may be dissatisfied with the progress of the consultation and begin to resist data collection efforts.

A school district that seeks a consultant to help with selection of an appropriate battery of group tests to give all third and fifth graders has had difficulty making a decision on this matter because there are two strong factions in the school—those who feel standardized group testing is helpful and those who do not. The consultant approaching this problem soon realizes that not only do the district officials need to know more about the psychometric properties of the various tests they are considering, but they also need a better means of conflict resolution. In order to provide help in this matter, the consultant may have to collect data on the attitudes of the staff toward the group testing program and survey the staff regarding their views about how this conflict should be resolved. The preparation of an appropriate survey is time consuming, as are recording and analyzing the resulting data and working out a satisfactory method for discussing the data with all factions in the dispute. The administrators who originally contacted the consultant felt than an exert could provide important answers in a week, while the consultant, seeing the nature of the problem, might feel that three months would be a more appropriate time interval.

Making clear the requirements for data collection and the consultee's responsibilities for problem solution are only two areas requiring a careful, thoughtful, and thorough orientation. While contract negotiation can go a long way toward orienting the consultee, it will not cover many points that will need to be discussed. In both contract negotiation and in orientation, repeated exploration of the consultant's and consultee's expectations is desirable in order to avoid misunderstandings that can undermine the consultation process.

Stage 3—Problem Identification

The problem-identification stage of consultation can be divided into two parts. In the first phase, the consultant must determine how the consultee interprets the problem. This is accomplished through interviewing and active listening, the same basic process used in other forms of problem solving such as counseling, therapy, and even some forms of teaching. However, it is important in most consultation situations to determine not only the consultee's conception of the problem, but also the perception held by the consultee's colleagues and clients, and the administrative personnel in his or her organization. This process may reveal that what was defined by the consultee as a client problem (e.g., the teacher feels he has a number of very slow children in his classroom and is at a loss to know how to cope with the problem) is best thought of and approached as an organizational problem (e.g., the allocation of classroom aides in this school had not taken into account the heterogeneity in student abilities in this teacher's classroom, so the consultant began to explore with the principal the possibility of providing an aide for the classroom).

The second phase of the problem-identification stage consists of the consultant's making an independent determination of the problem and its causes. At least two determinations must be made at this time. The first is to identify the appropriate organizational level of the problem. Is it best thought of as a general organizational problem, a subgroup problem, an individual consultee problem, or a client problem? Of course, any problem affects all levels of an organization and is caused, in part, by factors at all levels of the organization. However, it is the consultant's task to make a preliminary determination about the most appropriate level at which to approach the problem.

The second determination that must be made is what type of problem is being manifested at that level. At the client level, a classification of student problems is available and readily recognized by school psychologists: is the problem predominantly cognitive, behavioral, physical, emotional, or interpersonal? School psychologists have been in the business of diagnosing problems at this level throughout the history of the discipline, so nothing further need be said about the classification of student or client problems. If the problem is at the consultee level, the Caplanian classification is often helpful (see page 275). At the subgroup or organizational level, the classification system discussed by Blake and Mouton (1976) can be helpful (see page 276). At all of these organizational levels various classification systems are available, so the above systems are only presented as examples. Further, none of these systems is exhaustive, so adjustments must be made by the consultant no matter what system is used.

It is important that the consultant utilize some sort of rational classification system, because the general nature of subsequent treatment or intervention will be determined by the manner in which the problem is defined. Consider Caplan's classification of individual consultee problems. If the teacher lacks self confidence, a Rogerian type of intervention is highly appropriate (one that emphasizes acceptance of the consultee as a person and a professional). This same approach by itself would not be appropriate for problems such as lack of understanding, since a problem defined in this way demands that new knowledge be presented. The task of the consultant then becomes more one of teaching than a counseling intervention. If the problem is one of lack of skill, the consultant becomes a trainer or coach, watching the behavior of the consultee and providing appropriate feedback on positive and negative instances. Finally, if the consultee lacks professional objectivity, the task is more like therapy; that is, his or her attitudes regarding the client have to be restructured. This kind of intervention may consist of listening for emotionally laden descriptions of the problem, determining if cognitive distortions are present (e.g., stereotypes), and some forms of confrontation. These examples indicate that problem diagnosis is not a vacuous exercise, but is an essential first step in designing an intervention.

Note that the definition of the problem and the organizational level of the problem as conceptualized by the consultee or others in the consultee organization may have no relation to the consultant's definition of the level and type of problem. In fact, a consultant's major contribution may be to redefine the problem. Once a problem is seen from another point of view, the solution may be much clearer. Often redefinition clarifies the problem to the extent that the intervention can be carried out in large part by the organization or consultee without the consultant's help.

Stage 4 — Intervention

The intervention stage can be conveniently divided into three phases — recommendations, adjustment of recommendations, and implementation. The recommendation phase involves the communication by the consultant of his or her analysis of the problem and the method recommended for dealing with it. The major task of the consultant in communicating a diagnosis and recommendation is to set out a general frame of reference that orients the consultee toward seeing the problem in a given way and seeing the recommended action to be taken as a natural extension of that frame of reference. Thus, a consultant may define a problem as a client problem resulting primarily from the side effects of medication being prescribed by the child's pediatrician. The intervention that follows logically from this definition is to discuss the medication with the parents and the physician, and perhaps to have the physician vary the medication level while simultaneously monitoring the child's behavior in school to check for the effects of dosage changes. If the consultant saw the problem as a student-teacher interaction problem, the consultant would most likely attempt to modify the behavior of the teacher and observe subsequent changes in child's behavior.

It can be seen from these examples that the placement of the problem in a conceptual, causal context is one of the most important aspects of the consultation process. During this phase, if the consultation is to succeed, the consultant's ideas about the causal context must be accepted by the consultee. During the recommendation phase, then, the personal qualities (expertise and likeability) of the consultant play a critical role. Only if the consultant is perceived by the consultee to be knowledgeable and if he or she can communicate this knowledge in an effective way, will the consultee be persuaded that the problem is most appropriately viewed in a particular causal context.

Many consultants fail at this critical time because they attempt too much; that is, they lay out a detailed intervention instead of a more general recommendation. This leads to failure because a consultant is not an expert, for example, on how to intervene in Mr. Brown's second-grade class in inner-city Boston. The consultant is an expert, perhaps, in child management or inner-city school problems, but the consultant can never know Mr. Brown and his class as well as Mr. Brown does. So the consultant who jumps into a detailed intervention almost always makes significant errors in judgment about what is likely to work in a particular setting.

The process of adjusting the intervention recommendation should occur in phase two of the intervention stage. This phase is separated from the initial phase because the social forces at work are much different from those in phase one. If it is carried out correctly, phase one ends with the consultant and consultee agreeing on a general view of the problem and a general approach to its solution. At this point the source for ideas shifts from the consultant to the consultee, for now it is the consultee who is the primary source for ideas regarding the specifics of the intervention. Further, the consultant's perception of the expertise and likeability of the consultee is critical at this stage. In order for the consultee to adapt the basic idea to the specifics of his or her situation successfully, the consultant must respect the consultee and the consultee must be able to communicate his or her ideas effectively.

We can see, then, that influence in the consultation situation flows in two ways — first, from the consultant to the consultee in the general problem-definition phase, and then from the consultee to the consultant during the recommendations, refinement and adjustment phase. The reciprocal nature of influence is the hallmark of consultation, distinguishing it from other professional roles like teaching and therapy.

Phase three simply involves actually carrying out the mutually decided intervention. Since the content of the intervention specific to a particular problem is the focus of attention during this phase, little can be said about it here. However, one point must be made by the consultant during this phase: that is that the consultant and consultee should plan to meet frequently during the intervention phase to make any adjustments that are necessary. Even a well-thought-out, mutually agreed on intervention rarely works exactly as it was designed to, often because of changes in the organizational environment. So the intervention is not simply put in place but is monitored and adjusted as necessary.

Stage 5 — Assessment

The primary focus of attention in stage five is the evaluation of the effectiveness of the intervention. In situations in which the primary role of the consultant is to provide a service, as opposed to researching some aspect of the consultation process, assessment is often given very little attention. Unfortunately, the only way many consultants judge their consultative success is by whether they are asked to consult by the same consultee again.

In order to be effective, assessment has to be built into the project from the beginning. If, for example, adjustments are going to be made to the intervention (as discussed in stage four), then a monitoring procedure can be used for ongoing assessment and the long-term follow-up assessment.

In making decisions about what types of assessments to make, the reciprocal influence model outlined above should be used. First, the consultant should plan the general form the evaluation should take (the variables to be considered, for example); then the consultee, who will be carrying out the evaluation, should make final decisions about its details.

Finally, two levels of evaluation should be considered in almost all consultation interventions. Judgments from the consultee should be sought (e.g., how effective was the consultant? Did he or she communicate clearly?), as well as behavioral assessment of changes in client behavior (e.g., did the child's behavior actually change in the appropriate direction when the teacher's behavior changed?). It is also advisable to assess the impact of consultee behavior and attitude changes on the subgroup or the organization.

Stage 6 — Ending the Consultation

Ending the consultation is an important step and it needs appropriate handling. The most frequent mistake is to terminate a consultation passively rather than actively. The consultant must directly state when he or she feels relieved of any further obligations regarding a particular problem. With outside consultants, this is reasonably easy to do, because the consultant physically removes himself or herself from the situation. However, even in this case a consultant may receive phone calls for help that he or she perceives to be inappropriate. The internal consultant has greater problems because continued service may be a contractual obligation. However, even the internal consultant must terminate service for one problem before beginning work on another. If no definite termination is made, the consultee may continue to seek aid which the consultant cannot provide because of other obligations, resulting in frustration on the part of both parties.

RESEARCH IN CONSULTATION

Medway (1979) conducted a review of research in consultation. The studies reviewed assessed the effectiveness of consultation in school settings. He found that in twenty-two of the twenty-nine studies reviewed, some positive effects were observed; however, he strongly criticized this literature on methodological grounds. Specifically, few studies utilized any control or comparison groups (ten of the eleven studies with positive outcomes used no control group), important variables were left uncontrolled (e.g., characteristics of consultation participants), and follow-up data were seldom collected.

This review and others (e.g., Mannino and Shore 1975) indicate that empirical research in consultation is not highly developed. This is related in part to the difficulty of doing good field-based research in this area. One factor that creates difficulties for consultation researchers is that the opportunity to do consultation is primarily under the control of the consultee. For a relationship to be truly consultative, the consultee must approach the consultant and not the reverse. The persons planning research, therefore, find it difficult to control such important variables as type of presenting problem and characteristics of the consultee (e.g., age, experience, ability to implement the intervention planned, etc.).

This problem is operative in other types of intervention research such as in investigations of outcomes in therapy. However, consultation research is perhaps more troublesome than therapy research for two additional reasons. First, these interactions, unlike most therapeutic interactions, do not take place in one circumscribed location. Consultations occur spontaneously in corridors, cafeterias, and teachers' lounges. This makes some types of data collection virtually impossible (e.g., videotaping interactions for later analysis, or direct observation by someone other than the consultant). Second, the consultation takes place in the work environment of the consultee. This heightens the consultee's sensitivity to issues of confidentiality. Persons in therapy are also sensitive about confidentiality, but they meet the therapist in a location distant from home and work. The relative anonymity provided by distance from known persons helps make some research procedures possible that are unlikely to be practical in consultation situations.

Another important consideration in consultation research is that many consultation relationships are maintained by brief, casual contacts carried out over long periods of time (perhaps years). Substantial consultative projects involving concentrated consultant effort over a time period that fits research plans (several weeks or months) are rare.

All these difficulties will limit most consultation researchers to three general types of reasearch: case studies, retrospective studies, and analogue studies.

The case study will remain an important source of data in consultation for some time to come. Case studies appear frequently in research areas in which the exploration of the variables in the domain is an early stage of development, and in areas where it is important to document rare, naturally occurring events that have implication for the broader research area (e.g., diagnostic studies of rare diseases in medicine, biographical studies of unusually creative or gifted persons). Consultation fits these criteria on both counts.

Two colleagues and I carried out a case study (Martin, Duffey, and Fischman 1973) which demonstrated both the strengths and weaknesses of this approach. Two doctoral-level interns in school psychology were placed in one moderate-sized elementary school for a full academic year. One of their main functions was to consult with teachers. The school also had the services of a counselor who consulted on mental health problems. This situation created a rather unique opportunity to study the effects of saturating one school with mental health expertise. Data consisted of logs kept by the interns recording their activities on a half-hour basis throughout the year. Also, a questionnaire was distributed to teachers at the end of the year to help evaluate the services offered. One aspect of the study was to determine what percentage of the interns' time was spent in consultation. The results indicated that about one-third of their time was spent in this activity. An additional aspect of the study was to determine how the teachers felt about the training and personal demeanor of the interns and how they felt about the services offered. In general, teachers felt the interns were technically well trained and interpersonally skilled. However, they felt dissatisfied about the amount of service offered. They felt they needed more of the psychologists' time than they were given.

This study seemed to show that even with a psychologist-teacher ratio of one to ten, teachers felt they needed more mental health consultation than they got. This interesting finding seems to indicate that the more help a teaching staff gets from well-trained school psychologists, the more they want. It is difficult to know exactly how to interpret this finding, however, due to the methodological problems associated with case studies. No control or comparison groups were studied, only one evaluation assessment was made, and the characteristics of this school (it had been recently desegregated) may have been a prime factor in the results obtained. Finally, what treatment was really evaluated? These interns engaged in a wide variety of verbal behaviors, consultative tactics, and suggested many types of intervention strategies. Given all these interpretative problems, what did the study accomplish? Primarily it helped to raise questions about teacher satisfaction that deserve further study. Raising questions is the major outcome of all case studies.

An alternative approach is the retrospective study. In this type of research, practitioners are asked to describe and answer questions about past consultation experiences. In one such study, Martin and Curtis (1981) surveyed 164 school psychologists and asked them to think of the most successful and unsuccessful consultation experiences they had been involved in. They were then asked several questions about these experiences, including why they thought each consultation succeeded or failed. An analysis of their responses indicated that these consultants tended to blame the consultee for failure more often than they gave them credit for success. This result was interpreted as consistent with the social psychology theory of attribution.

By using retrospective methods, it was possible for the sample size of this study to be sufficiently large to allow much greater generalizability of the results than is justified from typical small-sample studies. Also, the study compared two outcomes from the same set of subjects, which offered substantial control of important variables. However, these advantages were accrued at great cost, because the data collected were based on the recollections of the respondents. It is likely that these data were biased in numerous ways, but the extent and nature of these biases remains unknown.

Another approach often used in the consultation literature is the analogue study. Analogue studies are laboratory-like investigations designed to simulate certain aspects of the condition or process under study. This simulation is then studied in a more controlled environment than would be possible if the process were studied in the field.

Crowe (1982) has developed a fictional transcript of a consultation-like interaction between a school psychologist and a teacher. This interaction was designed to be neutral with regard to the consultant's process skills. Undergraduate education majors were asked to read the transcript and then evaluate the consultant's skill in dealing with the teacher. The experimental treatment consisted of four sets of introductions to the transcript, each of which varied the level of expertise attributed to the consultant and the extent to which the consultant was a likeable person. For example, the introduction given some subjects suggested the consultant was very experienced and knowledgeable but was personally distant and aloof. Another introduction implied the consultant possessed great expertise and was easy to relate to. The results of this study indicated that perceptions regarding the likeability of the consultant clearly related to how effective the consultant was perceived to be.

This approach allows for a highly controlled study to be carried out with large samples. It does so, however, at the cost of what is sometimes referred to as *ecological validity*. That is, how do we know that the evaluation of this contrived consultation situation relates to the evaluation of consultation as practiced in the field? We don't, but it provides important clues regarding field practice.

Each of these methods provides only an approximation of reality and an approximation of the research method of preference. That method is to study a large number of real-life consultation experiences in which intervention procedures, consultant and consultee characteristics, and problems presented (to mention only some of the most important variables) are carefully described and analyzed.

CONCLUSION

In this chapter I have attempted to orient the student to the consultation process. It is my hope that this introduction will encourage a more detailed study of the process (see the suggestions for further reading which follow) and will stimulate the student to begin practicing systematic consultation in the earliest stages of his or her field experience.

There is a real need at the present time for school psychologists who can demonstrate to the public, school administrators, teachers, and students the benefits that can result from systematic consultation. School systems are operating for the most part on a clinical model of service delivery. Therefore, the preventive, consultative model is often studied by school psychologists in training, but it is seldom practiced on the job. Only when the utility of consultation can be documented will it begin to have an impact on the thinking of the consumers of psychological services. Thus, school psychologists not only have to consult well, they have to be able to demonstrate empirically that this type of service is the best, most cost-effective service they provide.

REFERENCES

Aaronson, E., Willerman, B., & Floyd, J. The effects of a pratfall on increasing interpersonal attraction. *Psychonomic Science,* 1966, *4,* 227–228.

Bergan, J. R. *Behavioral consultation.* Columbus, Ohio: Merrill, 1977.

Blake, R. R., & Mouton, J. S. *Consultation.* Reading, Mass.: Addison-Wesley, 1976.

Caplan, G. *The theory and practice of mental health consultation.* New York: Basic Books, 1970.

Crowe, D. *Effects of expert and referent power in consultation process.* Doctoral dissertation, University of Georgia, 1982.

Dinkmeyer, P., & Carlson, J. *Consultation.* New York: Wiley, 1973.

Lippitt, G. L. A study of the consultation process. *Journal of Social Issues,* 1959, *15,* 43–50.

Mannino, F. V., & Shore, M. F. The effects of consultation: A review of empirical studies. *American Journal of Community Psychology,* 1975, *3,* 1–21.

Martin, R. P. Expert and referent power: A framework for understanding and maximizing consultation effectiveness. *Journal of School Psychology,* 1978, *16,* 49–55.

Martin, R. P., & Curtis, M. Consultants' perceptions of causality for success and failure of consultation. *Professional Psychology,* 1981, *12,* 670–676.

Martin, R. P., Duffey, J., & Fischman, R. A time analysis and evaluation of an experimental internship program in school psychology. *Journal of School Psychology,* 1973, *11,* 263–268.

Medway, F. J. How effective is school consultation? A review of recent research. *Journal of School Psychology,* 1979, *17,* 275–281.

Meyers, J., Parsons, R. D., & Martin, R. *Mental health consultation in the schools.* San Francisco: Jossey-Bass, 1979.

SUGGESTED READINGS

Blake, R. R. & Mouton, J. S. *Consultation.* Reading, Mass: Addison-Wesley, 1976. (Discusses a wide-ranging conceptualization of consultation types and applications including business applications.)

Brown, D., Wyne, M. D., Blackburn, J. E., & Powell, W. C. *Consultation.* Boston: Allyn and Bacon, 1979. (Written from a counselor and special-education viewpoint discussing predominantly education applications.)

Caplan, G. *The theory and practice of mental health consultation.* New York: Basic Books, 1970. (A psychiatric approach, one of the major books in consultation by a founding father in the area.)

Meyers, J., Parsons, R. D., & Martin, R. *Mental health consultation in the schools.* San Francisco: Jossey-Bass, 1979. (Broad introductory coverage designed for and written by school psychologists.)

Schmuck, R. A., & Miles, M. B. (Eds.). *Organization development in schools.* Palo Alto: National Press Books, 1971. (The book looks at several forms of organization level consultation in school settings. It has a group dynamics emphasis.)

12

Remedial Intervention in Education

NADEEN L. KAUFMAN AND ALAN S. KAUFMAN

PERHAPS THE MOST difficult task for the school psychologist is writing the last part of a case report, the portion that is supposed to contain relevant educational recommendations. Public Law 94-142 requires that Individual Educational Plans (IEPs) be prepared for each handicapped child who is assessed. Although these IEPs typically result from a multidisciplinary effort, the role of the school psychologist is vital. In former times, school psychologists could assess, diagnose, and place children without paying much more than lip service to educational intervention; consequently, many otherwise competent professionals were deficient in areas pertaining to the educational implications of test results. Such deficiencies can no longer be tolerated, and school psychology training programs around the country have taken steps to provide systematic experiences in educational intervention, as well as in other related nonassessment areas such as consultation and counseling.

This chapter has as its primary goal to provide an overview of research on remedial intervention, particularly research that is relevant to the school psychologist's task of delineating educational recommendations. No attempt will be made to cover the many research avenues in this area because they are too diverse and multifaceted, and the quality of the investigations varies widely. Rather, certain topics have been selected to illustrate key points and to lead the reader in the direction in which remediation research seems to be heading.

The first topic treated is research concerned with training children to reduce their tendency to make reversal errors. This area of research is typical of the process involved in determining the efficacy of one or more methods for treating a host of fairly specific educational problems. The treatments are administered uniformly to groups of children without regard to individual differences, and the success of a method depends upon producing statistically significant differences between various treatment groups. The research on reversal errors is intended to illustrate two points: (a) that remedial intervention can be documented to be statistically effective in producing the desired outcomes; and (b) there are many intervening variables which limit generalizations from research results, particularly when generalizing from group data to an individual.

Treated next will be the bulk of research conducted on the Illinois Test of Psycholinguistic Abilities (ITPA) training program. There are numerous training programs, usually rigorous in scope with carefully specified steps and procedures, which are tied directly into a theoretical model and/or the results of a multiscore test battery. The ITPA program is a popular structured approach of this sort, as are methods developed by Frostig, Getman, Kephart, and others (Myers and Hammill 1976). The goal of this section is to make school psychologists aware of the "validity" evidence for such comprehensive programs, so they will be able to judge whether their recommendations should sometimes include advocating the implementation of these kinds of language or perceptual-motor remedial systems.

The last half of this chapter covers in some depth a topic that has been the focus of much recent empirical investigation and one that looms as the key to future remediation strategies: the individualization of instruction. This research often goes by the name *aptitude-treatment interaction* (ATI), and it operates out of the basic assumption that a single educational intervention approach cannot be thought of as uniformly the "best," even if significant group differences are obtained when this method is used. Rather, the type of educational treatment, as well as the rate and mode of presenting the materials, are likely to vary as a function of the characteristics of the learner — e.g., level of intelligence, need for independence, style of solving problems, or degree of anxiety. The task for the school psychologist, then, is to match the materials and methods of remedial intervention to the specific cognitive and personality profile of each individual child, taking into account the characteristics of the teacher as well.

TRAINING TO REDUCE REVERSAL ERRORS

Reversal errors, which may take the form of orientation problems (*b-d* confusions) or sequencing difficulties (reading *was* for *saw*), occur normally in young children but usually disappear almost completely by the age of 8 (Davidson 1934, 1935; Gibson, Gibson, Pick, and Osser 1962). The occurrence of reversal errors in children above age 8 has been shown to discriminate significantly between disabled and normal readers (Doehring 1968, Lyle and Goyen 1968). In addition, predictive validity correlational studies have shown that children who tend to reverse letters at the end of grade K or the beginning of grade 1 are more likely to be poor readers at the end of grade 1 or 2 than youngsters who do not have a reversal problem (deHirsch, Jansky, and Langford 1966, Goins 1958, N. Kaufman 1980a, Teegarden 1933). Significant correlation coefficients are invariably obtained between reversal errors and later reading achievement, with impressive values in the .50s and .60s obtained when reliable measures of the reversal tendency are used (N. Kaufman 1980b).

Because of the demonstrated relationship between reversals and reading, it is understandable that many studies have been undertaken to train children not to make reversal errors. These investigations have employed diverse techniques for training children to reduce their tendency to reverse, and most studies have found significant and substantial reductions in reversal errors for the experimental groups when compared to the control populations (e.g., Powell 1974, Wass 1972, Williams 1975).

Lavine (1977) suggests that merely exposing reversible visual stimuli to children will improve their discrimination of them. However, it is well documented that the orientation of a stimulus is a feature of low salience for young children when compared to other features such as contour, color, or size (McGurk 1972, Ricciuti 1963). Consequently, many investigators have designed training programs which call attention to the distinctive features of visual forms that relate to directionality. For example, Hendrickson and Muehl (1962) had 5-to-7½-year-old subjects push a handle under an arrow pointing in the direction of the reversible letters *b* and *d*. A second experimental group was also trained using arrows, but requiring an inconsistent motor response, and a control group was given irrelevant pretraining. Both experimental groups performed significantly better than the control group on the criterion measure, which demanded transfer of training, suggesting that the use of arrows to focus on the directional qualities of the stimuli was effective. The nature of the motor response did not matter, however, as the two experimental groups did not differ significantly from each other. Indeed, Koenigsberg (1973) found that exercises which trained on the relevance of orientation were effective in reducing reversal errors, and that sensory-motor training contributed virtually no additional benefit.

Further support for the effectiveness of distinctive-feature training in reducing reversal errors comes from studies by: (*a*) Williams (1975), who used discrimination and reproduction tasks with a sample of black 4 and 5 year olds; (*b*) Wohlwill and Wiener (1964), who trained 4-to-6-year-olds with both match-to-sample and motor methods; (*c*) Lyle and Cameron (1976), who used left and right markers to train 4-year-olds to discriminate the *b-d-p-q* group; and (*d*) Wass (1972), who found that all three methods he used to help kindergarten children detect critical differences in visual stimuli were highly effective, but that these methods (perceptual training, verbal training, feedback training) did not differ from each other in effectiveness.

Powell (1974) contrasted distinctive-feature training (sorting cards which focused attention on shape orientation and sequence) with prototype training (sorting cards with omitted portions of the "target" shape, designed to build a memory image or prototype of the stimulus). She discovered that the critical-feature method was effective in reducing reversal errors for kindergarten children and was far superior to the prototype approach. Smothergill (1971) also found a distinctive-feature training method to be quite effective but, in contrast to Powell's results, this method was not demonstrated to be superior to a prototype technique. The discrepancy in research results may be due to the different interpretations given by Powell and Smothergill to the characteristics of prototype training.

There is ample documentation that training procedures which call attention to the distinctive features of reversible stimuli and highlight them in some way are very effective for remediating reversal problems. However, the consistency of the research on this point does not necessarily translate directly to specific remedial suggestions. Should the reversible stimuli be presented simultaneously, so the child views the different visual forms at the same time, or is a successive presentation preferred? Bryant (1973) found simultaneous presentations to be easier to solve correctly than successive exposures of stimuli, but Williams and Ackerman (1971) discovered that successive presentations of very similar reversible stimuli led to greater learning than training methods utilizing simultaneous presentations. Smothergill (1971), however, found that learning occurred about equally well regardless of the mode of presentation.

Another reasonable question is how much training is necessary to effect change. Tighe and Tighe (1968) observed that four experiences per stimulus did not lead to later learning, but eight or twelve experiences were equally effective in reducing reversal errors. Insufficient training time may have accounted for McNeil, Kievit, and Lindstrom's (1974) finding of only a partial benefit from their distinctive-feature training approach.

Evans and Bilsky (1975) trained ninety educable mentally retarded children on reversals and demonstrated that distinctive-feature or differentiation training employing very similar distractors was more effective than training using quite dissimilar distractor letters, but this finding emerged for only one of their four dependent variables. Training did not significantly improve performance on the other three criteria for the group as a whole, although the authors performed subsequent analyses to detect significant interaction effects. Operating from this ATI frame-work, Evans and Bilsky found numerous significant interactions involv-ing chronological age and mental ability. In general, they found training with similar letters, as compared to training using other stimuli (e.g., color and form discrimination, and irrelevant tasks such as card games and drawing), significantly improved the reversals performance of younger and less intelligent retarded youngsters, but not that of the older and brighter subjects.

It is interactions such as these that must be known and under-stood before proper educational recommendations can be made. Of equal importance is detailed knowledge of the skill or skill areas that are to be remediated. In the case of reversal errors, a considerable body of infor-mation has accumulated (N. Kaufman 1980b); many findings in the theo-retical literature need to be learned before effective training can be imple-mented, most notably research on factors such as neurological variables which are believed to influence reversal errors.

Neurological considerations merit attention since reversal errors have been associated with various types of neurological impairment for over half a century (Hinshelwood 1917, Orton 1925). Much research has been generated from neurological hypotheses, particularly the line of in-vestigation involving the nature of mirror images. Neurological propo-nents feel that the central nervous system's bilateral symmetry about the vertical axis makes it intrinsically difficult to discriminate mirror-images (e.g., Rudel and Teuber 1963). However, Barroso and Braine's (1974) re-sults with 3½-to-5½-year-olds cast serious doubt on the role of bilateral symmetry of the body. They observed the same error pattern with stimuli that were not truly mirror-image stimuli.

Vellutino (1978) rejected Orton's neurological position based on data from several sources, and concluded that the key to reversal errors is verbal intrusion errors and verbal mediation problems (i.e., errors associ-ated with applying verbal labels) rather than a visual processing defi-ciency. Nevertheless, there are still a number of researchers who are ac-tively pursuing neurological explanations of reversals, such as Frank and Levinson (1976), who trace the difficulty to a cerebellar-vestibular circuit. Perhaps reversal errors are neurologically based for some children and not others, which would suggest different approaches for remediation if etiology can be determined.

The child's age is also an interacting variable regarding reversals training. There is evidence that even infants (Cornell 1974) and toddlers (Gellerman 1933a, 1933b) are perceptually aware of differences in the ori-entation of stimuli, but reversal errors are often made by young children because of the low salience of orientation as a stimulus dimension. Consequently, reversals are common for four and five-year-olds (Gibson et al., 1962). Logically remediation would not be appropriate until about the second grade, since reversal errors are not unusual even for six-year-olds. The results of research on the value of distinctive-feature training suggest that this approach might be useful to teach orientation to preschool or first-grade children in a conventional classroom setting, but utilizing this approach for educational intervention on a one-to-one remedial basis is not warranted until the child is old enough for reversal errors to be unusual.

When determining the method to recommend to teachers for orientation training, psychologists should be aware of other consistent research findings as well. For example, the positioning of stimuli affects difficulty level. Up-down discriminations are easier than left-right comparisons, and skewed positions are easier to discriminate than aligned ones (Davidson 1935, Huttenlocher 1967a, 1967b; Rudel and Teuber 1963). In addition, match-to-sample methods of assessing orientation and sequencing ability have been observed to be more effective than other techniques, such as copying the stimulus or responding verbally (Asso and Wyke 1971, Cronin 1967).

Remediation studies on reversal errors have been used to illustrate that educational intervention can be proven effective, but that even the teaching of a "simple" phenomenon turns out to be quite complex. Proper translation of psychoeducational data to educational action requires thorough grounding in the literature, dynamic assessment of the child's cognitive and emotional profile, and finally selecting an appropriate intervention plan from the sensible alternatives so as to provide the best possible match to the child's profile.

ILLINOIS TEST OF PSYCHOLINGISTIC ABILITIES (ITPA) TRAINING MODEL

The ITPA is a twelve-subtest psycholinguistic battery developed from Osgood's (1957) theory of communication (Kirk, McCarthy, and Kirk 1968). It measures the psycholinguistic processes of reception (intake of information), association (mental manipulation), and expression (output) in both the visual and auditory channels of communication. The ITPA includes six tasks at the representational level of organization (complex mediating processes), and six at the automatic level (highly organized processes, e.g., memory or perceptual closure).

Each ITPA subtest is considered to measure an important communication function; taken together, they are believed to represent foundation skills necessary for success in academic areas. Consequently, deficiencies in one or more areas require direct remediation, and this intervention frequently takes place at the level assessed by each subtest (Kirk and Kirk 1971). According to Hammill and Larson (1974):

> Psycholinguistic training is based upon the assumption that discrete elements of language behavior are identifiable and measurable, that they provide the underpinning for learning, and that if defective they can be remediated. When using this approach, an additional assumption is made that the cause of the child's learning failure is within himself and that strengthening weak areas will result in improved classroom learning (pp. 5–6).

A number of comprehensive programs for remediating language problems has been developed and used fairly widely (e.g., Bush and Giles 1969, Minskoff, Wiseman, and Minskoff 1972). Much research has been generated, and the varieties of investigations on psycholinguistic (as well as perceptual-motor) training have been integrated and summarized (Arter and Jenkins 1979, Hammill and Larson 1974, Newcomer and Hammill 1976). The type of remediation in which the child's strengths and weaknesses on skills presumed to be essential prerequisites of school-related learning form the basis of instructional programs has been referred to by Arter and Jenkins (1979) as *differential diagnosis-prescriptive teaching*. The purpose of this section is to determine whether this type of remedial programming, illustrated by the ITPA approach, is effective. Can these supposed prerequisite skills be taught? Does mastery of the presumed foundation abilities actually transfer to academic areas? Do remedial approaches which exploit a child's strength in a modality translate to improvement in academic skills such as reading?

Teaching the Specific Psycholinguistic Skills

Hammill and Larsen (1974) summarized data from thirty-eight studies which used the ITPA or a portion of it as the criterion for demonstrating improvement in language ability following a psycholinguistic training program. They grouped the studies in several ways to evaluate differential effects of the training. Significant gains in individual subtests were the exception rather than the rule for studies with retarded, disadvantaged, preschool, and elementary school children. Across all groups, a majority of studies (52%) showed post-training gains in the ITPA Verbal Expression subtest, and 48% of the studies showed gains in Auditory Association. Of the nine subtests evaluated in most studies, the mean percent of significant gains was only 35%; in fact, the mean percent for the three automatic subtests was only 27. Quite clearly, the vast majority of the children tended *not* to improve in their psycholinguistic skills as a result of systematic language training. This lack of success was apparently upheld regardless of the nature of the activities, the approach used (individual prescriptions or a set program), the age level of the samples, or the nature of the samples (retarded or disadvantaged).

Hammill and Larsen (1974) concluded "that the idea that psycholinguistic constructs, as measured by the ITPA, can be trained by existing techniques remains nonvalidated" (p. 11), but this conclusion has not gone unchallenged. Minskoff (1975) criticized Hammill and Larsen for lumping together many diverse studies without considering specific variables such as the nature of the subjects, nature of the treatment, and inadequacies of experimental design. In particular, she considered the nearly forty studies to contain innumerable methodological flaws; to employ treatments that varied widely on the key factors of content, time, group vs. individual approach, and teacher competence; and to include inappropriate subjects such as mentally retarded children, even though psycholinguistic training programs are intended only for bona fide learning-disabled children.

Lund, Foster, and McCall-Perez (1978) openly challenged Hammill and Larsen's (1974) conclusions by reevaluating the twenty-four studies of the thirty-eight cited in the original critique which they were able to locate. These authors noted that six studies cited by Hammill and Larsen were quite positive, in that gains were observed in at least six ITPA subtests per study. Lund et al. (1978) pointed out that the six successful investigations were also among the better studies in that they tended to employ long, comprehensive, and structured treatment programs. They also claimed that Hammill and Larsen inaccurately reported the results of four negative studies, reached conclusions from two studies with insufficient data, and anticipated gains in all areas when several studies intended to remediate only one or two skills.

Despite the vociferous challenges, Hammill and his colleagues have not backed down. Newcomer, Larsen, and Hammill (1975) agreed with Minskoff's (1975) call for better designed and controlled studies, but otherwise dispute her criticisms. For example, they object to her claim that the programs are only intended for the learning disabled, since they are used in current practice for many other types of children, and Minskoff's own program (Minskoff et al., 1972) is geared for developmental use and for the mentally retarded, not just for the learning disabled. Newcomer et al. (1975) also note that it is the methodologically weak studies which are more likely to show positive results because of uncontrolled variables and other factors.

In response to Lund et al. (1978), Hammill and Larsen (1978) explained that with one small exception they did not report or interpret data inaccurately. They also accused Lund et al. of trying to claim positive results when the data were clearly negative, and they cited the results of a subsequent study that attempted to follow Minskoff's (1975) fifteen guidelines for psycholinguistic remediation, and used the Minskoff et al. (1972) program as the treatment, but still produced negative results.

Hammill and Larsen (1974) reiterated their original position that the effectiveness of psycholinguistic training is *unvalidated*—not proven ineffective, worthless, or invalid, but simply unvalidated. We concur with this conclusion based on present data. However, we also strongly support the position taken by Minskoff (1975) that the real issue is to determine what types of psycholinguistic methods are most effective for which children under what conditions.

Transfer of Training

Even if psycholinguistic programs are ultimately shown to be effective in significantly improving specific psycholinguistic skills, such a finding is not nearly as important as the issue of transfer of training. The crux of the effectiveness of psycholinguistic training is whether or not such intervention transfers to academic skills. Do children who improve as a result of these remedial programs show significant gains in school-related areas such as reading and mathematics?

Surprisingly, there has been little research attempting to answer this question for psycholinguistic training. Most transfer studies have been validation attempts for visual-perceptual training approaches, such as those advocated by Kephart-Getman, Frostig, and Doman-Delacato (Arter and Jenkins 1979). When all of these transfer studies are grouped together, including one that was apparently conducted using the ITPA program, the results are unimpressive. Arter and Jenkins (1979) report that trained groups significantly outstripped controls on pertinent criteria only about one-third of the time. This is hardly better than chance.

While direct evidence of transfer from the ITPA training program to academics is apparently unavailable, there is an accumulation of discouraging indirect evidence. The ITPA subtests do not correlate very highly with reading, spelling, or arithmetic achievement, as the median coefficients derived from a substantial number of studies fell below .35 for virtually all subtests (Newcomer and Hammill 1976). In addition, the

ITPA subtests were found to be largely lacking in diagnostic validity—
i.e., none of the subtests consistently or effectively discriminated between
groups known to differ in reading ability (Newcomer and Hammill 1976).

The questionable effectiveness of the ITPA training program in
producing significant gains in the ITPA skill areas, coupled with the disappointing results of criterion-related and diagnostic-validity investigations, make it extremely unlikely that psycholinguistic training programs
will prove overly successful in enhancing academic achievement.

Modality-Based Remediation

The final question regarding the ITPA approach is whether or
not remediation that is prescribed based on an individual's strength in
either the auditory-vocal or visual-motor modality has proven successful
in improving academic achievement. This issue is related to the ATI technique, and is quite different from the previous section which explored
whether training on weaknesses would transfer to the academic arena.
Rather, modality-based remediation stipulates that a child who performs
relatively well on auditory-perceptual tasks should be given academic instruction via the stronger auditory channel, with the reverse holding true
for the "visual learner" (Johnson and Myklebust 1967).

Arter and Jenkins (1977) reviewed fifteen pertinent studies where
reading instruction was geared to a child's preferred modality (including
kinesthetic), and in fourteen the children learned about equally well,
whether or not their instructional plan matched their preferred modality.
Similar reviews by Silverston and Deichmann (1975) and Larrivee (1981)
reached equally negative conclusions regarding the use of modality-
matching for teaching beginning reading, improving reading achievement
scores, or generating acquisition of basic skills. The negative results reported by Bateman (1968), Smith (1971), and Waugh (1973) are noteworthy because they used ITPA subtests to identify a child's preferred
modality.

Larrivee (1981) did provide a small amount of evidence to suggest
that the preferred modality approach *was* effective in teaching spelling.
She also mentioned two variables which might confound a simplistic application of auditory or visual-channel teaching, namely, some consistent
developmental findings as well as the different and changing roles of auditory and visual discrimination in learning to read.

Larrivee (1981) criticized the modality-preference studies on several grounds, particularly the small size and unrepresentative nature of
the samples and the questionable reliability of the instruments used to as-

sess preference (including ITPA subtests). Nevertheless, she still accepted the overwhelming bulk of negative findings as support for the futility of basing beginning reading instruction on so-called preferred modality.

Implications for School Psychologists

Psycholinguistic training programs have not been validated in any sense of the word. The same conclusion can be reached for the various visual-perceptual and auditory-perceptual training programs, for reasons almost identical to the ones documented above for the ITPA approach (Arter and Jenkins 1979, Hammill, Goodman, and Wiederholt 1974).

As a general rule, school psychologists should *not* recommend the application of any current comprehensive psycholinguistic training program where the goal is to remediate psycholinguistic deficiencies. Such time-consuming methods simply do not have empirical support. It would seem more reasonable to make some limited remedial suggestions regarding modality preference so long as (*a*) several instruments are used to determine preference to improve the reliability of the assessment, (*b*) the child's progress in the remediation program is monitored carefully, and (*c*) different procedures are immediately employed if the modality matching seems unsuccessful.

Perceptual-motor training programs, in a rigorous, time-consuming format, are also not recommended. Some aspects of the various visual or auditory perceptual training programs might occasionally be suggested, so long as the three cautions indicated above for psycholinguistic training are followed. An added caution is Hammill and Bartel's (1978) warning that "perceptual-motor training is viewed as more acceptable for preschool than for kindergarten or school-aged children, and is never recommended as a substitute for teaching language, reading, or arithmetic skills" (p. 372).

APTITUDE — TREATMENT INTERACTION (ATI)

The field of aptitude-treatment interaction was born following Cronbach's (1957) plea to psychologists to put an end to the segregation of experimental psychology from the investigation of individual differences. The merger of experimental manipulation (in search of generalizable laws and theories) with correlational research brought forth the now flourishing field of aptitude-treatment interactions (Cronbach 1975, Cronbach and Snow 1977). In this field, researchers are more interested in significant *interactions* in analysis of variance studies than in significant main effects, since the main goal is to discover the best treatment for a child based on his or her individual characteristics. Whereas learning theorists such as Thorndike and Hull searched for laws of learning that are generalizable to all people, ATI researchers operate from the basic assumption that "treatment A" or "law B" may work well for some individuals (e.g., bright children) but be ineffective or inaccurate for others (average or dull children).

Since the word *aptitude* implies differences in cognitive functioning or intelligence, it is understandable that a new label, *trait-treatment interaction* (TTI), was coined by researchers more interested in variables associated with personality or behavior than with cognition (Berliner and Cahen 1973). Tobias (1976) suggests that *attribute*-treatment interaction is the most appropriate term, since this would retain the popular ATI abbreviation while better reflecting the range of research presently being conducted within both the personality and cognitive domains. In this chapter, we are interpreting the ATI in accordance with Tobias' suggestion.

The abundance of research generated in the ATI area has produced many provocative findings for professionals involved with remedial intervention. Some lines of ATI research have yielded consistently negative results, such as the approach discussed earlier regarding the match of a child's strong sensory modality with a specific remedial approach. However, other areas of investigation have produced many significant interactions, with a bulk of these studies summarized by Cronbach and Snow (1977).

Unfortunately, the significant interactions have often been inconsistent from study to study, preventing the formulation of a series of ATI laws (Cronbach 1975). Significant ATIs were found to vary with sex of the subjects, nature of the content being taught, and other variables that were sometimes uncontrolled or unknown (Cronbach and Snow 1977). Nevertheless, certain consistencies have been found by Cronbach (1975) in his overview of the ATI research, and these findings are worth studying by school psychologists and others with responsibility for recommending specific interventions.

First, teachers can reduce the degree to which the student's level of intelligence controls learning by including pictures and diagrams in the lessons. This goal can also be facilitated by using more didactic lessons and relying less on a student's ability to induce generalizations. A second consistency concerns social class, broadly defined. On the average, children from blue-collar families seem to learn better with didactic teaching, structured and explicit requirements, and immediate rewards. In contrast, the methodologies long advocated by educational theorists seem to be effective only with middle-class children: "problem-oriented, ego-motivated, supportive methods of teaching" (Cronbach, 1975, p. 121).

Tobias (1976) found consistent results in several ATI studies in which students' prior familiarity with the subject was varied. Prior familiarity, which is essentially the same as level of achievement in a given subject area, was found to interact in a predictable way with instructional methodology. The higher the level of prior achievement, the lower the instructional support that is needed for effective learning to occur; in contrast, students with little prior knowledge of a content area need much instructional support. Little instructional support occurs when material is simply presented as a stimulus. Instructional support can be increased by organizing the materials and providing feedback, e.g., by providing instructional objectives, eliminating irrelevant information, and monitoring content mastery with criterion questions. From a programmed instruction perspective, a branched, flexible program would be desirable for students with much prior knowledge, whereas a linear program should be more effective for students with low achievement in the content area (Tobias 1976). The ATI literature is voluminous, and much of the pertinent research has been summarized by Cronbach and Snow (1977); consequently only a few selected topics, all relevant to the school psychologist's task of translating cognitive and emotional profiles to educational recommendations, are treated below. These include the "attribute" variables of cognitive processing and cognitive style, the issue of student-teacher interactions, and the goals of the intervention.

Cognitive Processes

Although aptitude was originally defined as intelligence or general scholastic aptitude in the early ATI cognitive-domain studies, it has increasingly and primarily been defined from various cognitive theories. The shift has been from a psychometric and quantitative definition of aptitude to a process-oriented definition focusing on the method of problem solving and other qualitative aspects of the problem-solving situation. A recent, comprehensive, two-volume compilation called *Aptitude, Learning, and Instruction* (Snow, Federico, and Montague 1980) provides insightful cognitive process analyses of learning, problem solving, and aptitude; also a valuable reference in this area is *Cognition, Development, and Instruction,* edited by Kirby and Biggs (1980).

There is a diversity of cognitive theories discussed in the above texts, such as those by Robert Sternberg, Jean Piaget, J. P. Das, Earl Hunt, and John Anderson, and each provides a legitimate basis for ATI prescriptions. These processing theories share an emphasis on the use of cognitive mechanisms in the acquisition and retention of knowledge, and the application of these mechanisms for solving problems. Federico (1980) states definitively:

> It is these cognitive processes that should be considered in the design and development of adaptive instructional systems. Customary measures of abilities, aptitudes, and other attributes have been produced primarily for predictive purposes. These selection instruments were not created as tests of cognitive processes that mediate distinct types of learning and performance. Therefore, traditional psychometric measures are not indices that suggest how to support and facilitate the processes of acquiring knowledge or evoking performance. (p. 9)

Federico (1980) goes on to explain that the intervening processes used by individual children to learn, store, and retrieve information have to be measured in order to select each child's most appropriate instructional approach.

The cognitive processing theory espoused by Das, Kirby, and Jarman (1975, 1979), derived from Luria's (1966) model of successive and simultaneous processing, is used here to illustrate the role cognitive theory can play in educational applications of ATI research. This processing dichotomy resembles closely the distinction made by Neisser (1967) between serial and parallel processing, and the duality of analytic-sequential (left hemisphere) vs. gestalt-holistic (right hemisphere) processing put forth by cerebral specialization theorists (Bogen 1969, Levy 1972, Nebes 1974). Successive processing is linear and temporal in nature, requiring the handling of information in serial order; the system is typically not surveyable at any point in time. In contrast, for simultaneous processing the stimuli are frequently totally surveyable. The gestalt-like integration of stimuli is necessary for correct solution of these problems, most of which have spatial overtones (Das, et al. 1975, 1979). According to Luria (1966), successive processing is associated with the fronto-temporal regions of the brain, and simultaneous processing with the occipital-parietal regions.

Some studies have shown that effective treatment seems to be a function of an indivdual's processing style. Krashen, Seliga, and Hartnett (1973) taught Spanish to English-speaking adults via two methods: an analytic, deductive, sequential approach requiring learning explicit rules prior to practice; and a simultaneous, holistic approach involving conversation and induction. The most successful students taught by the analytic-sequential approach were identified as having a sequential style of processing information, whereas the most successful adults taught by the conversational method did not display consistent preferences. Pask and Scott (1972) used a classification test to categorize students as "serialists" and "holists," and proceeded to teach new material to these students using either a serial or holistic treatment. When students' problem-solving styles were matched to their treatment approach, near perfect performance resulted. Students mismatched between processing style and treatment scored much lower on the criterion measure.

One process-oriented ATI study was conducted in the schools by Hartlage and his colleagues (Hartlage 1975) and summarized by Reynolds (1981). First-grade children were identified by a group measure as having strengths in auditory sequencing, visual sequencing, and auditory/visual space. Unlike the typical modality preference studies (Larrivee 1981), these children were identified as having processing strengths from a neuropsychological paradigm, not from a simplistic "visual learner-auditory learner" model. The group with visual sequencing strengths was taught using the initial teaching alphabet (ITA) approach, those with auditory sequencing strengths with a heavily linguistic-phonics approach, and children with strengths in auditory/visual space (essentially simultaneous processing) were taught with a "traditional orthographic, whole-word, look-say approach" (Reynolds 1981). The control group was assigned randomly to a reading instructional method. The total group of children whose reading program matched their processing strength obtained a mean standard score in Wide Range Achievement Test (WRAT) Reading of 129 at the end of first grade, compared to a mean of 106 for the controls. Teachers' ratings of global reading ability agreed with the WRAT data.

Application of processing theory to ATI intervention also requires understanding educational goals in terms of their processing requirements. The reading process seems to depend primarily on successive processing during decoding and other "early reading" tasks, with a shift to a dependency on simultaneous processing when trying to achieve higher levels of fluent reading (Cummins and Das 1977, Kirby 1980). Once normal readers acquire the conceptual-linguistic operations requisite for competent reading, their reading success may relate primarily to simultaneous processing and be largely independent of successive processing. Reading-disabled children and others experiencing reading difficulties, however, may have initial deficiencies in successive processing which "may delay the differentiation of conceptual-linguistic operations from more elementary forms of sequential linguistic processing" (Cummins

and Das 1977, p. 247). This hypothesis is given some support by a variety
of studies which show or imply that low levels of successive processing
may limit the reading achievement of students who are reading disabled
or retarded, or who are low achievers or from a low social class (Blackman, Bilsky, Burger, and Mar 1976, Das, Leong, and Williams 1978, Das,
Manos, and Kanungo 1975, Doehring 1968, Kinsbourne and Warrington
1966, Leong 1976).

One possible remedial solution for reading difficulties is to attempt to enhance children's successive processing skills. Two studies have
shown that nonacademic tasks and special instructional procedures can
be used to teach problem-solving strategies and, hence, improve successive processing (D. Kaufman and P. Kaufman 1979, Krywaniuk 1974). It
is significant that the instruction given in these studies also transferred to
improved performance in word reading and mathematics. Kirby (1980)
has urged the remediation of processing strategies whenever such attempts have been shown to be successful and when they are practical to
implement. However, despite the positive results of two training studies,
caution is needed regarding the teaching of processing strategies. There is
still the bulk of negative results regarding the training of deficient skills in
psycholinguistic and perceptual-motor areas to contend with, as well as
the major limitations of deficit training that are suggested by findings in
neurology and genetics (Adams and Victor 1977, Hartlage 1975, Reynolds
1981). Basically, contemporary neuropsychological models consider the
training of deficits as doomed to failure since damaged or dysfunctional
areas are the targets of the teaching (Reynolds 1981).

When remediation of a processing deficiency proves inadvisable,
Kirby (1980) recommends the traditional ATI approach of exploiting processing strengths in the teaching of the pertinent subject matter. This
method was given some support by studies cited (Hartlage 1975, Krashen,
et al. 1973, Pask and Scott 1972), but more ATI investigations with
school-age children in areas such as reading and mathematics are necessary before direct application of this processing theory to the classroom
can be thought of as having empirical support. It is to be hoped that such
research will be more successful than the studies which matched sense modality to treatment, since the latter line of investigation was not process
oriented and did not account for the changing demands of reading
achievement at different stages of the reading process.

Gunnison, N. Kaufman, and A. Kaufman (1982) proposed methods for remediating different reading-related skills from either a sequential or simultaneous vantage point. They described methods for remediating various decoding, lexical access, and text organization skills, and
identified each training approach as involving sequential processing, si-

multaneous processing, or a combination of both. For example, the lexical access skill of recognizing the meanings of single words through direct identification can be trained in three ways: (*a*) by rehearsing the word's pronunciation (sequential); (*b*) by associating the word with a concrete object, experience, picture, or image (simultaneous); and (*c*) by rehearsing the word's pronunciation in an appropriate, student-produced oral sentence context (sequential and simultaneous).

Logue (1977) analyzed math errors from the framework of Luria's (1966) theory. He discussed, for example, how children with simultaneous processing deficiencies are likely to experience difficulty in spatially related arithmetic reasoning problems, such as sorting out comparative relationships (If Joe is taller than Bob, and Sam is taller than Joe, who is the shortest?) or identifying reference points in space, whereas children with poor successive processing would have special difficulty with the temporal sequencing required for oral arithmetic. Logue (1977) does not provide a proposed remedial program, but he does include suggestions for teachers, such as noting which children loudly verbalize their mental calculations, rely too heavily on fingers for problem solving, and are overdependent on pencil and paper (at a point where these behaviors are no longer age appropriate), since they are likely candidates for a neurologically-related successive processing deficiency.

Applications of process-oriented treatments to the classroom will require additional systematic ATI research to determine if they are effective, as noted above. In this regard, Cronbach (1975) offers an important word of warning. In a number of experiments conducted in his laboratory and elsewhere, the hypothesis that individuals with high spatial ability (closely akin to simultaneous processing) should learn better with many diagrams and few words was not borne out. Cronbach suspects that significant interactions were not obtained because of failure to control for the complexity of the content. Students with good spatial processing skills will probably benefit from diagrams when instruction is complex; however, students with low-spatial skills will probably benefit more from diagrams for simple instruction, since the children with good spatial skills are able to visualize the relationships without benefit of the diagrammatic aids.

Thus, consider the teaching of mathematics to a child high in successive processing and low in simultaneous processing. Strict adherence to a training program that focused on sequential, rule-governed learning, at the expense of visual-spatial, concrete materials would probably penalize the child in learning basic mathematics concepts and facts. This child would probably need the "simultaneous" materials as a crutch because of an inability to visualize spontaneously the referents for the quantitative "building block" facts. Once the foundations skills are mastered, then a more sequential approach to the learning of complex mathematical operations would probably be appropriate.

Cognitive Style

Cognitive processing, like intelligence, is part of the aptitude domain. In contrast, cognitive style refers more to how a person approaches a wide variety of problems in the cognitive, behavioral, personality, perceptual, and social domains. Cognitive styles are concerned with the process or form of an activity (how we perceive, learn, relate to people) rather than the content; they are pervasive and are stable over time. Unlike strict aptitudes, both extremes of bipolar cognitive styles are "good", and have adaptive value in certain circumstances (Witkin, Moore, Goodenough, and Cox 1977). Two of the more well known cognitive styles are field dependence-field independence (Witkin, et al. 1977) and impulsive-reflective (Kagan 1966); the former will be used to illustrate the relationship of cognitive style to ATIs.

Based on laboratory tasks such as orienting one's body in a darkened room or paper-and-pencil measures of orientation, individuals are categorized as field dependent or field independent. Field-independent people tend to be flexible in problem-solving situations, to impose structure when it is lacking, to have an impersonal orientation, to be interested in abstract and theoretical concerns, and they are not overly dependent on cues from the environment. Field-dependent individuals are quite attuned to their social environment, utilize prevailing social frameworks, enjoy being with people, are better liked, and are heavily influenced by cues in the environment (Witkin, et al. 1977).

Field-dependent individuals are better at learning and remembering materials with a social content (Ruble and Nakamura 1972, Witkin, et al. 1977), but field-independent people make better use of mediation in learning and are more able to structure and organize information when the material is not already organized (Schwen 1970, Witkin, et al. 1977). Regarding reinforcement, field-independent individuals perform better than field-dependent people with intrinsic motivation, but this difference evaporates when either material rewards or praise are introduced (Steinfeld 1973). In addition, field-dependent individuals are more affected by criticism than those who are field independent (Witkin, et al. 1977). All of these findings are consistent and are supported by many investigations.

Quite obviously, remediation approaches and the organization of remedial materials need to be quite different to be maximally effective with children identified as field dependent or field independent as the result of a psychoeducational evaluation. WISC-R profiles can be helpful in identifying a child's cognitive style, since high scores on Picture Completion, Block Design, and Object Assembly are associated with field independence (A. Kaufman 1979). The interested reader should consult Witkin, et al.'s (1977) review of the studies cited above, of other relevant investigations, and of other topics such as interaction between a teacher's and student's cognitive styles.

Teacher-Student Interactions

A popular avenue of ATI research has been the study of interactions between characteristics of the teacher and his or her students; many such studies are chronicled by Cronbach and Snow (1977). A few illustrations should help document the potential value of such studies.

Domino (1968) evaluated college students' performance in introductory psychology courses as a function of both the teachers' and students' needs for achievement via conformity, as opposed to achievement via independence. He found that students performed significantly better when their achievement needs matched the teaching styles of their teachers. Instructors who dominated the class, demanding conformity, produced better results for students with a need to achieve via conformity than for students with a high need for independent achievement. In contrast, these latter students functioned exceptionally well with teachers who demanded independent work. This interesting finding has been cross-validated numerous times (Cronbach 1975). Peterson (1977), in exploring these same achievement needs in high school students, found that teachers who controlled and structured the presentation of social studies material produced relatively good performance by high ability-high anxiety students, as opposed to students with other combinations of ability and anxiety level.

Janicki and Peterson (1981) compared direct instruction (controlled, structured) with a small-group variation of direct instruction for a two-week unit on fractions in fourth and fifth grade. They found significant interactions with students' aptitudes, attitudes, and locus of control. For example, children with an external locus of control (those who do not need to control a situation) fared well with direct instruction, whereas those with an internal locus of control benefited from the small-group setting, perhaps because they had some choices to make and could thus provide some of their own structure in that learning environment.

It is evident that the significant ATIs frequently found in studies of teacher-student interaction necessitate that the personality and teaching style of the teacher or remedial specialist, and their match to the child's personality and needs, be weighed carefully when making specific educational recommendations. School psychologists need to know the teachers and special educators in their system quite well, so that variables pertaining to their styles and behaviors can be incorporated when choosing the most appropriate educational alternative for a given child.

Goals of the Treatment

Sometimes the goal of the intervention is the key variable in determining the type of treatment. This point is well illustrated by Singer (1977) in his review of instructional strategies for psychomotor skills. Singer suggests different strategies depending on the purpose for the treatment. For example, if the goal of the learning situation is to promote transfer to similar skills and situations, then research supports use of a problem-solving, discovery, or trial-and-error strategy. However, when transfer is not the issue and the goal is simply to achieve a high level of performance in that skill, then a guided and prompted approach is advised (Singer 1977).

Implications for School Psychologists

The ATI research is provocative, and there are consistent findings that can be applied directly, but by and large the specific results of these studies are not as interesting as the notion of studying interactions. Cronbach (1975) has noted that interactions have interactions and the more research is conducted, the more aware investigators become that it is almost impossible to come up with a systematic set of laws and rules. In other words, the more we know about a set of interactions, the more we realize that a number of other factors contribute to the interaction. Snow (1977) believes that theory and ATI are not incompatible terms, but practitioners cannot wait for theory in this area before applying the notions of ATI to their practical recommendations.

The fact that so many significant interactions occur in the literature, despite the inconsistencies, impels us to abandon any notions that certain methods should be universally applied to specific problems. The identical educational problem found in five children may require five totally different treatments. Indeed, research has indicated that the nature of ATIs may vary significantly at different points in time during science instruction, perhaps because the aptitudes needed for one outcome are different from those needed for subsequent outcomes (Burns 1980).

The prevalence of cognitive processing theories in the ATI research should encourage school psychologists to study many of these cognitive theories and try to understand their educational implications. This interest in cognitive processing will naturally shift a psychologist's interest in intelligence from a quantitative profile of scores to a qualitative analysis of learning styles and mental operations. This shift alone lends itself to educational action. It is simply easier to think in terms of educational intervention if we are concerning ourselves with problem-solving strategy, learning style, and mediating variables than if we focus on standard scores in various content areas. The WISC-R can be interpreted in the context of cognitive processing theories (A. Kaufman 1979), but it would be desirable if many new tests were developed directly from theory, such as the one we have constructed (A. Kaufman and N. Kaufman, 1983).

Ultimately remediation becomes a very individual and personal thing, with the school psychologist's main task one of solving the "problem of the match." Some sources which may be valuable in this endeavor are the volumes on cognition and instruction cited earlier (Kirby and Biggs 1980, Snow, et al. 1980), as well as books with a more practical orientation (Dunn and Dunn 1978, Hammill and Bartel 1978, Kauffman 1980), including a recent work devoted to hyperactive children (Whalen and Henker 1980).

GENERAL REMEDIAL SUGGESTIONS

Although the key word in this chapter is "individualization," there are still some approaches, ideas, and suggestions which generalize to many circumstances where educational recommendations are required. The goal of the last part of this chapter is to synthesize and organize some of these generalizations, and present them in a format that may be of practical benefit.

Planning educational strategies is often the least structured task the school psychologist has to face when writing a case report. Anyone who has not functioned as a classroom teacher or remedial specialist may feel justifiably hesitant to tell the teacher of a child who has been psychoeducationally "diagnosed" what now needs to be done and how to go about doing it. The preceding discussion of studies evaluating educational interventions make it clear that choosing such strategies for each individual child is a highly complex matter. The job does not end with these suggestions: negative feedback will surely follow if the suggestions do not produce the desired outcomes, so constant monitoring of recommendations is a must.

Defining the school psychologist's role in planning remediation rests on one's professional philosophy, as well as on the consultation relationship maintained with the faculty and staff of the school. It is not necessarily part of the school psychologist's job to prescribe specific educational materials or instructional programs, although remaining up to date and familiar with such materials is essential for the most efficient functioning. Nevertheless, the school psychologist's job is not to *be* the child's teacher, but rather to communicate with teachers about a child's strengths and weaknesses, and what they imply in terms of the most-likely-to-succeed teaching methodologies. It is the teacher's job to select the actual materials, once he or she understands the child's functioning and individual needs. The better skilled the child's teacher is, the more correct educational choices are likely to be made. It therefore seems quite fair to view remedial programs as simply ideal teaching situations.

The degree to which teachers have internalized child development research, cognitive psychology, and theories of learning all greatly influence how curriculum contents are selected, what teaching procedures will be utilized, and the teachers' expectations for individual children. Despite the fact that teacher-training institutions have become far more content oriented in recent years (e.g., Brodinsky 1978), sometimes the most astute recommendations that the school psychologist can make fit into the category of reteaching basic educational psychology. Whereas cognitive processing is important for choosing a methodology, learning theory has much value for other aspects of intervention. There are numerous educational principles which one may wrongly assume are known and understood by the classroom teacher. Even those principles that are known and understood are frequently not applied where appropriate. One important source for suggesting recommendations becomes a self-made list of generalized educational principles which can be personalized to fit the individual needs of the child in question. There are many classic textbooks in the field of educational psychology that can be sources of ideas. What follows is a brief example of the kinds of pointers that may become good remedial interventions when selected with a unique child in mind.

1. Check out the child's ability to transfer input from one sensory channel to another sensory channel before you prescribe multisensory stimulation. Whereas many teachers present new information in as many different ways as possible, all designed to reinforce and intensify the learning experience, a child having difficulty integrating information re-

ceived from several sensory sources will be greatly hindered when bombarded with too much "noisy" interference. A recent empirical study documented this potentially adverse effect of multisensory training as a remedial technique (Luchow and Shepherd 1981).

2. Be aware of all the feedback available in remedial settings and use it. This includes feedback both the child and the teacher receive from each other: vocal or motor, manifest or covert, and the internal mediation with self-correction (as with programmed instruction).

3. Develop abilities functionally and in natural settings (not just artificially contrived ones). Integrate new reading skills by having a multitude of easy reading materials for the child to "practice" on and review.

4. Encourage slow learners, educable mentally retarded, brain damaged, and learning disabled youngsters to generalize newly acquired learning, which they may not do spontaneously. Do this by providing set variations of initial learning bits, and by pointing out similarities or unity of information. Also, present the same information in many different ways to create adequate redundancy to promote necessary generalizations.

5. Remediate prerequisite deficits first. Lessons should progress from simple to more complex tasks; use minimal steps of increasing difficulty, following behavioral task analysis when necessary (Bryant 1965). Remember that children are often at different readiness levels for different skill areas.

6. Help a child with memory problems by employing distributed review. Develop automatic skills by spacing out demands for practice.

7. Use other pupils to set up cooperative remedial sessions, rather than relying solely on one-to-one tutoring. This can reduce competition and provide needed social experiences.

8. Encourage highly interesting and relevant material selections. Short, structured tasks with highly interesting, creative material and liberal use of proven reinforcers should be high priority for unmotivated students.

9. Maintain a high success rate to avoid error learning and feelings of inadequacy. Teach to the child's tolerance level (Bryant 1965).

10. Get some improvement each session; don't persist with the same approach if not successful. Work on one new skill at a time to avoid interference and overloading.

Finally, listed below are some concrete suggestions for the classroom teacher of ways to modify the learning environment to help meet the child's individual needs.

11. The teacher can manipulate space by using partitions, cubicles, and special rooms, or even by varying the size of work paper or desk surfaces. The teacher exerts control, then gradually decreases the imposed

structure as the children begin to internalize their own set of limits and controls.

12. The teacher can vary the "time" factor. For example, if a child has a very short attention span, give quicker lessons! Time allotments can be increased slowly, and quiet activities alternated with active ones. Planned breaks in long lessons are desirable.

13. The number of factors that the child must manipulate in any learning situation can be varied. The teacher can control the number of pieces of work to be dealt with (fewer pages assigned, fewer spelling words), the extraneous stimuli in the environment (teacher's own verbalizations, pictures on the wall), and the use of multi- or unisensory learning.

14. Language utilized must clarify rather than disturb learning. Check the child's understanding of basic concepts in the wording of directions. The teacher can emphasize meaning with gestures.

15. The interpersonal relationship between the teacher and student needs to be developed. Rapport is an essential learning tool. With it, learning frequently takes place in spite of inappropriate techniques or materials.

REFERENCES

Adams, R. D., & Victor, M. *Principles of neurology.* New York: McGraw-Hill, 1977.

Arter, J. A., & Jenkins, J. R. Examining the benefits and prevalence of modality considerations in special education. *Journal of Special Education,* 1977, *11,* 281-298.

Arter, J. A., & Jenkins, J. R. Differential diagnosis — prescriptive teaching: A critical appraisal. *Review of Educational Research,* 1979, *49,* 517-555.

Asso, D., & Wyke, M. Discrimination of spatially confusable letters by young children. *Journal of Experimental Child Psychology,* 1971, *11,* 11-20.

Barroso, F., & Braine, L. G. "Mirror-image" errors without mirror-image stimuli. *Journal of Experimental Child Psychology,* 1974, *18,* 213-225.

Bateman, B. The efficacy of an auditory and a visual method of first grade reading instruction with auditory and visual learners. In H. K. Smith (Ed.), *Perception and reading.* Newark, Delaware: International Reading Association, 1968.

Berliner, D. C., & Cahen, L. S. Trait-treatment interaction and learning. *Review of Research in Education,* 1973, *1,* 58-94.

Blackman, L. S., Bilsky, L. H., Burger, A. L., & Mar, H. Cognitive processes and academic achievement in EMR adolescents. *American Journal of Mental Deficiency,* 1976, *81,* 125-134.

Bogen, J. E. The other side of the brain: Parts I, II, and III. *Bulletin of the Los Angeles Neurological Society,* 1969, *34,* 73–105; 135–162; 191–203.

Brodinsky, B. Back to the Basics: The movement and its meaning. In F. Schultz (Ed.), *Annual editions: Readings in education 78/79.* Guilford, Conn.: Duskin, 1978.

Bryant, N. D. Some principles of remedial instruction for dyslexia. *The Reading Teacher,* 1965, *18,* 567–572.

Bryant, P. E. Discrimination of mirror images by young children. *Journal of Comparative and Physiological Psychology,* 1973, *82,* 415–425.

Burns, R. B. Relation of aptitudes to learning at different points in time during instruction. *Journal of Educational Psychology,* 1980, *72,* 785–795.

Bush, W. J., & Giles, M. T. *Aids to psycholinguistic teaching.* Columbus, Ohio: Charles E. Merrill, 1969.

Cornell, E. H. Infants' discrimination of photographs of faces following redundant presentations. *Journal of Experimental Child Psychology,* 1974, *18,* 98–106.

Cronbach, L. J. The two disciplines of scientific psychology. *American Psychologist,* 1957, *12,* 671–684.

Cronbach, L. J. Beyond the two disciplines of scientific psychology. *American Psychologist,* 1975, *30,* 116–127.

Cronbach, L. J., & Snow, R. E. *Aptitudes and instructional methods: A handbook for research on interactions.* New York: Irvington, 1977.

Cronin, V. Mirror-image reversal discrimination in kindergarten and first grade children. *Journal of Experimental Child Psychology,* 1967, *5,* 577–585.

Cummins, J., & Das, J. P. Cognitive processing and reading difficulties: A framework for research. *Alberta Journal of Educational Research,* 1977, *23,* 245–256.

Das, J. P., Kirby, J., & Jarman, R. F. Simultaneous and successive syntheses: An alternative model for cognitive abilities. *Psychological Bulletin,* 1975, *82,* 87–103.

Das, J. P., Kirby, J. R., & Jarman, R. F. *Simultaneous and successive cognitive processes.* New York: Academic Press, 1979.

Das, J. P., Leong, C. K., & Williams, N. H. The relationship between learning disability and simultaneous-successive processing. *Journal of Learning Disabilities,* 1978, *11,* 618–625.

Das, J. P., Manos, J., & Kanungo, R. N. Performance of Canadian Native, black, and white children on some cognitive and personality tasks. *Alberta Journal of Educational Research,* 1975, *21,* 183–195.

Davidson, H. P. A study of reversals in young children. *Journal of Genetic Psychology,* 1934, *45,* 452–465.

Davidson, H. P. A study of the confusing letters b, d, p, and q. *Journal of Genetic Psychology,* 1935, *47,* 458–468.

De Hirsch, K., Jansky, J. J., & Langford, W. S. *Predicting reading failure.* New York: Harper and Row, 1966.

Doehring, D. G. *Patterns of impairment in specific reading disability.* Bloomington, Ind.: Indiana University Press, 1968.

Domino, G. Differential prediction of academic achievement in conforming and independent settings. *Journal of Educational Psychology*, 1968, *59*, 256–260.

Dunn, R., & Dunn, K. *Teaching students through their individual learning styles: A practical approach.* Reston, Va.: Reston Publishing Co., 1978.

Evans, R. A., & Bilsky, L. H. Effects of letter-reversals training on the discrimination performance of EMR children. *American Journal of Mental Deficiency*, 1975, *80*, 99–108.

Federico, P. Adaptive instruction: Trends and issues. In R. E. Snow, P. Federico, & W. E. Montague (Eds.), *Aptitude, learning, and instruction* (Vol. 1). Hillsdale, N.J.: Lawrence Erlbaum, 1980.

Frank, J., & Levinson, H. N. Dysmetric dyslexia and dyspraxia. *Academic Therapy*, 1976, *11*, 133–143.

Gellerman, L. W. Form discrimination in chimpanzees and two-year-old children. 1. Form (triangularity) per se. *Journal of Genetic Psychology*, 1933, *42*, 3–29. (a)

Gellerman, L. W. Form discrimination in chimpanzees and two-year-old children. 11. Form vs. background. *Journal of Genetic Psychology*, 1933, *42*, 29–50. (b)

Gibson, E. J., Gibson, J., Pick, A., & Osser, H. A developmental study of the discriminability of letter-like forms. *Journal of Comparative and Physiological Psychology*, 1962, *55*, 897–906.

Goins, J. T. *Visual perceptual abilities and early reading progress.* (Supplementary Educational Monographs, No. 87). Chicago: University of Chicago Press, 1958.

Gunnison, J., Kaufman, N. L., & Kaufman, A. S. Application of sequential and simultaneous processing to reading disabilities and remedial intervention. *Academic Therapy*, 1982, *17*, 297–307.

Hammill, D. D., & Bartel, N. R. *Teaching children with learning and behavior problems* (2nd ed.). Boston: Allyn and Bacon, 1978.

Hammill, D. D., Goodman, L., & Wiederholt, J. L. Visual-motor processes: Can we train them? *The Reading Teacher*, 1974, *27*, 470–479.

Hammill, D. D., & Larsen, S. C. The effectiveness of psycholinguistic training. *Exceptional Children*, 1974, *41*, 5–14.

Hammill, D. D., & Larsen, S. C. The effectiveness of psycholinguistic training: A reaffirmation of position. *Exceptional Children*, 1978, *44*, 402–414.

Hartlage, L. C. Neuropsychological approaches to predicting outcome of remedial educational strategies for learning disabled children. *Pediatric Psychology*, 1975, *3*, 23–28.

Hendrickson, L. N., & Muehl, S. The effects of attention and motor response pretraining on learning to discriminate *b* and *d* in kindergarten children. *Journal of Educational Psychology*, 1962, *53*, 236–241.

Hinshelwood, J. *Congenital word blindness.* London: H. K. Lewis, 1917.

Huttenlocher, J. Children's ability to order and orient objects. *Child Development*, 1967, *38*, 1169–1176. (a)

Huttenlocher, J. Discrimination of figure orientation: Effects of relative position.

Journal of Comparative and Physiological Psychology, 1967, *63,* 359–361. (b)

Janicki, T. C., & Peterson, P. L. Aptitude-treatment interaction effects of variations in direct instruction. *American Educational Research Journal,* 1981, *18,* 63–82.

Johnson, D., & Myklebust, H. *Learning disabilities: Educational principles and practices.* New York: Grune and Stratton, 1967.

Kagan, J. Reflection-impulsivity: The generality and dynamics of conceptual tempo. *Journal of Abnormal Psychology,* 1966, *71,* 17–24.

Kauffman, J. M. Teaching exceptional children to use cognitive strategies. *Exceptional Education Quarterly,* 1980, *1,* whole issue.

Kaufman, A. S. *Intelligent testing with the WISC-R.* New York: Wiley-Interscience, 1979.

Kaufman, A. S., & Kaufman, N. L. *Kaufman Assessment Battery for Children (K-ABC).* Circle Pines, Minn.: American Guidance Service, 1983.

Kaufman, D., & Kaufman, P. Strategy training and remedial techniques. *Journal of Learning Disabilities,* 1979, *12,* 416–419.

Kaufman, N. L. Differential validity of reversal errors as predictors of first-grade reading achievement for blacks and whites. *Psychology in the Schools,* 1980, *17,* 460–465. (a)

Kaufman, N. L. Review of research on reversal errors. *Perceptual and Motor Skills,* 1980, *51,* 55–79. (b)

Kinsbourne, M., & Warrington, E. K. Developmental factors in reading and writing backwardness. In J. Money (Ed.), *The disabled reader.* Baltimore: Johns Hopkins Press, 1966.

Kirby, J. R. Individual differences and cognitive processes: Instructional application and methodological difficulties. In J. R. Kirby & J. B. Biggs (Eds.), *Cognition, development, and instruction.* New York: Academic Press, 1980.

Kirby, J. R., & Biggs, J. B. (Eds.) *Cognition, development, and instruction.* New York: Academic Press, 1980.

Kirk, S. A., & Kirk, W. D. *Psycholinguistic learning disabilities: Diagnosis and remediation.* Urbana, Ill.: University of Illinois Press, 1971.

Kirk, S. A., McCarthy, J. J., & Kirk, W. D. *Examiner's manual: Illinois Test of Psycholinguistic Abilities* (Rev. ed.). Urbana, Ill.: University of Illinois Press, 1968.

Koenigsberg, R. S. An evaluation of visual versus sensorimotor methods for improving orientation discrimination of letter reversals by preschool children. *Child Development,* 1973, *44,* 764–769.

Krashen, S., Seliga, R., & Hartnett, D. Two studies in adult second language learning. *Kritikon Litterarum,* 1973, *3,* 220–228.

Krywaniuk, L. W. *Patterns of cognitive abilities of high and low achieving school children.* Unpublished doctoral dissertation, University of Alberta, 1974.

Larrivee, B. Modality preference as a model for differentiating beginning reading instruction: A review of the issues. *Learning Disabilities Quarterly,* 1981, *4,* 180–188.

Lavine, L. O. Differentiation of letterlike forms in pre-reading children. *Developmental Psychology*, 1977, *13*, 89–94.

Leong, C. K. Lateralization in severely disabled readers in relation to functional cerebral development and synthesis of information. In R. M. Knights & D. J. Bakken (Eds.), *The neuropsychology of learning disorders: Theoretical approaches*. Baltimore: University Park Press, 1976.

Levy, J. Lateral specialization of the human brain: Behavioral manifestations and possible evolutionary basis. In J. A. Kiger (Ed.), *Biology of behavior*. Corvallis, Ore.: Oregon State University Press, 1972.

Logue, G. Learning disabilities and math inadequacy. *Academic Therapy*, 1977, *12*, 309–319.

Luchow, J. P., & Shepherd, M. J. The effects of multisensory training in perceptual learning. *Learning Disabilities Quarterly*, 1981, *4*, 38–43.

Lund, K. A., Foster, G. E., & McCall-Perez, F. C. The effectiveness of psycholinguistic training: A reevaluation. *Exceptional Children*, 1978, *44*, 310–319.

Luria, A. R. *Higher cortical functions in man*. New York: Basic Books, 1966.

Lyle, J. G., & Cameron, R. Discrimination of right-left orientation with directional markers. *Perceptual and Motor Skills*, 1976, *43*, 1279–1282.

Lyle, J. G., & Goyen, J. Visual recognition, developmental lag, and strephosymbolia in reading retardation. *Journal of Abnormal Psychology*, 1968, *73*, 25–29.

McGurk, H. The salience of orientation in young children's perception of form. *Child Development*, 1972, *43*, 1047–1052.

McNeil, J., Kievit, J., & Lindstrom, E. The value of feature analysis in learning to recognize letters. *Reading Improvement*, 1974, *11*, 32–35.

Minskoff, E. Research on psycholinguistic training: Critique and guidelines. *Exceptional Children*, 1975, *42*, 136–144.

Minskoff, E., Wiseman, D. E., & Minskoff, J. G. *The MWM program for developing language abilities*. Ridgefield, N.J.: Educational Performance Associates, 1972.

Myers, P. I., & Hammill, D. D. *Methods for learning disorders* (2nd ed.), New York: Wiley, 1976.

Nebes, R. D. Hemispheric specialization in commissurotomized man. *Psychological Bulletin*, 1974, *81*, 1–14.

Neisser, U. *Cognitive Psychology*. New York: Appleton-Century-Crofts, 1967.

Newcomer, P. L., & Hammill, D. D. *Psycholinguistics in the schools*. Columbus, Ohio: Charles E. Merrill, 1976.

Newcomer, P. L., Larsen, S. C., & Hammill, D. D. A response. *Exceptional Children*, 1975, *42*, 144–148.

Orton, S. T. Word blindness in school children. *Archives of Neurology and Psychiatry*, 1925, *14*, 581–615.

Osgood, C. E. Motivational dynamics of language behavior. In *Nebraska Symposium on Motivation*. Lincoln: University of Nebraska Press, 1957.

Pask, G., & Scott, B. C. E. Learning strategies and individual competence. *International Journal of Man-Machine Studies*, 1972, *4*, 217–253.

Peterson, P. L. Interactive effects of student anxiety, achievement orientation, and teacher behavior on student achievement and attitude. *Journal of Educational Psychology,* 1977, *69,* 779–792.

Powell, J. N. Teaching discrimination of shape orientation and sequence to kindergarten boys (Doctoral dissertation, University of Minnesota, 1974). *Dissertation Abstracts International,* 1974, *35,* 898A. (University Microfilms No. 74-17, 275).

Reynolds, C. R. Neuropsychological assessment and the habilitation of learning: Considerations in the search for the aptitude x treatment interaction. *School Psychology Review,* 1981, *10,* 343–349.

Ricciuti, H. N. Geometric form and detail as determinants of comparative similarity judgments in young children. In *A basic research program on reading* (Final Report, Cooperative Research Project No. 639). Washington, D.C.: U.S. Office of Education, 1963.

Ruble, D. N., & Nakamura, C. Y. Task orientation versus social orientation in young children and their attention to relevant social cues. *Child Development,* 1972, *43,* 471–480.

Rudel, R. G., & Teuber, H. L. Discrimination of direction of line in children. *Journal of Comparative and Physiological Psychology,* 1963, *56,* 892–898.

Schwen, T. M. The effect of cognitive styles and instructional sequences on learning a hierarchical task (Doctoral dissertation, Indiana University, 1970). *Dissertation Abstracts International,* 1970, *31,* 2797A–2798A. (University Microfilms No. 70-23, 380).

Silverston, R. A., & Deichmann, J. W. Sense modality research and the acquisition of reading skills. *Review of Educational Research,* 1975, *45,* 149–172.

Singer, R. N. To err or not to err: A question for the instruction of psychomotor skills. *Review of Educational Research,* 1977, *47,* 479–498.

Smith, C. M. The relationship of reading method and reading achievement to ITPA sensory modalities. *Journal of Special Education,* 1971, *5,* 143–149.

Smothergill, D. W. Effects of temporal relationship between stimuli on children's discrimination learning. *Perceptual and Motor Skills,* 1971, *32,* 511–515.

Snow, R. E. Individual differences and instructional theory. *Educational Researcher,* 1977, *6,* 10–15.

Snow, R. E., Federico, P., & Montague, W. E. (Eds.). *Aptitude, learning, and instruction* (2 vols.). Hillsdale, N.J.: Lawrence Erlbaum, 1980.

Steinfeld, S. L. Level of differentiation and age as predictors of reinforcer effectiveness. (Doctoral dissertation, Hofstra University, 1973). *Dissertation Abstracts International,* 1973, *34,* 2912B–2913B. (University Microfilms No. 73-25, 324.)

Strauss, A. A., & Kephart, N. C. *Psychopathology and education of the brain-injured child* (Vol. 2). New York: Grune & Stratton, 1955.

Strauss, A. A., & Lehtinen, L. *Psychopathology and education of the brain-injured child* (Vol. 1). New York: Grune & Stratton, 1947.

Teegarden, L. Tests for the tendency to reversal in reading. *Journal of Educational Research,* 1933, *27,* 81–97.

Tighe, T. J., & Tighe, L. S. Perceptual learning in the discrimination processes of children: An analysis of five variables in perceptual pretraining. *Journal of Experimental Psychology,* 1968, *77,* 125-134.

Tobias, S. Achievement treatment interactions. *Review of Educational Research,* 1976, *46,* 61-74.

Vellutino, F. R. Toward an understanding of dyslexia: Psychological factors in specific reading disability. In A. L. Benton and D. Pearl (Eds.), *Dyslexia: An appraisal of current knowledge.* New York: Oxford University Press, 1978.

Wass, I. R. Reduction of the reversal of letters b, d, p, q, as a function of systematic training (Doctoral dissertation, University of Illinois at Urbana-Champaign, 1972). *Dissertation Abstracts International,* 1972, *33,* 5570A-5571A. (University Microfilms No. 73-10, 080).

Waugh, R. P. Relationship between modality preference and performance. *Exceptional Children.* 1973, *40,* 465-469.

Whalen, C. K., & Henker, B. (Eds.), *Hyperactive children.* New York: Academic Press, 1980.

Williams, J. P. Training children to copy and to discriminate letterlike forms. *Journal of Educational Psychology,* 1975, *67,* 790-795.

Williams, J. P., & Ackerman, M. D. Simultaneous and successive discrimination of similar letters. *Journal of Educational Psychology,* 1971, *62,* 132-137.

Witkin, H. A., Moore, C. A., Goodenough, D. R., & Cox, P. W. Field-dependent and field-independent cognitive styles and their educational implications. *Review of Educational Research,* 1977, *47,* 1-64.

Wohlwill, J. F., & Wiener, M. Discrimination of form orientation in young children. *Child Development,* 1964, *35,* 1113-1125.

Index

THE SCHOOL PSYCHOLOGIST

was composed in 10-point Compugraphic Times Roman with two points of leading
by Metricomp, Inc.,
with display type in Optima by Dix Typesetting Co., Inc.;
printed on 50-pound, acid-free Glatfelter Antique Cream,
Smythe-sewn and bound over boards in Joanna Arrestox B,
also adhesive bound with Corvon 220-13 covers,
by Maple-Vail Book Manufacturing Group, Inc.;
and published by

SYRACUSE UNIVERSITY PRESS
SYRACUSE, NEW YORK 13210